About This Book

"Oldmeadow's comprehensive and insightful presentation of the life and work of Frithjof Schuon and his function within the perennialist movement takes full advantage of the most recently translated documents. It is a faithful compilation of facts and ideas whose main merit is to show the importance of Schuon's role for our times. . . . This book will be valuable for anyone in search of a thorough introduction to the *sophia perennis*."

—**Jean-Pierre Lafouge**, Marquette University, editor of *For God's Greater Glory: Gems of Jesuit Spirituality*

"This book is much more than an excellent introduction to the life and work of Frithjof Schuon and the perennial wisdom that he taught. It is an insightful and urgent call to apply to our lives those timeless principles and values that are vitally relevant to the host of issues that confront us in the modern world."

—**M. Ali Lakhani**, editor of *Sacred Web: A Journal of Tradition and Modernity*

"One can think of very few contemporary scholars who can match Oldmeadow's knowledge of the literary corpus of Frithjof Schuon, and of its seminal role within the perennial philosophy. This work . . . points to the ways in which Schuon's exposition of the perennial philosophy can resolve many of the most hotly debated issues within philosophy and religion today."

—**Reza Shah-Kazemi**, author of *Paths to Transcendence: According to Shankara, Ibn Arabi, and Meister Eckhart*

"The great value of Professor Oldmeadow's book is its systematic and comprehensive treatment of Schuon's thought. In this it is almost unique. It demands serious scholarly recognition and engagement with Schuon's thought, while at the same time providing a valuable introduction to his oeuvre. This is a highly commendable and timely work."

—**Timothy Scott**, La Trobe University, co-editor of *Vincit Omnia Veritas: Collected Essays*

"This is as important a book in the field of the *philosophia perennis* as I have encountered. Oldmeadow has given us a mountain ledge view of the realm of Traditionalism and Perennialism as expounded by its greatest sage, Frithjof Schuon, and he has done so with impeccable scholarship as well as with a stunning breadth of insight that is as spiritually rich as it is intellectually rigorous. . . . Rarely has Schuon's pneumatic genius been better understood and better served. This is an eloquent gem of a book engaging our profoundest faculties."

—**Mark Perry**, author of *On Awakening and Remembering: To Know Is to Be*

About Frithjof Schuon

"In reading Schuon I have the impression that I am perhaps going along parallel to him, and once in a while I will get a glimpse of what he means in terms of my own tradition and experience. . . . I think that he has exactly the right view. . . . I appreciate him more and more."

—**Thomas Merton**, from correspondence to Marco Pallis in *The Hidden Ground of Love*

"[Schuon] is, without doubt, one of the most penetrating philosophical minds of the twentieth century, if not well beyond."

—**Keith Critchlow**, Professor Emeritus, The Prince's School of Traditional Arts, and President of the Temenos Academy

"Schuon is unsurpassed—and I would add unequalled—as a writer on comparative religion. . . . If I were asked who is the greatest writer of our time, I would say Frithjof Schuon without hesitation."

—**Martin Lings**, author of *Ancient Beliefs and Modern Superstitions*

"[Schuon is] the greatest metaphysical and religious thinker of our century. . . . Intellectually *à propos* religion, equally in depth and breadth, the paragon of our time. I know of no living thinker who begins to rival him."

—**Huston Smith**, University of California, Berkeley, author of *The World's Religions*

"In Schuon's writings we find the serenity of the vision of 'that which eternally exists, really and unchangeably'. . . . His work is full of calm and profound illumination."

—**Kathleen Raine**, co-founder of the Temenos Academy, author of *Defending Ancient Springs*

"Schuon seems like the cosmic intellect itself impregnated by the energy of divine grace surveying the whole of the reality surrounding man and elucidating all the concerns of human existence in the light of sacred knowledge."

—**Seyyed Hossein Nasr**, The George Washington University, author of *Knowledge and the Sacred*

"Schuon's thought does not demand that we agree or disagree, but that we understand or do not understand. Such writing is of rare and lasting value."

—**Times Literary Supplement**

"Frithjof Schuon is well known as one of the greatest metaphysicians of the twentieth century and as Traditionalism's wisest and most profound exponent."

—**Christopher Bamford**, author of *The Voice of the Eagle: The Heart of Celtic Christianity*

World Wisdom
The Library of Perennial Philosophy

The Library of Perennial Philosophy is dedicated to the exposition of the timeless Truth underlying the diverse religions. This Truth, often referred to as the *Sophia Perennis*—or Perennial Wisdom—finds its expression in the revealed Scriptures as well as the writings of the great sages and the artistic creations of the traditional worlds.

Frithjof Schuon and the Perennial Philosophy appears as one of our selections in the Perennial Philosophy series.

The Perennial Philosophy Series

In the beginning of the twentieth century, a school of thought arose which has focused on the enunciation and explanation of the Perennial Philosophy. Deeply rooted in the sense of the sacred, the writings of its leading exponents establish an indispensable foundation for understanding the timeless Truth and spiritual practices which live in the heart of all religions. Some of these titles are companion volumes to the Treasures of the World's Religions series, which allows a comparison of the writings of the great sages of the past with the perennialist authors of our time.

Frithjof Schuon, 1965

Frithjof Schuon
and the
Perennial Philosophy

by

Harry Oldmeadow

Foreword by

William Stoddart

World Wisdom

Frithjof Schuon and the Perennial Philosophy
© 2010 World Wisdom, Inc.

Library of Congress Cataloging-in-Publication Data

Oldmeadow, Harry, 1947-
Frithjof Schuon and the perennial philosophy / by Harry Oldmeadow ; foreword by
William Stoddart.
        p. cm. -- (The perennial philosophy series)
"Select Schuon bibliography"--P.
Includes bibliographical references and index.
ISBN 978-1-935493-09-9 (pbk. : alk. paper) 1. Schuon, Frithjof, 1907-1998. 2.
Religion--Philosophy. 3. Tradition (Philosophy) I. Title.
BL51.O4 2010
200.1--dc22

                                                                2010001855

Printed on acid-free paper in Canada

Cover photograph of Frithjof Schuon by Roland Michaud

For information address World Wisdom, Inc.
P.O. Box 2682, Bloomington, Indiana 47402-2682
www.worldwisdom.com

CONTENTS

FOREWORD

Frithjof Schuon is one of the greatest exponents ever of perennial wisdom; his unique feature is that, amongst all the great sages, he is the only one who is equally at home—and in a masterly fashion—in all of its many and varied historic forms: Vedanta, Taoism, Platonism, Palamitism, Scholasticism, and Sufism. And yet, to a world that treats with respect the legion of post-Medieval philosophers—from the humanistic Descartes and Kant down to the absurd and narcissistic philosophers of the twentieth and twenty-first centuries—, he remains largely unknown. The wisdom in question is that of *intellectus purus*, universal metaphysics, intrinsic orthodoxy. This wisdom, as expounded in the writings of Schuon, has been variously called *philosophia perennis*, *sophia perennis*, and *religio perennis*.

Schuon himself clarifies:

> The term *philosophia perennis*, which has been current since the time of the Renaissance and of which neo-scholasticism made much use, signifies the totality of primordial and universal truths—and therefore of the metaphysical axioms—whose formulation does not belong to any particular system. One could speak in the same sense of a *religio perennis*, designating by this term the essence of every religion; this means the essence of every form of worship, every form of prayer and every system of morality, just as the *sophia perennis* is the essence of all dogmas and all expressions of wisdom. We prefer the term *sophia* to that of *philosophia*, for the simple reason that the second term is less direct and because in addition it evokes associations of ideas with a completely profane and all too often aberrant system of thought.

Schuon's predecessors were not the great devotional mystics, such as Saint John of the Cross; they were sages, or sapiential teachers, such as Shankara, Plato, Dionysius the Areopagite, Meister Eckhart, and Angelus Silesius. Schuon extolled both wisdom and sanctity—he saw these as being inextricably wed—but he nevertheless stressed that the element "wisdom" was even more lacking today than the element "sanctity". At the same time, Schuon loved all goodness: all that was simple and pure. For example, of Saint Theresa of Lisieux ("the Little Flower"), he said: "Her littleness was her greatness." Schuon's guiding star was (in his own adaptation of the juridical formula): "the Good, the whole Good, and nothing but the Good."

In the noble words of Schuon's poetic prose one tastes the awesomeness of the Absolute and the bliss of Paradise; but, in addition to his prose, there is the remarkable cycle of more than three thousand didactic poems which Schuon wrote in his native German during the last three years of his life. These have been compared to Rumi's *Mathnawi*, and many of them are redolent of the Psalms of David: they are an expression of man's nostalgia and longing for ultimate satisfaction in the Lord. Their main theme is trustful prayer to an ever-merciful God, and benevolence towards men of goodwill; but first and foremost, the poems are instruments of instruction. As such, they are a powerful propulsion towards the inward. The essential contents of Schuon's long sequence of poems are truth, beauty, and images of noble and sacred love reminiscent of the Song of Solomon—each of these factors being a potential vehicle of salvation.

At the beginning of a religion, the urgent command is to preach to all nations. On the contrary, in the "latter days" in which Schuon lived, his mission was to teach the truth—the whole and uncolored truth—only to those who seek it, urgently need it, and are satisfied by nothing else. It was with this in mind that Schuon often said: "I am not interested in numbers." Nevertheless, Schuon also had a message for the whole world, and he himself summed this up in one word: prayer. Prayer, on the basis of sincerity and humility, is man's sole—and infinitely precious—link with God.

It is good that all of Schuon's books are now available in English, and it is only natural that his followers should seek to introduce him to the public; only thus can those who need him find him. Nevertheless, the authors of books about Schuon are in nowise under the illusion that his profound metaphysical and spiritual insights will be understood by the majority. For many, in fact, they could be disturbing and unsettling—though this too might not be without its benefits, for we find a parallel in the words of Christ: "I come not to bring peace, but a sword." Christ said further: "Many are called but few are chosen." This touches on the respective roles of "exoterism" (the common religion) and "esoterism" (the deeper and wider purview of those, and only those, who have a vocation for it, and who need it). In reality, "esoterism", in the sense intended, is a danger for no one; indeed, it is a hidden blessing; all this is discussed in detail in Schuon's writings. Schuon demonstrates how esoterism is the intellectual *principle* capable of explaining the formal contradictions between the various religions which, in the "scientific age", have been triumphantly paraded as a proof of their falseness; and also how it constitutes a spiritual *way* whereby we may reach truth or reality despite the confusion and blindness which a technological age has engendered—often imperceptibly—in our minds and imaginations. Schuon writes: "Just as rationalism can remove faith, so esoterism can restore it." In this sense, "esoterism" is a synonym for *religio perennis*.

Schuon's writings are nothing if not exacting; but the truth is implacable. It is also liberating: "Ye shall know the truth, and the truth shall make you free." Oldmeadow's book deftly presents to the wider public an author who is relatively unknown, and whose work newcomers are likely to find difficult. For those already familiar with Schuon and his writings, much will already be known; but Oldmeadow's presentation is satisfyingly fresh and full of insight. He explicates Schuon's principal theses with precision and clarity in a way that will help the new reader to understand the more difficult and unfamiliar points. As in Oldmeadow's other works, one is struck both by the comprehensiveness of his exposition and the awesome breadth of his reading. He covers virtually everything! This is surely a case where one may justifiably have recourse to the cliché: "He leaves no stone unturned and no avenue unexplored!" Nevertheless, the many facets of Frithjof Schuon will never be covered by one sole author. In this respect, Oldmeadow's painstaking presentation of Schuon's works is an important complement to the biographies of Schuon by Jean-Baptiste Aymard and Michael Fitzgerald.

As just mentioned, many people, in making their first approach to Schuon, find his writings difficult. There appear to be three reasons for this. Firstly, Schuon often uses unfamiliar *vocabulary*, not only as regards European words, but also in his frequent use of foreign terms, especially Sanskrit and Arabic. I must immediately say that, on a careful second reading of a given article or chapter, the reader will discover that all the terms used are in fact fully explained. Secondly, he introduces many unfamiliar *concepts*. Once again, on a close second reading, it will be found that these concepts are fully explained. The chief difficulty here seems to lie in the fact that not many people have a clear idea as to what is meant by the "higher levels of reality"; I am referring to what tradition calls "the Five Divine Presences". This doctrine is crucial, but I will not expand on it here, as Oldmeadow presents it in full in this book. Thirdly, even in the modern world, there are authors who occasionally examine things in depth, but who, very quickly, return again to the surface. In the case of Schuon, he starts at a considerable depth, and he *remains* at that depth! Readers are unaccustomed to such a thing.

It is my experience that these three difficulties can be overcome. When this occurs, the reading of Frithjof Schuon becomes, not exactly easy, but a great joy. In fact, it will be discovered that his style is both simple and poetic.

Apart from a hunger for the Absolute, what Schuon demands from his readers is total objectivity, total detachment, and total lack of pretension. For Schuon, virtue, or humility, is an indispensable component of true knowledge.

One point remains: In my opening paragraph, I sharply contrasted Ancient and Medieval philosophy with post-Renaissance philosophy. Schuon explains this great divide in the history of philosophy by pointing out that, whereas Greek and Medieval philosophies were based on certainty, Cartesian and all subsequent philosophies were based on doubt. Traditional philosophy was effectively marginalized by the Renaissance and, even more brutally, by the Enlightenment.

Dr. Oldmeadow has performed an important service in providing us with such a sensitive and detailed presentation of the Schuonian *oeuvre*.

William Stoddart
Windsor, February 2009

INTRODUCTION

For many people in the contemporary world life is perplexing, fraught as it is with challenges, difficulties, and sufferings of one kind and another. Sooner or later thoughtful people find themselves confronting irresistible questions to which there seem to be no readily apparent or satisfactory answers. Does God exist? What is the meaning and purpose, if any, of human life? What is the "good life", and how is it to be lived? What lies beyond death? Why does evil and suffering exist in the world? What is my right relation with my fellows, and with the rest of the natural order? Like Siddhartha, we cannot ignore forever the "great signs" of suffering—sickness, physical decrepitude, death, impermanence—to which we are all subject. Nor can we ignore the fact that our civilization as a whole seems to have lost its bearings, and is now largely governed by an acquisitive materialism. We find ourselves troubled and confused amidst the din, the freneticism, the spiritual sterility of modern life. Sometimes we fail to recognize that our perplexities are, at root, a symptom of a spiritual hunger which, left unsatisfied for too long, can spiral us into ennui, cynicism, despair, even self-destruction.

In our time many people suppose that a "progressive" modern science can provide us with answers to life's fundamental questions; the Genome Project will reveal all and Stephen Hawking will produce a Theory of Everything! Others, understanding both the drastic limits and the Promethean hubris of such a science, turn towards some sort of "religious" or "spiritual" solution. Or perhaps a "self-help" guru or psychiatrist will show us the path to happiness and contentment? Alas, much of what passes these days as "therapy", "religion", and "spirituality" is counterfeit; all too often we are given stones rather than bread.

The most profound and satisfying answers to life's most searching questions cannot simply be fashioned by purely human initiative, for such an enterprise is a symptom of the very darkness we wish to dispel. No individual can "think through" these questions alone: as Frithjof Schuon has remarked, *contra* the existentialists and relativists, "truth is not a personal affair".[1] Nor, in the end, will any of the modern sciences be of much use, whatever partial insights they might yield. Ultimately we must have recourse to a wisdom which infinitely surpasses the "thought" of any single individual and which, in its deepest sources, is actually supra-human. Many modern people scoff at the very idea—but there *is* such a wisdom and it can be found in manifold forms throughout the ages, all over the globe. This is none other than the "perennial philosophy", which has informed all integral mythological and religious traditions since the dawn of time.

---

[1] *Light on the Ancient Worlds*, "Fall and Forfeiture", 24.

Although this timeless wisdom, in its full plenitude, cannot be identified with any particular religion or philosophy, it is only *through* specific and concrete religious forms that most people will ever understand something of this wisdom or experience the realities to which it bears witness. This is in the nature of things. However, there are those few individuals who have been blessed with the metaphysical and contemplative intelligence to penetrate the forms which veil the quintessential wisdom itself. There have always been such individuals—we find them amongst the great sages and saints of the various traditions.

Even rarer are those who are not only able to conform themselves to the Truth at the center of the *sophia perennis*—and this is the deepest sense of *spirituality*—but who are also able to understand and to expound perennial (that is to say, timeless and immutable) principles and doctrines in a systematic fashion, intelligible to those with eyes to see and ears to hear—and this is the quintessence of *intellectuality*. To put it as succinctly as possible, such persons are able to give us an adequate (but never exhaustive) account of Reality, encompassing but surpassing the particular religious forms through which they have come to such an understanding. This science of the Real is *metaphysics*: thus, such figures we can call metaphysicians. Amongst their number, leaving aside the *avataras* and the great founders of religion, we may count such figures as Plato, Plotinus, Meister Eckhart, Ibn Arabi, Chuang Tzu, Nagarjuna, and Shankara, to mention a few of the very first rank. Providence ensures that the Truth, no matter how dark and confused the times, is never without a voice in the world: were it not so the world would vanish in an instant.

But each era in human history must hear the Truth fashioned in a way which answers the peculiar needs of the moment. As Schuon remarks in one of his Prefaces, "Everything has already been said, and even well said; but it is always necessary to recall it anew".[2] In our own time this function has fallen, in different ways, to a small handful of men and women who are immune to the follies of the age and who, through divine grace, are able by their example and teaching to re-awaken those truths which we actually bear within ourselves. One may mention such figures as Sri Ramana Maharshi, Anandamayi Ma, Black Elk, and Shaykh Ahmad al-Alawi. Although their teachings have a universal dimension, such figures have remained within the cadre of their own traditions.

However, there are also those whose destiny it is to reveal "the essential unity and universality and at the same the formal diversity of tradition and revelation"[3]—that is, those few who are able to communicate the perennial

[2] *In the Face of the Absolute*, "Preface", 5.
[3] S.H. Nasr, *Sufi Essays*, 126.

philosophy in a way which does not privilege any particular tradition but which respects all orthodox religious perspectives. Doubtless their expositions will be fragranced by the perfume of the particular religion which provides their own spiritual homeland—and, let it be plainly said that adherence to an orthodox tradition is a necessity even for the most elevated metaphysician. But the function of these few is to take us to the heart of each and every tradition, to that Center from which everything originates, to that Light which, in the words of the Koran, is of neither the East nor the West. Such figures—and the subject of this book is one—exemplify the state of which Ibn Arabi wrote in such memorable lines:

> My heart is open to every form: it is a pasture for gazelles, and a cloister for Christian monks, a temple for idols, the *Kaaba* of the pilgrim, the tables of the *Torah*, and the book of the Koran. I practice the religion of Love; in whatsoever direction His caravans advance, the religion of Love shall be my religion and my faith.[4]

Such luminaries are few in number and we must be wary of the many impostors who in recent times have claimed to speak in the name of the "perennial philosophy".

The most authoritative exponents of the *sophia perennis* in our own time have been René Guénon and Frithjof Schuon, followed by Ananda Coomaraswamy and Titus Burckhardt. Often under their guidance, a larger group of perennialists, or traditionalists as they are sometimes called, has emerged;[5] we will meet a number of them in these pages. The perennialists, by definition, are committed to the explication of the perennial wisdom which lies at the heart of the diverse religions and behind the variegated forms of the world's different traditions. At the same time, as traditionalists, they are dedicated to the preservation and illumination of the traditional forms

[4] Ibn Arabi, quoted in *Understanding Islam*, "Islam", 37.
[5] Ananda Coomaraswamy occasionally used "traditionalist" in a straightforward way to describe an outlook in conformity with traditional principles. Guénon, on the other hand, applied it pejoratively to certain individuals who, in reaction to the relentless march of modernism, were calling for some kind of traditional restoration in the West, although they were themselves unaware of the true nature of tradition: "people who" as Guénon wrote, "have only a sort of tendency or aspiration towards tradition without really knowing anything at all about it" (*Reign of Quantity and the Signs of the Times*, 251-252). He called these people "traditionalists" and their vague objectives "Traditionalism", which he contrasted with "the true traditional spirit". Nonetheless, in the light of developments since Guénon's time, such a term is now necessary to identify those who espouse the traditional outlook. In North America the term "perennialist" now also enjoys some currency. In this work I have used the terms "traditionalist and "perennialist" interchangeably. It should also be noted that if we sometimes refer to these perennialists as a "school" or "movement", this is merely an expedient: their unanimous testimony about the *sophia perennis* could not be encompassed by a mere "school" or "movement".

which give each religious heritage its *raison d'être* and guarantee its formal
integrity and, by the same token, ensure its spiritual efficacy. Amongst these
perennialists/traditionalists we find Marco Pallis, Martin Lings, Leo Schaya,
Whitall Perry, Seyyed Hossein Nasr, and William Stoddart. Many years ago
Ananda Coomaraswamy suggested that

> if we are to consider what may be the most urgent practical problem
> to be resolved by the philosopher, we can only answer . . . a control
> and revision of the principles of comparative religion, the true end of
> which science . . . should be to demonstrate the common metaphysical
> basis of all religions and that diverse cultures are fundamentally related
> to one another as being the dialects of a common spiritual and intel-
> lectual language.[6]

This is the task to which the perennialists have devoted themselves.
Insofar as the accent is on "the metaphysical basis of all *religions*" (as distinct
from other sapiential and mythological traditions which also enshrine the
Wisdom of the Ages) we can speak of the *religio perennis*. This study focuses
on the work of its pre-eminent exponent, Frithjof Schuon, whose writings
express truths "of which the traditional dialectics are the vestitures; hence it
is not as a historian of ideas, but as a spokesman of the *philosophia perennis*
that . . . [he] expound[s] diverse formulations of the truth that is everywhere
and always the same".[7]

In an interview in 1991, asked to summarize his philosophy, Schuon
replied:

> There are four elements that are essential: There is first *discernment*
> between the Absolute and the relative. . . . Then *prayer*, because if you
> understand what is essential and what is Absolute, you want to assimi-
> late it. . . . The third thing is intrinsic *morality*: beauty of the soul. . . .
> The fourth dimension is *beauty*: beauty of forms.[8]

Elsewhere Schuon stated that "the *Sophia perennis* is to know total Truth
and, in consequence, to will the Good and to love Beauty" (prayer being
implicit in all three arms of this formulation).[9] Or again, Schuon's most
compressed summation of his message: "Truth, Prayer, Virtue, Beauty."[10]
These might well serve as the coordinates around which a discussion of
Schuon's teachings could be organized. And indeed each of these will figure

[6] A.K. Coomaraswamy, *What is Civilization? and Other Essays*, 18.
[7] *In the Face of the Absolute*, "Preface", 4.
[8] Quoted in M. Fitzgerald, *Frithjof Schuon: Messenger of the Perennial Philosophy*, xx (italics mine). (This work is subsequently cited by title only.)
[9] *Roots of the Human Condition*, "Pillars of Wisdom", 93.
[10] Frithjof Schuon, quoted in William Stoddart's Foreword to *Frithjof Schuon: Messenger of the Perennial Philosophy*, xiv.

prominently in what follows. However, there is much else in Schuon's message which does not immediately fit into such a schema. Whilst paying due attention to the philosophical and spiritual terrain signposted by these four themes in the Schuonian *oeuvre* we will also have to pursue some other avenues of inquiry.

This study is structured in five parts. "Frithjof Schuon and Perennialism" furnishes a historical and biographical context for what follows. "Timeless Truths and Immutable Principles" outlines traditional metaphysical/cosmological principles, rehearses Schuon's understanding of the "transcendent unity of religions" (one of his signature themes), considers the cardinal notion of "tradition", and situates both theology and philosophy in a metaphysical frame. The third section, "Religious Forms and Sacred Symbols" explores Schuon's writings on the great religious traditions of East and West, on the spiritual heritage of the American Indians in whom Schuon had such a close personal interest, and on sacred art and symbolism as vehicles for metaphysical truths and spiritual messages. It also includes an overview of Schuon's own painting and poetry. "Signs of the Times" presents, in skeletal form, Schuon's arraignment of modernism in its various guises, his repudiation of a prevailing worldview which by its nature is anti-traditional. The concluding section, "The Spiritual Life", concerns several aspects of spiritual anthropology and of the spiritual path itself, to which Schuon so often returns in his writings. Thus, to identify as concisely as possible the themes which structure the present study, one might say: context, principles, forms, errors, way.

*   *   *

The relation of this book to an earlier work needs some explanation. Thirty years ago I wrote of Schuon and the perennialist "school" in an academic dissertation which eventually saw the light of day, in revised form, as *Traditionalism: Religion in the Light of the Perennial Philosophy* (2000). At the time of writing, it was one of the earliest attempts to provide the general reader with a systematic and coherent account of perennialism as espoused by Schuon and others. This volume recapitulates parts of that study but it focuses more exclusively on Schuon rather than on the perennialist movement as a whole. For instance, chapter 4 of *Traditionalism* provided an account of the emergence of the perennialist "school" and of the principal organs of traditionalist discourse. None of that material is reproduced here.

As *Traditionalism* was written in an academic context it addressed various methodological and epistemological problems arising out of the comparative scholarly study of religion/s. Such problems are less likely to interest the general reader and are not canvassed in this book. Furthermore, much of *Traditionalism* drew its anecdotal and illustrative material from the 1960s and 70s, material which is now less pertinent. Also, I nowadays feel less inclined to *argue* with those who do not share the outlook evinced by Schuon. As Guénon once acerbically remarked, "Individualism introduces everywhere the addiction to discussions".[11] Schuon himself no doubt shared something of Guénon's view when the latter wrote:

> Those who are qualified to speak in the name of a traditional doctrine are not required to enter into discussion with the "profane" or to engage in polemics: it is for them simply to expound the doctrine such as it is, for the sake of those capable of understanding it, and at the same time to denounce error wherever it arises. . . . Their function is not to engage in strife and in doing so to compromise the doctrine, but to pronounce the judgement which they have the right to pronounce if they are in effective possession of the principles which should inspire them infallibly.[12]

Then, too, there is the fact that *Traditionalism* made too little of aspects of the Schuonian corpus which at the time struck me less forcibly than they do now: his writings on the Divine Presences, "spiritual anthropology", "culturism", the doctrine of cycles, and the heritage of the American Indians received much less attention there than they do here. As the earlier book focused on perennialism as a whole it also left out of account Schuon's paintings and poetry.

A very considerable body of recently translated Schuonian writings has enabled a more nuanced consideration of many subjects, as well as providing us with some glimpses into a personality and a life which had previously been more or less opaque to those outside Schuon's immediate circle. Whilst some material from *Traditionalism* is directly incorporated in the present work, with only minor modifications, other parts of that book have been substantially revised and rewritten. About half of the material here is entirely new.[13] *Traditionalism* was only published in modest numbers and is now difficult to acquire. It is certainly not a work which I want to disavow. Be that as it may, the present study provides a more adequate introduction to Frithjof Schuon's work and to the providential role he has fulfilled in our time. If it brings new readers to Schuon's writings and to the spiritual life which they extol, it will, whatever its deficiencies, have served a noble end.

---

[11] Guénon, quoted in M. Tamas, *The Wrath of Gods*, 118.

[12] R. Guénon, *Crisis of the Modern World*, 65.

[13] For readers interested in the relation of the two books: chapters 1, most of 5, 12, 13 and 14 of *Traditionalism* have been omitted altogether while the remaining chapters have been edited and revised, with new material added. In the present work chapters 3, 7, 10, 11, 12, 16 and 17 are entirely new.

Introduction

Over the last three decades a number of other studies have appeared, some dealing with the more abstruse aspects of Schuon's metaphysical expositions, as well as many essays and articles addressing other facets of his work. Professor Nasr's Introduction to *The Essential Writings of Frithjof Schuon* (1986)[14], a compilation of many of Schuon's most seminal essays, provided a lucid and percipient introduction to Schuon's *oeuvre*. James Cutsinger's *Advice to the Serious Seeker* (1997), subtitled *Meditations on the Teaching of Frithjof Schuon*, provides a guide for wayfarers treading the path signposted in Schuon's writings. Jean-Baptiste Aymard and Patrick Laude's *Frithjof Schuon: Life and Teachings* (2004) includes both metaphysical and biographical material. In addition there is a burgeoning European literature on Schuon and perennialism.[15] In their different ways all these works are invaluable and it is a pleasure to acknowledge my many debts to them. I should also like to mention Patricia Adrichem's unpublished doctoral thesis, *Frithjof Schuon and the Problem of Religious Diversity* (2005), a work which has often steered me back to particular points in Schuon's writings. Deon Valodia's *Compass for the Journey: Terms Used by Frithjof Schuon* (2004) has also been useful.

There is, I believe, still a good purpose to be served by an exposition which starts from scratch, so to speak—which provides any intelligent and receptive reader with a context for Schuon's writings and some tools which might make them more immediately intelligible. I add the word "receptive" because intelligence alone (at least as it is usually understood nowadays) will not suffice. As Schuon himself has remarked:

> That which is lacking in the present world is a profound knowledge of the nature of things; the fundamental truths are always there, but they do not impose themselves because they cannot impose themselves on those unwilling to listen.[16]

Schuon's writings, while crystalline in their expression, are nevertheless difficult for many first-time readers. They also range over a vast and unending terrain. As Nasr has observed:

> Schuon is at once metaphysician, theologian, traditional philosopher and logician, master of the discipline of comparative religion, expositor of traditional art and civilization, authority in the science of man and society, spiritual guide, and a critic of the modern world in not only

---

[14] The second edition of this work is entitled, The Essential Frithjof Schuon (2005).
[15] There are also various journal issues and *festschrifts* devoted to Schuon, in English, French, and in several other languages. Some of these are referred to elsewhere in this study and in the Select Schuon Bibliography.
[16] "No Activity Without Truth", 28.

its practical but also its philosophical and scientific aspects. His knowledge, moreover, embraces East and West.[17]

It hardly needs saying, then, that no single study can offer anything more than a partial account of Schuon's work. This book is intended primarily as an introductory guide rather than for readers already versed in Schuon's work, though it may be that they too will find something of interest within these covers. Finally, the reader's attention is drawn to Michael Fitzgerald's *Frithjof Schuon: Messenger of the Perennial Philosophy* (2010), an intimate biography, drawing on the author's friendship with Schuon and on a mass of private writings which have hitherto been inaccessible to all but Schuon's closest associates. The present work is intended to serve as a companion volume and complement to this biography: whilst each book can stand alone, for a fuller understanding readers are urged to read both.

Harry Oldmeadow
Bendigo, February 2009

---

[17] S.H. Nasr, Introduction to *Essential Frithjof Schuon*, 2.

I

Frithjof Schuon and Perennialism

The formulation of the traditional point of view was
a response of the Sacred . . . to the elegy of doom of
modern man lost in a world depleted of the sacred,
and therefore, of meaning.

(Seyyed Hossein Nasr, *Knowledge and the Sacred*, 65)

1

Frithjof Schuon: A Sage for the Times

The remembrance of God is our true homeland.[1]

A Biographical Sketch

Frithjof Schuon was born in Basle, in 1907, the second son of German parents. His father, Paul Schuon, was an accomplished concert violinist and a professor at the Basle Conservatory of Music. The Schuon brothers were raised in an atmosphere redolent of medievalism, German romanticism, and Lutheran piety. Late in life Frithjof Schuon recalled the ambience of the family home, "nurtured by the Middle Ages, at once chivalrous, enchanted, and mystical. . . . Almost every evening our parents read to us stories of knights or Red Indians, as well as fairy tales and myths".[2] Erich, the elder brother, became a Trappist monk and spent most of his life in the Abbaye Notre Dame de Scourmont in Belgium. Frithjof was schooled in both French and German but left school at sixteen to work as a textile designer in Paris.

Even as a young schoolboy Schuon evinced a deep spirituality, recounting that "on the long way to school"—alongside the Rhine—"I talked to God, and I thought that everyone else did the same."[3] By the age of ten he was reading Plato. From an early age he devoted himself to a study of philosophy, religion, and metaphysics, reading the classical and modern works of European philosophy, and the sacred literatures of the East. Amongst the Western sources, Plato and Eckhart left a profound impression while the *Bhagavad Gita* was his favourite Eastern reading.[4] Of Schuon's youthful writings, one of his biographers has remarked:

> His own discourse was rather of a mystical nature and in his intimate diary one sees a great melancholy, a feeling of irrepressible solitude, a nostalgia for the Eternal Feminine, an unutterable aspiration toward the Beautiful and the Sovereign Good.[5]

---

[1] Letter to Leo Schaya, March 1983, quoted in J-B. Aymard and P. Laude, *Frithjof Schuon: Life and Teachings*, 27.

[2] *Frithjof Schuon: Messenger of the Perennial Philosophy*, 2.

[3] *Frithjof Schuon: Messenger of the Perennial Philosophy*, 3.

[4] B. Perry, *Frithjof Schuon: Metaphysician and Artist*.

[5] J-B. Aymard and P. Laude, *Frithjof Schuon: Life and Teachings*, 11.

After the death of his beloved father in 1920, and a period of intense suffering, Schuon entered the fold of the Catholic Church. In his *Memoirs* he writes:

> In Catholicism I loved the liturgical manifestation of the sacred, the beauty of the Mass in the Gothic-style churches, the worship of the Blessed Virgin and the rosary; but I could not stop with this, for I had early read the *Bhagavad Gita* and profoundly experienced the sacred art of the Far East.[6]

He felt at home in this religious milieu but was alienated by the narrow-mindedness and calcified exclusivism of the Latin Church. Nonetheless, even after his formal commitment to Islam he retained a mystical affinity for both Christ and His Mother, in 1965 experiencing the overwhelming presence of the Blessed Virgin.[7]

In 1924, through his friend Lucy von Dechend, Schuon came into contact with the writings of René Guénon "which served to confirm his own intellectual rejection of the modern civilization while at the same time bringing into sharper focus his spontaneous understanding of metaphysical principles and their traditional applications."[8] He had for several years immersed himself in the texts of the Vedanta as well as other Eastern scriptures, finding in them the metaphysical wisdom to which he was thenceforth to devote his life. He felt a particular affinity to both the Hindu tradition and to Taoism which he found "peerless and unique".[9] From his earliest years Schuon was also fascinated by traditional art, especially that of Japan and the Far East. One commentator has drawn attention to the importance of aesthetic intuition in Schuon's extraordinary understanding of traditional religious and social forms: "It suffices for him to see . . . an object from a traditional civilization, to be able to perceive, through a sort of 'chain-reaction', a whole ensemble of intellectual, spiritual, and psychological ideas."[10] This may seem an extravagant claim but those who have read Schuon's work will not doubt it for a moment. Nor is it any surprise that Schuon was himself a distinguished painter, drawing his subjects and themes from the spiritual traditions of both East and West, from the heritage of the American Indians, and from his own mystical visions.

---

[6] Frithjof Schuon, quoted in *Frithjof Schuon: Messenger of the Perennial Philosophy*, 11-12.

[7] On these experiences and Schuon's veneration of the Virgin see J-B. Aymard and P. Laude, *Frithjof Schuon: Life and Teachings*, 41-42.

[8] B. Perry, *Frithjof Schuon: Metaphysician and Artist*. See also W. Perry, "The Revival of Interest in Tradition" in *The Unanimous Tradition*, ed. R. Fernando, 14-16.

[9] Unpublished writings, courtesy of World Wisdom.

[10] B. Perry, *Frithjof Schuon: Metaphysician and Artist*.

After working for a time in Mulhouse, in Alsace, Schuon underwent a year and a half of military service before returning to his design work in Paris. There, in 1930, his interest in Islam prompted a close study of Arabic, first with a Syrian Jew and afterwards at the Paris mosque.[11] Of his own spiritual trajectory he later wrote:

> Being *a priori* a metaphysician, I have had since my youth a particular interest in Advaita Vedanta, but also in the spiritual method of realization of which Advaita Vedanta approves. Since I could not find this method—in its strict and esoteric form—in Europe, and since it was impossible for me to turn to a Hindu guru because of the laws of the castes, I had to look elsewhere. . . . I finally decided to look for a Sufi master; the outer form did not matter to me.[12]

After a series of providential signs, in 1932 Schuon found himself in Mostaghanem in Algeria, at the feet of Shaykh Ahmad al-Alawi, the Sufi sage and founder of the Alawi order.[13] Schuon has characterized this modern-day saint as

> someone who represents in himself . . . the idea which for hundreds of years has been the life-blood of that [the Islamic] civilization. To meet such a one is like coming face to face, in mid-twentieth century, with a medieval Saint or a Semitic Patriarch.[14]

Early in 1933 Schuon was formally initiated as a Sufi and given the traditional name Isa (Jesus) Nur ad-Din ("light of the religion").[15] In late 1936 a series of profound experiences revealed to Schuon his role as a spiritual guide; already in 1935 he became a *muqaddam* and in late 1936 was invested as a Shaykh.[16] Although he never proselytized, from this time on he fulfilled

---

[11] B. Perry, *Frithjof Schuon: Metaphysician and Artist.*

[12] Frithjof Schuon, letter of January 1996, quoted by James Cutsinger in Introduction to *Prayer Fashions Man*, xviii.

[13] On the Shaykh al-Alawi see M. Lings, *A Sufi Saint of the Twentieth Century*. There is a moving portrait of the Algerian Shaykh by Schuon, facing page 160. See also M. Valsan, "Notes on the Shaikh al-Alawi, 1869-1934".

[14] Frithjof Schuon, "*Rahimahu Llah*", *Cahiers du Sud*, 1935, quoted in M. Lings, *A Sufi Saint of the Twentieth Century*, 116.

[15] As his biographer explains, "Following the Sufi custom, the new name of Schuon's *Tariqah* was added to his personal name. Schuon's complete traditional name thus became Shaykh Isa Nur ad-Din Ahmad ash-Shadhili ad-Darqawi al-Alawi al-Maryami. The term Shaykh refers to his spiritual function; the name Isa (Jesus) was received when he entered Islam in Mostaghanem; the name Nur ad-Din ("light of the religion") when he was initiated into Sufism; and the name Ahmad during his second trip to Mostaghanem in 1935; next follow the names of the three major figures in the history of his spiritual lineage; and finally the name of his *Tariqah*—the *Maryamiyyah*." (*Frithjof Schuon: Messenger of the Perennial Philosophy*, 100).

[16] This is how Michael Fitzgerald, and Schuon himself, have described this investiture: "Then, at the end of 1936, the twenty-eight year old Schuon awoke one morning with the unshak-

the role of a spiritual master, and various communities grew up under his leadership. Although his teachings were universal and esoteric, and although he accepted disciples from different traditions, he always insisted that his followers cleave to an orthodox religious tradition within which they could observe the essential rites and disciplines.

In the years before the war Schuon several times visited North Africa, sometimes in the company of his close schooldays friend, Titus Burckhardt, spending time in Algeria, Morocco, and also Egypt where he met René Guénon, with whom he had been corresponding for some years. In many respects Schuon's work was to be a restatement and elaboration of principles first given public expression by Guénon, and their application in many domains beyond Guénon's reach.[17] It was in these years that Schuon launched his public writings as an expositor of metaphysical doctrines and of religious forms.

The contemplative climate of India exercised a strong attraction but a visit to the sub-continent was cut short by the outbreak of war, which obliged Schuon to return to Europe. He served for some months in the French army before being captured by the Germans. His father had been a native of southern Germany while his mother had come from German-Alsatian stock. Such a background ensured some measure of freedom but

able certitude that he had been invested with the function of spiritual guide. 'This happened, moreover, at a time when I least expected such a thing. . .'. During the same night, several of his friends had had visionary dreams of Schuon, all of which confirmed the receipt from on high of this new role. It was not Schuon but others who first announced this new function. 'When next I went to Basle, the friends there told me, one after the other, that they had seen in the clearest of dream-visions that I had become Shaykh.' Schuon was initially hesitant to accept the responsibility of guiding spiritual seekers in their lives of prayer. When René Guénon learned of Schuon's experience, he encouraged him to overcome his reluctance and accept the responsibility of aiding those who wished to follow him on a path towards God. Schuon, in writing of some of the reasons for his initial hesitation, also wrote of his ultimate certainty regarding his new function: 'I sometimes asked myself if I have the right to be Shaykh. I had forgotten, in those moments, that this function did not depend at all on my choice, that it had been placed on me at a given moment and completely unexpectedly. I became Shaykh at a providential time when I was in doubt about any spiritual possibility in the West, and when I was ready to give up everything. Heaven placed the function on me suddenly, without transition, like a ray of light falls in a dark room; it was totally contrary to my state of mind, but it was irresistible. . . . When I ask myself the question of knowing whether I am worthy of my function, the problem is unsolvable for me; but when I remember that this function was placed on me by Heaven, as also our method, there is no longer room for any uncertainty; praise be to God.' Frithjof Schuon thus acceded to the responsibility of spiritual guide conferred on him by the providence of Heaven." (*Frithjof Schuon: Messenger of the Perennial Philosophy*, 39).

[17] Martin Lings: "There is nothing in Guénon that is not to be found in Schuon. There is much in Schuon that is not to be found in Guénon" (quoted in *Frithjof Schuon: Messenger of the Perennial Philosophy*, 54).

when the Nazis threatened to forcibly enlist Alsatians in the German army, Schuon seized an opportunity to escape across the rugged Jura Mountains into Switzerland. He was detained by the Swiss military until he could verify that he had been born in Basle. He settled in Lausanne and, some years later, took out Swiss nationality.[18]

Two of the most profound books of the century—unsurpassed in unraveling some of the darkest enigmas of our times—appeared within a few years of each other. The first, in 1945, was René Guénon's *magnum opus, The Reign of Quantity and the Signs of the Times;* the second, appearing meteor-like in 1948, was *The Transcendent Unity of Religions,* Schuon's first major work in which he spells out the metaphysical foundations of the *religio perennis.* We will return frequently to this book, but for the moment it is worth noting that Schuon's book exposed several divergences from Guénon, particularly concerning Christian esoterism and the efficacy of the sacraments.[19] It was perfectly apparent that whatever debts Schuon owed to the elderly French metaphysician, with whom he remained on cordial terms despite some strenuous disagreements, he had attained full intellectual independence. It was also now evident that Schuon was embarking on a program even more far-reaching than that of Guénon, namely, not only the exposition of metaphysical and cosmological doctrines but, in their light, the penetration of religious forms and sacred art from around the globe and from all the major religious and sapiential traditions.

In 1949 Schuon married Catherine Feer, the daughter of a Swiss diplomat. It was she who introduced him to the beauties of the Swiss Alps.[20] Schuon's love of nature, which runs through his work like a haunting melody, was further deepened during two periods which the couple spent with the Plains Indians of North America. "For Schuon, virgin nature carries a message of eternal truth and primordial reality, and to plunge oneself therein is to rediscover a dimension of the soul which in modern man has become atrophied."[21] Schuon himself, writing in the context of Red Indian receptivity to the lessons of nature, said this:

> Wild Nature is at one with holy poverty and also with spiritual child-likeness; she is an open book containing an inexhaustible teaching of truth and beauty. It is in the midst of his own artifices that man most easily becomes corrupted, it is they who make him covetous and impious; close to virgin Nature, who knows neither agitation nor

---

[18] B. Perry, *Frithjof Schuon: Metaphysician and Artist.*

[19] On the divergences of Guénon and Schuon see *Frithjof Schuon: Messenger of the Perennial Philosophy,* 54-57, 192-194.

[20] See C. Schuon, "Frithjof Schuon: Memories and Anecdotes", 47-48.

[21] B. Perry, *Frithjof Schuon: Metaphysician and Artist.*

falsehood, he had the hope of remaining contemplative like Nature herself.[22]

Schuon and his wife had previously developed friendly contacts with visiting Indians in Paris and Brussels in the 1950s. During their first visit to North America in 1959, the Schuons were officially adopted into the Red Cloud family of the Lakota tribe, that branch of the Sioux nation from which came the revered "medicine-man" Black Elk (Hehaka Sapa).[23] Schuon, Coomaraswamy, and Joseph Epes Brown were all instrumental in efforts to preserve the precious spiritual heritage of the Plains Indians.[24]

During the forty years he lived in Switzerland Schuon traveled in Europe, North Africa, the Middle East, and the United States, maintaining close friendships with representatives of all the great religious traditions. Amongst those whom he counted as close personal friends were the perennialists Titus Burckhardt, Leo Schaya, and Whitall Perry, and Chief Thomas Yellowtail of the Crow Indians. Martin Lings and Seyyed Hossein Nasr were amongst his best-known Islamic disciples, each to make their own distinctive contribution to the perennialist "school". Of the many distinguished scholars, teachers, and spiritual leaders with whom Schuon came into contact we may mention the Russian Archimandrite and later Archbishop Anthony Bloom, Staretz Sophrony of Athos, Father Thomas Merton, Shaykh Hassan of Morocco, the renowned Hindu saint Swami Ramdas, Pandit Hari Prasad Shastri, Shin and Zen Buddhist priests and masters such as Shojun Bando, Sohaku Ogata, and Shinichi Hisamatsu, the Tibetan teacher Lobsang Lhalungpa, and Marco Pallis, who was often to act as Schuon's emissary in the East. Schuon also had a special relationship with the Jagadguru of Kanchipuram, the living representative of the spiritual tradition that stretches back through sixty-eight generations to the great Vedantic sage Shankara. It is also worth noting that Schuon experienced several intense dreams and visions in which he encountered such figures as Ramakrishna and Ramana Maharshi, two of the most lucent sages of the recent Hindu tradition.

Two elements became increasingly important to Schuon during the Swiss years, and he continued to advocate them until his death: *dhikr* (remembrance of God), also known as "invocation" or "prayer of the heart",

---

[22] *Light on the Ancient Worlds* (1965), "The Shamanism of the Red Indians", 84.

[23] For some account of the Schuons' personal experiences with the Plains Indians see *Feathered Sun*, Parts 2 and 3, *Frithjof Schuon: Messenger of the Perennial Philosophy*, 84-94, 204-208, and J-B. Aymard and P. Laude, *Frithjof Schuon: Life and Teachings*, 40-41.

[24] See R. Lipsey, *Coomaraswamy: His Life and Work*, 227-228.

and the *khalwah* (retreat).[25] This was perfectly in accord with the quintessential esoterism which he explicated in his writings.[26]

Schuon moved to the United States in 1980, making his home in Bloomington, Indiana. He devoted his later years to his voluminous metaphysical
writings and poetry, to the guidance of the Sufi community of which he was
the spiritual master, and to counseling many seekers of different faiths from
around the world. Schuon crossed to the further shore in 1998. The funeral
ceremony included the recitation of a couplet he wrote a few years before
his passing:

> Because I made my heart a holy shrine,
> My soul belongs to God, and God is mine.

His tomb, attended by deer, is in the lovely woods in which he had walked
and meditated daily.

Schuon's daily life, governed by a rigorous spiritual discipline, remained
much the same throughout his adult years. His wife Catherine has afforded
us some glimpses of his daily routines in Lausanne, and thereby reveals
something of his temperament and disposition:

> [Frithjof Schuon] was leading a highly disciplined life, punctuated by
> times of prayer; ever hard on himself, he was on the contrary indulgent
> with his disciples, taking into account the difficult work conditions of
> the modern world. He never changed his habits during all the years we
> lived together. He would get up at dawn and perform his prayers. "As
> long as one has not said one's prayers, one is not a human being." After
> a simple breakfast, he would walk down to the lake alone. . . . He had
> a strict need for these hours of solitude outdoors. At ten o'clock he
> would receive visitors and in the afternoon, after having retired for an
> hour, he would write articles or letters. He answered all his mail with
> admirable patience and generosity. . . . Often he would write until late
> at night and would get up and go back and forth in his room, less to
> ponder what he wished to express than to remember God. Every day
> he would read one page in the Koran (in Arabic) and he also loved to
> read the Psalms—Psalms 23, 63, 77 and 124 were his favourites. . . .
>
> We would eat sitting either on the floor or at a small Moroccan
> table or in the kitchen, in silence. "One should respect the food.". . .
> When seated, he would never lean back. . . . He would always walk in
> a straight, upright fashion, even during the last months of his life. . . .
> He would wash only with cold water; to take a hot bath occurred to
> him as little as to smoke a hookah! If it is true that some of his habits
> stemmed from the fact that we had always been poor, they correspond

---

[25] See J-B. Aymard and P. Laude, *Frithjof Schuon: Life and Teachings*, 27.
[26] Concerning some controversy surrounding Frithjof Schuon's methods, see *Frithjof Schuon: Messenger of the Perennial Philosophy*, 52-53, 189-192.

on the other hand to his ascetic nature. Everything he did, he would do well, without hurry, with recollected mien.[27]

Of Schuon's personal qualities, William Stoddart has written this:

Schuon was a combination of majesty and humility; of rigor and love. He was made of objectivity and incorruptibility, coupled with compassion. In meeting with him many times during a period of nearly five decades, the immediate personal qualities which constantly struck me were his infinite patience and infinite generosity.[28]

Huston Smith, who met with many spiritual masters from all over the world, stated: "With the possible exception of the Dalai Lama, Frithjof Schuon is the only person I have known who invariably made me feel, on leaving him, that I had been in the presence of a different order of human being."[29]

In *The Conference of the Birds*, the great Sufi mystic, Farid ad-Din Attar, enjoins the spiritual seeker to "Put on the mantle of nothingness". Schuon covered his own life with the cloak of anonymity, maintaining a deliberate obscurity and detachment from public affairs.[30] In a letter to a friend he spoke of "holy solitude", explaining that

A relationship with God leads to a certain solitude, because God is not the world, and the world is not God; in this solitude there is a sweetness from the next world, because God is the supreme Good. It is in this sense that an old proverb says O *beata solitudo, o sola beatitudo.*[31]

Like Guénon, Schuon had no interest in noisy acclaim, nor was he in any sense the worldly "intellectual"—quite the contrary. In one of his early books we find the following:

The more serious among [Eastern] spiritual teachers are showing an increasing tendency to withdraw themselves as far as possible from the public gaze in order that the wisdom they have to impart may become sufficiently hard of access to filter out, as it were, the unqualified,

---

[27] C. Schuon, "Frithjof Schuon: Memories and Anecdotes", 53-54.

[28] W. Stoddart, Foreword to *Frithjof Schuon: Messenger of the Perennial Philosophy*, xv. Schuon's wife confirms that "humility was at the base of his character" ("Frithjof Schuon: Memories and Anecdotes", 38).

[29] H. Smith, "Providence Perceived: In Memory of Frithjof Schuon", 31.

[30] His biographer tells us that Schuon resisted the entreaties of his friends and followers to publish his autobiographical work of the early 1970s, *Memories and Meditations* (also often referred to as *Memoirs*). By his own wish they remain unpublished (*Frithjof Schuon: Messenger of the Perennial Philosophy*, 173-174). It is also a striking fact that Schuon delivered only one public address in his entire life, in Basle in 1935.

[31] Frithjof Schuon, letter to Leo Schaya, March 23, 1983, quoted in *Frithjof Schuon: Messenger of the Perennial Philosophy*, 164.

leaving the door open to those only who, guided thither by the divine Grace, are prepared to pay the proper price.[32]

This seems to have been the posture that Schuon himself adopted, one not excluding friendly relations with other spiritual teachers and representatives of the different traditions.

From one point of view it would be quite impertinent for an outsider, such as the present author, to mount any "assessment" of Schuon's role as a spiritual guide: only those blessed to be his disciples, in some more or less direct sense, are in a position to understand and comment on Schuon's spiritual function. Furthermore, much of his spiritual teaching remains unpublished, given only to those who sought him out for spiritual advice.[33] On the other hand, it *is* possible to make a few modest observations, based on the published sources. It is clear that Schuon was a personal guide to adherents of different faiths, who sought him out despite his relative anonymity. Such individuals had a close relationship with him and often committed themselves to the life of perpetual prayer. At the same time Schuon was also an impersonal spiritual guide to many people in the wider world; his work served to guide people back to their own religions and to the life of prayer as practiced respectively in these different traditions. From an interview with Mrs. Schuon:

> Q: What is his function in the world?
> A: His function in the world is really to bring people back to practice their religion, which is so important, and to bring them back to a path that leads to God. And he has done it through his books. I know that many, many people have gone back and practiced their religion very seriously after having read his books. He wants to help people to go back to where we belong. Here we are only passing on this earth.[34]

As Schuon himself remarked in one of his later works, "Even if our writings had on average no other result than the restitution, for some, of the saving barque that is prayer, we would owe it to God to consider ourselves profoundly satisfied."[35]

In recent years much confusion, obfuscation, and discord has accumulated around the person and the role of Frithjof Schuon, not to mention the inevitable incomprehensions and hostilities of those who are incapable of

---

[32] *Language of the Self* (1959), "Self-Knowledge and the Western Seeker", 50.

[33] Readers interested in this facet of Schuon's life are directed to the several sources which have become available since his passing. In particular see J-B. Aymard and P. Laude, *Frithjof Schuon: Life and Teachings*, M. Fitzgerald, "Frithjof Schuon: Providence without Paradox", and R. Fabbri, "The Milk of the Virgin: The Prophet, the Saint, and the Sage".

[34] Film interview conducted by Michael Fitzgerald.

[35] *Play of Masks*, "Foreword", vii.

understanding even the simplest messages of Tradition, let alone grasping the esoteric wisdom which Schuon was ever expressing anew. However, various tensions, controversies, and polemical eruptions have arisen within "perennialist" circles, calling for some comment. Some of the forces at work here include: over-zealous and misguided attempts to isolate René Guénon as the exclusive master of metaphysics in our time, and the final arbiter on all matters pertaining to tradition; the "passional blindness" and pious extravagances of some representatives of religious orthodoxy who believed, wrongly, that Schuon had compromised the integrity of religious forms; and the squalid calumnies leveled at this noble soul by some lost individuals under the sway of a malevolence which thinks nothing of defiling the reputations of the most saintly of men and women. Jean-Baptiste Aymard, one of Schuon's biographers, reminds us of analogous cases involving no less than St. Theresa of Ávila, Padre Pio, and Ramana Maharshi. He also cites Schiller's somber observation that "the world seeks to blacken what shines and to drag into the dust what is sublime".[36] In Aymard and Laude's biography each of these groups critical of Schuon is quietly disarmed through a sober consideration of the facts of Schuon's relationship to Guénon (many of which had not previously come to light in published form), through an explanation of the somewhat different roles that each providentially fulfilled, through a careful and persuasive explication of Schuon's stance in regard to religious forms, and through an affirmation of those qualities which made Schuon quite incapable of the offences with which his detractors had vilified him.

Schuon's *Oeuvre*

Before turning to a conspectus of Schuon's writings I offer a brief reminiscence which may strike a chord with some of his other readers. Some thirty and more years ago, browsing through a magazine in rather desultory fashion, my eye caught a review of *The Sword of Gnosis*, an anthology of writings on "Metaphysics, Cosmology, Tradition, Symbolism", edited by Jacob Needleman. The review was sufficiently arresting for me to seek out a copy of the book. It was with growing excitement that I first encountered the writings of several figures whose work I would come to know well over the years ahead—René Guénon, Titus Burckhardt, Martin Lings, Marco Pallis, Seyyed Hossein Nasr, among others. But the effect of Frithjof Schuon's several essays in this anthology was quite mesmeric: here, in the exposition of traditional doctrines and principles, was a clarity, a radiance, and a depth which seemed to me, as indeed it still does, to be of a more or less miraculous order. Nasr has written of the appearance of Guénon's first book (*Introduction to the Study of the Hindu Doctrines*, 1921), in these terms:

---

[36] J-B. Aymard and P. Laude, *Frithjof Schuon: Life and Teachings*, 51.

> It was like a sudden burst of lightning, an abrupt intrusion into the modern world of a body of knowledge and a perspective utterly alien to the prevalent climate and world view and completely opposed to all that characterizes the modern mentality.[37]

This, precisely, is how Schuon's essays struck me. My own intellectual and spiritual life was changed forever. At that time, Schuon's books were not easily available in Australia. It was in the face of some difficulties that I rapidly accumulated not only Schuon's works but those of other perennialists. I soon felt the force of Ananda Coomaraswamy's remark that, "if you ever really enter into this other world, you may not wish to return: you may never again be content with what you have been accustomed to think of as 'progress' and 'civilization'."[38] And so it proved!

Schuon's published work forms an imposing corpus and covers a staggering range of religious and metaphysical subjects without any of the superficialities and simplifications which we normally expect from someone covering such a vast terrain. His works on particular religions have commanded respect from leading scholars and practitioners within the traditions in question. Over five decades he was a prolific contributor to journals such as *Études Traditionnelles, Connaissance des Religions, France-Asie, Islamic Quarterly, Tomorrow* and its successor, *Studies in Comparative Religion,* and *Sophia Perennis.* All his major works, written in French, have now been published in English. Since his death Schuon's prodigious poetic output, as well as some of his correspondence, has appeared in English translation. The corpus available in English, leaving aside the poetic collections, amounts to some thirty-odd books.

Schuon's works are governed by an unchanging set of metaphysical principles. They exhibit nothing of a "development" or "evolution" but are, rather, restatements of the same principles from different vantage points and brought to bear on divergent phenomena. Schuon's vision was complete from the outset. The recent translation and publication of his first book, which he commenced in 1927 and which was published in German in 1935, makes this perfectly evident. In the words of his biographer, "A comparison of this early book to his later works demonstrates that Schuon's foundational principles were already fully formed".[39] When considering Schuon's writings one is immensely impressed by his learning, but there is something here far

---

[37] S.H. Nasr, *Knowledge and the Sacred,* 101.

[38] A. Coomaraswamy, "Medieval and Oriental Art", in *Coomaraswamy 1: Selected Papers, Traditional Art and Symbolism,* 45-46.

[39] *Frithjof Schuon: Messenger of the Perennial Philosophy,* 29. The book in question was *Leitgedanken zur Urbesinnung,* the English translation by Gillian Harris appears in *Sacred Web* 20, 2008, under the title *Primordial Meditation: Contemplating the Real.*

beyond mere "erudition": Schuon not only knows "about" an encyclopedic range of religious manifestations and sapiential traditions but understands them "from the inside", in a way which, for want of a better word, we can only call intuitive. His writings in the limitless field of metaphysics, cosmology, and religion are without equal. Nonetheless, his intuitions took place in cooperation with an immense learning acquired through reading as well as direct personal encounters and experiences. It is worth noting that Schuon was fluent, in both written and spoken form, in German, French, English, and Arabic, could converse in Italian, read Sanskrit and Latin, and had a working familiarity with Greek, Spanish, Lakota, and Chinese.[40]

All of Schuon's work is concerned with a re-affirmation of traditional metaphysical principles, with an explication of the esoteric dimensions of religion, with the penetration of mythological and religious forms, and with the critique of a modernism which is either indifferent or nakedly hostile to the Wisdom of the Ages. Traditionalists are, by definition, committed to expounding the *sophia perennis* which lies at the heart of the diverse religions and within their manifold forms. Schuon's general position—or better, the position to which Schuon adhered—was defined in his first work to appear in English, *The Transcendent Unity of Religions* (1953), a book of which T.S. Eliot remarked, "I have met with no more impressive work in the comparative study of Oriental and Occidental religion."[41] In peerless fashion this book elaborated the distinction between the exoteric and esoteric dimensions of religious traditions and, by uncovering the metaphysical convergence of all orthodox religions, provided a coherent and irrefutable basis for a properly constituted religious ecumenism—one might well say the *only* possible basis.

Much of Schuon's work has been explicitly directed to the Islamic tradition to which he has devoted four books: *Understanding Islam* (1963), *Dimensions of Islam* (1969), *Islam and the Perennial Philosophy* (1976), and *Sufism: Veil and Quintessence* (1981),[42] while *Christianity/Islam: Essays on Esoteric Ecumenicism* (1985) and *In the Face of the Absolute* (1989) cover

---

[40] *Frithjof Schuon: Messenger of the Perennial Philosophy*, 179.

[41] Quoted by Huston Smith, Introduction to *Transcendent Unity of Religions* (1975), ix.

[42] In regard to two of these books Michael Fitzgerald has noted: "In accordance with [Schuon's] preference we [i.e., his publishers] have not listed either *Dimensions of Islam* or *Islam and the Perennial Philosophy* among his English language compilations." According to Schuon, "My doctrinal message is in my French books and their translations. It is only indirectly and imperfectly in the English compilations *Dimensions of Islam* and *Islam and the Perennial Philosophy*, which were produced for contingent reasons and do not correspond to my intentions" (Unpublished document, quoted in *Frithjof Schuon: Messenger of the Perennial Philosophy*, 221). The essays from these two books can be found in revised form in the more recent editions of his other books, particularly in the posthumously published *Form and Substance in the Religions* (2002).

Christian and Islamic traditions. *Understanding Islam* was one of only a few Schuon works conceived as a book (rather than as a collection of articles). Seyyed Hossein Nasr, himself an eminent Islamicist, wrote of it, "I believe his work to be the most outstanding ever written in a European language on why Muslims believe in Islam and why Islam offers to man all that he needs religiously and spiritually."[43]

Whilst many of Schuon's works have a Sufic fragrance, his work has by no means been restricted to the Islamic heritage. Two major works explore Hinduism and Buddhism: *Language of the Self* (1959) and *In the Tracks of Buddhism* (1969).[44] It is worth noting that although Schuon's destiny led him to a Sufi spiritual master and thus to Islam as his religion, his intellectuality found its deepest inspiration in Advaita Vedanta, particularly in the *Upanishads* and in the teachings of the eighth-century sage Shankara. However, Schuon's exposition of the *religio perennis* knows no boundaries and there are countless illuminating references in his work to all manner of religious phenomena and doctrines, drawn from all over the world.

Spiritual Perspectives and Human Facts (1954) is a collection of aphoristic essays including studies of Vedanta and sacred art, and a meditation on the spiritual virtues. My own most conspicuous memory of first reading this book, apart from a sense of its crystalline beauty, is of Schuon's compelling contrast between the principles which govern all traditional art and the pomposity, vacuity, and grotesqueness of much that masquerades as art in the post-medieval world and which has long since ceased to "exteriorize either transcendent ideas or profound virtues".[45] Schuon's writings on art are often embellished with striking epigrams. Who could forget one as telling as this:

> When standing before a [medieval] cathedral, a person really feels he is placed at the center of the world; standing before a church of the Renaissance, Baroque, or Rococo periods, he merely feels himself to be in Europe.[46]

Gnosis: Divine Wisdom (1959), *Logic and Transcendence* (1975), and *Esoterism as Principle and as Way* (1981) are largely given over to the exposition of metaphysical principles. The first includes a resplendent section on the Christian tradition while *Logic and Transcendence* contains Schuon's

---

[43] See S.H. Nasr, *Ideals and Realities of Islam*, 10. Nasr has been no less emphatic in commending later works. See his Prefaces to *Dimensions of Islam* and *Islam and the Perennial Philosophy* and his Introduction to *Essential Frithjof Schuon*.

[44] The latter appeared in revised and expanded form and newly translated as *Treasures of Buddhism* (1993).

[45] *Spiritual Perspectives and Human Facts*, "Aesthetics and Symbolism in Art", 32.

[46] *Transcendent Unity of Religions*, "Concerning Forms in Art", 65n.

most explicit refutation of some of the philosophies and ideologies of the modern West. His early arraignment of such characteristically modern philosophies of negation and despair as relativism, rationalism, "concretism", existentialism, and psychologism put us in mind of the sword of discriminating wisdom wielded by the Bodhisattva Manjushri! The later parts of the book concern aspects of the spiritual life, culminating in this passage:

> To the question of what are the foremost things a man should do, situated as he is in this world of enigmas and fluctuations, the reply must be made that there are four things to be done or four jewels never to be lost sight of: first, he should accept the Truth; second, bear it continually in mind; third, avoid whatever is contrary to Truth and the permanent consciousness of truth; and fourth, accomplish whatever is in conformity therewith.[47]

Schuon suggested some years ago that *Logic and Transcendence* was his most representative and inclusive work.[48] That distinction is perhaps now shared with *Esoterism as Principle and as Way*, which includes Schuon's most deliberate explanation of the nature of esoterism, and with *Survey of Metaphysics and Esoterism* (1986), which is a masterly work of metaphysical synthesis.

Stations of Wisdom (1961) is an exploration of certain religious and spiritual modalities while *Light on the Ancient Worlds* (1965) includes a range of essays on such subjects as the Hellenist-Christian "dialogue", shamanism, monasticism, and the *religio perennis*. The last decade of Schuon's life was astonishingly productive, seeing the appearance of *To Have a Center* (1990), *Roots of the Human Condition* (1991), *Echoes of Perennial Wisdom* (1992), *The Play of Masks* (1992), *The Transfiguration of Man* (1995), and the translation of an early work, *The Eye of the Heart* (1997). The later writings exhibit a masterly lightness of touch and a style that is increasingly synthetic and poetic. The title chapter of *To Have a Center* furnishes us with Schuon's only extended statement concerning the literary and artistic "culture" of the last two hundred years. Other essays in these books cover such subjects as intellection, prayer, integral anthropology, and art. *Echoes of Perennial Wisdom* is a compilation of epigrammatic passages and apophthegms taken mainly from works which at that time were still unpublished.

Schuon's effulgent writings on the spiritual treasury of the Plains Indians have been collected, together with reproductions of some of his paintings, in *The Feathered Sun: Plains Indians in Art and Philosophy* (1990). This is one of Schuon's most "personal" books, textured as it is with direct references to his own experience. A further token of this aspect of the book is

[47] *Logic and Transcendence*, "Man and Certainty", 265-266.
[48] Schuon's comment about *Logic and Transcendence* is recorded in Whitall Perry's review in *Studies in Comparative Religion*, 9:4, 1975, 250.

that one cannot imagine any of his predecessors or contemporaries writing anything like it. The book, in both text and image, is also pervaded by the pathos which marks the disappearance of a spiritual economy and a way of life of exceptional beauty and nobility. There is a peculiar poignancy in the fact that Schuon was adopted into both the Crow and Sioux tribes, remembering their heroic resistance to the encroachments of "civilization". Furthermore, one cannot but see in Schuon himself precisely those qualities which he extolled in the Indians—"a stoical and combative heroism with a priestly bearing [which] conferred on the Indian of the Plains and Forest a sort of majesty at once aquiline and solar".[49]

Patrick Laude has noted five "points of view" from which "the distinction between the Divine and what lies outside it" might legitimately be envisaged, namely: meta-theistic metaphysics such as we find in Advaita Vedanta or Taoism; a monotheistic theology which emphasizes the "fundamental hiatus" between God and his Creation; the Logocentric outlook pre-eminent in Christianity and in the Avataric perspective of Hinduism; angelolatry and various forms of so-called polytheism in which angels/deities "essentially represent Divine aspects"; and, lastly, primordial Shamanism which calls for "an ecological participation in the supernatural vocation of Nature" and a thorough-going integration of psychic energies and powers into the spiritual life.[50] The plasticity of Schuon's spiritual sensibility (in some respects reminiscent of that of Paramahamsa Ramakrishna) enabled him, according to the exigencies of the moment, to take the viewpoint of each of these perspectives. Further, as Laude observes elsewhere, "There is no author more categorical than Schuon when the dazzling evidence of principles imposes itself, but there is no one more attentive to the paradoxes, the compensations, and the complex play of necessary exceptions."[51]

In the last few years of his life Schuon composed twenty-three collections comprising around 3,200 short poems in German, and nearly 100 in English, adding to a body of poetry written earlier in Arabic and German. In these poems, the principles and insights expressed in his other writings find a lyric voice in the most simple and concise form. This long cycle of poems has been compared to Rumi's *Mathnawi* and to the Psalms of David. As William Stoddart has observed:

> They are an expression of nostalgia, of mankind's longing for, and ultimate satisfaction in, the Lord. . . . They are an inexhaustible, and

---

[49] *Feathered Sun*, "The Shamanism of the Red Indians", 39-40.
[50] J-B. Aymard and P. Laude, *Frithjof Schuon: Life and Teachings*, 98-103. See also *Survey of Metaphysics and Esoterism*, "Outline of Religious Typologies", 103-113.
[51] J-B. Aymard and P. Laude, *Frithjof Schuon: Life and Teachings*, 120.

ever new, purifying fountain—a crystalline and living expression of the *religio perennis*. They epitomize truth, beauty, and salvation.[52]

Many of Schuon's paintings are reproduced in *The Feathered Sun* and *Images of Primordial and Mystic Beauty: Paintings by Frithjof Schuon* (1992). His earliest works, in the main, were sketches of the heads of men from different ethnic backgrounds whilst in mid-life he produced a magnificent series of canvases depicting the mythology and ceremonial life of the Plains Indians of North America. His favourite subject in his later years was the Virgin, sometimes rendered in a visual style somewhat reminiscent of Hindu art. "The subjects treated by Schuon", Laude observes, "are essentially of two types":

> The world of the American Indians envisaged in its sacerdotal hiera-tism and heroic dignity, and the world of femininity, from its virginal innocence in the genre of Gauguin to the mysterious inwardness in the icons of the Virgin.[53]

Jean-Baptiste Aymard cautions that

> One will understand nothing of Schuon's teachings if one is unaware of the importance for him of the sacred and beautiful, and his inclina-tion—as with every "visual" type, towards anything that manifests Beauty as such. An important part of his message is the following: in a centrifugal world of mediocrity and ugliness, the contemplation of beauty is a concrete response, a source of interiorization, a door to the True.[54]

Both Schuon's poetry and his visual art recall the vital role of Beauty. As one of his biographers has suggested, "If sapiential intelligence is the directing principle of Schuon's work, beauty is its main mode of manifes-tation and assimilation."[55] Beauty itself entails three dimensions, each of which can be linked with the Vedantic ternary, *Sat-Cit-Ananda*, and each readily apparent in Schuon's life, teaching, and handiwork: "a doctrine of Beauty which pertains to the domain of metaphysical consciousness" (*Cit*); "a methodical and spiritual awareness of the beautiful as a means of grace" (*Sat*); "a creative joy, a dimension of beatitude (*Ananda*), which is expressed by his poetical and pictorial productions and by a contemplative receptivity to feminine beauty as a privileged mirror of the Divine."[56]

---

[52] W. Stoddart, Introduction to *World Wheel Volumes I-III: Poems by Frithjof Schuon*, xiv-xv.
[53] J-B. Aymard and P. Laude, *Frithjof Schuon: Life and Teachings*, 117.
[54] J-B. Aymard and P. Laude, *Frithjof Schuon: Life and Teachings*, 52.
[55] J-B. Aymard and P. Laude, *Frithjof Schuon: Life and Teachings*, 125
[56] J-B. Aymard and P. Laude, *Frithjof Schuon: Life and Teachings*, 108.

In the last few years several thematic anthologies of Schuon's writings have been published, including *René Guénon: Some Observations* (ed. William Stoddart, 2004), *The Fullness of God: Frithjof Schuon on Christianity* (ed. James Cutsinger, 2004), *Prayer Fashions Man: Frithjof Schuon on the Spiritual Life* (ed. James Cutsinger, 2005), and *Art from the Sacred to the Profane: East and West* (ed. Catherine Schuon, 2006). There is now also a burgeoning literature on Schuon's life and work. Readers are directed to the following: *The Essential Frithjof Schuon* (1986, 2005), which includes Seyyed Hossein Nasr's magisterial introduction; *Religion of the Heart* (1991), a *festschrift* compiled for Schuon's eightieth birthday, edited by Nasr and William Stoddart; James Cutsinger's *Advice to the Serious Seeker: Meditations on the Teaching of Frithjof Schuon* (1997); the Frithjof Schuon Memorial Issue of *Sophia* (4:2, 1998); *Frithjof Schuon: Connaissance et Voie d'Intériorité, Biographie études et témoignages*, edited by Bernard Chevilliat (1999); *Frithjof Schuon: Les Dossiers H* (2002), edited by Jean-Baptiste Aymard and Patrick Laude; *Frithjof Schuon: Life and Teachings* (2004) by Jean-Baptiste Aymard and Patrick Laude; *Frithjof Schuon (1907-1998): Notas biográficas, estudios, homenajes*, edited by Josep Prats and Esteve Serra (2004); the Winter 2007 issue of *Sacred Web* dedicated to Schuon on the occasion of his birth centenary; and a more intimate biography based on his diaries, letters, and other personal writings, *Frithjof Schuon: Messenger of the Perennial Philosophy* (2010), by Michael Fitzgerald.

*   *   *

In *Understanding Islam* Schuon had this to say about the nature of sacred Books:

> That is sacred which in the first place is attached to the transcendent order, secondly, possesses the character of absolute certainty and, thirdly, eludes the comprehension and power of investigation of the ordinary human mind. . . . The sacred is the presence of the center in the periphery, of the immutable in the moving; dignity is essentially an expression of it, for in dignity too the center manifests outwardly; the heart is revealed in gestures. The sacred introduces a quality of the absolute into relativities and confers on perishable things a texture of eternity.[57]

Without wishing to make any extravagant claims such as might conflate Schuon's writings with holy Scriptures, I do not think it too much to avow that these qualities are everywhere manifested in his own *oeuvre*. The pervasive sense of the sacred, the love of prayer, of sacred symbols and of the

---

[57] *Understanding Islam*, "The Koran", 45.

"modes of Divine Presence", the miraculous sensitivity to "theophanic manifestations" and "celestial perfumes", the discernment of the "metaphysical transparency of phenomena", the capacity to grasp the "principial within the manifested", to see "the vertical ray", to see God everywhere—these qualities overflow in Schuon's work and constitute a providential and incomparable gift to an age apparently determined to turn its back on the sacred.[58]

A fitting epitaph for Frithjof Schuon's life is provided by Seyyed Hossein Nasr, writing of the "integrated" man of Sufism:

> His thoughts and actions all issue from a single center and are based on a series of immutable principles. He has been cured of that hypocrisy in which most men live and therefore, since the veil of otherness which hides the inner light in the majority of men has been removed, like the sun he reflects his light wherever he happens to be. In him, the Islamic ideal of unifying the contemplative and active ways is realized. . . . And because by virtue of his becoming integrated he reflects Divine Unity and has become the total theophany of the Divine Names and Qualities, he acts and lives in such a manner that there is a spiritual fragrance and beauty about all he does and says. Somehow he is in touch with that *barakah* which runs through the arteries of the Universe.[59]

[58] The quoted phrases are Schuon's and come from fragments of correspondence published in *Transfiguration of Man*, 113.
[59] S.H. Nasr, *Sufi Essays*, 50.

2

Other Perennialists

> There are those whose vocation it is to provide the keys with which
> the treasury of wisdom of other traditions can be unlocked, revealing to
> those who are destined to receive this wisdom the essential unity and
> universality and at the same time the formal diversity of tradition and
> revelation. (*Seyyed Hossein Nasr*)[1]

> By directing our gaze toward the perennial wisdom of the traditional
> worlds, these authors show us that what our world most requires is
> nothing short of a wholesale reorientation of its outlook, for "as a man
> thinks, so he becomes". (*Huston Smith*)[2]

René Guénon, Ananda Coomaraswamy, and Frithjof Schuon have played
different but complementary roles in reaffirming the perennial philosophy,
each fulfilling a function corresponding to their distinct sensibilities and
gifts. They have been referred to as "the Great Triumvirate" of the perennialist, or traditionalist, school.[3] The distinctive role of Schuon can only be
fully understood against the backdrop provided by the work of Guénon and
Coomaraswamy. For this reason, and because of their role in the emergence
of the perennialist "school" of which Schuon became the foremost exponent, it is worth providing an overview of the life and work of each.

René Guénon (1886-1951)

René Guénon was born in Blois in 1886. He grew up in a strict Catholic
environment and was schooled by Jesuits. As a young man he moved to Paris
to pursue studies in mathematics at the Collège Rollin. Maths remained a
lifelong interest and a few years before his death he published a short math-

---

[1] S.H. Nasr, *Sufi Essays*, 126.

[2] H. Smith, Foreword to *The Essential Sophia*, ed. S.H. Nasr and K. O'Brien, vii.

[3] As was made clear in the Introduction, I do not altogether agree with the idea of the "Great
Triumvirate", sharing William Stoddart's view that Guénon must be regarded as the founder
of the perennialist "school" which is "brought to full fruition" by Schuon. These two figures
really tower above all other perennialists. Stoddart designates Coomaraswamy and Burckhardt
as the two "leading continuators of this current of intellectuality and spirituality". See W.
Stoddart, *Remembering in a World of Forgetting*, 51. Nonetheless, there are good reasons for
comparing the respective roles of Guénon, Coomaraswamy, and Schuon in some detail, as is
done in this chapter. The most obvious reason for including Coomaraswamy is the fact that
he was the most immediately and widely influential of the three figures, being much better
known, during his lifetime, in both the East and the West than the other two.

ematical treatise, *The Metaphysical Principles of the Infinitesimal Calculus* (1946). However, Guénon's energies were soon diverted from academic studies and in 1905 he abandoned his preparation for *Grandes Écoles*. For the next seven years, seized by what Anatole France called "the vertigo of the invisible", Guénon submerged himself in *fin-de-siècle* French occultism.[4] He became a leading member in several secret societies—theosophical, spiritualistic, masonic, and "gnostic". He was soon to become one of the most unsparing critics of these occultist movements. Although Guénon was to disown the philosophical and historical assumptions on which such movements were built and to contrast their "counterfeit spirituality" with what he came to see as genuine expressions of esoteric wisdom, he remained implacably opposed to contemporary European civilization.

Some of the occultist movements stimulated a study of ancient esoteric traditions in Egypt, Persia, India, and China, and turned attention towards the sacred writings of the East. Precisely how Guénon came to a serious study of Taoism, Hinduism, and Islam remains unclear. Whitall Perry has suggested that the "catalyzing element" was Guénon's contact in Paris with some Indians of the Advaita school.[5] In any event, Guénon's life entered a new phase in 1912, marked by his marriage to a devout Catholic. He emerged from the subterranean world of the occultists and now moved freely in an intensely Catholic milieu, leading a busy social and intellectual life. The years 1912 to 1930 were the most public of Guénon's life. He attended lectures at the Sorbonne, wrote and published widely, gave public lectures himself and maintained many social and intellectual contacts. He published his first books in the early 1920s and soon became well known for his work on metaphysical subjects.

The years 1927 to 1930 saw another transition in Guénon's life, culminating in his move to Cairo in 1930 and his open commitment to Islam.[6] Guénon's unhappy involvement in an ecclesiastical controversy and adverse Catholic criticism of his *The King of the World* (1927) compounded a growing disillusionment with the Church and hardened Guénon's suspicion that it had surrendered to the "temporal and material". In January 1928 Guénon's wife died rather abruptly. Following a series of fortuitous circumstances

[4] France's phrase is cited in M. Eliade, *Occultism, Witchcraft, and Cultural Fashions*, 51.
[5] W. Perry, "The Revival of Interest in Tradition", 8-9.
[6] In the case of both Guénon and Schuon it is inappropriate to speak of a "conversion" to Islam. Guénon: "I cannot let it be said that I 'converted to Islam' for this way of presenting things is completely false; whoever is aware of the essential unity of traditions is therefore 'unconvertible'... but one may 'settle', if one may say so, in such or such a tradition depending upon circumstances, and above all for reasons of an initiatory order" (from Alain Daniélou, "René Guénon et la tradition hindoue", 138). On Guénon's entry into Islam see also *René Guénon: Some Observations*, "René Guénon: A Note", 6.

Guénon left on a three-month visit to Cairo.[7] He was to remain there until his death in 1951.

In Cairo Guénon was initiated into the Sufic order of Shadhilites and invested with the name Abdel Wahed Yahya. He married again and lived a modest and retiring existence—

> Such was his anonymity that an admirer of his writings was dumb-founded to discover that the venerable next door neighbor whom she had known for years as Sheikh Abdel Wahed Yahya was in reality René Guénon.[8]

Much of Guénon's energy was directed in the 1930s to a massive correspondence with his readers in Europe, often people in search of some kind of initiation. Most of his published work after his move to Cairo appeared in *Études Traditionnelles* (until 1937 *Le Voile d'Isis*), a formerly theosophical journal that under Guénon's influence was transformed into the leading European forum for traditional thought. The war provided Guénon with enough respite from his correspondence to devote himself to the writing of some of his major works, including *The Reign of Quantity and the Signs of the Times* (1945).

The American traditionalist, Whitall Perry, who knew Guénon personally, speaks of his "outer anonymity" and of this "austere yet benevolent figure . . . ungraspable and remote".[9] Ananda Coomaraswamy wrote of him:

> The least important thing about Guénon is his personality or biography. . . . The fact is he has the invisibility that is proper to the complete philosopher: our teleology can only be fulfilled when we really become no one.[10]

There is indeed something elusive about René Guénon the man. He left a formidable legacy of writings which testify to his achievements as a metaphysician, but his personal life remains obscure.

Guénon occupies a special position in the perennialist movement by virtue of being the first to articulate the fundamental metaphysical and cosmological principles through which the *sophia perennis* might be rediscovered and expressed anew in the West. Schuon recognized Guénon as a "providential interpreter, at least on the doctrinal level" for the modern

---

[7] J.P. Laurant, "Le problème de René Guénon", 60.

[8] W. Perry, "Coomaraswamy: The Man, Myth, and History", 160.

[9] W. Perry, "Coomaraswamy: The Man, Myth, and History", 160, and "The Man and the Witness", 6.

[10] Letter to Kurt Leidecker, November 1941, *Selected Letters*, 49-50.

West.[11] In a like sense, Jean-Pierre Laurant refers to Guénon's "hieratic role".[12] Guénon's indictment of the "reign of quantity" also provides the platform from which more detailed critiques could be made by later traditionalists. His reaction to modernism was integral to his role and constitutes a kind of clearing of the ground, enabling us to understand

> some of the darkest enigmas of the modern world, enigmas which the world itself denies because it is incapable of perceiving them although it carries them within itself, and because this denial is an indispensable condition for the maintenance of the special mentality whereby it exists.[13]

Guénon was a prolific writer. He published seventeen books during his lifetime, and at least twelve posthumous collections and compilations have since appeared. Amongst his most important works are *Man and His Becoming According to the Vedanta* (1925), *Crisis of the Modern World* (1927), *The Symbolism of the Cross* (1931), *The Great Triad* (1946), and his masterwork, *The Reign of Quantity and the Signs of the Times* (1945).[14] The *oeuvre* exhibits certain recurrent motifs and preoccupations and is, in a sense, all of a piece. As early as 1909 we find Guénon writing of "the Primordial Tradition which, in reality, is the same everywhere, regardless of the different shapes it takes in order to be fit for every race and every historical period."[15] As the English writer Gai Eaton observed, Guénon

> believes that there exists a Universal Tradition, revealed to humanity at the beginning of the present cycle of time, but partially lost. . . . His primary concern is less with the detailed forms of this Tradition and the history of its decline than with its kernel, the pure and changeless knowledge which is still accessible to man through the channels provided by traditional doctrine.[16]

The existence of a Primordial Tradition embodying a set of immutable metaphysical and cosmological principles from which derive a succession of traditions each expressing these principles in forms determined by a given

---

[11] Frithjof Schuon, "L'Oeuvre", quoted in W. Perry, "Coomaraswamy: The Man, Myth, and History", 160.

[12] J-P. Laurant, "Le problème de René Guénon", 63.

[13] R. Guénon, *The Reign of Quantity and the Signs of the Times*, 11.

[14] Dates are for the first French editions. The first English translations appeared, respectively, in 1928, 1942, 1958, 1991 and 1953.

[15] R. Guénon, "Le Démiurge", *La Gnose* 1909, quoted in M. Bastriocchi, "The Last Pillars of Wisdom", 351.

[16] G. Eaton, *The Richest Vein*, 188-189.

Revelation and by the exigencies of the particular situation, is axiomatic in Guénon's work.[17]

Guénon's work, from his earliest writings onwards, can be seen as an attempt to give a new expression and application to the unchanging principles which inform all traditional doctrines. In his writings he ranges over a vast domain—Vedanta, the Chinese tradition, Christianity, Sufism, folklore and mythology from all over the world, the secret traditions of gnosticism, alchemy, the Kabbalah, and so on, always intent on excavating their underlying principles and showing them to be formal expressions of the one Tradition. Several key themes run through his writings and one meets again and again with such notions as these: the idea of metaphysics transcending all other doctrinal orders, and thus the hierarchic superiority and infallibility of intellective knowledge; the identification of metaphysics and the "formalization", so to speak, of gnosis (or *jnana* if one prefers); the distinction between the exoteric and esoteric domains; the contrast of the modern Occident with the traditional Orient; the spiritual bankruptcy of modern European civilization; a cyclical view of Time, based largely on the Hindu doctrine of cosmic cycles; a contra-evolutionary view of history.

Guénon gathered together doctrines and principles from diverse times and places but emphasized that the enterprise was a *synthetic* one which envisaged formally divergent elements in their principial convergence rather than a *syncretic* one which press-ganged incongruous forms into a factitious unity.[18] He repeatedly turned to Oriental wisdoms, believing that it was only in the East that various sapiential traditions remained more or less intact. It is important not to confuse this Eastward-looking stance with the kind of sentimental exoticism nowadays so much in vogue. As Coomaraswamy noted:

> If Guénon wants the West to turn to Eastern metaphysics, it is not because they are Eastern but because this is metaphysics. If "Eastern" metaphysics differed from a "Western" metaphysics—one or the other would not be metaphysics.[19]

Marco Pallis, one of Guénon's translators, made the same point in suggesting that if he turns so often to the East it is because the West is in the position of the

---

[17] The relationship between the Primordial Tradition and the various traditions needs clarification in that while each tradition in fact derives its overall form and principal characteristics from a particular Revelation, it nevertheless carries over (in many of its aspects) certain essential features of the tradition which precedes it.

[18] See R. Guénon, *The Symbolism of the Cross*, x-xi, and *Crisis of the Modern World*, 9, 108ff.

[19] A. Coomaraswamy, *The Bugbear of Literacy*, 72-73.

foolish virgins who, through the wandering of their attention in other directions, had allowed their lamps to go out; in order to rekindle the sacred fire, which in its essence is always the same wherever it may be burning, they must have recourse to the lamps still kept alight.[20]

The contrast between the riches of traditional civilizations and the spiritual impoverishment of modern Europe sounds like a refrain through Guénon's writings. Throughout,

> Guénon's mission was twofold: to reveal the metaphysical roots of the "crisis of the modern world" and to explain the ideas behind the authentic and esoteric teachings that still remained alive . . . in the East.[21]

For those in the West who accept Guénon's premises he is a voice crying in the wilderness. However, as both Schuon and Perry have stressed, Guénon's function cannot strictly be termed "prophetic", the age of prophecy being over. Schuon:

> If on the doctrinal plane the Guénonian work has a stamp of unicity, it may not be useless to point out that this is owing not to a more or less "prophetic" nature—a supposition that is excluded and which Guénon had already rejected beforehand—but to an exceptional cyclical conjuncture whose temporal aspect is this "end of the world" in which we live, and whose spatial aspect is—by the same token—the forced convergence of civilizations.[22]

It is also worth noting that Guénon never assumed the role of a spiritual master; he consistently refused those who requested initiation from him.[23] Guénon remarked in a letter to Martin Lings, "I would never have wanted to have any [disciples], not for anything in the world!"[24]

Like other traditionalists, Guénon did not perceive his work as any kind of essay in creativity or personal "originality", often insisting that in the metaphysical domain there was no room for "individualist considerations" of any kind. He certainly did not see himself building a new "philosophy" or creating a new "school of thought". In a letter to a friend Guénon wrote, "I have no other merit than to have expressed to the best of my ability some

---

[20] Quoted in G. Eaton, *The Richest Vein*, 199.

[21] J. Needleman, Foreword to *The Sword of Gnosis*, 11-12.

[22] From Frithjof Schuon, "L'Oeuvre", quoted in W. Perry, "Coomaraswamy: The Man, Myth, and History", 160. For some reflections by Schuon on Guénon see *René Guénon: Some Observations*.

[23] See J-P. Laurant, "Le problème de René Guénon", 62-64.

[24] Guénon quoted in *Frithjof Schuon: Messenger of the Perennial Philosophy*, 185.

traditional ideas."[25] When reminded of the people who had been profoundly influenced by his writings he calmly replied, "such disposition becomes a homage rendered to the doctrine expressed by us in a way which is totally independent of any individualistic consideration".[26] It was Guénon's role to remind a forgetful world, "in a way that can be ignored but not refuted", of first principles and to restore a lost sense of the Absolute".[27]

Ananda Coomaraswamy (1877-1947)

Ananda Coomaraswamy was a much more public figure than René Guénon. His life story has been admirably recounted by Roger Lipsey.[28] A few biographical facts: Coomaraswamy was born in Colombo in 1877, the son of a distinguished Tamil jurist, Sir Mutu Coomaraswamy, and his English wife. Thus, by nativity, Coomaraswamy belonged to both East and West. He was schooled in England but in his formative years frequently traveled between his two homelands. Coomaraswamy initially embarked on a career as a geologist. However, during field studies in Ceylon his exposure to traditional arts and crafts steered his life in a new direction. He soon established himself as a pioneering scholar in the traditional arts and crafts not just of Ceylon but of the whole Indian sub-continent as well as other parts of South-East Asia. He possessed prodigious scholarly gifts, including an astonishing aptitude for languages; he is said to have known thirty-six different languages![29] His ever-proliferating scholarly output saw him appointed, in 1917, as the first Keeper of Indian Art in the Museum of Fine Arts in Boston, where he spent the rest of his professional life. He died in Needham, Massachusetts, in 1947.

By the end of his life Coomaraswamy was thoroughly versed in the Scriptures, mythology, doctrines, and arts of many different cultures. He was an immensely erudite scholar, a profound thinker, a distinguished linguist, and an extraordinarily productive writer—a full bibliography running to upwards of a thousand items on geological studies, art theory and history, linguistics, philology, social theory, psychology, mythology, folklore, religion, and metaphysics. The great Orientalist, Heinrich Zimmer, remarked of Coomaraswamy, "the only man in my field who, whenever I read a paper of his, gives me a genuine inferiority complex".[30] Coomaraswamy lived in three continents and maintained many contacts, both personal and professional,

[25] W. Perry, "The Man and His Witness", 7.
[26] M. Bastriocchi, "The Last Pillars of Wisdom", 356.
[27] W. Perry, "Coomaraswamy: The Man, Myth, and History", 63.
[28] R. Lipsey, *Coomaraswamy: His Life and Work* (1977).
[29] See "Ananda Coomaraswamy" in *Wikipedia.*
[30] Zimmer, quoted in W. McGuire, "Zimmer and the Mellens", 38.

with scholars, antiquarians, artists, theologians, and spiritual practitioners from all over the globe.

We can discern in Coomaraswamy's life and work three focal points which shaped his ideas and writings: a concern with social and political questions connected with the conditions of daily life and work, and with the problematic relationship of the present to the past (this tension sometimes manifesting in contrasts between "West" and "East"); a fascination with traditional arts and crafts which impelled an immense scholarly enterprise; and thirdly, largely under the influence of Guénon, an emerging preoccupation with religious and metaphysical questions, which was resolved in a "unique balance of metaphysical conviction and scholarly erudition".[31]

From the outset Coomaraswamy's interest in art was controlled by much more than either antiquarian or "aesthetic" considerations. For him the most humble folk art and the loftiest religious creations alike were an outward expression not only of the sensibilities of those who created them but of the whole civilization in which they were nurtured. There was nothing of the *art nouveau* slogan of "art for art's sake" in Coomaraswamy's outlook. His interest in traditional arts and crafts, from a humble pot to a medieval cathedral, was always motivated by the conviction that something immeasurably precious and vitally important was disappearing under the onslaughts of modernity. As his biographer remarks, "history of art was never for him either a light question—one that had only to do with pleasures—or a question of scholarship for its own sake, but rather a question of setting right what had gone amiss partly through ignorance of the past."[32]

During the late 1920s Coomaraswamy's life and work somewhat altered their trajectory. The collapse of his third marriage, ill-health and a growing awareness of death, an impatience with the constrictions of purely academic scholarship, and the influence of René Guénon all deepened Coomaraswamy's interest in spiritual and metaphysical questions.[33] He became more austere in his personal lifestyle, partially withdrew from the academic and social worlds in which he had moved freely over the last decade, and addressed himself to traditional metaphysics, especially those of classical India and pre-Renaissance Europe. He remarked in one of his letters that "my indoctrination with the *Philosophia Perennis* is primarily Oriental, secondarily

---

[31] From R. Lipsey, *Coomaraswamy: His Life and Work*, quoted in W. Perry, "The Bollingen Coomaraswamy Papers and Biography", 206.

[32] R. Lipsey, *Coomaraswamy: His Life and Work*, 20.

[33] See R. Lipsey, *Coomaraswamy: His Life and Work*, 161-175. On Coomaraswamy's move from "descriptive iconography" to metaphysics see his letter to Herman Goetz, June 1939, in *Selected Letters*, 26-27.

Mediaeval, and thirdly classic".[34] His later work is densely textured with references to Plato and Plotinus, Augustine and Aquinas, Eckhart and the Rhenish mystics, to Shankara, Lao Tzu, and Nagarjuna. He also immersed himself in folklore and mythology since these too carried profound teachings. Coomaraswamy remained the consummate scholar but his later work took on more urgency. He spoke of his "vocation"—and he was not one to use such words lightly—as "research in the field of the significance of the universal symbols of the *Philosophia Perennis*" rather than as "one of apology for or polemic on behalf of doctrines".[35]

Coomaraswamy discovered Guénon's writings through Heinrich Zimmer, some time in the early thirties and, a few years later, wrote:

> No living writer in modern Europe is more significant than René Guénon, whose task it has been to expound the universal metaphysical tradition that has been the essential foundation of every past culture, and which represents the indispensable basis for any civilization deserving to be so-called.[36]

Several commentators have detailed the creative reciprocal influences which flowed between Coomaraswamy and Guénon.[37] We shall not go over this ground again here. However, it is worth noting that Coomaraswamy told one of his friends that he and Guénon were "entirely in agreement on metaphysical principles" which, of course, did not preclude some divergences of opinion over the applications of these principles on the plane of historical phenomena.[38]

We can ratify Coomaraswamy's own words: "I have little doubt that my later work, developed out of and was necessitated by my earlier works on the arts and dealing with Indian philosophy and Vedic exegesis, is really the most mature and most important part of my work."[39] Some of his work is labyrinthine and not easy of access. It is often laden with a mass of technical detail and with linguistic and philological subtleties which test the patience of some readers. Of his own methodology as an exponent of metaphysics, Coomaraswamy wrote:

> We write from a strictly orthodox point of view . . . endeavoring to speak with mathematical precision, but never employing words of our

---

[34] Letter to Artemus Packard, May 1941, *Selected Letters*, 299.

[35] A. Coomaraswamy, "The Bugbear of Democracy, Freedom, and Equality", 134.

[36] Quoted in R. Lipsey, *Coomaraswamy: His Life and Work*, 170.

[37] See W. Perry, "The Man and the Witness", 3-7; M. Pallis, "A Fateful Meeting of Minds", 176-182; and M. Bastriocchi, "The Last Pillars of Wisdom", 350-359.

[38] W. Perry, "The Man and the Witness", 5.

[39] Coomaraswamy, quoted in R. Lipsey, *Coomaraswamy: His Life and Work*, 248. (Coomaraswamy's claim somewhat underplays the decisive "external" influence of Guénon's work.)

own, or making any affirmation for which authority could not be cited by chapter and verse; in this way making our technique characteristically Indian.[40]

Coomaraswamy was much more scrupulous than Guénon in this respect, the latter sometimes ignoring the niceties of scholarship at the cost of exposing some of his claims to academic criticism.

There is no finer exegesis of traditional Indian metaphysics than is to be found in Coomaraswamy's later works. His work on the Platonic, Christian, and Indian conceptions of sacred art is also immensely impressive.[41] Roger Lipsey has performed an invaluable service in bringing some of Coomaraswamy's finest essays on these subjects together in *Coomaraswamy, Selected Papers* (2 volumes). But it hardly matters what one picks up from Coomaraswamy's later years: all his mature work is stamped with rare scholarship, elegant expression, and a depth of understanding which makes most of the other scholarly work on the same subjects look vapid.[42]

The Roles of Guénon, Coomaraswamy, and Schuon

Coomaraswamy brought to the study of traditional metaphysics, sacred art, and religious culture an aesthetic sense and a scholarly aptitude not found in Guénon. The Frenchman had "no great sensitivity for human cultures".[43] In a sense Coomaraswamy brings the principles about which Guénon wrote, down to a more human level. His work evinces more of a sense of history, and a feel for the diverse and concrete circumstances of human experience. There is also a sense of personal presence in Coomaraswamy's writings that is absent in Guénon's work which, to some readers at least, must appear somewhat abstract and rarefied. As Gai Eaton put it, to move from Guénon's work to Coomaraswamy's is to "descend into a far kindlier climate, while remaining in the same country. . . . The icy glitter is replaced by a warmer glow, the attitude of calm disdain towards all things modern

---

[40] Coomaraswamy, quoted in V.S. Naravane, "Ananda Coomaraswamy: A Critical Appreciation", 206

[41] It is, however, worth pointing out that certain deficiencies in Coomaraswamy's work—for instance, concerning the *sacramental* role of art—were remedied by both Schuon and Burckhardt.

[42] Of his later books three in particular deserve much wider attention: *Christian and Oriental Philosophy of Art* (1939), *Hinduism and Buddhism* (1943), and *Time and Eternity* (1947). *The Bugbear of Literacy* (1979) (first published in 1943 as *Am I My Brother's Keeper?*) and two posthumous collections of some of his most interesting and accessible essays, *Sources of Wisdom* (1981) and *What is Civilization?* (1989), offer splendid starting-points for uninitiated readers. *Guardians of the Sun-Door: Late Iconographic Essays* (2007) is another important posthumous compilation.

[43] P. L. Reynolds, *René Guénon: His Life and Work* (unpublished manuscript), 6.

by a more human indignation."[44] Whitall Perry contrasts their roles through a metaphor which each would have appreciated:

> Guénon was like the vertical axis of a cross, fixed with mathematical precision on immutable realities and their immediate applications in the domain of cosmological sciences; whereas Coomaraswamy was the horizontal complement, expanding these truths over the vast field of arts, cultures, mythologies, and symbolisms: metaphysical truth on the one hand, universal beauty on the other.[45]

Schuon combined in himself something of the qualities of both Guénon and Coomaraswamy. His work includes psychic, moral, and aesthetic dimensions which are missing from Guénon's writings and are, in Jean Borella's words, "more open to the intelligence of beauty".[46] As Jean Tourniac has remarked:

> Another writer, M. Frithjof Schuon, for his part, had to develop the spiritual exegesis of traditional forms in a series of works of a different kind to those of Guénon, works of high color. . . . This word is not excessive, for beauty and color play a distinctive role in the work of F. Schuon . . . [which are] more "Christly" than those of Guénon which essentially hold themselves to defining the mechanisms of invariable principles.[47]

Schuon's work has a symmetry and an inclusive quality not found in the work of his precursors; there is a balance and fullness which give his writings something of the quality of a spiritual therapy. In this sense Schuon does not simply write *about* the perennial philosophy but gives it a direct and fresh expression proportioned to the needs of the age.

The contrast with Guénon can be clearly seen in the style and tone of language. If Guénon's expositions can be called "mathematical", Schuon's might be described as "musical"; this, of course, not implying any deficiency in precision but rather the addition of a dimension of beauty. As Professor Nasr has observed of Schuon's writings, "His authoritative tone, clarity of expression, and an 'alchemy' which transmutes human language to enable it to present the profoundest truths, make of it a unique expression of the . . . *sophia perennis*."[48] Marco Pallis refers to what he rather loosely calls "the gift of tongues": "the ability, that is to say, both to speak and to understand

---

[44] G. Eaton, *The Richest Vein*, 199.

[45] W. Perry, "The Man and the Witness", 7.

[46] J. Borella, "René Guénon and the Traditionalist School", 349.

[47] J. Tourniac, quoted in P.L. Reynolds, *René Guénon: His Life and Work*, 13 (translation mine).

[48] S.H. Nasr, Preface to *Islam and the Perennial Philosophy*, viii.

the various dialects through which the Spirit has chosen to communicate itself . . . the power to penetrate all traditional forms".[49]

Like Guénon, Schuon appears to have an intuitive grasp of metaphysical and cosmological principles but he does not subordinate facts to principles in a way which would leave his work vulnerable to scholarly attack. One sometimes senses in Guénon's work an impatience with and disdain for empirical and historical considerations. Schuon's commitment to first principles is no less steadfast but he is more sensitive to the exigencies and diversities of human experience and to the spiritual and psychological textures of different civilizations. In this sense he is closer to Coomaraswamy, with whom he also shares a discerning eye for the spiritual riches of traditional art. Although formidably learned, Schuon's approach is less academic and scholarly than Coomaraswamy's, less burdened with technical minutiae and the ever-proliferating qualifications which often make Coomaraswamy's work something of an obstacle course. As a writer he is more discursive and fluid, more poetic, than either Guénon or Coomaraswamy.

For Schuon the study of tradition has meant, primarily, the elucidation of religious forms within a metaphysical framework. Guénon's work was fixed on questions of principle and on the esoteric repositories of metaphysical wisdom. Coomaraswamy's interests were wide-ranging indeed but, for the most part, underpinned by his preoccupation with the relationships of Truth, Beauty, and Goodness. Schuon, on the other hand, moves in a boundless universe, being concerned with intellectual and spiritual life in all its aspects. He illuminates religion in all its dimensions: doctrinal, ethical, psychological, historical, social, aesthetic and so on. He is equally at home with the most abstruse subtleties of, say, Eckhart's exposition of metaphysical knowledge, and the simple pieties of a European peasant. The explanation of the exoteric-esoteric distinction is fundamental in Schuon's work but, unlike Guénon, he does not restrict himself to the latter domain alone. His books are more attuned to the legitimate claims of religious forms and of orthodox theologies than those of either of his precursors. He situates the exoteric and esoteric aspects of religion in a framework that gives to each its due.

Writing of the work of Schuon in relation to that of Guénon and Coomaraswamy, Whitall Perry suggested that

> The complement and copestone of this witness remained to be realized in the message of Schuon, coming freshly from the sphere of the *Religio Perennis,* in contradistinction to the *Philosophia Perennis* which was the legacy of the other two. His was the third pole, needed to complete the triangle and integrate the work on an operative basis.[50]

[49] M. Pallis, *The Way and the Mountain*, 78.
[50] W. Perry, "The Man and the Witness", 7.

Seyyed Hossein Nasr has compared the three figures this way:

> If Guénon was the master expositor of metaphysical doctrines and Coomaraswamy the peerless scholar and connoisseur of Oriental art who began his exposition of metaphysics through recourse to the language of artistic forms, Schuon seems like the cosmic intellect itself impregnated by the energy of divine grace surveying the whole of the reality surrounding man and elucidating all the concerns of human existence in the light of sacred knowledge.[51]

There is a nobility of spirit in Schuon's work which makes it something much more than a challenging and arresting body of ideas: it is a profoundly moving *theoria* which reverberates in the deepest recesses of one's being. Not without justification did Whitall Perry compare Schuon's work to that of Plato and Shankara.[52] In Schuon's work we find the richest, the most authoritative, and the most resonant expression of the *sophia perennis* in modern times. One might borrow the following words, applied to Meister Eckhart but equally true of Schuon:

> Being wholly traditional in the truest sense, and therefore perennial, the doctrine he expounds will never cease to be contemporary and always accessible to those who, naturally unsatisfied with mere living, desire to know how to live, regardless of time or place.[53]

Other Perennialists

As Ananda Coomaraswamy observed,

> There is a universally intelligible language, not only verbal but also visual, of the fundamental ideas on which the different civilizations have been founded. . . . We need mediators to whom the common universe of discourse is still a reality.[54]

Since Coomaraswamy's death in 1947 a group of just such mediators has emerged; collectively they can be called the perennialist "school", with Schuon at the center. The members of this loose-knit movement have not sought the limelight and many of them were obscured from public view. It will perhaps be useful to sketch out a few simple pen-portraits of some of these figures.

---

[51] S.H. Nasr, *Knowledge and the Sacred,* 107.
[52] W. Perry, "The Revival of Interest in Tradition", 15.
[53] C.F. Kelley, *Meister Eckhart on Divine Knowledge,* xv.
[54] A. Coomaraswamy, *The Bugbear of Literacy,* 80, 88.

Titus Burckhardt (1908-1984)

After the passing of Guénon and Coomaraswamy, the most authoritative exponent of traditional thought, Schuon aside, was Titus Burckhardt.[55] As William Stoddart has stated, within the perennialist movement there have been two great "originators", Guénon and Schuon, and two great "continuators", Coomaraswamy and Burckhardt.[56] Born into a patrician family in Florence in 1908, Titus was the son of the Swiss sculptor Carl Burckhardt and great-nephew of the renowned art historian, Jacob Burckhardt. As a young schoolboy he became a companion of Frithjof Schuon, his senior by one year; this was the beginning of "an intimate friendship and a deeply harmonious intellectual and spiritual relationship that was to last a lifetime".[57] As a young man, Burckhardt spent many years in North Africa where he received initiation into a Sufi order. He mastered Arabic and assimilated the classics of Sufism in their original versions. In later years he was to share these treasures with a wider public through his irreplaceable translations of Ibn Arabi, Jili, and the eighteenth century Moroccan spiritual master, Mulay al-Arabi ad-Darqawi.[58] Later, back in Switzerland, he was for several years a director of the publishing firm Urs Graf Verlag, which specialized in producing facsimile editions of such outstanding medieval illuminated manuscripts as the Book of Kells and the Lindisfarne Gospels. He also served as a consultant on the preservation and restoration of traditional cities such as Fez and Siena. Burckhardt died in Lausanne in 1984.

Burckhardt wrote principally in his native German. Most of his works have now been translated into English; these include *Introduction to Sufi Doctrine* (1959), *Sacred Art in East and West* (1967), *Alchemy: Science of the Cosmos, Science of the Soul* (1967), *Moorish Culture in Spain* (1972), and *Art of Islam* (1976). William Stoddart identifies the first of these books as Burckhardt's "chief metaphysical exposition, beautifully complementing the work of Schuon. . . . [It is] an intellectual masterpiece which analyzes comprehensively and with precision the nature of esoterism as such".[59] In the space of a few years Burckhardt also produced a remarkable series of

---

[55] For biographical information on Burckhardt see W. Stoddart, "Right Hand of Truth" and M. Lings, "Titus Burckhardt", both in the Titus Burckhardt Memorial Issue of *Studies in Comparative Religion*, 16: 1-2, 1984. This issue also includes contributions from Seyyed Hossein Nasr and Jean-Louis Michon. See also W. Stoddart, "Titus Burckhardt: An Outline of His Life and Works" in Burckhardt's *Mirror of the Intellect*, 3-9.
[56] W. Stoddart, *Remembering in a World of Forgetting*, 50. Stoddart here follows Schuon's own understanding of his role and those of the other three.
[57] W. Stoddart, "Titus Burckhardt: An Outline of His Life and Works", 5.
[58] A full bibliography of Burckhardt's work can be found in *Mirror of the Intellect*, 255-262, and in *The Essential Titus Burckhardt*, 312-321.
[59] W. Stoddart, *Remembering in a World of Forgetting*, 57.

monographs on sacred cities: *Siena: City of the Virgin* (1958), *Fez: City of Islam* (1960), and *Chartres and the Birth of the Cathedral* (1962). It was works such as these that later prompted Huston Smith to remark, "No one since the legendary A.K. Coomaraswamy has been able to demonstrate how entire civilizations define themselves through their art with the precision of Titus Burckhardt."[60]

Although he first followed in his father's footsteps as a sculptor and illustrator, Burckhardt was from childhood attracted to traditional art. This early interest provoked a study of medieval and Eastern doctrines and awoke in Burckhardt an understanding of the intellectual principles that govern all traditional forms. For Burckhardt, the relationship between art and metaphysics finds perfect expression in the words of Plato, "Beauty is the splendor of Truth". In the same vein a medieval artist had declared "*ars sine scientia nihil*" ("art without science is nothing").[61] Following the same line of thought Burckhardt has shown how, in a traditional society, every art is a science, and every science an art. Furthermore, Burckhardt "had a particular affinity with traditional art and craftsmanship and was skilled in the evaluation of traditional architecture, iconography, and other arts and crafts. In particular, he dwelt on how they had been—and could be—turned to account spiritually, both as meaningful activities which by virtue of their inherent symbolism harbor a doctrinal message, and above all as supports for spiritual realization and means of grace."[62]

Burckhardt had a deep interest in traditional cosmology ("the handmaid of metaphysics"), in the sacred sciences of the traditional worlds, and in the deviations of modern science which so often negated, inverted, or parodied traditional doctrines. His most important cosmological work is *Alchemy*, "a brilliant presentation of alchemy as the expression of a spiritual psychology and as an intellectual and symbolic support for contemplation and realization".[63] Another central work is "Traditional Cosmology and Modern Science" (a gathering together of several articles) which ruthlessly exposes the precarious foundations and the malign effects of materialist physics, Darwinian evolutionism, and Freudian psychology, three of the mainstays of the contemporary outlook. It was published in *The Sword of Gnosis* (1974), and is also included in Burckhardt's collected essays, *Mirror of the Intellect* (1987).

---

[60] Huston Smith, cited on the back cover of *The Essential Titus Burckhardt*.

[61] See A.K. Coomaraswamy, "*Ars Sine Scientia Nihil*" in *Selected Papers 1*, 229.

[62] W. Stoddart, *Remembering in a World of Forgetting*, 57.

[63] W. Stoddart, "Titus Burckhardt: An Outline of His Life and Works", 6.

Burckhardt's work is in one sense a prolongation of that of Frithjof Schuon, but at every turn it also bears witness to his own spiritual originality and imposing gifts. Of his close friend, Schuon wrote this:

> What was precious about Titus Burckhardt's personality was the combination of an extraordinarily penetrating and profound intelligence with great artistic talent. . . . He was at the same time very gifted for mystical contemplation. . . . He had in him an eternal youthfulness. . . . I can add that he was an excellent writer: we all know that.[64]

Burckhardt is still less widely known than Guénon, Coomaraswamy, and Schuon but in traditionalist circles his work is held in the highest regard. As Seyyed Hossein Nasr has written:

> Titus Burckhardt lived the truth of which he wrote. The exceptional light of intelligence which emanated from him pierced to the heart of the texts he studied and illuminated their meaning in a manner which is possible only by a person in whom the truth has descended from the plane of the mind to the center of the heart and become fully realized.[65]

Not for nothing did Stoddart call Burckhardt the "Right Hand of Truth".

Marco Pallis (1895-1989)

The only Buddhist in what might be called the "inner circle" of traditionalists was Marco Pallis.[66] He was born of Greek parents in Liverpool in 1895, educated at Harrow and Liverpool University, and served in the British army during the Great War. Later he studied music with Arnold Dolmetsch, whose approach, Pallis tells us, was shaped by "a radical rejection of the idea of 'progress', as applied to the arts, at a time when the rest of the musical profession took this for granted."[67] Dolmetsch himself was familiar with Coomaraswamy's work and it was through him that Pallis first heard of the scholar who was to become, along with Guénon, such a decisive influence.

Pallis twice visited southern Tibet on mountaineering trips in the 1930s. Consumed by an interest in the country's traditional culture, he returned for a third and more extended visit after the war when he lived and studied

---

[64] Frithjof Schuon, letter to Hans Küry, January 21, 1984, cited in J-B. Aymard and P. Laude, *Frithjof Schuon: Life and Teachings*, 9.
[65] Nasr, cited on back cover of *The Essential Burckhardt*.
[66] Information on Pallis taken from his own books, from his article "A Fateful Meeting of Minds: A.K. Coomaraswamy and René Guénon", 175-188, and from T. Merton, *Asian Journal*, 71-72. See also J. Fitzgerald, "From Marco Pallis to Thubden Tendzin: A Son of Tibet Returns", and Paul Goble's "Appreciation" in the new edition of *The Way and the Mountain* (2008).
[67] M. Pallis, "A Fateful Meeting of Minds", 176.

under Tibetan lamas near Shigatse, where he was initiated into one of the lineages.[68] On his way to Tibet in 1947 Pallis visited René Guénon, two of whose books he had already translated with his friend Richard Nicholson. He also visited Ceylon and South India, receiving the *darshan* of Ramana Maharshi at Tiruvannamalai. Pallis returned to England in 1951 and, with Nicholson and some other musicians, formed "The English Consort of Viols", a group dedicated to the preservation of early English music. In a sense this completed the circle which began with his studies under Dolmetsch in the 1920s. Pallis made several concert tours with this group. On one such tour to the U.S.A. he met Thomas Merton with whom he had already opened a correspondence.[69]

Marco Pallis wrote two books deriving from his experiences in Tibet: *Peaks and Lamas* (1939), which was reprinted several times and became something of a bestseller, and *The Way and the Mountain* (1960), recently republished. They are a unique blend of travelogue, discursive essays on the Tibetan civilization, and metaphysical expositions. He also wrote a number of articles for *Studies in Comparative Religion*, many of which can be found in *A Buddhist Spectrum* (1980). The work of Marco Pallis radiates a distinctively Buddhist ambience and fulfils a vital function, this tradition receiving comparatively little attention from other perennialists—aside from Schuon's *Treasures of Buddhism*.

Martin Lings (1909-2005)

The foremost English traditionalist, Martin Lings, was born in Burnage, Lancashire, in 1909.[70] After studying English at Oxford, where his tutor was C.S. Lewis, he was appointed Lecturer in Anglo-Saxon at the University of Kaunas. An interest in Islam took him to the Middle East and North Africa. He embraced Sufism in the 1930s and became a disciple of Frithjof Schuon. Of their first meeting he said:

> I knew when I was in his presence that I was in the presence of a true saint and also the spiritual master that I was seeking. When I say "true saint", I don't mean just a saintly man but a true saint of the first magnitude, such as one cannot expect to meet in the twentieth century.... I knew this with a certainty.[71]

In 1940 Lings traveled to Cairo to meet René Guénon with whom he was henceforth to have a close relationship, often acting as his secretary and

---

[68] A. Desjardins, *The Message of the Tibetans*, 20.

[69] See M. Pallis, "Thomas Merton, 1915-1968", 138-146.

[70] Information on Lings taken from his own publications. See also the many tributes which followed his death in 2005, in *Sophia* 11:1 and *Sacred Web* 15.

[71] Quoted from an interview, in M. Fitzgerald, "In Memoriam: Dr Martin Lings", 146.

emissary. He soon secured an appointment as Lecturer in Shakespeare at Cairo University where he taught for the next eleven years.

In 1952 Lings returned to England to take a doctorate in Arabic—in which he was already fluent—at London University. He worked for many years at the British Museum where he was Keeper of Oriental Manuscripts and Printed Books. As well as being a highly productive writer Lings was a tireless traveler. In the last six months of his life, in his mid-90s, he traveled to Egypt, Dubai, Pakistan, Malaysia, and South Africa, visiting the far-flung Sufi communities to which he had provided spiritual counsel for many years.

Martin Lings was an authority on Koranic manuscripts and calligraphy. His biography of the Shaykh Ahmad al-Alawi, *A Moslem Saint of the Twentieth Century* (1961), is a gem of Islamic spirituality. *The Book of Certainty* (1952), written under his Islamic name, Abu Bakr Siraj ad-Din, dealt with Sufic doctrines of faith, vision, and gnosis, while *What is Sufism?* (1975) is a more popular introductory work. In *Ancient Beliefs and Modern Superstitions* (1965) Lings took up certain themes from Guénon and Coomaraswamy to write a powerful indictment of modernism. He also published a fascinating study of Shakespeare's major plays, *The Secret of Shakespeare* (1966), as well as two volumes of poetry *The Elements* and *The Heralds.*[72] Later works include *The Quranic Art of Calligraphy and Illumination* (1976), *The Eleventh Hour* (1989), which deals with eschatological doctrines, and *Symbol and Archetype* (1991). Perhaps his most enduring work will be *Muhammad: His Life Based on the Earliest Sources* (1983) in which the Prophet's life is recounted with an authority and dignity appropriate to the subject.

Whitall Perry (1920-2005)

The most authoritative traditionalist of American background was Whitall Perry.[73] He was born near Boston in 1920. His early intellectual interests included Platonism and Vedanta. He traveled in the Middle and Far East both before and after World War II, with a brief interlude at Harvard University. In the course of his extensive travels he absorbed a great deal from Islamic, Hindu, and Buddhist cultures. He was one of several Harvard students, including Joseph Epes Brown, who in the 1940s came under the influence of Ananda Coomaraswamy who, in turn, introduced Perry to the writings of Guénon and Schuon. Between 1946 and 1952 Perry and his wife lived in Egypt where he developed close ties with René Guénon, after whose death he moved with his family to Switzerland. He soon became a

---

[72] The two volumes were subsequently published together as *Collected Poems* (2001).
[73] Material on Perry drawn from his own publications, especially "The Man and the Witness" and Marco Pallis' Foreword to W. Perry (ed.), *A Treasury of Traditional Wisdom*, 7-11.

close associate of Schuon, with whom he returned to the United States in 1980. (William Stoddart has pointed out that Perry was one of a very small handful of people who knew all four of the leading traditionalists—Guénon, Schuon, Coomaraswamy, and Burckhardt.[74])

Coomaraswamy once expressed the view that the time was ripe for someone well-versed in the world's great religious traditions and fluent in several languages to compile an encyclopedic anthology drawing together the spiritual Wisdom of the Ages in a single volume. This task was to be accomplished by Whitall Perry, whose seventeen-year labor bore fruit in *A Treasury of Traditional Wisdom* (1971).[75] This is a work of singular importance. In his Introduction Perry invites the reader

> To enter upon a spiritual journey. In this book he will encounter the heritage he shares in common with all humanity, in what is essentially timeless and enduring and pertinent to his final ends. Out of this myriad mosaic of material emerges a pattern of the human personality in the cosmos that is unerringly consistent, clear, and struck through with a resonance infallible in its ever renewed reverberations of the one same Reality.[76]

Thousands of quotations have been woven into an immense tapestry whose threads have been drawn from all the major religious and wisdom traditions. Each section of the book is introduced with a concise and acute commentary, often referring to the works of Guénon, Coomaraswamy, and Schuon to whom Perry acknowledges a debt of "profound gratitude" and "whose several roles", Perry tells us, "have been altogether indispensable in the formation of this work". While performing a valuable service in bringing their work to the attention of a wider audience, Perry has himself discharged an awesome labor in pulling together the many strands of traditional wisdom between the covers of a single volume in which the concrete reality of the *sophia perennis* is revealed and documented. It would, of course, be impossible to uncover every manifestation of the Primordial Wisdom in all its plenitude, but Perry has surely come as close as any one man could. It is a monumental and profoundly impressive achievement. Perry also wrote on a range of other subjects.[77]

[74] W. Stoddart, "In Memoriam: Whitall Perry", *Sacred Web*, 16, 2006, 189.
[75] For a review of this anthology see P. Moore in *Studies in Comparative Religion*, 6:1, 1972.
[76] W. Perry (ed.), *A Treasury of Traditional Wisdom*, 19.
[77] See *Gurdjieff in the Light of Tradition* (1978), *The Widening Breach: Evolutionism in the Mirror of Cosmology* (1995), and *Challenges to a Secular Society* (1996).

Seyyed Hossein Nasr (b. 1933)

An eminent Islamicist and of the living traditionalists the most widely known in academic circles, Seyyed Hossein Nasr was born in Tehran.[78] His father was physician to the Persian royal family, and instilled in his son a deep love and respect for the culture of Persian Sufism. At an early age the boy was memorizing the poetry of Hafiz, Rumi, Sadi, and other mystics. From the age of thirteen Nasr was educated in the United States and as a young man studied physics and the history of science at the Massachusetts Institute of Technology and at Harvard University. He first became aware of perennialist writings whilst studying at MIT, thereafter becoming a disciple of Schuon. He rapidly established himself as an authority on Islamic philosophy and science, and on Sufism, and began his teaching career in 1955 while still a doctoral student at Harvard. In 1958 he became Professor of Science and Philosophy at Tehran University and in 1964-65 occupied the first Aga Khan Chair of Islamic Studies at the American University at Beirut. In 1962 and 1965 he was a visiting lecturer at Harvard University and at the University of Chicago in 1966. Nasr became Chancellor of Aryamehr University in 1972 and was also the founding President of the Imperial Iranian Academy of Philosophy, which published the traditionalist journal *Sophia Perennis*. The purpose of the Imperial Academy, of which Nasr was the President, was stated thus:

> The goals of the Academy are the revival of the traditional intellectual life of Islamic Persia; the publication of texts and studies pertaining to both Islamic and pre-Islamic Persia; making the intellectual treasures of Persia in the field of philosophy, mysticism, and the like known to the outside world; making possible extensive research in comparative philosophy; making Persians aware of the intellectual traditions of other civilizations in both East and West; encouraging intellectual confrontations with the modern world; and finally, discussing from the point of view of tradition various problems facing modern man.[79]

The Iranian Revolution forced Nasr to flee the country and since that time he has lived in the United States. After some years in the Religious Studies Department at Temple University he is now the University Professor of Islamic Studies at the George Washington University. Nasr has lectured extensively not only in the U.S.A., but in Europe, the Middle East, Pakistan, India, Japan, and Australia. He has published widely, being the author of some fifty books and five hundred articles, and is a frequent con-

---

[78] Information about Nasr taken from notes accompanying his own publications, from William Chittick's "Introduction" to *The Essential Seyyed Hossein Nasr*, and the *Wikipedia* entry on Nasr.

[79] Quoted in the Editorial, *Studies in Comparative Religion*, 10:1, 1976, 3-4.

tributor to academic, Islamic, and traditionalist journals. Since the passing of Burckhardt, Schuon, and Lings, Nasr has been widely recognized as the pre-eminent living exponent of perennialism.[80] He was the first non-European invited by Edinburgh University to give the prestigious Gifford Lectures in Natural Theology, in 1981; these lectures were subsequently published under the title *Knowledge and the Sacred*—in Huston Smith's estimate, "one of the most important books of the twentieth century".[81] A volume in the esteemed Library of Living Philosophers series is also dedicated to the work of Seyyed Hossein Nasr.

*   *   *

Other perennialists include Lord Northbourne, Leo Schaya, Gai Eaton, Joseph Epes Brown, William Stoddart, Philip Sherrard, and Rama Coomaraswamy. Their works have been less seminal than those of the major figures— which is not to diminish the invaluable work they have done in bringing the treasures of Tradition to a wider audience. Indeed, each has made a distinctive contribution, as have many others whom we cannot introduce here.

Lord Northbourne (1896-1982) was educated at Eton and Oxford, and was for many years Provost of Wye College.[82] He was a pioneer of ecological farming methods and is credited with the term "organic farming", which appeared in his first book, *Look to the Land* (1940). Northbourne played a role in the development of traditionalism in two ways: firstly as author of two accessible and extremely useful books, *Religion in the Modern World* (1963) and *Looking Back on Progress* (1970); and secondly, as the translator of that cardinal work, Guénon's *The Reign of Quantity and the Signs of the*

---

[80] See, for instance, Huston Smith's Foreword and William Chittick's Introduction to *The Essential Seyyed Hossein Nasr*, vii-xiv.

[81] H. Smith, "Foreword" to *The Essential Seyyed Hossein Nasr*. (Nasr's predecessors as Gifford lecturers included William James, A.N. Whitehead, Paul Tillich, Arnold Toynbee, Albert Schweitzer, and Werner Heisenberg.) Nasr's most important works fall into three groups: those concerned with Islamic science and philosophy, which include *An Introduction to Islamic Cosmological Doctrines* (1964), *Science and Civilization in Islam* (1968), and *Islamic Science: An Illustrated History* (1976); works dealing with Islam more generally or with the mystical traditions of Sufism, *Three Muslim Sages* (1964), *Ideals and Realities of Islam* (1966), *Islamic Studies* (1967), *Sufi Essays* (1972), studies of Rumi and Sadr ad-Din Shirazi, and *Islamic Art and Spirituality* (1987); and thirdly, books in which specifically modern problems are investigated in the light of traditional metaphysics: *The Encounter of Man and Nature* (1968), *Islam and the Plight of Modern Man* (1976), *Traditional Islam in the Modern World* (1987), and *Religion and the Order of Nature* (1996).

[82] Information on Lord Northbourne can be found in the Foreword, Preface, and Introduction to *Of the Land and the Spirit: The Essential Lord Northbourne on Ecology and Religion* (2008), ed. Christopher James and Joseph Fitzgerald.

Times. Several of Northbourne's essays on ecology, agriculture, and religion have recently been published as *Of the Land and the Spirit* (2008).

Leo Schaya (1916-1985) was for a time editor of the French journal *Études Traditionnelles* and founding editor of *Connaissance des Religions*.[83] He was born in Switzerland and given a traditional Jewish upbringing. He later lived in France. He was an authority on Sufism and on the Kabbalah, subjects on which he published *The Universal Meaning of the Kabbalah* (1958) and *La doctrine soufique de l'unité* (1962), the former perhaps "the most lucid metaphysical synthesis of the sephirothic doctrine".[84] He was a close personal friend of Frithjof Schuon, with whom he exchanged many letters.

Gai Eaton (b. 1921) was born in Switzerland and educated at Charterhouse and Cambridge.[85] Under the influence of his friend, the writer L.H. Myers, he developed an early interest in Vedanta as well as Taoism and Zen Buddhism. He served in the British Army during World War II and later worked as a teacher, journalist, and diplomat in Egypt, India, and the Caribbean. He was one of the first people to write in English about the work of René Guénon: *The Richest Vein* (1949), a book commissioned by T.S. Eliot, includes an incisive essay on the writings of Guénon and Coomaraswamy, and remains a useful introduction to these two figures. While working at Cairo University he met Martin Lings and, partly under his influence, committed himself to Islam in 1951. In later years he published *King of the Castle* (1978), an inquiry into choice and responsibility in the modern world, and *Islam and the Destiny of Man* (1986), a work which directly confronts some of the political realities of the twentieth century.

Joseph Epes Brown (1920-2000) was the author of two important works: *The Spiritual Legacy of the American Indians* (1982) and *Animals of the Soul* (1992), which bring a fully traditional outlook to bear on the spiritual culture of the Plains Indians of North America. He also edited *The Sacred Pipe* (1953), based on Black Elk's account of the ritual forms of the Oglala Sioux. Some of his essays and lectures have been gathered together in *Teaching Spirits* (2001) of which Peter Matthiessen has remarked, "a wonderful, clear synthesis—perhaps the best we have—of American Indian spiritual traditions, so precious and so illuminating".[86] Until his recent death Brown was a professor of Religious Studies at the University of Montana, and a key figure in bringing the study of Indian traditions into American higher education. Of Brown, Seyyed Hossein Nasr has written, "America has

---

[83] See Y. Ibish and P.L. Wilson (eds.), *Traditional Modes of Contemplation and Action*, 475.

[84] J. Borella, "René Guénon and the Traditionalist School", 353.

[85] Information on Eaton from his own books and from M. Pallis' review of *King of the Castle* in *Studies in Comparative Religion*, 12: 1-2, 1978, 119-123.

[86] Matthiessen, quoted on the Amazon website.

not produced another scholar of the Native American traditions who combined in himself, as did Joseph Brown, profound spiritual and intellectual insight, and traditional understanding, the deepest empathy for those traditions, nobility of character and generosity".[87]

William Stoddart (b. 1925) was born in Scotland.[88] After graduating from Glasgow University where he studied European languages and medicine, he undertook further studies in Edinburgh and Dublin. In 1945 he discovered the writings of Coomaraswamy, and then those of Guénon and Schuon, later becoming closely associated with Schuon, his spiritual mentor, and Titus Burckhardt. He is the leading authority on the work of Titus Burckhardt, four of whose books he has translated from the German. In recent years he has played a leading part in making the vast corpus of Schuon's poetic work available in English translation. Stoddart is the author of *Sufism: The Mystical Doctrines and Methods of Islam* (1976), *Outline of Hinduism* (1993), *Outline of Buddhism* (1998), *Remembering in a World of Forgetting* (2007), and *What do the Religions Say about Each Other?* (2008). For many years he was assistant editor of *Studies in Comparative Religion*. Since 1982 he has lived in Windsor, Canada, and has travelled extensively.

Several Christian authors whose work is largely but not invariably in sympathy with perennialism should also be mentioned. Bernard Kelly (1907-1958), the English Catholic writer and Thomist philosopher, was something of a pioneer of "Christian perennialism", if one might be permitted such a term, as was Angus McNab (1906-1977), another Catholic, one of Guénon's translators, and author of *Spain Under the Crescent Moon*. Philip Sherrard (1922-1995) was a Lecturer in Orthodox Church History at London University and a member of the Greek Orthodox Church. As well as several fine works on aspects of the Orthodox tradition, he published *The Rape of Man and Nature* (1987)—which, along with Nasr's *Man and Nature*, is one of the most far-reaching analyses of the ravages of modern scientism—*Athos: The Holy Mountain* (1985), *The Sacred in Life and Art* (1990), and *Human Image, World Image: The Death and Resurrection of Sacred Cosmology* (1992). He also contributed to the translation of the *Philokalia*. Rama Coomaraswamy (1929-2006), son of the illustrious Ananda, was born in Massachusetts and educated in England at Wycliffe College.[89] He was sent with Marco Pallis

---

[87] Nasr quoted in the "Biography of Dr. Joseph Epes Brown", included in the commemorative edition of J.E. Brown, *The Spiritual Legacy of the American Indian*. On Brown see also H. Smith, "What They Have That We Lack: A Tribute to the Native Americans via Joseph Epes Brown", 85-95, and H. Oldmeadow, Review of the commemorative issue of *The Spiritual Legacy of the American Indian* in *Sophia* 12:2.

[88] On Stoddart's life and work see Mateus Soares de Azevedo's biography in W. Stoddart, *Remembering in a World of Forgetting*, 135-139.

[89] On Rama Coomaraswamy see M. Pallis, "A Fateful Meeting of Minds"; R. Lipsey, *Coomaras-*

to study Hindi and Sanskrit at the Haridwar Gurukul. He returned to America to study medicine and later practiced as a surgeon in Greenwich, Connecticut. He was a Roman Catholic and his book *The Destruction of the Christian Tradition* (1980) analyzed the Church's deviation from its own traditions with the Second Vatican Council. He was also the author of *The Invocation of the Name of Jesus: As Practised in the Western Church* (1999). With Alvin Moore Jr. he edited *Selected Letters of Ananda Coomaraswamy* (1987).[90]

*   *   *

To be a traditionalist is to be committed to one or another of the religious traditions. Perennialism demands not merely a mental assent but an engagement of the whole person, evinced by a direct participation in a living tradition. It does not allow of any free-wheeling syncretism or universalism such as would subvert the formal claims of any particular religion. Fine scholars and linguists though some of the traditionalists are, their interest in religion always incorporates what we might call the experiential or existential dimension and goes beyond the purely academic. The Romanian philosopher E.M. Cioran rightly remarked that it is impossible to imagine most academic scholars of comparative religion "at prayer"; on the other hand, the perennialists (some of whom *are* scholars of comparative religion) are, by definition, religious practitioners. They have experienced religion "on their knees", as it were, not merely by poring over dusty tracts in academic libraries.

There are many other scholars and writers whose works exhibit, in varying degree, a strong traditionalist influence—indeed, some of them are fully-fledged perennialists themselves. Among the most respected and influential of such writers we may here mention the following: in the USA, William Chittick, James Cutsinger, Victor Danner, Michael Fitzgerald, Huston Smith, Wolfgang Smith; in the United Kingdom, Keith Critchlow, Brian Keeble, the late Kathleen Raine; in Europe, Jean-Baptiste Aymard, Jean Biès, Jean Borella, Jean Hani, Patrick Laude, Jean-Louis Michon; in Japan, the late Rev Shojun Bando. A younger generation of perennialist scholars includes Waleed El-Ansary, Rodney Blackhirst, David Dakake, Maria Dakake, Renaud Fabbri, Joseph Fitzgerald, Ibrahim Kalin, Ali Lakhani, Joseph Lumbard, Timothy Scott, Reza Shah-Kazemi, and Algis Uzdavinys. The names of other perennialists can be found in the pages of such journals as *Études*

---

wamy: His Life and Work; and W. Stoddart and Mateus Soares de Azevedo, "Rama P. Coomaraswamy (1929-2006): In Memoriam".

[90] On Alvin Moore Jr. (1923-2005), another Christian perennialist, see the tributes which appeared in *Sacred Web* 15, 2005. One of these is from Rama Coomaraswamy.

Traditionnelles, Connaissance des Religions, Studies in Comparative Religion, Sophia Perennis, Sophia, Temenos Review, Sacred Web, Vincit Omnia Veritas, Oriens, and *Eye of the Heart* (although these journals were/are all perennialist in their orientation, it must be remembered that not all contributors were/are perennialists).

Over the last three decades World Wisdom Books (Bloomington, IN), Sophia Perennis et Universalis (New York) (now Sophia Perennis, San Raphael, CA), Fons Vitae (Louisville, KY), Golgonooza Press (Ipswich, UK), and Quinta Essentia (Cambridge, UK), have been the most important English-language publishers of traditionalist works. World Wisdom maintains a large website on which may be found details about many scholars and writers in sympathy with the perennialist outlook. Discussing the work of contemporary perennialists, Gai Eaton observed that

> These books and articles present variety in unity, very different voices speaking from a single standpoint. Few readers respond to them in a neutral or tepid fashion. For some they open up new horizons, often with a sense of shock, discovery, and delight, while others, who cannot bear to have their ingrained habits of thought and all the cherished assumptions of the age so ruthlessly challenged, are angered and outraged. They provoke ... a polarization of perspectives which serves to clarify thought and to define the demarcation line between the basic tendencies of our time, the traditional and the modernist.[91]

This insight applies not only to traditionalist writings as a whole but also to the Schuonian corpus in particular, to which we now turn.

---

[91] G. Eaton, *King of the Castle*, 219.

René Guénon

Ananda K. Coomaraswamy

Titus Burckhardt

Martin Lings

Seyyed Hossein Nasr

Marco Pallis

Whitall N. Perry

II

Timeless Truths
and Immutable Principles

Total Truth is inscribed in an eternal script in the very
substance of our spirit.

(Frithjof Schuon, *Light on the Ancient Worlds*, 119)

3

The Five Divine Presences

Dimensions of the Real

Indeed, God is ineffable, nothing can describe Him or enclose Him in words; but, on the other hand, truth exists, that is to say that there are conceptual points of reference which sufficiently convey the nature of God.[1]

Metaphysical doctrine is nothing other than the science of Reality and illusion, and it presents itself, from the starting-point of the terrestrial state—and thus with its cosmological extension—as the science of the existential or principial degrees. . . . It distinguishes within the Principle itself between Being and Non-Being, or in other words between the personal God and the impersonal Divinity; on the other hand, within manifestation, metaphysics—now become cosmology—distinguishes between the formless and the formal, the latter being in turn divided into two states, the one subtle or animic and the other gross or corporeal.[2]

What falsifies modern interpretations of the world and of man at their very base . . . is their monotonous and obsessive ignorance of the supra-sensible degrees of Reality, or of the "Five Divine Presences".[3]

The metaphysic elucidated by Schuon might be articulated in any number of ways, from a variety of viewpoints. Two metaphysical vocabularies which Schuon himself frequently deploys are those of Sufism and Advaita Vedanta ("one of the most adequate expressions possible of the *philosophia perennis*"[4]), each presenting essentially the same account of the Real, albeit in the differing "languages" of the traditions in question. Given what has already been said about the *sophia perennis* there is nothing surprising in this convergence; indeed, it could not be otherwise. Under different guises much the same account can be found in any integral tradition, especially in those

---

[1] *From the Divine to the Human,* "Structure and Universality of the Conditions of Existence", 70.

[2] *René Guénon: Some Observations,* "René Guénon: Definitions", 2.

[3] *Form and Substance in the Religions,* "The Five Divine Presences", 62.

[4] *Esoterism as Principle and as Way,* "Understanding Esoterism", 21. Elsewhere Schuon writes that "Advaita Vedanta . . . is the most direct possible expression of *gnosis*" (*Gnosis: Divine Wisdom,* "Gnosis: Language of the Self", 61).

which foreground metaphysics—Platonism, Pythagoreanism, Taoism, to cite three obvious instances. In other cases, where the accent, in the first place, is on a spiritual therapy, the metaphysical teachings will be veiled; Christianity and Buddhism might be adduced as examples.

To provide even a rudimentary outline of gnostic teachings as they are understood within a single tradition is no easy matter, still less when one is dealing with a metaphysical synthesis such as we find in Schuon's work. One might start with these words, from Schuon:

> The content of the universal and primordial Doctrine is the following, expressed in Vedantic terms: "*Brahma* is Reality; the world is appearance; the soul is not other than *Brahma*". These are the three great theses of integral metaphysics: one positive, one negative, one unitive.[5]

Alternatively, one might start with a Schuonian passage such as this, concerning God as the Absolute (here "God" designating the Divinity "in all its possible aspects", and unrestricted by any theological dogmatism):

> In metaphysics, it is necessary to start from the idea that the Supreme Reality is absolute, and that being absolute it is infinite. That is absolute which allows of no augmentation or diminution, or of no repetition or division. . . . And that is infinite which is not determined by any limiting factor and therefore does not end at any boundary; it is in the first place Potentiality or Possibility as such. . . . Without All-Possibility, there would be neither Creator nor creation, neither *Maya* nor *Samsara*.[6]

Further, let us recall that

> God is the Absolute, and being the Absolute, He is equally the Infinite; being both the Absolute and the Infinite, intrinsically and without duality, He is also the Perfect. Absoluteness is reflected in space by the point or the center; in time by the moment or the present; in matter, by ether, which vehicles energy; in form, by the sphere; in number, by unity.[7]

Another possible point of departure, adopted here, is Schuon's essay, "The Five Divine Presences", expounding a Sufi doctrine which furnishes a coherent "explanation" of the Real, and of the various levels of the cosmic and meta-cosmic hierarchy.

---

[5] *Eye of the Heart*, "Diverse Aspects of Initiatory Alchemy", 135-136.
[6] *Survey of Metaphysics and Esoterism*, "Summary of Integral Metaphysics", 15.
[7] *From the Divine to the Human*, "Structure and Universality of the Conditions of Existence", 69.

The Five Divine Presences

The Five Divine Presences as affirmed in Sufism, starting from "below" in the world of manifestation in which we find ourselves, and expressed in the most succinct fashion possible, are:

1. *nasut*: the human realm, the domain of the corporeal (since man is created out of "earth");

2. *malakut*: the subtle realm, the "realm of royalty" because it dominates the corporeal world;

3. *jabarut*: the realm of power, which is macrocosmically Heaven and microcosmically the human Intellect ("Heaven" within us);

4. *Lahut*: the realm of the Divine which coincides with the Uncreated Intellect, the Logos;

5. *Hahut*: "Aseity" or "Ipseity", the Supreme Principle, the Divine Essence, *Allahu ahad*.

In Sufism these five presences are sometimes signaled by a parallel set of terms which can be loosely translated as: body; soul; Spirit/Intellect; Unicity ("God has no partners"); Unity ("God has no parts"). In the language of Occidental metaphysics they are sometimes called the Universal Degrees, or the Multiple States of Being (the title of one of Guénon's major metaphysical works).[8]

As Schuon explains:

> To understand correctly the Arabic terminology mentioned above (*nasut, malakut, jabarut, Lahut, Hahut*), it must be appreciated that the Universe is considered as a hierarchy of divine "dominions", which is to say that God is "most present" in the supreme degree and "least present"—or the "most absent"—on the corporeal plane; it is here that He apparently "dominates" the least or least directly; but the word "apparently" is almost a pleonasm, for to admit Relativity and Manifestation is to admit illusion or appearance.[9]

The Five Divine Presences, translated into terms more accessible to those of Judeo-Christian background, and now starting from the "top" and allowing for some expedient simplifications, can be variously rendered thus:

---

[8] Schuon notes that in Buddhism the three higher degrees, in ascending order, are those of the *Bodhisattva, Buddha*, and *Nirvana* respectively (the latter two terms being interchangeable with *Dharmakaya* and *Shunya*). He adds, "The realities in question are the same whether the concepts are 'theist' or 'non-theist'; whoever admits first, the possibility of an Absolute, and secondly, the transcendence of this Absolute—without which the notion would be entirely relative and therefore false—can never be an atheist in the conventional sense of the word" (*Form and Substance in the Religions*, "The Five Divine Presences", 53-54n).

[9] *Form and Substance in the Religions*, "The Five Divine Presences", 55.

1. *Beyond Being*, the Godhead, the Divine Essence, the Divine Principle, the Absolute Unqualified (*the Divine Principle Itself*)

2. *Being*, the Personal God, the Creator, the Uncreated Logos (*the pre-figuration of Manifestation in the Principle*[10])

3. *Spirit*, the Angelic, Celestial, or Avataric Realm, the Intellect, the Created Logos [Latin: *Spiritus*; Greek: *Pneuma*; Arabic: *ar-Ruh*] (*the projection of the Principle in Manifestation*)

4. *Soul*, the Psychic Realm [Latin: *anima*; Greek: *psyche*; Arabic: *an-nafs*]

5. *Body*, the Corporeal Realm, Matter; the realm of "matter-energy, form, number, space, and time".[11]

Starting with a "manifestation that surrounds us, and in which we are as it were woven as threads in a piece of cloth", these Presences (or Degrees, or Hypostases) comprise a structured hierarchy of Reality in which we can establish certain "boundaries or syntheses":

> The totality of the corporeal and animic states forms the "natural" domain, that of "nature"; the totality of those two states and of supra-formal manifestation constitutes the cosmic realm; the totality of the cosmic realm and of Being is . . . the realm of relativity, of *Maya*; and all of the realms considered together with the supreme Self [*Atman* in the Hindu perspective] constitute the Universe in the highest sense.[12]

In some expositions the five degrees are consolidated in a three-tiered totality, as in this passage from Schuon:

> The three great degrees of reality are: formal manifestation (comprising the gross, corporeal, sensible plane and the subtle, psychic plane), non-formal manifestation (constituted by the universal Spirit, the supreme Angels), and non-manifestation (God, in His Essence as well as in His Word).[13]

The Doctrine of the Five Presences, here only adumbrated, discloses the "relationships" of the Absolute and the Relative, the Principle and Manifestation, God and the World. The metaphysical and cosmological teachings which are implicit in the Doctrine of the Five Presences will be unfolded in various parts of the present study. Many of the terms used in the second of

[10] "There must be a 'metaphysical precedent' *in divinis* which renders both the world and things possible" (*Survey of Metaphysics and Esoterism*, "Confessional Speculation: Intentions and Impasses", 154).

[11] *From the Divine to the Human*, "Structure and Universality of the Conditions of Existence", 65.

[12] *Form and Substance in the Religions*, "The Five Divine Presences", 54. ("Universe" here is obviously not restricted to the time-space relativities of a profane science.)

[13] *Treasures of Buddhism*, "Nirvana", 84n.

the lists above—"God", "Soul", and "Body"—will be familiar to everyone: the two Presences or Degrees most likely to cause difficulty are "Beyond Being" and "Spirit". Of the first, all that need be said presently is that the theological language of exoteric monotheism tends to stop short at the fourth degree, which is to say that the two highest degrees are often assimilated in the notion of the Personal Creator God; within esoteric Christianity—in Eckhart, for instance—the distinction between God and Godhead remains intact.[14] The terms "Spirit" and "Intellect" often generate confusion in the modern mind, the first because it is frequently collapsed into "Soul", the second because its meaning has been altogether degraded, to the extent that it is now generally understood to refer to nothing more than ratiocination, mental operations, or some vaguely defined "cleverness" or mental facility. We cannot too often be reminded of the distinction between intellective intuition and a merely cerebral "intelligence".

> The cult of intelligence and mental passion distances man from truth: intelligence narrows as soon as man puts his trust in it alone; mental passion chases away intellectual intuition just as the wind blows out the light of a candle.[15]

The term Intellect (which for the moment can be assimilated with "Spirit"), requires careful definition. Presently we will concern ourselves only with the Intellect as it is "experienced" by the human subject, all the while remembering that "The Intellect is not cerebral nor is it specifically human or angelic; all beings 'possess' it."[16]

Whenever the traditionalists use "Intellect" or its derivatives it is to be understood as a precise technical term taken from the Latin *intellectus* and from mediaeval scholasticism: the faculty which perceives the transcendent.[17] The Intellect receives intuitions and apprehends realities of a supra-phenomenal order. We remember Meister Eckhart's statement: "There is something in the soul which is uncreated and uncreatable . . . this is the Intellect".[18] It is, in Schuon's words, "a receptive faculty and not a power which produces: it does not 'create'; it receives and transmits; it is a mirror."[19] The Intellect is an impersonal, unconditioned, receptive faculty, whence the objectivity

---

[14] See Schuon's interesting footnote on Eckhart in *From the Divine to the Human*, "Transcendence is Not Contrary to Sense", 21n, and his reference to Eckhart's *Gott/die Gottheit* distinction in *Christianity/Islam*, "Dilemmas of Muslim Scholasticism", 159-160.

[15] *Spiritual Perspectives and Human Facts*, "Knowledge and Love", 140.

[16] *Spiritual Perspectives and Human Facts*, "Knowledge and Love", 142.

[17] See M. Lings, *What is Sufism?*, 48.

[18] Quoted in M. Lings, *A Sufi Saint of the Twentieth Century*, 27.

[19] *Stations of Wisdom*, "Orthodoxy and Intellectuality", 21.

of intellection. It is "that which participates in the divine Subject";[20] that which in man is "most conformable to God",[21] the "transpersonal essence of the subject".[22] Intellection is a "naturally supernatural" grace which is inseparable from our "consubstantiality with all that can be known, and so with all that is."[23]

In almost every culture the Intellect (under whatever name) is symbolically associated with the heart; hence the recurrence of such images as "the eye of the heart", "the cave of the heart" and suchlike, and formulations such as "Heart-Knowledge", or in popular usage "I knew in my heart" (as distinct from knowing "in the head"). This transcendent faculty, capable of direct contact with Reality, is to be found, under various names, in all traditions.[24] Schuon:

> It is indispensable to know at the outset that there are truths inherent in the human spirit that are as if buried in the "depths of the heart", which means that they are contained as potentialities or virtualities in the pure Intellect: these are principial and archetypal truths, those which prefigure and determine all others.[25]

And elsewhere:

> The Absolute is not an artificial postulate, explainable by psychology, but is "pre-mentally" evident and as actual as the air we breathe or the beating of our hearts; that intelligence when not atrophied—the pure, intuitive, contemplative intellect—allows no doubt on this subject, the "proofs" being in its very substance.[26]

However:

> Fallen man, and thus the average man, is as it were poisoned by the passional element, either grossly or subtly; from this results an obscuring of the Intellect and the necessity of a Revelation from the outside.[27]

Revelation—a divine communication addressed to a human collectivity—is there to compensate for the obscuration of innate Knowledge and, in doing so, "to awaken it, at least in principle".[28] (We will return to Revelation shortly.)

[20] *Stations of Wisdom*, "Manifestations of the Divine Principle", 88.

[21] *Echoes of Perennial Wisdom*, 23

[22] *Echoes of Perennial Wisdom*, 46.

[23] *Esoterism as Principle and as Way*, "The Way of Oneness", 240.

[24] See Marco Pallis, quoted in W. Perry (ed.), *A Treasury of Traditional Wisdom*, 733.

[25] *Survey of Metaphysics and Esoterism*, "Introduction: Epistemological Premises", 3.

[26] *Stations of Wisdom*, "Preface", 9.

[27] *Esoterism as Principle and as Way*, "Understanding Esoterism", 20.

[28] *From the Divine to the Human*, "Consequences Flowing from the Mystery of Subjectivity", 7.

Insofar as it is useful to distinguish between "Intellect" and "Spirit", in regard to the human situation, it can be said that the former signifies the "means" to theoretical or doctrinal understanding whereas the latter concerns practical realization. As one commentator has put it, "They pertain respectively to the objective (or discriminative) and the subjective (or unitive) modes of knowing."[29] The Intellect/Spirit is immortal, supra-formal, universal, and objective; the soul, on the other hand, whilst also immortal, is formal, individual, and subjective.

The Five Levels of Reality

<table>
<tr><td colspan="3" rowspan="2">The Divine

The Unmanifest
The Uncreated
The Metacosmic</td><td colspan="2">(1) BEYOND-BEING

(the Divine Essence, the Supra-Personal God)</td><td>ABSOLUTE</td><td>ATMA</td><td rowspan="2">DIVINE</td><td rowspan="3">HEAVEN</td><td rowspan="4">IMMORTAL</td></tr>
<tr><td>(2) BEING

(the Personal God, Creator, Judge; Divine Qualities)</td><td>UNCREATED LOGOS</td><td rowspan="4">RELATIVE</td><td rowspan="4">MAYA</td></tr>
<tr><td rowspan="3">EXISTENCE

The Manifest
The Created
The Cosmic</td><td colspan="2">Universal or Supra-formal Manifestation</td><td>(3) Spirit, Intellect

(Spiritual, Intellectual, or Angelic realm)</td><td>CREATED LOGOS</td><td rowspan="3">HUMAN</td></tr>
<tr><td rowspan="2">individual or formal manifestation</td><td>subtle</td><td colspan="2">(4) soul

(animic or psychic realm)</td><td rowspan="2">EARTH</td></tr>
<tr><td>gross</td><td colspan="2">(5) body

(corporeal realm)</td><td>MORTAL</td></tr>
</table>

[29] W. Stoddart, *Remembering in a World of Forgetting*, 46.

In a useful chart, William Stoddart consolidates Schuon's writings about the Five Divine Presences, making clear the various "boundaries and syntheses" to which Schuon alludes.

It is imperative to understand, near the outset of the present study, that the modern worldview is almost entirely ignorant of the suprasensorial dimensions of Reality; indeed, this ignorance is the very cornerstone of this outlook. As Schuon so clearly states, as did René Guénon before him, the whole edifice of modern (i.e., post-medieval Western) thought, particularly that branch of it that prides itself on the name "science", is essentially no more than a *negation*, a denial of a knowledge which infinitely surpasses it. Schuon:

> All of the philosophic and scientific errors of the modern world proceed essentially from the negation of the doctrine under discussion: in other words, what falsifies modern interpretations of the world and of man at their very base, thus depriving them of whatever validity they may have, is their monotonous and obsessive ignorance of the suprasensible degrees of Reality, or of the "Five Divine Presences".[30]

Two of the most blatant representative errors of an anti-traditional and horizontal modern mindset are evolutionism and psychologism. Each will be anatomized in later chapters. For now let us simply recall that, in Schuon's words:

> Evolutionism, that most typical offspring of the modern spirit, is no more than a kind of substitute [for traditional doctrines about the universal degrees]: it is a compensation on a "flat surface" for the missing dimensions. : . . One seeks the solution to the cosmogonic problem on the sensible plane and replaces real causes with imaginary causes that conform, in appearance at least, to the possibilities of the material world.[31]

An unabashed materialism is perhaps the most grotesque form of ignorance which is to be found amongst many moderns, but even when it is acknowledged that the psychic/animic realm cannot be reduced to "material" causes, the result—without recourse to traditional doctrines— is always a kind of psychologism which denies all supernatural causes and, by dint of the same ignorance, all principial truths. As Schuon remarks:

> According to this way of thinking man is doubtless more than just his body, but he is nevertheless reduced to being a human animal, which

---

[30] *Form and Substance in the Religions*, "The Five Divine Presences", 62.

[31] *Form and Substance in the Religions*, "The Five Divine Presences", 63.

means that he is no longer anything; *for man limited to himself is no longer human.*[32]

At this point it might also be as well to dispel a certain confusion arising out of Guénon's somewhat one-sided (though perhaps expedient) treatment, in works such as *The Reign of Quantity and the Signs of the Times*, of the psychic or animic realm. Patrick Laude clarifies some of the issues at stake:

> The French metaphysician [Guénon] envisaged the animic realm, and magic as the science pertaining to this realm, in an almost exclusively negative manner. He overwhelmingly considered it as the realm of delusions and temptations. . . . Guénon's priority was to counter the phenomenalism of occultists and other neospiritualists . . . [because] the obsession of the latter with all kinds of dangerous psychic manipulations needed to be denounced unambiguously. In this prophylactic perspective, the distinction between the psychic and the spiritual realms appears almost absolute, and the psychic realm can only be the domain of temptations and aberrations. It is the domain in which, to use one of Schuon's poetic formulas, the soul runs the risk of "drowning in its own nothingness".[33]

As we have already noted, Guénon was uncommonly alert to the dangers of confounding the psychic and spiritual realms. However, the danger in this partial view of the subtle realm is that, implicitly at least, it denies the unity of Being which metaphysics affirms, and does not allow for the fact that "the psychic plane is . . . a relatively external prolongation of the spiritual realm, just as the physical domain is like the external shell of the animic world".[34] As such, the psychic/animic realm can be integrated fully into the spiritual life through various alchemical transmutations which are evident, for instance, in shamanism and in the tantric practices of the Orient. More generally it might be said that much of the spiritual life, at least for the ordinary believer, is concerned with cleansing the subjective psyche and integrating it in the Spirit.

The Absolute, the Relative, and the Origin of *Maya*

Let us move now to several issues which arise out of the account above. Firstly, to the perennial question of why the world, the time-space universe, the realm of *maya*, exists at all, and, secondly, to the relationships between the unqualified Absolute (referred to variously as the Godhead, Beyond-

---

[32] *Form and Substance in the Religions*, "The Five Divine Presences", 64 (italics mine).

[33] J-B. Aymard and P. Laude, *Frithjof Schuon: Life and Teachings*, 100.

[34] J-B. Aymard and P. Laude, *Frithjof Schuon: Life and Teachings*, 101.

Being, *nirguna Brahman*, the *Tao* and the like), God as Creator, and the manifest world.

Whether one adopts a creationist or emanationist cosmogony, in both cases, "*Maya* is a necessary consequence of the infinity of *Atma*".[35] The Absolute is necessarily infinite Possibility, thus including the necessity of universal Manifestation.[36]

> As for the question of the "origin" of illusion [*maya*] it is among those questions that can be resolved . . . though this resolution cannot be adjusted to suit all logical needs. . . . The infinitude of Reality implies the possibility of its own negation and . . . since this negation is not possible within the Absolute itself, it is necessary that this "possibility of the impossible" should be realized in an "inward dimension" that is "neither real nor unreal", a dimension that is real on its own level while being unreal in respect of the Essence; thus we are everywhere in touch with the Absolute, from which we cannot emerge but which at the same time is infinitely distant, no thought ever circumscribing it.[37]

There is nothing abnormal or idiosyncratic in Schuon's formulation of a dimension which is "neither real nor unreal"; compare with this, for example, from St Augustine:

> I beheld these others beneath Thee, and saw that they neither altogether are, nor altogether are not. An existence they have because they are from Thee; and yet no existence, because they are not what Thou art. For only that really is that remains unchangeably.[38]

Approaching our question from another angle, Schuon writes:

> If the world is necessary by virtue of a mystery of the divine infinity—and there must be no confusing of the perfection of necessity with constraint, nor yet of the perfection of liberty with arbitrariness—the necessity of creative Being must come before that of the world, and with all the more reason: what the world is to Being, Being is—*mutatis mutandis*—to supreme Non-Being. Not only does *Maya* encompass manifestation: it is affirmed already *a fortiori* "within" the Principle; the divine Principle "desiring to be known"—or "desiring to know"—condescends to the unfolding of its inward infinity, an unfolding at first potential and then outward or cosmic. The relationship "God-world", "Creator-creature", "Principle-manifestation" would be inconceivable

---

[35] *Spiritual Perspectives and Human Facts*, "Vedanta", 103.

[36] *Survey of Metaphysics and Esoterism*, "Dimensions, Modes, and Degrees of the Divine Order", 25

[37] *Gnosis: Divine Wisdom*, "The Doctrine of Illusion", 57-58; *Logic and Transcendence*, "Evidence and Mystery", 89. See also *In the Face of the Absolute*, "Atma-Maya", *passim*.

[38] *Confessions* 9.vii.

were it not prefigured in God, independently of any question of creation.[39]

Elsewhere Schuon elaborates the Creator-creature relationship further:

> That we are conformed to God—made in His image—this is certain; otherwise we would not exist. That we are contrary to God, this is also certain; otherwise we would not be different from God. Apart from analogy with God, we would be nothing. Apart from opposition to God, we would be God. The separation between man and God is at one and the same time absolute and relative. . . . The separation is absolute because God alone is real, and no continuity is possible between nothingness and Reality; but the separation is relative—or rather "non-absolute"—because nothing is outside of God. In a sense it might be said that this separation is absolute from man to God and relative from God to man.[40]

As Nasr says, "to understand God as Reality is also to grasp the world as unreality, not nothingness pure and simple but as relative reality".[41]

To those who want variously to claim that the very idea of God is a "projection", a "wish-fulfillment", a "delusion", an "expedient", or whatever, Schuon says this:

> There are those who claim that the idea of God is to be explained only by social opportunism, without taking account of the infinite disproportion and the contradiction involved in such a hypothesis: if men such as Plato, Aristotle, or Thomas Aquinas—not to mention the Prophets, or Christ, or the sages of Asia—were not capable of noticing that God is merely a social prejudice or some other dupery of the kind, and if hundreds and thousands of years have been based intellectually on their incapacity, then there is no human intelligence, and still less any possibility of progress, for a being absurd by nature does not contain the possibility of ceasing to be absurd.[42]

As to the so-called "problem of evil" which modern philosophers have so often marshaled as an "argument" against the existence of God, all that need be said presently is this:

> If the world is the world, this is because it is not God; unable to be either Absoluteness or Infinity, it is relative and finite—hence the presence of evil, which by its privative nature proves *a contrario* that the

---

[39] *Light on the Ancient Worlds*, "Tracing *Maya*", 76.

[40] *Spiritual Perspectives and Human Facts*, "Knowledge and Love", 171.

[41] S.H. Nasr, *The Need for a Sacred Science*, 12.

[42] *Stations of Wisdom*, "Orthodoxy and Intellectuality", 36.

cosmic Substance, and consequently *a fortiori* the Divine Nature, is essentially Goodness.[43]

Likewise, "If there is a cosmos, a universal manifestation, there must also be a fall or falls, for to say "manifestation" is to say "other than God" and "remotion"."[44] Or yet again, (and here Schuon's argument is reminiscent of that of St Augustine):

> It is in the nature of the Good to wish to communicate itself: to say Good is to say radiation, projection, unfolding, gift of self. But at the same time, to say radiation is to say distance, hence alienation or impoverishment: the solar rays dim and become lost in the night of space. From this arises, at the end of the projection, the paradoxical phenomenon of evil, which nonetheless has the positive function of highlighting the good *a contrario*, and of contributing in its fashion to equilibrium in the phenomenal order.[45]

The world of *maya* is "illusory", not in the sense that it is a mirage or a fantasy, but in that its "reality" is only relative and contingent: it has no independence, no autonomy, no existence outside the Divine Principle Itself. It is an ever-changing multiplicity, a fugitive tissue of relativities, one which both veils and discloses the Absolute.

Maya is indeed "cosmic illusion" but

> She is also divine play. She is the great theophany, the unveiling of God "in Himself and by Himself" as the Sufis would say. *Maya* may be likened to a magic fabric woven from a warp that veils and a weft that unveils; she is the quasi-incomprehensible intermediary between the finite and the Infinite—at least from our point of view as creatures—and as such she has all the multi-colored ambiguity appropriate to her part-cosmic, part-divine nature.[46]

Thus,

> The term *maya* combines the meanings of "productive power" and "universal illusion"; it is the inexhaustible play of manifestations, deployments, combinations, and reverberations, a play with which *Atma* clothes itself even as the ocean clothes itself with a mantle of foam ever renewed and never the same.[47]

[43] *Logic and Transcendence*, "Dharmakara's Vow", 258.

[44] *Light on the Ancient Worlds*, "Fall and Forfeiture", 34.

[45] *Survey of Metaphysics and Esoterism*, "Summary of Integral Metaphysics", 18.

[46] *Light on the Ancient Worlds* (1965), "*Maya*", 89. See also A. Lakhani, "What Thirst is For", 13-14.

[47] *Logic and Transcendence*, "Evidence and Mystery", 89n.

It goes without saying that in this domain a material and empirical science is of no help:

> Modern science is a totalitarian rationalism that eliminates both Revelation and Intellect, and at the same time a totalitarian materialism, which ignores the metaphysical relativity—and hence the impermanence—of matter and the world; it does not know that the supra-sensible—which is beyond space and time—is the concrete principle of the world, and consequently that it is also at the origin of that contingent and changeable coagulation we call "matter". The science called "exact" is in fact an "intelligence without wisdom", just as post-scholastic philosophy is conversely a "wisdom without intelligence".[48]

Before leaving the realm of metaphysical speculation (and let us not be confused by the modern misunderstanding of this latter term but rather remember the link between this word and "speculum") we might profitably recall another of Schuon's dictums: "The Infinite is what it is; a man may understand it or not. Metaphysics cannot be taught to everyone but if it could be there would be no atheists."[49]

Next we might ask, what is the nature of the manifested world? What are we dealing with in this time-space ensemble? What are we to make of the phenomena of this world—the creatures, the forms and processes of nature, the qualities which inhere in the natural order? "When we look around us", asks Schuon, "what do we see?"

> First existence; second, differences; third, movements, modifications, transformations; fourth, disappearances. All these things together manifest a state of universal Substance: that state is at once a crystallization and a rotation, a heaviness and a dispersion, a solidification and a segmentation. Just as water is in ice and the movement of the hub in the rim, so is God in phenomena; He is accessible in them and through them, this being the whole mystery of symbolism and immanence. God is "the Outward" and "the Inward", "the First" and "the Last".[50]

The "kingdom of Nature" can be "considered as the majestic, pure, limitless raiment of the Divine Spirit",[51] and as "the art of God".[52] It is in this context that we might best understand the many apophthegms which characterize Schuon's writings on nature. A small sample:

[48] *Light on the Ancient Worlds*, "Man in the Universe", 98-99.
[49] *Spiritual Perspectives and Human Facts*, "Contours of the Spirit", 51.
[50] *Light on the Ancient Worlds* (1965), "Man in the Universe", 111-112.
[51] *Feathered Sun*, "The Sacred Pipe", 70.
[52] *Logic and Transcendence*, "Concerning the Love of God", 191.

For the sage every star, every flower, is metaphysically a proof of the Infinite.[53]

The sun, not being God, must prostrate itself every evening before the throne of Allah.[54]

God reveals Himself to the plant in the form of the light of the sun. The plant irresistibly turns itself toward the light; it could not be atheistic or impious.[55]

The fruits of the earth and the rain from the sky, which make life possible, are nothing if not manifestations of the Goodness that penetrates everywhere and warms the world, and which we carry within ourselves, in the depths of our chilled hearts.[56]

The Logos, Bridge between the Divine and the Human

What of the "relationship", so to speak, of the Absolute and the relative, of *Atma* and *maya*, of God and man? The key is to be found in the third Divine Presence which, considered from different angles, is variously signaled by the terms Intellect, Created Logos, Revelation—the "bridge" between the two higher degrees (Beyond-Being/Godhead, and Being/Creator God) and the two lower degrees (the animic and corporeal realms).

> If in the world there is necessarily both good and evil, and if the good manifests by definition the Divine qualities and therefore Goodness, it follows that Goodness has also to manifest itself as such and this it does through Revelation; and once it exists it compels assent, since man cannot but choose the good. In and through Revelation man rejoins the saving Goodness, the Infinite that includes all, the Absolute which is That which is and which alone is.[57]

"Revelation is to the macrocosm what intellection is to the microcosm".[58] Revelation is the means by which the Absolute is made known to all mankind. The Uncreated Logos is the "prefiguration of the relative in the absolute"[59], "the prototype of the cosmos in the Principle, or of the world in God";[60] the Created Logos, the "reflection of the Absolute in the relative",[61] enters the manifested world by way of a divine Messenger, the

[53] *Spiritual Perspectives and Human Facts*, "Thought and Civilization", 4.
[54] *Light on the Ancient Worlds*, "Tracing *Maya*", 79.
[55] *Spiritual Perspectives and Human Facts*, "Knowledge and Love", 142.
[56] *Light on the Ancient Worlds*, "Man in the Universe", 96.
[57] *Logic and Transcendence*, "Dharmakara's Vow", 258.
[58] *Survey of Metaphysics and Esoterism*, "Introduction: Epistemological Premises", 4.
[59] Frithjof Schuon, quoted in W. Stoddart, *Remembering in a World of Forgetting*, 58.
[60] *Christianity/Islam*, "The Idea of 'The Best' in Religions", 98. Compare John 1:1-5.
[61] Frithjof Schuon, quoted in W. Stoddart, *Remembering in a World of Forgetting*, 59.

avatara, revealing Truth to a particular human collectivity in time and space; thus "Revelation is in one sense the infallible intellection of the total collectivity".[62] Man's sense of the Absolute is re-awakened (after "the Fall") on the one hand, through Revelation, a downward descent of the Divine Principle, and on the other through Intellection, a vertical ascent back to the Divine. As James Cutsinger glosses Schuon:

> Nothing can resist God's entry. Being Infinite, He cannot but enter space, and the force or impact of this entry results in a kind of radiation or reverberation through time. The former can be pictured as a vertical descent, like dropping a stone into a pool of water, while the latter corresponds to centrifugal ripples moving horizontally toward the shore. These ripples are an image of tradition.[63]

"Revelation speaks an absolute language, because God is absolute",[64] but

> When the divine Light descends onto the human plane—"incarnating" itself, to some extent—it undergoes an initial limitation, and this results from human language and the requirements of a given collective mentality or cycle of humanity.[65]

Again, William Stoddart has provided a very serviceable diagram which demonstrates some of the "relationships" at issue here.

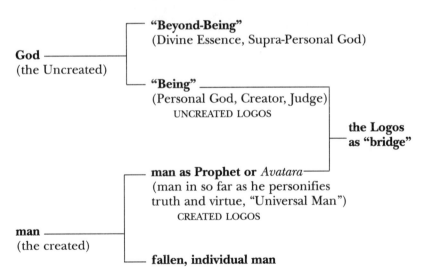

[62] *Light on the Ancient Worlds*, "Fall and Forfeiture", 25.

[63] J. Cutsinger, *Advice to the Serious Seeker*, 3.

[64] *Gnosis: Divine Wisdom*, "Diversity of Revelation", 18.

[65] *Christianity/Islam*, "The Idea of 'The Best' in Religions", 107.

Metaphysics and the Spiritual Life

The human is an axial or amphibious being who lives in both the material and spiritual worlds, in a way which is not quite true of other living beings, and is thus a bridge between them. Schuon reminds us that

> The human state is a central state, and consequently man's intelligence, his will, and his soul have a central character, in other words a character of totality, hence also of objectivity. Human intelligence is total, for it can conceive the Transcendent, the Absolute, or the Substance. . . . The human will is total, for it can choose the Absolute. . . . The will is made for the total Good. . . . The human soul is total for it can love the Absolute, or the Infinite. . . . The soul is made for total Happiness . . . heavenly beatitude and earthly harmony.[66]

This understanding is, of course, quite incompatible with the notion that man is simply another biological organism. And indeed, as Schuon points out, there are the "immediately visible" features which distinguish man from the animals: "first of all, his vertical posture; secondly, the gift of speech; thirdly, the creative, productive, and constructive faculty, which means art in all its degrees and all its forms".[67] This view is utterly at odds with that most seductive of scientistic hypotheses, Darwinian evolutionism. As Blake so well understood, "Man is either the ark of God or a phantom of the earth and of the water".[68] As "the ark of God", man is the guardian and custodian of the natural order, the pontifex, the caliph, "the vicegerent of God on earth" in Koranic terms.[69]

Intellection, or intellectual intuition, is an activity of the Intellect in which the illumination of universal knowledge is spontaneous and infallible; moreover, it "implies a certain detachment with regard to the world and the 'I', and demands *a posteriori* an ascesis conforming to its nature".[70] Because metaphysics is attuned to the sacred and the divine it demands something of those who would unlock its mysteries:

> If metaphysics is a sacred thing, that means it could not be . . . limited to the framework of the play of the mind. It is illogical and dangerous

---

[66] Unpublished writings, courtesy of World Wisdom. Similarly, in the words of Seyyed Hossein Nasr, "Man's central position in the world is not due to his cleverness or inventive genius but because of the possibility of attaining sanctity and becoming a channel of grace for the world around him. . . . The very grandeur of the human condition is precisely that he has the possibility of reaching a state 'higher than the angels' and at the same time of denying God" (*Ideals and Realities of Islam*, 24-25).

[67] Unpublished writings, courtesy of World Wisdom.

[68] Blake, cited by K. Raine in "The Underlying Order: Nature and the Imagination" in *Fragments of Infinity*, ed. A. Sharma, 208.

[69] See J-L. Michon, "The Vocation of Man According to the Koran".

[70] *Stations of Wisdom*, "Orthodoxy and Intellectuality", 50.

to talk of metaphysics without being preoccupied with the moral con-comitances it requires, the criteria of which are, for man, his behavior in relation to God and to his neighbor.[71]

Moreover, Intellection "must not be confused with spiritual realization"; for realization means that "our 'being', and not merely our 'thought', partici-pates in the 'objects' which the mirror reflects".[72]

> The total exigency of Sacred Doctrine—of "theosophy" in the proper sense of the word—results from the fact that human intelligence is by definition capable of objectivity and transcendence and implies *ipso facto* the same capacity for the will and for the feeling soul; whence the freedom of our will and the moral instinct of our soul. And just as our intelligence is fully human only through truths concerning God and our last ends, so too is our will fully human only through its operative participation in these truths; and similarly, our soul is human only by its morality, its detachment, and its magnanimity, hence by its love of the Truth and the Way.[73]

Metaphysics cannot be a matter of intelligence only but of the will and the affections. Indeed, the three are inseparable:

> To say that free will and moral sensibility are part of the intelligence of *homo sapiens*, means that there is no consequential and plenary meta-physical knowledge without the participation of these two faculties, the volitive and the affective: to know completely is to be . . . "where your treasure is, there will be your heart be also".[74]

Later in this work we will consider Schuon's writings on the spiritual life, which is implicit in any metaphysical understanding and without which doctrines such as those under discussion are likely to remain no more than sterile abstractions. To actualize metaphysical truths within oneself requires, in normal circumstances, a religious commitment:

> The normal condition of the Path is a traditional and ritual framework, which is to say a formal religion; to be more precise, at least the indis-pensable minimum of it, and without a sentimental attachment incom-patible with the metaphysical and hence universalist perspective.[75]

---

[71] *Spiritual Perspectives and Human Facts* (1969), "The Spiritual Virtues", 173.

[72] *Stations of Wisdom*, "Orthodoxy and Intellectuality", 31.

[73] *Survey of Metaphysics and Esoterism*, "Summary of Integral Metaphysics", 23.

[74] *Survey of Metaphysics and Esoterism*, "Summary of Integral Metaphysics", 23.

[75] Frithjof Schuon, unpublished writings, courtesy of World Wisdom. Exceptions to the rule, such as are alluded to in the Hindu Scriptures, are of no relevance or concern to the vast majority.

4

Tradition, Traditions, and the Perennial Philosophy

That is "traditional" which is transmitted from a divine source.[1]

In all epochs and in all countries there have been revelations, religions, wisdoms; tradition is a part of mankind just as man is part of tradition.[2]

Tradition speaks to each man the language he can understand, provided he be willing to listen; this reservation is essential, for tradition, we repeat, cannot become bankrupt; it is rather of man's bankruptcy that one should speak, for it is he who has lost the intuition of the supernatural and the sense of the sacred.[3]

Outside tradition there can assuredly be found some relative truths . . . but outside tradition there does not exist a doctrine that catalyzes absolute truths and transmits liberating notions concerning total reality.[4]

"Tradition" is today a tarnished word, often evoking the "dead weight" of the past, "cultural baggage" which should now be jettisoned. Sometimes it signals little more than blindly-observed custom, or some institution or practice which has persisted over generations. In like manner the term "traditionalist" is sometimes associated pejoratively with a "nostalgia for the past", and with "romanticism" and "folklore".[5] These jaundiced uses of the word must be abandoned if we are to understand what "Tradition" and its derivatives mean in the perennialist lexicon. As Guénon observed, "the very idea of tradition has been destroyed to such an extent that those who aspire to recover it no longer know which way to turn".[6]

---

[1] *From the Divine to the Human*, "The Sense of the Sacred", 109.

[2] *Light on the Ancient Worlds*, "Fall and Forfeiture", 35. See also W. Perry, "The Revival of Interest in Tradition".

[3] *Play of Masks*, "No Initiative Without Truth", 77.

[4] Frithjof Schuon, "No Activity Without Truth" in *The Sword of Gnosis*, ed. J. Needleman, 36.

[5] For some comments from Schuon about these associations see *Logic and Transcendence*, "Introduction", 6.

[6] R. Guénon, *The Reign of Quantity and the Signs of the Times*, 251.

"Wisdom Uncreate": The Perennial Philosophy

St. Augustine speaks of "Wisdom uncreate, the same now as it ever was and ever will be".[7] This timeless wisdom has carried many names: *Philosophia Perennis, Lex Aeterna, Hagia Sophia, Din al-Haqq, Akalika Dhamma,* and *Sanatana Dharma* are among the better known. In itself and as such this truth is formless and beyond all conceptualizations. Any attempt to define it is to try to catch the wind in a net. This universal wisdom, in existence since the genesis of time and the spiritual patrimony of all humankind, can also be designated as the Primordial Tradition. Guénon refers, in one of his earliest articles, to "the Tradition contained in the Sacred Books of all peoples, a Tradition which in reality is everywhere the same, in spite of all the diverse forms it assumes to adapt itself to each race and period".[8] In this sense tradition is synonymous with the perennial philosophy, which is eternal, universal, and immutable.[9] "Tradition" in its purest metaphysical sense is one and the same timeless Wisdom which can be found in all the sacred Scriptures, and which underpins all religious traditions. This is a first principle, a *sine qua non* of traditionalist thought. It has met with a good deal of skepticism, even derision, in modern times, which only goes to show how far we have "progressed" in our foolishness. On the other hand, the credibility of the principle, if one might so put it, has also been compromised by its appropriation by a rag-tag of "gurus" and "spiritual" movements claiming adherence to some vague universalist "essence" without really understanding its nature. More often than not such people are shameless iconoclasts who repudiate the very forms in which the perennial wisdom is necessarily clothed; they are, thereby, anti-traditional.

Schuon and other perennialists point out that all the great religious teachings, albeit in the differing vocabularies appropriate to the spiritual perspective in question, affirm a primordial truth or wisdom. We remember Krishna's declaration in the *Bhagavad Gita* of the pre-existence of his message, proclaimed at the beginning of time.[10] Likewise Christ, speaking in his cosmic function as incarnation of the Truth, states, "Verily I say unto you, before Abraham was, I am".[11] Affirmations of the principle are to be found over and over in the integral traditions.[12] "Tradition" in its most pristine

---

[7] Quoted in S. Radhakrishnan, "Fragments of a Confession", 80.

[8] R. Guénon in *La Gnose*, 1909, quoted in W. Perry (ed.), *A Treasury of Traditional Wisdom*, 20.

[9] See A. Coomaraswamy, "Vedanta and Western Tradition" in *Selected Papers 2*, 7. See also S.H. Nasr, *Knowledge and the Sacred*, 74.

[10] *Bhagavad Gita* IV.5.i.

[11] John 8.58. For a brief commentary see M. Pallis, *A Buddhist Spectrum*, 157.

[12] A sample of quotes taken from W. Perry (ed.), *A Treasury of Traditional Wisdom*: Chou Li: "The true doctrine has always existed in the world and has never perished" (794); St Augus-

sense is this selfsame primordial truth and as such takes on the status of a first cause, a cosmic datum, a principial reality woven into the very fabric of the universe. As such it is not amenable to "proof": it is a self-evident, self-validating principle in the face of which it is possible only to understand or not understand. As Coomaraswamy points out, "a first cause, being itself uncaused, is not probable but axiomatic".[13] Thus the Primordial Tradition or *sophia perennis* is of supra-human origin and is in no sense a product or evolute of human thought: it is "the birth-right of humanity".[14] It is, in Marco Pallis' words, "formless and supra-personal in its essence" and thus "escapes exact definition in terms of human speech and thought":

> Only the divine Suchness is unborn and therefore undying, limitless and therefore not limiting, free and therefore the seat of Deliverance. The voice of tradition is the invitation to that freedom whispered in the ear of existential bondage; whatever echoes that message in any degree or at any remove may properly be called traditional; anything that fails to do so, on the other hand, is untraditional and humanistic.[15]

The primary meaning of "Tradition", then, at least as Guénon uses it, is synonymous with *philosophia perennis*. However, this second term itself, calls for some comment. The idea is as ancient as you like, but the expression itself seems to have first been used by the theologian and Vatican librarian, Augustinus Steuchus (sometimes called Agostino Steuco) in his work *De philosophia perenni libri X* (1540). Steuchius coined the term to signify "the Christian pinnacle of wisdom to which all other philosophical currents in one way or another point". In other words, the term signified a timeless wisdom which informed the teachings of the sages of antiquity (Pythagoras, Plato, Aristotle, and Plotinus), but which reached its culmination in Christianity. A century and a half later, Gottfried von Leibniz detached the term from scholastic theology and characterized the perennial philosophy as that "common, eternal philosophy that underlies all religions, and in particular the mystical streams within them".[16] In a letter of 1714 Leibniz foreshadowed an analysis of all philosophies, ancient and modern,

---

tine: "The very thing that is now called the Christian Religion was not wanting amongst the ancients from the beginning of the human race" (793); Plotinus: "There must first be one from which the many arise. This one is competent to lend itself to all yet remain one. . . . This is identity in variety" (776).

[13] A. Coomaraswamy, *Time and Eternity*, 42n. (By "uncaused" Coomaraswamy here means unconditioned, outside the realm of phenomenal contingencies.)

[14] A. Coomaraswamy, letter to Vasudeva Saharan Agrawala, March 1939, *Selected Letters*, 168.

[15] Marco Pallis, quoted in *The Unanimous Tradition*, ed. R. Fernando, 1.

[16] "Perennial Philosophy", *Wikipedia*. The full title of the work by Steuchius was *De philosophia perenni sive veterum philosophorum cum theologica christiana consensu libri X*.

which would "draw the gold from the dross, the diamond from its mine, the light from the shadows; and this would be in effect a kind of perennial philosophy [*perennis quaedam philosophia*]".[17] The term now no longer entailed a privileged position for Christianity which, in its mystical and metaphysical dimension, was simply one of many expressions—in both East and West—of the perennial philosophy. Since the early eighteenth century this has come to be the most widely understood sense of the term. In more recent times it was popularized by Aldous Huxley's *The Perennial Philosophy* (1944), a thematic compilation of religious and mystical passages, drawn from all over the globe, through which Huxley hoped to lay bare an "immemorial and universal" wisdom—

> The metaphysic that recognizes a divine Reality substantial to the world of things and lives and minds; the psychology that finds something in the soul similar to, or even identical with, divine Reality; the ethic that place's man's final end in the knowledge of the immanent and transcendent Ground of all being.[18]

Huxley's understanding of the perennial philosophy was, in fact, rather partial and idiosyncratic, and his search for the "Highest Common Factor" in religions quite misguided (a matter to which we will return in chapter 15). In the East the metaphysical unanimity of the world's great religious traditions had already been explicitly affirmed by the great nineteenth century Indian saint Ramakrishna.

Schuon himself was not averse to the term *philosophia perennis*/perennial philosophy, which appears frequently in his writings. And, indeed, before his passing Schuon suggested that his foreshadowed biography should be subtitled "Messenger of the Perennial Philosophy". He defined the perennial philosophy this way:

> The term *philosophia perennis* . . . signifies the totality of the primordial and universal truths—and therefore of the metaphysical axioms—whose formulation does not belong to any particular system.[19]

In another place he referred to the perennial philosophy as "the inward and permanent Revelation" which "coincides with our kernel of immortality", a kind of "inward Religion" which becomes obscured or forgotten, thereby

---

[17] "Perennial Philosophy", *Dictionary of the History of Ideas*, Electronic Text Center, University of Virginia Library.

[18] A. Huxley, *The Perennial Philosophy*, vii.

[19] Frithjof Schuon, "The Perennial Philosophy", 21. This article is also reproduced in the Appendix of the present volume.

necessitating the various and outward Revelations of the different traditions.[20]

Schuon also often used the terms *religio perennis*, referring to "the essence of every religion; this means the essence of every form of worship, every form of prayer, and every system of morality", and the *sophia perennis*, "the essence of all dogmas and all expressions of wisdom". Of this second term he also remarks that *sophia* is to be preferred to *philosophia* (though not invariably) because it is more direct and because the latter "evokes in addition associations of ideas with a completely profane and all too often aberrant system of thought".[21] Concerning the term "philosophy", in another place Schuon writes: "Fundamentally we have nothing against the word 'philosophy', for the ancients understood by it all manner of wisdom; in fact, however, rationalism . . . has given the word 'philosophy' a limitative coloring. . . . If Kant is a 'philosopher', then Plotinus is not, and vice versa."[22]

Tradition, the Traditions, and "Traditional"

Before considering other significations of "Tradition", "traditions", and "traditional" we must also take note of the fact that Schuon himself uses the word "Tradition" much more sparingly than Guénon, for the following reason:

> We say "primordial Religion", and not "Tradition", because the first of these terms has the advantage of expressing an intrinsic reality (*religere* = "to bind" the earthly with the heavenly), and not simply an extrinsic reality like the second (*tradere* = "to hand down" scriptural ritual and legal elements). Moreover, one may with reason ask if there could be any question of "tradition" in an age in which spiritual knowledge was innate or spontaneous, or again, if the necessity of a "tradition", and thus of an outward handing down, does not *ipso facto* involve the necessity of a plurality of formulations.[23]

Etymologically "tradition" simply means "that which is transmitted" and this is the key to its second meaning. Here tradition cannot simply be equated with a formless and immutable Truth but rather is that Truth as it finds expression, through the medium of a divine Revelation, in the myths, rituals, symbols, doctrines, iconographies, and other forms of different primal and religious civilizations. The Truth as such is formless and so cannot be con-

---

[20] *Esoterism as Principle and as Way*, "The Primordial Tree", 88.
[21] Frithjof Schuon, "The Perennial Philosophy", 21. For a discussion of early Christian adumbrations of the idea of the *religio perennis* (called by Tertullian *Lex Aeterna*) see G. Castleman, "Golgotha, Athens, and Jerusalem: Patristic Intimations of the *Religio Perennis*".
[22] *Essential Frithjof Schuon*, "Sophia Perennis", 534.
[23] *Esoterism as Principle and as Way*, "The Supreme Commandment, 157n.

veyed, as such, within forms: thus it is aspects of Truth, or partial truths, as it were, which are transmitted by traditional forms. It is in this sense that Schuon usually deploys the term, as in a passage such as this:

> Moreover, our position is well known: it is fundamentally that of meta-physics, and the latter is by definition universalist, "dogmatist" in the philosophical sense of the term, and traditionalist; universalist because free of all denominational formalism; "dogmatist" because far from all subjectivist relativism—we believe that knowledge exists and that it is a real and efficacious adequation—and traditionalist because the traditions are there to express, in different ways but unanimously, this quintessential position—both intellectual and spiritual—which in the last analysis is the reason for being of the human mind.[24]

So, we have two related but distinct meanings for the word "tradition": a timeless, formless, and immutable wisdom; and the formal embodiments of this wisdom which are transmitted through time. To these two senses can be added a third: "tradition" may sometimes refer to the living process of the transmission itself. It may also refer, fourthly, to the channels of transmission. A simple convention will avert some potential misunderstandings. *Tradition*: the primordial wisdom, or Truth, the *philosophia perennis* (the sense in which Guénon most often uses the term); *tradition*: a formal embodiment of Truth under a particular mythological or religious guise which is passed down through time (the primary sense of the word in Schuon's writings); or the vehicle for the transmission of this formal embodiment; or the process of transmission itself (these latter being quite secondary uses). This is not as confusing as it might look: once the distinction between the first sense and the other three has been grasped then the meaning carried by the word becomes clear in the context in which it is used. We can follow the same kind of expedient to distinguish two meanings of "truth": *Truth*: synonymous with Tradition; *truth*: an expression of Truth and, as such, incomplete.

When Guénon uses the word "tradition" he is more often than not referring to what we shall now call Tradition. The Frenchman was not much interested in history in general, nor in the annals of the different religions. However, other perennialists frequently use the word "tradition/s" to refer to different religious and spiritual heritages as they are manifested in time, channels for the transmission of truths of supra-human origin, couched in the forms which have been providentially adapted to suit the needs and receptivities of the peoples and civilizations in question—in Marco Pallis' words, "an effective communication of principles of more-than-human

---

[24] *From the Divine to the Human*, "Preface", 1. (This translation provided by William Stoddart.)

origin . . . through use of forms that will have arisen by applying those principles to contingent needs."[25]

Plainly tradition here means vastly more than the observance of custom; similarly, it cannot be understood as a mere temporal continuity nor assimilated to any historical process. Brian Keeble:

> Tradition is far beyond being merely an accumulation of human endeavor and invention even if it does have a history. Granting that the external characteristics and expression of a tradition are colored by and reflect the passage of time, nonetheless, to equate tradition with a form of historical continuity is to ignore its supra-formal essence in the name of which it remains free and objective in relation to spatio-temporal determinations.[26]

The reference here to "supra-formal essence" is, of course, the key to the relationship between Tradition and tradition, and thus to the deciphering of the perennial philosophy. As Guénon insisted, "there is nothing and can be nothing truly traditional that does not contain some elements of a superhuman order."[27] In our context, then, the term cannot be applied to anything of purely human provenance—which is to say most of modern culture, even if traces of traditional forms inevitably persist. It must always be remembered that

> Tradition cannot be improvised from human means for by the terms of a tradition the human state as such is by definition a mode of ignorance—a blindness that cannot, by merely having recourse to itself, overcome its own unknowingness.[28]

On the other hand, tradition cannot simply be equated with religion, which is one form of tradition but not exhaustive. Thus "tradition" is more inclusive than "religion" though the relationship of the latter to the former is always intimate. A tradition may appear in a guise which cannot strictly be termed "religious", this word implying the presence of certain formal elements which may be absent. A tradition may, for instance, be embedded in a mythico-ritual complex which might more properly be described as mythological rather than religious. Or again, one might refer to an esoteric wisdom which may be associated with religious forms but which is distinct from them, as a tradition—one can speak, for example, of the Pythagorean or the alchemical tradition. However, these qualifications notwithstanding, in most cases where the word "tradition" is used in perennialist discourse,

[25] M. Pallis, *The Way and the Mountain*, 203.
[26] B. Keeble, "Tradition, Intelligence, and the Artist", 236.
[27] R. Guénon, *The Reign of Quantity and the Signs of the Times*, 253.
[28] B. Keeble, "Tradition, Intelligence, and the Artist", 239.

the writer has in mind a religious tradition including, of course, whatever esoteric currents might be associated with it: tradition always encompasses more than the visible exoteric forms. Schuon identifies the essential and operative aspects of tradition this way:

> To the question of what a man should do first of all, situated as he is in this world of enigmas and fluctuations, we would reply that there are four things to be done or four jewels never to be lost sight of: first, to accept the truth; second, to bear it continually in mind; third, to avoid whatever is contrary to truth and the permanent consciousness of truth; and fourth, to accomplish whatever is in conformity therewith. *All religion and all wisdom* is reducible, extrinsically and humanly, to these four laws; indeed, enshrined in *every tradition* is an immutable truth, then a law of "attachment to the Real," of "remembrance" or "love" of God, and finally prohibitions and injunctions; and these make up a fabric of elementary certainties which encompasses and resolves human uncertainty, and thus reduces the whole problem of earthly existence to a geometry at once simple and primordial.[29]

Marco Pallis also provides us with a helpful capsule definition of tradition:

> Wherever a complete tradition exists this will entail the presence of four things, namely: a source of . . . Revelation; a current of influence or Grace issuing from that source and transmitted without interruption through a variety of channels; a way of "verification" which, when faithfully followed, will lead the human subject to successive positions where he is able to "actualize" the truths that Revelation communicates; finally there is the formal embodiment of tradition in the doctrines, arts, sciences, and other elements that together go to determine the character of a normal civilization.[30]

Revelation, grace, method, forms: these four constituents of any integral tradition call for some commentary.

Revelation. We will start with a metaphorical explanation—indeed, strictly speaking, no other kind is possible. In his study of Sufism, Martin Lings articulates the "idea" of Revelation in these terms:

> From time to time a Revelation "flows" like a great tidal wave from the Ocean of Infinitude to the shores of our finite world. . . . From "time to time": this is a simplification which calls for a commentary; for since there is no common measure between the origin of such a wave and its destination, its temporality is bound to partake, mysteriously, of the Eternal, just as its finiteness is bound to partake of the Infinite. Being

---

[29] *Echoes of Perennial Wisdom*, 83 (italics mine).
[30] M. Pallis, *The Way and the Mountain*, 9.

temporal, it must first reach this world at a certain moment in history; but that moment will in a sense escape from time. "Better than a thousand months" is how the Islamic Revelation describes the night of its own advent. There must also be an end which corresponds to the beginning; but that end will be too remote to be humanly foreseeable. . . . There is only one water but no two waves are the same. Each wave has its own characteristics according to its destination, that is, the particular needs of time and place towards which and in response to which it has providentially been made to flow.[31]

One form of misunderstanding can easily be anticipated and should be immediately countered by a passage from Schuon, read as an addendum to the account just given:

To say that Revelation is "supernatural" does not mean that it is contrary to nature, for nature can be taken to represent by extension all that is possible on any given level of reality, but that it does not originate at the level to which—rightly or wrongly—the epithet "natural" is usually applied; this "natural level" is none other than that of physical causes, hence of sensory and psychic phenomena considered in relation to those causes.[32]

This leaves open the way for an understanding of Revelation compatible with whatever religious tradition is in question, not excluding Buddhism which, on the face of it at least, might appear to pose the most difficulties as far as the principle is concerned. (In this context Schuon does not hesitate to speak of the Buddha's "transcendent nature, without which there could be no question of the efficacy of his Law or of the saving power of his Name".[33])

Two related errors must also be resisted. Revelation is in no sense to be understood in any psychological sense.[34] This is a prejudice to which the neo-Hindus have been prone, failing as they sometimes do to respect the crucial distinction between the psychic and spiritual domains. The second fallacy, which is really the same misconception in different clothing, is the notion that Revelation can occur under the pressure of purely human initiatives. Here Revelation must be sharply distinguished from intellection and from inspiration; these terms will be elaborated in our discussion of metaphysics. There is, then, no necessity to restrict the meaning of "Revela-

---

[31] M. Lings, *What is Sufism?*, 11-12. See also S.H. Nasr, *Sufi Essays*, 30.

[32] *Light on the Ancient Worlds*, "Fall and Forfeiture", 25. See also *Spiritual Perspectives and Human Facts*, "Vedanta", 117-118.

[33] *Treasures of Buddhism*, "Treasures of Buddhism", 8.

[34] See *Language of the Self* (1959), "Self-Knowledge and the Western Seeker", 56-59; and *Light on the Ancient Worlds*, "Keys to the Bible", 117-118.

tion" to its characteristic formulation in the Abrahamic traditions, nor to identify it with the historic events pertaining to the successive Revelations wherein those traditions originated, namely the Sinaitic Revelation, the Incarnation, and the Descent of the Koran. Looked at from another angle—and this is the one usually taken by Guénon—Revelation can be understood as a "remembering anew", through a divine unveiling of the Primordial Tradition in respect of a given branch of humanity. Schuon, too, avails himself of this perspective in writing:

> It has been said more than once that total Truth is inscribed in an eternal script in the very substance of our spirit; what the different Revelations do is to "crystallize" and "actualize", in differing degrees according to the case, a nucleus of certitudes.[35]

Revelation must take on some form; we can thus say that it communicates truths rather than Truth, since to form is to limit. As Schuon states, "A traditional perspective or 'mythology' is to total truth what a geometric form is to space. . . . Each fundamental geometric form . . . is an adequate image of the whole of space, but each excludes the others."[36] Nevertheless, and somewhat paradoxically, the Revelations, being of divine origin, also communicate something of the virtuality of Absolute Truth:

> Revelation speaks an absolute language because God is absolute, not because the form is absolute; in other words, the absoluteness of the Revelation is absolute in itself, but relative in its form.[37]

To some mentalities this must remain a conundrum while to others it will be as clear as the day.

Secondly, the principle of Grace (in Arabic, *barakah*). This is related to but not exhausted by the dogmatic senses of the word in the theological perspectives of the Semitic monotheisms. It is a beneficent and catalyzing influence which issues from the same divine source as the Revelation and which will be mediated through the Revelation. If the primary principle of Revelation is accepted then this Grace follows just as warmth comes from the sun. As Schuon affirms, "Tradition conveys and transmits not only truths, but also celestial forces that no human ingenuity could replace".[38] The uninterrupted flow of this divine influence is of critical import: the spiritual legacy derived from a Revelation must be handed down through an

---

[35] *Light on the Ancient Worlds*, "*Religio Perennis*", 119. See also *Logic and Transcendence*, "Man and Certainty", 261 and *Esoterism as Principle and as Way*, "Introduction", 10-11.

[36] *Spiritual Perspectives and Human Facts*, "Contours of the Spirit", 58.

[37] *Gnosis: Divine Wisdom*, "Diversity of Revelation", 30.

[38] *Treasures of Buddhism*, "Virtues and Symbols of Shinto", 203n.

unbroken chain which may take various forms—initiatic, apostolic, or some other; hence the concern in all integral traditions with spiritual lineages.

The third factor characterizing a tradition will be a spiritual method, a Way, whereby one may conform one's being to the truths communicated by the Revelation and preserved in the tradition. The tradition in question provides "a method of concentrating upon the Real, of attaching oneself to the Absolute and living according to the Will of Heaven".[39] Schuon:

> The Path presents itself first of all as the polarity of "doctrine" and "method", or as metaphysical truth accompanied by contemplative concentration. In short, everything in it is reducible to these two elements: intellection and concentration or discernment and union. For us, who are in the realm of relativity since we exist and think, metaphysical truth is in the first place discrimination between the Real and the unreal or "less real"; and concentration or the operative act of the spirit—prayer in its very broadest sense—is in a way our response to the truth which offers itself to us; it is Revelation entering into our consciousness and becoming in some degree assimilated by our being.[40]

Finally one finds the formal embodiments of the tradition, the elements which give expression to saving truths and which will be found in all branches of a traditional civilization. In this context Gershom Scholem has written that tradition "embodies the realization of the effectiveness of the Word in every concrete state and relationship entered into by a society."[41] Tradition is the "application and full extension in every domain" of Revelation.[42] Thus the Revelation infuses the arts and crafts, the sciences and the social life of a traditional civilization, as well as on its theology and spiritual means. In this sense, then, tradition is indeed "the chain that joins civilization to Revelation"[43] and "the mediator between time and eternity".[44] As Nasr insists:

> Tradition is inextricably related to revelation and religion, to the sacred, to the notion of orthodoxy, to authority, to the continuity and regularity of transmission of the truth, to the exoteric and the esoteric as well as to the spiritual life, science, and the arts.[45]

Of the many formal elements which necessarily appear in any tradition the perennialists have paid especially close attention to sacred art. We shall devote a later chapter to this subject, but for the moment we can note

---

[39] S.H. Nasr, *Ideals and Realities of Islam*, 15.

[40] *Understanding Islam*, "The Path", 127.

[41] G. Scholem, "Tradition and Commentary as Religious Categories in Judaism", 148.

[42] W. Perry, "The Revival of Interest in Tradition", 3.

[43] Lord Northbourne, *Religion in the Modern World*, 34.

[44] A.K. Saran, "The Crisis of Hinduism", 93.

[45] S.H. Nasr, *Knowledge and the Sacred*, 68.

the implications of Schuon's affirmation that, "Traditions emerge from the Infinite like flowers; they can no more be fabricated than can the sacred art which is their witness and their proof."[46]

Traditional Worlds

A tradition is not static, a fossil-like form that persists in a frozen state through time. Traditions are dynamic: if needs be, they can grow, branch out, blossom. However, the principle of continuity which preserves the link with the Revelation must always be respected if the tradition is to remain an integral one. Titus Burckhardt explains the principle with the aid of the following image: "The growth of a tradition resembles that of a crystal, which attracts homologous particles to itself, incorporating them according to its own laws of unity."[47] In the final phrase—"its own laws of unity"—we find the key to the principle of orthodoxy. The great doctrinal elaborations which follow a Revelation, usually at some historical distance, do not, essentially, constitute an "addition" to the tradition, but an unfolding of principles and perspectives which until then have remained implicit. One thinks of a Nagarjuna, a Shankara, an Aquinas, an Ibn Arabi. Such figures disavow any personal "originality", claiming only to be elaborating the spiritual teaching to which they are heirs. Burckhardt again: "Doctrine grows, not so much by addition of new knowledge, as by the need to refute errors and to reanimate a diminishing power of intuition".[48] For the traditionalists there is always something providential about the appearance of the great doctors of theology and metaphysics. Schuon:

> It is therefore our increasing weakness, and with it the risk of forgetfulness and betrayal, which more than anything obliges us to externalize or make explicit what at the beginning was included in an inward and implicit perfection; Saint Paul needed neither Thomism nor cathedrals, for all profundities and splendors were in himself and all around him in the sanctity of the early community. And this, far from supporting iconoclasts of all kinds, refutes them completely; more or less late epochs—the Middle Ages, for example—have an imperious need for externalizations and developments, just as water from a spring, if it is not to be lost on its way, needs a channel made by nature or by the hand of man; and just as the channel does not transform the water and is not meant to do so—for no water is better than spring water—so the externalizations and developments of a spiritual patrimony are there,

---

[46] *Treasures of Buddhism*, "Treasures of Buddhism", 8.
[47] T. Burckhardt, *Alchemy*, 17.
[48] T. Burckhardt, *An Introduction to Sufi Doctrine*, 17.

not to change that patrimony, but to transmit it as fully and effectively as possible.[49]

Traditional cultures, then, are oriented towards our ultimate ends and governed by a coherent religious or mythological vision derived from a Revelation. This view of society has all manner of implications and applications. Let us consider a few. The perennialists, unlike most modern social theorists, find no absolute or self-evident value in "society" as such or, indeed, in what is called "civilization", in the modern sense of this term. Nor are they susceptible to the "demagogic obsession with purely 'social' values" which is nowadays so widespread, "even amongst 'believers'".[50] As Schuon points out:

> When people talk about "civilization" they generally attribute a quali-
> tative meaning to the term; now civilization only represents a value
> provided it is supra-human in origin and implies for the "civilized" man
> a sense of the sacred. . . . A sense of the sacred is fundamental for every
> civilization because fundamental for man; the sacred—that which is
> immutable, inviolable, and so infinitely majestic—is in the very sub-
> stance of our spirit and of our existence.[51]

Traditional societies are grounded in an awareness of this reality. Society itself represents nothing of permanent or unconditional value but only insofar as it provides a context for the sense of the sacred and the spiritual life which it implies.[52] A traditional society will not necessarily be self-consciously aware of being "traditional": the prevailing conditions will appear to be natural and normal, no other possibility having intruded itself.

We can see that this vision of a religious culture is diametrically opposed to the Marxist/Durkheimian thesis about the relationship between religion and society. It is not society which fashions religion in its own image but religion which shapes the society, whose whole rationale is embedded in the sense of which Schuon speaks. In traditional societies, "It is the spiritual, not the temporal, which culturally, socially, and politically is the criterion of all other values."[53] It is from this platform that the traditionalists reaffirm the values of civilizations other than our own and from which the most tren-chant critique of modernism can be mounted. Western "civilization" is now,

---

[49] *Light on the Ancient Worlds*, "Light on the Ancient Worlds", 5.

[50] *Transfiguration of Man*, "Reflections on Ideological Sentimentalism", 18.

[51] *Understanding Islam*, "Islam", 26.

[52] One of the most eloquent statements of this principle can be found in A. Govinda, *The Way of the White Clouds*, xi-xii.

[53] *Transfiguration of Man*, "Usurpations of Religious Feeling", 28. See also *Treasures of Buddhism*, "Treasures of Buddhism", 13ff; *Light on the Ancient Worlds*, "Light on the Ancient Worlds", 18; and Abu Bakr Siraj ad-Din, "The Spiritual Function of Civilization", 104ff.

in Guénon's words, "devoid of any traditional character with the exception of the religious [i.e. exoteric] element",[54] which, in many quarters, is itself in disarray.

Coomaraswamy's biographer has noted the dangers of using the idea of tradition as a simplistic device for separating the Blessed from the Cursed. One does sense, it must be admitted, the occasional over-schematization in the social critiques of both Guénon and Coomaraswamy, necessitated no doubt by their pioneering roles, but this is not a charge that can be sustained against Schuon. In any case, there is nothing of that cloudy sentimentality which looks back to a romanticized past in any of these writers. The reproach of wanting to "turn back the clock" is not one that anyone who has understood the traditionalist position would make. As Schuon remarks, a "nostalgia for the past" is, in itself, nothing; all that is meaningful is "a nostalgia for the sacred" which can be "located nowhere else than in the liberating 'now' of God".[55]

No amount of quotation can capture the cadences and resonances which grace Schuon's writings on traditional civilizations. Readers must turn to these writings for themselves. Nevertheless, it will perhaps be useful to close this part of our inquiry with a lengthy but highly germane passage from Schuon:

> When the modern world is contrasted with traditional civilizations, it is not simply a question of looking on each side for what is good and bad; since good and evil are everywhere, it is essentially a question of knowing on which side the lesser evil is to be found. If someone tells us that such and such a good exists outside tradition, we respond: no doubt, but it is necessary to choose the most important good, and this is necessarily represented by tradition; and if someone tells us that in tradition there exists such and such an evil, we respond, no doubt, but it is necessary to choose the lesser evil, and again it is tradition that contains it. It is illogical to prefer an evil which involves some benefits to a good which involves some evils.
>
> Certainly, to confine oneself to admiring the traditional worlds is still to stop short at a fragmentary point of view, for every civilization is a "two-edged sword"; it is a total good only by virtue of those invisible elements that determine it positively. In certain respects, every human society is bad; if its transcendent character is entirely removed—which amounts to dehumanizing it since the element of transcendence is essential to man though always dependent on his free consent—then at the same time society's whole reason for existing is removed, and there remains only an ant-heap. . . . It is one of the most pernicious of

[54] Guénon, quoted in R. Lipsey, *Coomaraswamy: His Life and Work*, 266. (This was written, obviously, before the Vatican II Council of 1962-1965.)

[55] *Christianity/Islam*, "On the Margin of Liturgical Improvisations", 12.

81

errors to believe that the human collectivity, on the one hand, or its well-being, on the other, represents an unconditional or absolute value, and thus an end in itself.

Regarded as social phenomena and independently of their intrinsic value—though there is no sharp dividing line between the two—traditional civilizations, despite their imperfections, are like sea-walls built to stem the rising tide of worldliness, error, subversion, of the fall that is ceaselessly renewed. . . . To reject traditional frameworks because of human abuses amounts to asserting that the founders of religion did not know what they were doing, that abuses are not inherent in human nature, that they are therefore avoidable even in societies numbering millions of men, and that they are avoidable thanks to purely human means; no more flagrant contradiction than this can be imagined.[56]

Clearly there is much here that might call for comment, and we shall return to some of the issues it raises in our discussion of the confrontation of traditionalism and modernism. For the moment we shall let the passage stand as it is and move on to an intimately related subject—the nature of religion.

---

[56] *Light on the Ancient Worlds*, "Fall and Forfeiture", 33. See also *To Have a Center*, "To Have a Center", 11-12.

5

The Transcendent Unity of Religions

Essentially all religions include decisive truths, mediators, and miracles, but the disposition of these elements, the play of proportions, can vary according to the conditions of the revelation and its human receptacles.[1]

Orthodoxy is the principle of formal homogeneity proper to any authentically spiritual perspective.[2]

Exoterism consists in identifying transcendent realities with the dogmatic forms, and if need be, with the historical facts of a given Revelation, whereas esoterism refers in a more or less direct manner to these same realities.[3]

Human nature in general and human intelligence in particular cannot be understood apart from the religious phenomenon, which characterizes them in the most direct and most complete way possible: grasping the transcendent—not the "psychological"—nature of the human being we thereby grasp the nature of revelation, religion, tradition; we understand their possibility, their necessity, their truth. And in understanding religion, not only in a particular form . . . but in its formless essence, we also understand the religions, that is to say, the meaning of their plurality and diversity; this is the plane of *gnosis*, of the *religio perennis*, where the extrinsic antinomies of dogmas are explained and resolved.[4]

Amongst the perennialists Schuon writes with sovereign authority on the subject of religion as such. The quotations above flag four motifs: the necessary diversity of Revelations and thus of religious forms (embracing both doctrine and method); the principle of orthodoxy; the distinction between the exoteric and esoteric domains; and, the transcendent unity of religions.

Revelation, Doctrine, Method
Schuon's view of religion turns on the axiomatic notion of multiple and diverse Revelations. He perceives humankind neither as a monolithic psy-

---

[1] *Spiritual Perspectives and Human Facts*, "Contours of the Spirit", 68.
[2] *Stations of Wisdom*, "Orthodoxy and Intellectuality", 13.
[3] *Logic and Transcendence*, "Oriental Dialectic and Its Roots in Faith", 144.
[4] *Light on the Ancient Worlds*, "Religio Perennis", 125.

chic entity nor as an amorphous agglomerate, but as being long since divided into several distinct branches, each with its own peculiar traits which determine its receptivity to truth and shape its apprehensions of reality. Needless to say there is no question here of any kind of racialism or ethnocentrism which attributes a superiority or inferiority to this or that ethnic collectivity. Nor, however, is there any sentimental prejudice in favor of the idea that the world's peoples are only "superficially" and "accidentally" different: "We observe on earth the existence of diverse races, whose differences are 'valid' since there are no 'false' as opposed to 'true' races."[5] Each branch of humanity exhibits a psychic and spiritual homogeneity which may transcend barriers of geography and biology. An example: that shamanism should extend through parts of Northern Europe, Siberia, Mongolia, Tibet, and the Red Indian areas betokens a certain spiritual temperament shared by the peoples in question, one quite independent of physical similarities and leaving aside the question of "borrowings" and "influences".[6]

To the diverse human collectivities are addressed Revelations which are determined in their formal aspects by the needs at hand. Thus,

> What determines the differences among forms of Truth is the difference among human receptacles. For thousands of years already humanity has been divided into several fundamentally different branches constituting as many complete humanities, more or less closed in on themselves; the existence of spiritual receptacles so different and so original demands a differentiated refraction of the one Truth.[7]

For this reason "a revelation always conforms to a racial genius, though this by no means signifies that it is restricted to the specific limits of the race in question".[8] And so it is that

> The plurality of religions is no more contradictory than the plurality of individuals: in Revelation, God makes Himself as it were an individual in order to address the individual; homogeneity in relation to other Revelations is inward and not outward. If humanity were not diverse, a single Divine individualization would suffice; but man is diverse not only from the point of view of ethnic temperaments, but also from that of spiritual possibilities; the diverse combinations of these two things make possible and *necessary* the diversity of Revelations.[9]

---

[5] *Gnosis: Divine Wisdom*, "Diversity of Revelation", 20. (Schuon's writings on the subject of race are examined in detail in chapter 16.)

[6] *Light on the Ancient Worlds*, "American Indian Shamanism", 59.

[7] *Gnosis: Divine Wisdom*, "Diversity of Revelation", 17.

[8] *Language of the Self*, "The Meaning of Race", 153n.

[9] *From the Divine to the Human*, "To Refuse or to Accept Revelation", 133 (italics mine).

We have already met with the idea that Truth is one. Revelation marks a "formalization" of Truth and thus cannot be identical with it.

> Truth is situated beyond forms, whereas Revelation, or the Tradition derived from it, belongs to the formal order, and this indeed by definition; but to speak of form is to speak of diversity, and thus plurality.[10]

In a sense the Revelations are communicated in different divine languages. Just as we should baulk at the idea of "true" and "false" languages, so we need to see both the necessity and the validity of multiple Revelations.[11]

It is in the nature of things that the principle of multiple Revelations is not accessible to all mentalities and its implications must remain anathema to the majority of believers. Nevertheless, from a metaphysical viewpoint, anyone today wishing to understand religion as such and the inter-relationships of the various traditions must have a firm grip on this principle. It is supported by Scriptural and traditional authority, though the penetration of the passages in question will be beyond the reach of most believers. As the Semitic traditions have been the ones most prone to extravagant claims of exclusivism, we shall cite a few passages from their Scriptures which are suggestive in the light of the foregoing:

> Other sheep have I which are not of this fold. (John 10:16)

> In my Father's house are many mansions. (John 14:2)

> For each we have appointed a law and traced out a path, and if God had wished, verily He would have made you one people. (Koran 5:53)

> And we never sent a messenger save with the language of his folk, that he might make the message clear for them. (Koran 14:4)[12]

Just as there are multiple Revelations, so too, it might be said, there are many "faces of God", as intimated in our earlier discussion of the Five Divine Presences. Here it is a matter of understanding "the mystery of the hypostatic face", as Schuon puts it:

> There is not only a personal God—who is so to speak the "human" or "humanized face" of the supra-personal Divinity—but . . . there is also, below and resulting from this first hypostatic degree, what we may term the "confessional face" of God: it is the Face that God turns towards a particular religion, the Gaze he casts upon it, and without which it

---

[10] *Gnosis: Divine Wisdom*, "Diversity of Revelation", 29.

[11] *Gnosis: Divine Wisdom*, "Diversity of Revelation", 20. (This is neither to suggest that all "religions" which claim to derive from a "Revelation" do so in fact, nor to deny that there is such a thing as a pseudo-religion.)

[12] See S.H. Nasr, *Sufi Essays*, 126n2.

could not even exist. In other words: the "human" or "personal Face" of God takes on diverse modes corresponding to so many religious, confessional, or spiritual perspectives, so that it could be said that each religion has its God, without thereby denying that God is One. . . . The Divine Being contains all spiritual possibilities and consequently all the religious and mystical archetypes.[13]

Revelation must be sharply distinguished from other intuitions and disclosures of the divine. In the perennialist vocabulary, "Revelation" always signifies the fountainhead of a whole religious tradition. When Martin Buber wrote that "Revelation is continual, and everything is fit to become a sign of revelation", he was using the word in a different sense.[14] Likewise, Archbishop Temple in writing "Unless all existence is a medium of revelation, no particular revelation is possible".[15] The referent here is what Mircea Eliade would call a "hierophany" and what the perennialists might describe as an "archetypal illumination".[16] In our discussion "Revelation" will be used in the traditionalist sense and thus signaled by the use of the capital. Furthermore, Revelation must be distinguished from "inspiration", which can encompass myriad workings of divine influence.[17] The neglect of this distinction in some quarters has produced abuses too numerous to catalogue but the Protestant tendency to idolatrize Scripture is a case in point.[18]

As each religion proceeds from a Revelation, it is, in Nasr's words, both

> *the* religion and *a* religion, *the* religion inasmuch as it contains within itself the Truth and the means of attaining the Truth, *a* religion since it emphasizes a particular aspect of Truth in conformity with the spiritual and psychological needs of the humanity for whom it is destined.[19]

---

[13] *Survey of Metaphysics and Esoterism*, "The Mystery of the Hypostatic Face", 91-92.

[14] M. Buber, *A Believing Humanism*, 113.

[15] From W. Temple, *Nature, Man and God*, quoted in J. Wach, *The Comparative Study of Religions*, 44.

[16] See M. Pallis, *A Buddhist Spectrum*, 152.

[17] This distinction has been scrupulously preserved in the Judaic, Islamic, and Hindu traditions, which is not to suggest that it is one of which all the adherents of these traditions will be aware.

[18] To clarify: the words of Christ are at the level of Revelation, whereas much of the New Testament falls into the category of inspiration (by the Holy Spirit). Christ is thus the "Word made flesh" whereas the Torah and Koran are the "Word made book". In Christianity, the Revelation—Christ—is often confused with the Scriptures which are, to varying degrees, inspired. See Schuon's remarks on the Epistles of the New Testament, which are inspired in a "secondary degree" (*In the Face of the Absolute*, "The Human Margin", 92-93). On the distinction between Revelation and inspiration see also *Spiritual Perspectives and Human Facts*, "Vedanta", 117-118, and *Understanding Islam*, "The Koran", 40n.

[19] See S. H. Nasr, *Ideals and Realities of Islam*, 15.

In other words each religion is sufficient unto itself and contains all that is necessary for man's sanctification and salvation. Nevertheless, it remains limited by definition. The recognition and reconciliation of these two apparently antagonistic principles is crucial. Schuon puts the matter this way:

> A religion is a form—hence a limit—which contains the Limitless, if this paradox is permissible; every form is fragmentary because of its necessary exclusion of other formal possibilities; the fact that these forms—when they are complete, that is to say when they are perfectly "themselves"—represent totality each in its own way, does not prevent them from being fragmentary in respect of their particularization and their reciprocal exclusion.[20]

The diversity of Revelations raises the question of the "status", so to speak, of the Messengers through whom the Revelations have been communicated. Each Messenger fulfils the appropriate function in a certain modality, or spiritual key, which determines the "tone" of the tradition which emanates from the Message. Thus, as Nasr tells us,

> When one says *the* Prophet it means the prophet of Islam . . . when one says *the* Incarnation it refers to Christ who personifies this aspect. And although every prophet and saint has experienced "enlightenment", *the* Enlightenment refers to the experience of the Buddha which is the most outstanding and universal embodiment of this experience.[21]

Much more might be said on this subject, but the following remarks from Schuon disallow some of the more obvious confusions which might arise:

> The great Messengers, if they are assuredly one by their principle, in their gnosis, and in the Logos, are not however of necessity equal on the phenomenal plane, that of manifestation on earth; what are equivalent are the Messages when each is taken in its entirety. It is necessary, in any case, not to confuse the phenomenal or cosmic with the spiritual reality; it is the latter which is one and the former which is diverse.[22]

Given this framework it hardly needs saying that the great religious founders must not be confounded with other religious figures, no matter how formidable. Schuon goes to some lengths to point out why Vivekananda's sentimental trinity of Jesus, the Buddha, and Ramakrishna is quite unacceptable from many different points of view—not because the sanctity

---

[20] *Understanding Islam*, "The Path", 174.

[21] See S.H. Nasr, *Ideals and Realities of Islam*, 67.

[22] *Gnosis: Divine Wisdom*, "The Sense of the Absolute", 14. See also *Stations of Wisdom*, "Manifestations of the Divine Principle", 91-93. Concerning Buddhism particularly, see *Treasures of Buddhism*, "Message and Messenger", 31-36.

of the latter is in any way in doubt but because his spiritual function is of a quite different order, Ramakrishna being as a river besides the oceanic nature of the other two.[23]

All religions necessarily entail doctrine and method. As Schuon insists:

> The quintessence of all tradition and all spirituality is discernment between the Real and the illusory and concentration on the Real. Everything is contained in this twofold definition. In a more outward sense this is doctrine and method; there are many doctrines and many methods, but there is only one discernment between the Real and the illusory, the Absolute and the contingent, the Infinite and the finite, just as there is only one concentration on the Real, only one Union, only one Deliverance.[24]

Similarly:

> Starting from the axiom that integral spirituality comprises by definition a doctrine and a method, we would say that the first is linked, to some degree or other, to discriminative and contemplative intelligence—active and passive, if one will—whereas the second comprises operative will and stimulating and interiorizing sensibility.[25]

Essentially, method might be thought of as the remembrance or love of God, and the disciplined observance of certain ritual and moral obligations. As Schuon so beautifully expresses it:

> Enshrined in every tradition is an immutable truth, then a law of "attachment to the Real", of "remembrance" or "love" of God, and finally prohibitions and injunctions; and these make up a fabric of elementary certainties which encompasses and resolves human uncertainty, and thus reduces the whole problem of earthly existence to a geometry at once simple and primordial.[26]

Further:

---

[23] See *Understanding Islam* (1976) "The Prophet", 87fn. Schuon's argument is presented more fully in chapter 15 which includes a more detailed discussion of Ramakrishna and Vivekananda.

[24] *Prayer Fashions Man*, "Appendix", 187.

[25] *From the Divine to the Human*, "Outline of a Spiritual Anthropology", 78n. Doctrine and method are not only the foundations of any integral religion but of *sophia* itself: "The key to the eternal *sophia* is pure intellection or in other words metaphysical discernment. To 'discern' is to 'separate': to separate the Real and the illusory, the Absolute and the contingent, the Necessary and the possible, *Atma* and *Maya*. Accompanying discernment, by way of complement and operatively, is concentration, which unites: this means becoming fully aware—from the starting point of earthly and human *Maya*—of *Atma*, which is both absolute and infinite" (Frithjof Schuon, "The Perennial Philosophy", 21).

[26] *Echoes of Perennial Wisdom*, 83.

All the dogmas, all the prescriptions, and all the means of a religion have their sufficient reason in the three fundamental vocations of man: discernment, practice, and virtue.[27]

Orthodoxy

By what means can it be established whether something deserves the dignity of the term "religion"? The answer to this question has been suggested by much that has already been said about tradition. Further ambiguities are dispelled by the principle of orthodoxy, which Schuon articulates thus:

> Orthodoxy is the principle of formal homogeneity proper to any authentically spiritual perspective; it is therefore an indispensable aspect of all genuine intellectuality; in other words, the essence of every orthodoxy is the truth, and not mere fidelity to a system that might possibly turn out to be false. To be orthodox means to participate, through the medium of a doctrine that can properly be called "traditional", in the immutability of the principles which govern the Universe and fashion our intelligence.[28]

It follows that

> in order to be orthodox a religion must possess a mythological or doctrinal symbolism establishing the essential distinction [between the Real and the illusory] . . . and it must provide a path that guarantees both the perfection of concentration and its continuity; in other words a religion is orthodox if it provides a sufficient, if not always exhaustive, idea of the Absolute and the relative, and thus of their reciprocal relationships.[29]

Schuon amplifies this elsewhere:

> For a religion to be considered intrinsically orthodox—extrinsic orthodoxy depending on specific formal elements that cannot be applied literally outside of the perspective to which they belong—it must be founded on a doctrine of the Absolute which, taken as a whole, is adequate. . . . This religion must then advocate and achieve a spirituality that is proportioned to this doctrine, which is to say that it must comprise sanctity both in notion and in fact. Therefore, the religion must be of divine and not of philosophical origin, and consequently it must be the vessel for a sacramental or theurgic presence.[30]

---

[27] *Echoes of Perennial Wisdom*, 80.

[28] *Stations of Wisdom*, "Orthodoxy and Intellectuality", 13.

[29] *Light on the Ancient Worlds*, "*Religio Perennis*", 121.

[30] *Form and Substance in the Religions*, "Form and Substance in Religions", 13. See also commentary by Leo Schaya in Y. Ibish and P.L. Wilson (eds.), *Traditional Modes of Contemplation and Action*, 462ff.

The insistence on *divine origin*, *adequate doctrine*, and an *effective spiritual method* is by now clear enough. How are these to be put to the test?

Firstly, the origin of the religion in question: according to the traditionalists any claim to a Revelation such as would provide the impetus for a whole new religious tradition in post-Koranic times can immediately be disqualified.

> It is quite out of the question that a "revelation", in the full sense of the word, should arise in our time, one comparable, that is to say, to the imparting of the great *sutras* or any other primary scriptures: the day of revelations is past on this globe and was so already long ago. The inspirations of the saints are of another order.[31]

This statement derives from the sacred Scriptures themselves, especially the Koran, and from the doctrine of cycles. The Koranic Revelation must needs be the last great Revelation in this cycle. Muhammad is the "Seal of the Prophets", no later prophecies of this order being possible.[32] History has only gone to confirm it. Under this view there can, in fact, be no new religions as such: there can only be conformity to the traditional orthodoxies on one side or a surrender to the confusions of the age on the other. As Schuon observes:

> It is essential to grasp that after a certain cyclic period and the hardening of the terrestrial ambience which it comprises, God no longer speaks, at least not as Revealer. In other words, after a certain period, whatever is put forward as new religion is inevitably false; the Middle Ages mark *grosso modo* the final limit.[33]

The traditionalists have been implacable in the face of the various heterodox and quasi-spiritual movements of which there has been such a spate in recent times. Amongst their targets are the movements of "reformist" bent (neo-Hinduism, liberal theology, "Christian Marxism"), those of syncretic intention and esoteric trappings (Theosophical Society), those centered on charismatic "gurus" who are not faithful purveyors of any orthodox doctrine (Gurdjieff, Krishnamurti, Rajneesh), or those claiming a new divine dispensation (Mormonism, Subud). Although these groups and persons are rarely identified by name in perennialist writings, it is clear that they violate

---

[31] Frithjof Schuon, "No Activity Without Truth", 35. See also *Stations of Wisdom*, "Orthodoxy and Intellectuality", 17.

[32] See S.H. Nasr, *Ideals and Realities of Islam*, 33-36.

[33] *Understanding Islam*, "The Koran", 47. (We should also note a qualification made by Schuon concerning Sikhism: "As for the Sikh brotherhood, this is an esotericism analogous to that of Kabir, the special position of which is explained by the quite exceptional conditions arising from the contiguity of Hinduism and Sufism; but here too it is a case of the very latest possibility" [*Understanding Islam*, "The Koran", 48n].)

traditional principles. Plainly, it is such movements Schuon has in mind when he writes about heterodoxies which

> always tend to adulterate either the idea of the divine Principle or the manner of our attachment to it; they offer either a worldly, profane, or—if one prefers—"humanist" counterfeit of religion, or else a mysticism containing nothing but the ego and its illusions.[34]

Secondly, the adequacy of the doctrine: this can only be determined by a metaphysical discernment, itself nurtured within the integral traditions. (More on metaphysics in our next chapter.) A third test of religion is offered by the Biblical maxim: "By their fruits ye shall know them."[35] Any orthodox tradition, by being such, will necessarily bring forth saints and sages who are living testimony to the efficacy of the spiritual economy in question. Men indeed do not gather grapes from thorns nor figs from thistles. However, here again an acute metaphysical sensitivity is necessary to recognize spirituality in all its strange and sometimes scandalous guises. Finally, it is worth adding that another criterion is a fully-fledged sacred art—both "witness and proof" of tradition, as Schuon tells us.

What of the attitude of one orthodoxy to another? We have already encountered Schuon's reference to "formal elements which cannot apply literally outside their own perspective". This provides the key. From the exoteric vantage point of any particular tradition there can only be *one* orthodoxy—that is, the one determining the outlook in question. As Swami Abhishiktananda (Fr Henri Le Saux) put it, "Every *dharma* is for its followers the supreme vehicle of the claims of the Absolute".[36] Thus, for instance, from a Hindu viewpoint Buddhism must appear as unorthodox, the test in this case being the acceptance of Vedic authority. Here the Hindu viewpoint is both "right" and "wrong". This paradox is resolved in an illuminating passage from Schuon:

> What perhaps renders somewhat difficult the definition of orthodoxy is that in fact it presents two principal modes, one being essential or intrinsic and the other formal or extrinsic: the latter concerns its accordance with truth in some particular revealed form, the former its accordance with essential and universal truth, whether or not this agrees with a given particular form, so that these two modes may sometimes oppose one another outwardly. For example, Buddhism is on the one hand extrinsically heterodox in relation to Hinduism, because it is separated from the basic forms of the latter, and on the other hand it is intrinsically orthodox because it accords with the universal truth from

[34] *Light on the Ancient Worlds*, "*Religio Perennis*", 121.
[35] Matthew 7:20.
[36] Abhishiktananda, *The Further Shore*, 25.

which it derives. By contrast, the Brahmo-samaj, like every other form of "progressive" neo-Hinduism, is heterodox twice over, firstly in relation to Hinduism and secondly in relation to truth itself.[37]

Whilst on the subject of "reformist" movements let us remind ourselves that there is a good deal of talk these days about the traditional religions being "played out", "inadequate to the problems of the age", "irrelevant to contemporary concerns" and so on. "New solutions" are needed, "appropriate to the times". This kind of thinking is by no means restricted to those who are openly hostile to religion; it is to be found amongst many people who, being deeply concerned about our spiritual welfare, sense that something has gone wrong. The traditionalists are the first to agree that we have indeed gone astray. However, the solution is not to be found in any "program" which starts from the belief that the religions must be "reformed" in order to conform to the needs of "our times". Such a stance is part of the very problem which the reformers apparently want to remedy.

> Nothing is more misleading than to pretend, as is so glibly done in our day, that the religions have compromised themselves hopelessly in the course of the centuries or that they are now played out. If one knows what a religion really consists of, one also knows that the religions cannot compromise themselves and they are independent of human doings. . . . The fact that a man may exploit a religion in order to bolster up national or private interests in no wise affects religion as such. . . . As for an exhausting of the religions, one might speak of this if all men had by now become saints or Buddhas. In that case only could it be admitted that the religions were exhausted, at least as regards their forms.[38]

It is we who are compromised by our failure to conform to the timeless truths which tradition preserves.

The Exoteric and Esoteric Dimensions of Religion

Generally we are accustomed to drawing sharp dividing lines between the religious traditions. Schuon has no wish to blur the distinctions; his vigorous defense of the principle of orthodoxy precludes any misunderstanding on this point. However, this notwithstanding, Schuon draws another kind of dividing line which in some senses is more fundamental—that between the

---

[37] *Language of the Self,* "Orthodoxy and Intellectuality", 1. See also S.H. Nasr, *Knowledge and the Sacred,* 78-80.

[38] Frithjof Schuon, "No Activity Without Truth", 29. See also *Stations of Wisdom,* "Preface", 11.

exoteric and esoteric. A diagrammatic representation of the idea may be helpful.[39]

TRUTH

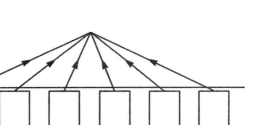

Esoteric Domain

Exoteric Domain:
the Formal
Traditions

The Revelations

ORIGIN

There is no question here of the lines being blurred. They issue from a single point of Origin and converge on their "destination", on the far side of the exoteric-esoteric divide. The apex of this diagram can be thought of as Truth, Reality, the Absolute. The point of Origin and the point of "arrival", or better, fulfillment, are in fact one and the same. Below the dividing-line, in the exoteric domain, we see the separate, distinct religious traditions, each cleaving to an ensemble of formal elements deriving from a Revelation. In the esoteric domain, above the line, the different traditions converge on the Truth through a variety of means—esoteric doctrines, initiations, spiritual disciplines, intellection, the plenary experience. The necessity and the formal integrity of the different traditions is in no way compromised under this view, which fully respects the formal differences between the religions on the plane where such distinctions, even antagonisms, find their proper place. It is only through the exoteric realm that the esoteric can be reached: the universality of every great spiritual patrimony rests on "formal elements of divine institution".[40]

[39] This is an elaborated version of a diagram offered by Huston Smith in his Introduction to *Transcendent Unity of Religions*, xii.
[40] *Light on the Ancient Worlds*, "*Religio Perennis*", 120.

The diagram above can be complemented by another, drawing on the symbolism of the circle.

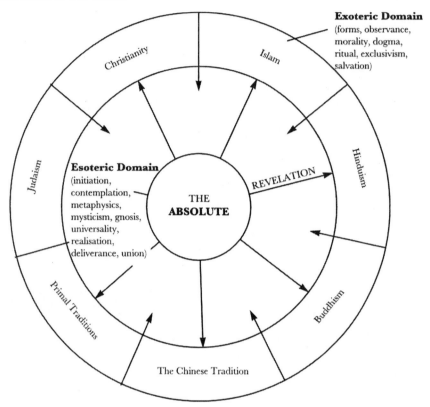

A couple of points should not go unnoticed. The exoteric domain does not derive from the esoteric but from a Revelation. This in itself is sufficient to throw out of court any suggestion that exoteric forms can be dispensed with. *Within* the circumference of the formal exoterisms are to be found convergent esoterisms. At a time when it is sometimes suggested that the esoteric dimension can exist *in vacuo* or that it can be detached from the formal tradition in question, this is a point which needs some stressing.[41]

In discriminating between the exoteric and the esoteric we are, in a sense, speaking of "form" and "spirit". Exoterism rests on a necessary formalism:

Exoterism never goes beyond the "letter"; it puts its accent on the Law—not on a realization of one kind or another—hence also on action

---

[41] This kind of assumption is evident in the pretensions of people who claim to be "Sufis" without being Muslims. See S.H. Nasr, *Sufi Essays*, 169n, and S.H. Nasr, *Knowledge and the Sacred*, 77.

and merit. It is essentially a "belief" in a "letter"—a dogma considered in its formal exclusiveness—and an obedience to a ritual and moral Law. Moreover, exoterism never goes beyond the individual; it is centered on heaven rather than on God, which amounts to saying that this difference has no meaning for it; the Absolute is conceived only with respect to the relative.[42]

Huston Smith has offered a useful gloss on Schuon's exoteric-esoteric distinction in these terms:

> For the exoteric God's personal mode is his only mode; for the esoteric this mode resides in one that is higher and ultimately modeless.... For the exoteric the world is real in every sense; for the esoteric it has only a qualified reality.... For the exoteric God is primarily loved; for the esoteric He is primarily known; though in the end the exoteric comes to know what he loves and the esoteric to love what he knows.[43]

It follows that exoterism must thereby embody certain inevitable and in a sense therapeutic limits or "errors" which from a fuller perspective can be seen in both their positive and negative aspects. Religion, in its formal aspect, is made up of what the Buddhists call *upaya*, "skillful means" which answer the necessities of the case, what Schuon calls "saving mirages" and "celestial stratagems".[44] The limiting definitions of exoteric formalism are "comparable to descriptions of an object of which only the form and not the colors can be seen".[45] Partial truths which might be inadequate in a sapiential perspective may be altogether proper on the formal exoteric plane:

> The formal homogeneity of a religion requires not only truth but also errors—though these are only in form—just as the world requires evil and as Divinity implies the mystery of creation by virtue of its infinity.

> Absolute truth exists only in depth, not on the surface.

> Religions are "mythologies", which as such are based on real aspects of the Divine and on sacred facts—hence on realities but on aspects alone; this limitation is at once inevitable and completely effective.[46]

In other words the forms of exoterism represent certain accommodations which are necessary to bring various truths within the purview of

---

[42] *Spiritual Perspectives and Human Facts*, "Contours of the Spirit", 78.
[43] H. Smith, Introduction to *Transcendent Unity of Religions*, xxvii. See also *Understanding Islam*, "The Path", 132.
[44] *Survey of Metaphysics and Esoterism*, "The Irrefutable Religion", 185n.
[45] *Understanding Islam*, "The Koran", 85.
[46] *Spiritual Perspectives and Human Facts*, "Contours of the Spirit", 72.

the exoteric mentality: "In religious exoterisms, efficacy at times takes the place of truth, and rightly so, given the nature of the men to whom they are addressed."[47] As such they are adequate to the collective needs in question. An example: in discussing the exoteric Christian dogmas about heaven and hell, Schuon has this to say:

> We are made for the Absolute, which embraces all things and from which none can escape, and this is marvelously expressed by the monotheistic alternative between the two "eternities" beyond the grave. . . . The alternative may be insufficient from the point of view of total Truth, but it is psychologically realistic and mystically efficacious; many lives are squandered and lost for the single reason that a belief in hell and Paradise is lacking.[48]

The statements of a formal exoterism can be seen as partial truths, as intimations of Truth, as metaphors and symbols, as bridges to the formless Reality.[49] Herein lies the point of Schuon's repeated affirmations of orthodoxy, such as this: "Orthodoxy includes and guarantees infinitely precious values which man could not possibly draw from himself."[50]

Just as there exists within each tradition an exoteric and an esoteric dimension so too there exist corresponding spiritual dispositions. It is in the nature of things that only a small minority will be blessed with the metaphysical intelligence necessary to penetrate the formal aspects of religion. For the normal believer the exoteric domain is the only domain. Remember, too, that

> the unity of the different religions is not only unrealizable on the external level, that of the forms themselves, but ought not to be realized at that level, even were this possible, for in that case the revealed forms would be deprived of their sufficient reason.[51]

If "exoterism consists in identifying transcendent realities with dogmatic forms" then esoterism is concerned "in a more or less direct manner with these same realities".[52] Esoterism seeks the apprehension of Reality as such, not Reality as understood in such and such a perspective and "under the veil of different religious formulations".[53] While exoterism sees "essence" or "universal truth" as a function of particular forms, esoterism sees the forms

[47] *Transfiguration of Man*, "Thought: Light and Perversion", 8.
[48] *Light on the Ancient Worlds*, "Light on the Ancient Worlds", 16.
[49] See *Understanding Islam*, "The Path", 132.
[50] *Spiritual Perspectives and Human Facts*, "Vedanta", 113.
[51] *Transcendent Unity of Religions*, "Preface", xxxiv.
[52] *Logic and Transcendence*, "Oriental Dialectic and Its Roots in Faith", 144. See also *Esoterism as Principle and as Way*, "Understanding Esoterism", 37.
[53] *Esoterism as Principle and as Way*, "Understanding Esoterism", 19.

as a function of "essence".[54] To put it another way, exoterism particularizes the universal, while esoterism universalizes the particular:

> What characterizes esoterism to the very extent that it is absolute, is that on contact with a dogmatic system, it universalizes the symbol or religious concept on the one hand, and interiorizes it on the other; the particular or the limited is recognized as the manifestation of the principial and the transcendent, and this in its turn reveals itself as immanent.[55]

Esoterism is "situated" on the plane of metaphysical intellection and mystical realization. Moreover, "the word 'esoterism'—according to its etymology—signifies gnosis inasmuch as it *de facto* underlies the religious, and thus dogmatic doctrines".[56] In other words, the science of metaphysical principles is also called esoterism when situated within the cadre of an integral religious tradition. Furthermore, the word designates "*a priori* doctrines and methods that are more or less secret because they are regarded as transcending the limited capacities of average men".[57] If gnosis as such is under consideration then the question of orthodoxy cannot arise, this being a principle which is only operative on the formal plane:

> If the purest esoterism comprises the whole truth—and that is the reason for its existence—the question of orthodoxy in the religious sense clearly cannot arise: direct knowledge of the mysteries could not be Muslim or Christian just as the sight of a mountain is the sight of a mountain and not something else.[58]

Nevertheless, the exoteric and esoteric realms are continually meeting and interpenetrating, not only because there is such a thing as a "relative esoterism" but because "the underlying truth is one, and also because man is one".[59] Furthermore, even if esoterism transcends forms, it has need of doctrinal, ritual, moral, and aesthetic supports on the path to realization.[60] And yet, from another point of view we should remember that although "The presence of an esoteric nucleus in a civilization that is specifically exoteric in character guarantees to it a normal development and a maximum of stability", it is also the case that "this nucleus . . . is not in any sense a part,

---

[54] *Esoterism as Principle and as Way*, "Understanding Esoterism", 37.

[55] *Esoterism as Principle and as Way*, "Understanding Esoterism", 37.

[56] *Esoterism as Principle and as Way*, "Understanding Esoterism", 18.

[57] *Esoterism as Principle and as Way*, "Understanding Esoterism", 7.

58 *Understanding Islam*, "The Path", 167-168. See also *Sufism: Veil and Quintessence*, "Human Premises of a Religious Dilemma", 87-88.

[59] *Esoterism as Principle and as Way*, "Understanding Esoterism", 16.

[60] *Esoterism as Principle and as Way*, "Understanding Esoterism", 29.

even an inner part, of the exoterism, but represents, on the contrary, a quasi-independent 'dimension' in relation to the latter."[61]

What of the attitude, so to speak, of the exoteric to the esoteric? Given the factors already mentioned it is not surprising that the exoteric elements in a religious tradition should be preserved and protected by authorities whose attitude to esoterism will be, at best, somewhat ambivalent, sometimes openly hostile. In addressing itself to the defense of the *credo* and of the forms which appear as guarantors of truth, the exoteric resistance to esoterism is entirely commendable. The esoteric can see and respect this guardianship of the "incalculable values" of orthodoxy. On the other hand, in Huston Smith's words:

> The exoteric's assessment of the esoteric is likely to be less charitable, not because exoterics are less endowed with that virtue, but because a portion of the esoteric position being obscured from him, he cannot honor it without betraying the truth he does see.[62]

It is in this context that we should understand Coomaraswamy's remark, frequently made in his correspondence with "exoterics": "even if you are not on our side, we are on yours."[63]

Sometimes the exoteric defendants of orthodoxy overstep themselves and in doing so beget results that are both destructive and counter-productive, especially when a religious tradition is endangered by a preponderantly exoteric outlook:

> The exoteric viewpoint is, in fact, doomed to end by negating itself once it is no longer vivified by the presence within it of the esoterism of which it is both the outward radiation and the veil. So it is that religion, according to the measure in which it denies metaphysical and initiatory realities and becomes crystallized in literalistic dogmatism, inevitably engenders unbelief; the atrophy that overtakes dogmas when they are deprived of their internal dimension recoils upon them from outside, in the form of heretical and atheistic negations.[64]

---

[61] *Transcendent Unity of Religions*, "The Limitations of Exoterism", 9-10. On this subject, Guénon wrote: "True esoterism is something quite different from the outward religion, and if it has some connections with it, this is only to the extent that it finds in the religious forms a mode of symbolic expression; moreover it matters little whether these forms are those of this religion or that since what is in question is the essential unity of the doctrine lying hidden behind their apparent diversity" (Guénon, quoted in *Spiritual Perspectives and Human Facts*, "Appendix: Selections from Letters and Other Previously Unpublished Writings", 237).

[62] H. Smith, Introduction to *Transcendent Unity of Religions*, xvi.

[63] For one of many instances where Coomaraswamy uses this phrase see letter to Joachim Wach, August 1947, *Selected Letters*, 113.

[64] *Transcendent Unity of Religions*, "The Limitations of Exoterism", 9.

How much of post-medieval Christian history bears witness to this truth![65] As to the theological ostracisms that have befallen some of the mystics and metaphysicians seeking to preserve the esoteric dimension within their respective religious traditions, Schuon reminds us of Aesop's fable about the fox and the grapes, a story which is "repeated in all sectors of human existence".[66] On the other hand, some comfort can be derived from the fact that, "When the religious phenomenon, hard-pressed as it were by a badly interpreted experience, appears to be at the end of its resources, esoterism springs forth from the very depths of this phenomenon to show that Heaven cannot contradict itself".[67]

Formal Diversity, Transcendent Unity

In the face of religious diversity Schuon poses the question that has vexed many minds: "Seeing that there is only one Truth, must we not conclude that there is only one Revelation, one sole Tradition possible?"[68] Indeed, one frequently comes across formulations such as the following: "It is sometimes asserted that all religions are equally true. But this would seem to be simply sloppy thinking, since the various religions hold views of reality which are sharply different if not contradictory."[69] This kind of either/or thinking, characteristic of much that nowadays passes for philosophy, is in the same vein as a dogmatism which

> reveals itself not only by its inability to conceive the inward or implicit illimitability of a symbol, but also by its inability to recognize, when faced with two apparently contradictory truths, the inward connection that they implicitly affirm, a connection that makes of them complementary aspects of one and the same truth.[70]

It is precisely this kind of incapacity which must be overcome if the transcendent unity of the religions is to be understood.

---

[65] A spiritually alert minority has recently given much thought to the implications of this principle. The intuition and affirmation of its lessons was perhaps the most important aspect of the work of the late Thomas Merton. Merton's work has too often been seen as an enterprise in dialogue, which indeed it was, without any thought as to what end this was to be directed. The end Merton had in view was, of course, precisely the revivification of the contemplative and esoteric dimension within the Catholic tradition.

[66] *Form and Substance in the Religions*, "The Human Margin", 214.

[67] *From the Divine to the Human*, "To Refuse or to Accept Revelation", 138.

[68] *Gnosis: Divine Wisdom*, "Diversity of Revelation", 17.

[69] O. Thomas, "Introduction" to *Attitudes to Other Religions* (1969), quoted by Huston Smith, Introduction to *Transcendent Unity of Religions*, xiiin.

[70] *Transcendent Unity of Religions*, "Conceptual Dimensions", 3.

> A religion is not limited by what it includes, but by what it excludes; doubtless, this exclusion does not harm the most profound content of religion—for each religion is inherently a totality—but it will take revenge all the more surely on this intermediary level . . . the arena of theological speculations and of moral and mystical ardors. . . . Outward contradictions can conceal an intrinsic compatibility or identity, which in fact amounts to saying that each of the contradictory theses contains a truth and, thereby an aspect of total truth and a means of access to it.[71]

Examples of "contradictory" truths which effectively express complementary aspects of a single reality can be found not only across the traditions but within them. One might instance, by way of illustration, the Biblical or Koranic affirmations regarding predestination and free will.[72]

From an esoteric viewpoint the exclusivist claims of one or another religion have no absolute validity. It is true that the "arguments of every intrinsically orthodox religion are absolutely convincing if one puts oneself in the intended setting".[73] It is also true that orthodox theological dogmatisms are entitled to a kind of "defensive reflex" which makes for exclusivism. However—and this is crucial—

> *The exoteric claim to the exclusive possession of a unique truth, or of Truth without epithet, is . . . an error purely and simply;* in reality, every expressed truth necessarily assumes a form, that of its expression, and it is metaphysically impossible that any form should possess a unique value to the exclusion of other forms; for a form, by definition, cannot be unique and exclusive, that is to say it cannot be the only possible expression of what it expresses.[74]

The argument that the different religions cannot all be repositories of the truth because of their formal differences and antagonisms rests on a failure to understand this principle. The lesson to be drawn from the multiplicity of religious forms is quite different:

> The diversity of religions, far from proving the falseness of all the doctrines concerning the supernatural, shows on the contrary the supraformal character of revelation and the formal character of ordinary human understanding: the essence of revelation—or enlightenment—is one, but human nature requires diversity.[75]

---

[71] *Form and Substance in the Religions*, "The Human Margin", 213.

[72] *Transcendent Unity of Religions*, "Conceptual Dimensions", 4.

[73] *Spiritual Perspectives and Human Facts*, "Thought and Civilization", 9.

[74] *Transcendent Unity of Religions*, "The Limitations of Exoterism", 18 (italics mine).

[75] Frithjof Schuon, "No Activity Without Truth", 4. See also M. Pallis, *A Buddhist Spectrum*, 157.

In connection with this need for diversity, which is explained by the fact that humanity is divided into different branches, we might recall Junayd's maxim that "the color of the water is the color of the vessel containing it".[76] Or, if a more abstract formulation be preferred, this from Aquinas: "the thing known is in the knower according to the mode of the knower".[77]

Schuon has deployed many images to clarify the relationship of the religions to each other. He likens them to geometric forms. Just as it would be absurd to imagine that spatial extensions and relationships could only be expressed by one form, so it is absurd to assert that there could be only one doctrine giving an account of the Absolute. However, just as each geometric form has some necessary and sufficient reason for its existence, so too with the religions.

To affirm that the Truth informing all religious traditions is one and that they essentially all vehicle the same message in different forms is not to preclude qualitative discriminations concerning particular aspects of this and that tradition. Schuon extends the geometric analogy: the differentiated geometric figures are

> irreplaceable—otherwise they would not exist—and they are in no sense various kinds of imperfect circles; the cross is infinitely nearer the perfection of the point or the circle than is the oval or the trapezoid, for example. Analogous considerations apply to traditional doctrines as regards their differences of form and their merits as an equation.[78]

The inter-relationships of the religions is an issue today which has taken on a new urgency in the cyclical conditions in which we live. In former times, just as man appeared as "man" and not as "yellow man" or "black man", and just as each language seemed to its practitioners to be language as such, so too each religion, for most believers, appeared as "religion" without further qualification. (To choose one example from a multitude of possibilities, the Tibetans referred to their beliefs and practices not as "Mahayana Buddhism" or as "the Vajrayana" but simply as *tehen*—"the way".[79]) At the present juncture in history the perennialist outlook provides the only satisfactory resolution of the formal diversity (with the inevitable antagonisms which it entails) and the inner unity of the different traditions. More than ever we must share the perception of Tierno Bokar, the twentieth century black Muslim saint from Mali, that

---

[76] Quoted in A.K. Coomaraswamy, "Sri Ramakrishna and Religious Tolerance" in *Selected Papers 2*, 37.

[77] A.K. Coomaraswamy, "Sri Ramakrishna and Religious Tolerance" in *Selected Papers 2*, 36.

[78] *Light on the Ancient Worlds*, "Religio Perennis", 122.

[79] A. Desjardins, *The Message of the Tibetans*, 20.

The rainbow owes its beauty to the variety of its shades and colors. In the same way, we consider the voices of various believers that rise up from all parts of the earth as a symphony of praises addressing God, Who alone can be Unique.[80]

The Limits of Religious Expansionism

By way of a footnote to our discussion of the four themes heralded at the beginning of this chapter, two other points deserve brief mention, concerning Schuon's views with respect to the limits of religious expansion and the inclusive nature of the great traditions. A corollary to the principle of multiple Revelations is the fact that there are certain providential limits to the possible expansion of each tradition, confirmed by the relative inefficiency of religious expansionism beyond its appointed boundaries: "if God were on the side of one religious form only, the persuasive power of this form would be such that no man of good faith would be able to resist it."[81]

Another thread in the same web is the idea that all the great religious traditions will include under their canopy spiritual perspectives and methods appropriate to a spectrum of different temperaments and dispositions. Beyond the characteristics and prevalent spiritual climate of any one tradition each

> particular spiritual perspective is usually discoverable somewhere within the framework of a tradition that [apparently] excludes it; thus "theism" reappears in a certain sense, notably in the form of Amidism, within the framework of Buddhism despite its characteristic non-theism.[82]

To attempt, as historians often do, to explain away the cult of the Buddha Amitabha in the Pure Land Schools as a "deviation" resulting from Nestorian influences is to fail to understand that analogous phenomena are bound to appear where circumstances are favorable and that "the fundamental pos-

---

[80] Amadou Hampaté Bâ, *A Spirit of Tolerance: The Inspiring Life of Tierno Bokar*, 126. Recall, too, the wise words of the great German theologian, Rudolf Otto: "We in the West now realize that we have no monopoly of religious truth. We must in honesty change our attitude towards other faiths, for our watchword must be 'Loyalty to truth'. This changed attitude, however, does not weaken, but rather, instead, reinforces one's faith in God, for He is seen to be not a small or partial being but the Great God who is working throughout all times and places and faiths" (Otto, quoted in P. Almond, "Rudolf Otto and Buddhism", 69).
[81] *Transcendent Unity of Religions*, "The Limitations of Exoterism", 15. See *Transcendent Unity of Religions*, "Limits of Religious Expansion", 79-94 and also *Form and Substance in the Religions*, "Form and Substance in the Religions", 14.
[82] *Treasures of Buddhism*, "Originality of Buddhism", 18-19.

sibilities of man cannot but emerge in some fashion in a framework as vast as a great Revelation".[83]

* * *

We will bring this chapter to its close with some remarks from Marco Pallis about Schuon's *The Transcendent Unity of Religions*:

> It marshals all the basic information needed in order that this pressing problem of religions and their relations to one another may be properly stated—wherever this is done one is already halfway to a solution. From the very outset, the author lays himself out to deal with the fundamental problem of letter and spirit, or otherwise expressed, of exoterism and esoterism. . . . He points the way to an effective answer by showing that here is not a case of choice between two alternatives situated on the same plane but rather of recognizing that they refer to things belonging to different orders (thus implying a hierarchical, not a symmetrical relationship between them). . . . It is this knowledge in fact which confers mastery over forms and constitutes the primary qualification required of one who would build a bridge, for his own sake and for the sake of others, between religion and religion, even while the stream of formal distinction continues to flow in between.[84]

---

[83] *Treasures of Buddhism*, "Treasures of Buddhism", 10.
[84] M. Pallis, *The Way and the Mountain*, 75.

6

Metaphysics: Science of the Real

The source of our knowledge of God is at one and the same time the Intellect and Revelation. In principle the Intellect knows everything, because all possible knowledge is inscribed in its very substance, and it promises absolute certainty because its knowledge is a "being", or a participation in being, and not merely a "seeing".[1]

The Infinite is what it is; a man may understand it or not. Metaphysics cannot be taught to everyone but if it could be there would be no atheists.[2]

[Metaphysical] doctrine is to the Truth what the circle or spiral is to the center.[3]

There can be no effective metaphysics without heaven's help.[4]

"When a man talks to you in a way that you don't understand about a thing he does not understand, them's metaphysics". The clown's definition of "metaphysics" in Voltaire's *Philosophical Dictionary* may well hold good for modern academic philosophers, as may Bradley's dictum that "Metaphysics is the finding of bad reasons for what we believe upon instinct."[5] "Metaphysics" is one of those words, like "dogma" or "mystical", which has been so sullied that it is now a somewhat treacherous term. In this chapter, within a Schuonian framework, we consider three questions: What is metaphysics? What is its relationship, in terms of procedures, criteria, and ends, to philosophy? And to theology?

Without a clear definition of terms certain misunderstandings will be more or less inevitable. The following words must be understood precisely: tradition, Revelation, Intellect, gnosis, metaphysics, and mystical. The first three terms have been discussed in the two preceding chapters, so let us turn to Schuon's "definitions" of the others.

[1] *Logic and Transcendence*, "Concerning the Proofs of God", 71.
[2] *Spiritual Perspectives and Human Facts*, "Contours of the Spirit", 51.
[3] *Understanding Islam*, "The Path", 183.
[4] *Form and Substance in the Religions*, "The Five Divine Presences", 52.
[5] F.H. Bradley, *Appearance and Reality* quoted in S. Radhakrishnan, "Reply to My Critics" in A. Schilpp (ed.), *The Philosophy of Sarvepalli Radhakrishnan*, 791.

Gnosis: "The word gnosis . . . refers to supra-rational and thus purely intellective, knowledge of metacosmic realities."[6] It must not be confused with the historical phenomenon of gnosticism, the Graeco-Oriental syncretism of latter classical times.[7] Its Sanskrit equivalent is *jnana*, knowledge in its fullest sense, what Eckhart calls "divine knowledge".

Metaphysic: "the science of the Absolute and of the true nature of things".[8] Similarly "metaphysical": "concerning universal realities considered objectively".[9] Furthermore,

> Metaphysics has as it were two great dimensions, the one "ascending" and dealing with universal principles and the distinction between the Real and the illusory, and the other "descending" and dealing on the contrary with the divine life in creaturely situations, and thus with the fundamental and secret "divinity" of beings and of things, for "all is *Atma*."[10]

Mystical: "concerning the same realities considered subjectively, that is, in relation to the contemplative soul, insofar as they enter operatively into contact with it";[11] or, concerning "all inward contact (other than the purely mental), with realities that are directly or indirectly Divine".[12]

Metaphysics

As Guénon observed more than once, metaphysics cannot properly be defined, for to define is to limit, while the domain of metaphysics is the Real and thus limitless. Consequently, metaphysics "is truly and absolutely unlimited and cannot be confined to any formula or any system".[13] Its end,

---

[6] *Understanding Islam*, "The Path", 138.
[7] See *To Have a Center*, "Gnosis Is Not Just Anything", 67-68, and *Roots of the Human Condition*, "On Intelligence", 10-11.
[8] *Logic and Transcendence*, "Rationalism, Real and Apparent", 34. Similarly, from Nasr: "Metaphysics, which in fact is one and should be named metaphysic . . . is the science of the Real, of the origin and end of things, of the Absolute and in its light, the relative" (S.H. Nasr, *Man and Nature*, 81).
[9] *Logic and Transcendence*, "Understanding and Believing", 204n.
[10] *Understanding Islam*, "The Path", 182. (The descending "dimension" is cosmology.)
[11] *Logic and Transcendence*, "Understanding and Believing", 204n. Schuon is, of course, not unaware of the linguistic and connotative ambiguities surrounding this term. See *Spiritual Perspectives and Human Facts*, "Contours of the Spirit", 90n. See also S.H. Nasr, *Sufi Essays*, 26n.
[12] *Logic and Transcendence*, "Introduction", 2. Schuon goes on to add: "it is only right that they [the terms 'mystical' and 'mysticism'] should suggest above all a spirituality of love because they are European terms and Europe is Christian."
[13] R. Guénon, "Oriental Metaphysics", 43-44.

in the words of John Tauler, is "that pure knowledge that knows no form or creaturely way".[14] Moreover, as Schuon states:

> Metaphysical Truth is both expressible and inexpressible: inexpressible, it is not however unknowable, for the Intellect opens onto the Divine Order and therefore encompasses all that is; and expressible, it becomes crystallized in formulations which are all they ought to be since they communicate all that is necessary or useful to our mind. Forms are doors to the essences, in thought and in language as well as in all other symbolisms.[15]

These considerations must always be kept in mind in any attempt at a "definition", necessarily provisional and incomplete. Following Schuon, Nasr defines metaphysics this way:

> It is a science as strict and as exact as mathematics and with the same clarity and certitude, but one which can only be attained through intellectual intuition and not simply through ratiocination. It thus differs from philosophy as it is usually understood. Rather, it is a *theoria* of reality whose realization means sanctity and spiritual perfection, and therefore can only be achieved within the cadre of a revealed tradition. Metaphysical intuition can occur everywhere—for the "spirit bloweth where it listeth"—but the effective realization of metaphysical truth and its application to human life can only be achieved within a revealed tradition which gives efficacy to certain symbols and rites upon which metaphysics must rely for its realization.
>   This supreme science of the Real . . . is the only science that can distinguish between the Absolute and the relative, appearance and reality. . . . Moreover, this science exists, as the esoteric dimension within every orthodox and integral tradition and is united with a spiritual method derived totally from the tradition in question.[16]

This accords with the traditional but not with the modern conception of philosophy—of *philo-sophia*, "love of wisdom", as a practical concern. In India, for example, philosophy was never only a matter of epistemology but an all-embracing science of first principles and of the true nature of Reality,

---

[14] Quoted in C.F. Kelley, *Meister Eckhart on Divine Knowledge*, 4.

[15] *Survey of Metaphysics and Esoterism*, "Introduction: Epistemological Premises", 11. Approaching the same issue from a slightly different angle Schuon writes this: "In the sight of the Absolute, envisaged as pure Self and unthinkable Aseity, metaphysical doctrine is assuredly tinged with relativity, but it nonetheless offers absolutely sure reference points and 'adequate approximations' such as the human spirit could not do without; and this is what the simplifiers in pursuit of the 'concrete' are incapable of understanding. Doctrine is to the Truth what the circle or the spiral is to the center" (*Understanding Islam*, "The Path", 183).

[16] S.H. Nasr, *Man and Nature*, 81-82. See also Coomaraswamy's undated letter to "M", *Selected Letters*, 10: "traditional Metaphysics is as much a single and invariable science as mathematics."

and one wedded to the spiritual disciplines provided by religion. The ultimate reality of metaphysics is the Supreme Identity in which all oppositions and dualities are resolved, those of subject and object, knower and known, being and non-being; thus a Scriptural formulation such as "The things of God knoweth no man, but the Spirit of God".[17]

The nature of metaphysics is more easily grasped through a contrast with philosophy (in the modern sense) and theology. Before that, some preliminary points. Because the metaphysical realm lies "beyond" the phenomenal plane the validity of a metaphysical principle can be neither proved nor disproved by any kind of empirical demonstration, by reference to material or historical realities.[18] The aim of metaphysics is not to *prove* anything whatsoever but to make doctrines intelligible and to demonstrate their consistency, and also to provide symbols for spiritual assimilation and realization.

Secondly, metaphysics is concerned with a direct apprehension of reality which entails a recognition of the Absolute, of God, and our relationship therewith. It thus takes on an imperative character for those capable of metaphysical discernment.

> The requirement of recognizing the Absolute is itself absolute, it concerns man as such and not man under a given condition; it is even a fundamental aspect of human dignity—and above all of that intelligence that makes up man—that we accept Truth because it is true and for no other reason.[19]

Moreover, because metaphysics is attuned to the Divine it demands something of those who would unlock its mysteries: "man is so made that his intelligence has no effective value unless it is combined with a virtuous character."[20] Metaphysicians seek not only to expound immutable principles and doctrines but to live by them, to conform their being to the truths they convey: in other words, the pursuit of metaphysics engages the whole person or it is as nothing.[21] As Schuon insists:

> The moral exigency of metaphysical discernment means that virtue is part of wisdom; a wisdom without virtue is in fact imposture and hypocrisy. . . . Plenary knowledge of Divine Reality presupposes or demands moral conformity to this Reality, as the eye necessarily con-

---

[17] I Corinthians 2:11. The Absolute may be called God, the Godhead, *nirguna Brahman*, the Tao, *nirvana* and so on, according to the vocabulary at hand. See *Light on the Ancient Worlds* (1965), 96n-97n on the use of "God".

[18] See R. Guénon, "Oriental Metaphysics", 53.

[19] *Treasures of Buddhism*, "Christianity and Buddhism", 103.

[20] *To Have a Center*, "Survey of Integral Anthropology", 40.

[21] See A. Coomaraswamy, "Vedanta and Western Tradition", 9.

forms to light; since the object to be known is the sovereign Good, the knowing subject must correspond to it analogically.[22]

Thirdly, metaphysics assumes man's capacity for absolute and certain knowledge:

> The capacity for objectivity and for absoluteness is an anticipated and existential refutation of all the ideologies of doubt: if man is able to doubt this is because certitude exists; likewise the very notion of illusion proves that man has access to reality. . . . If doubt conformed to the real, human intelligence would be deprived of its sufficient reason and man would be less than an animal, since the intelligence of animals does not experience doubt concerning the reality to which it is proportioned.[23]

Metaphysics, therefore, is immutable and inexorable, and the "infallible standard by which not only religions, but still more 'philosophies' and 'sciences' must be 'corrected' . . . and interpreted".[24] Metaphysics can be ignored or forgotten but not refuted "precisely because it is immutable and not related to change *qua* change".[25] Metaphysical principles are true and valid once and for all and not only for this particular age or mentality, and could not, in any sense, "evolve". They can be validated directly in the plenary and unitive experience of the mystic. Thus Martin Lings can write of Sufism—and one could say the same of any intrinsically traditional esoterism—that it

> has the right to be inexorable because it is based on certainties and not on opinions. It has the obligation to be inexorable because mysticism is the sole repository of Truth, in the fullest sense, being above all concerned with the Absolute, the Infinite, and the Eternal; and "If the salt have lost its savor, wherewith shall it be salted?" Without mysticism, Reality would have no voice in the world. There would be no record of the true hierarchy, and no witness that it is continually being violated.[26]

One might easily substitute the word "metaphysics" for "mysticism" in this passage, the former being the formal and objective aspect of the "subjective" experience. However, this is not to lose sight of the fact that any and every metaphysical doctrine will take it as axiomatic that every for-

---

[22] *Roots of the Human Condition*, "Pillars of Wisdom", 86.

[23] *Logic and Transcendence*, "The Contradiction of Relativism", 13. See also *Esoterism as Principle and as Way*, "Understanding Esoterism", 15ff.

[24] Coomaraswamy, letter to J.H. Muirhead, August 1935, in *Selected Letters*, 37.

[25] S. H. Nasr, *Sufi Essays*, 86. See also *Stations of Wisdom*, "Orthodoxy and Intellectuality", 42.

[26] M. Lings, *What is Sufism?*, 93.

mulation is "but error in the face of the Divine Reality itself; a provisional, indispensable, salutary 'error' which, however, contains and communicates the virtuality of the Truth".[27]

Metaphysics and Philosophy

In a discussion of Shankara's Advaita Vedanta, Coomaraswamy exposed some of the crucial differences between metaphysics and modern philosophy:

> The Vedanta is not a "philosophy" in the current sense of the word, but only as the word is used in the phrase *Philosophia Perennis*. . . . Modern philosophies are closed systems, employing the method of dialectics, and taking for granted that opposites are mutually exclusive. In modern philosophy things are either so or not so; in eternal philosophy this depends upon our point of view. Metaphysics is not a system, but a consistent doctrine; it is not merely concerned with conditioned and quantitative experience but with universal possibility.[28]

Modern European philosophy is dialectical, which is to say analytical and rational in its modes. From a traditional point of view it might be said that modern philosophy is anchored in a misunderstanding of the nature and role of reason; indeed, the idolatry of reason could hardly have otherwise arisen. Schuon spotlights some of the strengths and deficiencies of the rational mode in these terms:

> Reason is formal by its nature and formalistic in its operations; it proceeds by coagulations, by alternatives, and by exclusions—or, it can be said, by partial truths. It is not, like pure intellect, formless and fluid light; true, it derives its implacability, or its validity in general, from the intellect, but it touches on essences only through drawing conclusions, not by direct vision; it is indispensable for verbal formulation but it does not involve immediate knowledge.[29]

Burckhardt likens reason to "a convex lens which steers the intelligence in a particular direction and onto a limited field".[30] Like any other instrument it can be abused. Much European philosophy, adrift from its religious moorings, has surrendered to a despotic rationalism, to what Blake termed "Single Vision". In so doing it has violated a principle which was respected

---

[27] *Spiritual Perspectives and Human Facts* (1969), "Love and Knowledge", 162-163. Cf. Coomaraswamy: "every belief is a heresy if it be regarded as the truth, and not simply as a signpost of the truth" ("Sri Ramakrishna and Religious Tolerance" in *Selected Papers 2*, 38). See also *Sufism: Veil and Quintessence*, "Preface", xiii-xv.

[28] A. Coomaraswamy, "Vedanta and Western Tradition", in *Selected Papers 2*, 6.

[29] *Understanding Islam*, "Islam", 15. See also *Stations of Wisdom*, "Orthodoxy and Intellectuality", 18ff.

[30] T. Burckhardt, *Alchemy*, 36n.

wherever a metaphysical tradition and a religious framework for the pursuit of wisdom remained intact—the principle of adequation, articulated thus by Aquinas: "It is a sin against intelligence to want to proceed in an identical manner in typically different domains—physical, mathematical, metaphysical—of speculative knowledge."[31] Likewise Plotinus: "knowing demands the organ fitted to the object".[32] The transgressions and grotesqueries of modern philosophy spring, in large measure, from the violation of this principle. Many philosophers have been duped by the claims of a totalitarian scientism and thus suffer from a drastically impoverished view of reality and of the avenues by which it might be apprehended. The words of the Moravian alchemist, Michael Sendivogius, seem more apposite than ever: "philosophers are men whom too much [profane] learning and thought have made mad".[33] We might also profitably recall Plato's dictum that "The possession of all the sciences, if unaccompanied by the knowledge of the best, will more often than not injure the possessor".[34] This might well serve as an epitaph for modernity as a whole!

The place of reason, of logic and dialectic, in metaphysics is altogether more subordinate—an issue frequently misunderstood, sometimes with quite absurd results. Schuon: "In the intellectual order logical proof is only a quite provisional crystallization of intuition, the modes of which . . . are incalculable".[35] Or again:

> Metaphysics is not held to be true—by those who understand it—because it is expressed in a logical manner, but it can be expressed in a logical manner because it is true, without—obviously—its truth ever being compromised by the possible shortcomings of human reason.[36]

In metaphysics, contemplative intelligence takes precedence over ratiocination. Metaphysical formulations depend more on symbol and on analogy than on logical demonstration, though it is a grave error to suppose that metaphysics has any right to irrationality.[37] What many modern philosophers apparently fail to understand is that thought can become increasingly subtle

---

[31] Aquinas, quoted in S. H. Nasr, *Man and Nature*, 35.

[32] Plotinus, quoted in E.F. Schumacher, *A Guide for the Perplexed*, 49.

[33] Sendivogius, quoted in W. Perry (ed.), *A Treasury of Traditional Wisdom*, 735.

[34] Plato, quoted in W. Perry (ed.), *A Treasury of Traditional Wisdom*, 731.

[35] *Spiritual Perspectives and Human Facts* (1969), "Thought and Civilization", 10.

[36] *Esoterism as Principle and as Way*, "Understanding Esoterism", 28. Similarly, Guénon: "for metaphysics, the use of rational argument never represents more than a mode of external expression and in no way affects metaphysical knowledge itself, for the latter must always be kept essentially distinct from its formulation" (R. Guénon, quoted in *Stations of Wisdom*, "Orthodoxy and Intellectuality", 29n1).

[37] See *Esoterism as Principle and as Way*, "Understanding Esoterism", 28.

and complex without approaching any nearer to the truth. An idea can be subdivided into a thousand ramifications, fenced about with every conceivable qualification, and supported with the most intricate logic but, for all that, remain purely external and quantitative for "no virtuosity of the potter will transform clay into gold".[38] Furthermore,

> That a reasoning might simply be the logical and provisional description of an intellectual evidence, and that its function might be the actualization of this evidence, in itself supralogical, apparently never crosses the minds of pure logicians.[39]

Analytical rationality alone, no matter how useful a tool, will never generate metaphysical understanding. Metaphysicians of all ages have said nothing different. Shankara, for instance: "the pure truth of *Atman* . . . can be reached by meditation, contemplation, and other spiritual disciplines such as a knower of *Brahman* may prescribe—but never by subtle argument."[40] The Promethean arrogance of much modernist thought, often bred by scientistic and humanistic ideologies, is unmasked in its refusal to acknowledge the boundaries beyond which reason has no competence or utility. This has prompted some ludicrous claims about religion. As Schuon remarks:

> The equating of the supernatural with the irrational is characteristic. . . . It amounts to claiming that the unknown or the incomprehensible is the same as the absurd. The rationalism of a frog living at the bottom of a well is to deny the existence of mountains: this is logic of a kind but it has nothing to do with reality.[41]

A point often overlooked: metaphysics does not of necessity find its expression only in verbal forms. Metaphysics can be expressed visually and ritually as well as verbally. The Chinese and Red Indian traditions furnish pre-eminent examples of these possibilities. Moreover, writes Schuon:

> The criterion of metaphysical truth or of its depth lies, not in the complexity or difficulty of its expression, but in the quality and effectiveness of its symbolism, allowing for a particular capacity of understanding or style of thinking. Wisdom does not lie in any complication of words but in the profundity of the intention; assuredly the expression may according to the circumstances be subtle and difficult, but it may just as well not be so.[42]

[38] *Understanding Islam*, "The Path", 181.
[39] *Logic and Transcendence*, "Rationalism, Real and Apparent", 37.
[40] *Shankara's Crest Jewel of Discrimination*, 73.
[41] *Logic and Transcendence*, "Rationalism, Real and Apparent", 37.
[42] *Understanding Islam*, "The Path", 133.

Symbols offer a potent medium for the communication of mysteries which, by definition, elude ratiocination:

> Mystery is the essence of truth which cannot be adequately conveyed through language—the vehicle of discursive thought—but which may suddenly be made plain in an illuminating flash through a symbol, such as a key word, a mystic sound, or an image whose suggestive action may be scarcely graspable.[43]

—think of the Buddha's Flower Sermon, and, indeed, of the whole Zen tradition which it inaugurated.

The intelligibility of a metaphysical doctrine may depend upon a measure of faith in the traditional Christian sense of "assent to a credible proposition". As Coomaraswamy observes:

> One must believe in order to understand and understand in order to believe. These are not successive, however, but simultaneous acts of the mind. In other words, there can be no knowledge of anything to which the will refuses its consent.[44]

Schuon points out that just as Revelation calls for a measure of faith, so too the "certainties" of Intellection:

> It is well known that Revelation demands faith; it is less well known that Intellection also does so in its fashion, and this even seems paradoxical, since the Intellect, by definition, involves certitude. But certainty has degrees from the point of view of assimilation or integration, or indeed of sincerity; *credo ut intelligam*, but also: *intelligo ergo credo*. In the first case, faith consists in accepting truth obtained from the outside, and in accepting it in an instinctive, volitive, and sentimental manner; in the second case, faith consists, not in accepting what is evident, which would be a pleonasm, but in causing it to penetrate our whole being; as in the case of religious faith, this also engages both will and sentiment.[45]

"Faith is like an 'existential' intuition of its 'intellectual' object."[46] This mode of apprehension is something quite other than the philosophical thought that

> believes it can attain to an absolute contact with Reality by means of analyses, syntheses, arrangements, filtrations, and polishings—thought that is mundane by the very fact of this ignorance and because it is a

---

[43] *Treasures of Buddhism*, "Treasures of Buddhism", 11.

[44] A. Coomaraswamy, "Vedanta and Western Tradition" in *Selected Papers 2*, 8. See also S.H. Nasr, *Knowledge and the Sacred*, 6.

[45] *Esoterism as Principle and as Way*, "Introduction", 10.

[46] *Gnosis: Divine Wisdom*, "The Sense of the Absolute in Religions", 15.

vicious circle which not merely provides no escape from illusion, but even reinforces it through the lure of a progressive knowledge which in fact is inexistent.[47]

It is in this context that Schuon speaks of modern philosophy as "the codification of an acquired infirmity".[48] Unlike modern philosophy, metaphysics has nothing to do with personal opinion, or "originality" (at least in the current sense)—quite the contrary. Nor can there be any sense of personal "property" in the realm of metaphysics. As Guénon so forcibly reminds us:

> If an idea is true it belongs equally to all those capable of understanding it; if it is false there is no reason to be proud of having thought it. A true idea cannot be "new", since truth is not a product of the human mind; the truth exists independently of ourselves, and it is for us simply to comprehend it; outside of this knowledge there can be nothing but error.[49]

In a normal civilization, "it is almost inconceivable that a man should lay claim to the possession of an idea".[50]

Metaphysics is directed towards those unchanging realities which lie outside mental perimeters. The most a metaphysician will ever want to do is to reformulate some timeless truth so that it becomes more intelligible in the prevailing climate. A profane system of thought, on the other hand, is never more than a portrait of the person who creates it, an "involuntary memoir", as Nietzsche put it.[51] The metaphysician does not seek to invent or discover or prove a new system of thought but rather to crystallize direct apprehensions of Reality insofar as this is possible within the limited resources of human language, making use not only of logic but of symbol and analogy. Furthermore, the science of metaphysics normally proceeds in the context of a revealed religion, protected by the tradition in question, which

---

[47] *Logic and Transcendence*, "Rationalism, Real and Apparent", 34.

[48] *Transfiguration of Man*, "Thought: Light and Perversion", 4.

[49] R. Guénon, *Crisis of the Modern World*, 53.

[50] R. Guénon, *Crisis of the Modern World*, 52-53. Likewise Coomaraswamy: "There can be no property in ideas. The individual does not make them but *finds them*; let him see to it that he really takes possession of them, and work will be original in the same sense that the recurrent seasons, sunset, and sunrise are ever anew although in name the same" (quoted in N. Krsnamurti, "Ananda Coomaraswamy", 172). On his own role, Coomaraswamy wrote, "I regard the truth . . . as a matter of certainty, not of opinion. I am never expressing an opinion or any personal view, but an orthodox one" (letter to George Sarton, November 1934, *Selected Letters*, 31).

[51] Friedrich Nietzsche in *Beyond Good and Evil*, taken from *A Nietzsche Reader*, Extract 13. See also *Logic and Transcendence*, "Rationalism, Real and Apparent", 34 and *Transfiguration of Man*, "Thought: Light and Perversion", 4.

also supplies the necessary supports for the full realization of metaphysical doctrines.

Because the fundamental distinction between reason and Intellect has been obscured in recent European thought, then similarly, "the basic distinction between metaphysics as a *scienta sacra* or Divine Knowledge and philosophy as a purely human form of mental activity has been blurred or forgotten".[52] In the field of comparative religion this has led to any amount of confusion. As Nasr has noted, to speak of Hindu or Chinese "philosophy" and rationalistic European "philosophy" in the same breath is a contradiction in terms unless the word is used in two quite different senses. A failure to draw the necessary distinctions has

> Made a sham of many studies of comparative philosophy and has helped to reduce to nil the real significance of Oriental metaphysics. . . . To say that this or that statement of Hegel resembles the Upanishads or that Hume presents ideas similar to Nagarjuna's is to fall into the worst form of error, one which prevents any type of profound understanding from being achieved, either for Westerners wanting to understand the East or vice versa.[53]

The scope of the present work precludes a discussion of all Schuon's denunciations of specific philosophical follies, existentialism among them. Here modern "philosophy" does not succumb to totalitarian rationalism but *seems* to offer an escape from its clutches. Given that many seekers feel some attraction to "existentialist" modes of "thought", it is worth recalling a few remarks from Schuon's "Letter on Existentialism":

> Existentialism does not bring us one bit nearer the truth; to the rationalist error, which consists in reasoning about metaphysical or even simply cosmological realities in the absence of the indispensable intellectual data, existentialism adds the inverse error and substitutes, for reasoning good or bad, true or false, an experience which is in fact infra-intellectual, a cul-de-sac. . . . The thing which is absolutely lacking with the existentialists, and which reduces to nothing their theories as well as their moral attitudes, is an objective truth which is metaphysically integral, whether it be an orthodox theology or an authentic metaphysics. All their partial merits thus fall into a void. . . . Truths embedded in errors are fraught indirectly with the venom of their erroneous context. Existentialism has in fact, whether it be Protestant or atheistic, promoted nothing except individualism; never the understanding of metaphysical doctrines, never sanctity![54]

---

[52] S.H. Nasr, "Conditions for a Meaningful Comparative Philosophy", 54.

[53] S.H. Nasr, "Conditions for a Meaningful Comparative Philosophy", 55, 58.

[54] *Essential Frithjof Schuon*, "Letter on Existentialism", 492-495.

But to summarize modern philosophy as a whole: generally it is analytical, rationalistic, and quantitative; it is concerned with relationships and contingencies accessible to rational inquiry, or at least to the workings of the normal mind, these including imagination which is no less a mental process than ratiocination; European philosophers tend to see the development of philosophy as progressive, driven forward by the work of this or that philosopher who creates or discovers new insights, fresh perceptions, a different vocabulary of discourse, and so on; philosophy is usually seen as self-validating, not requiring any justification outside itself. Metaphysics, by contrast, is concerned with supra-mundane, transcendent, and unconditioned realities; it is qualitative, symbolical, and synthetic in its modes and is rooted in immutable principles; it is indifferent to the question of "proofs" and the metaphysician's purpose is not the resolution of some "problem" but the demonstration of something already intellectually evident; it does not evolve or progress; it is a practical pursuit intimately linked with spiritual disciplines, and depends for its realization on the presence of elements which could only be drawn from an integral tradition; its end is gnosis, transformation, and sanctification.

Metaphysics and Theology

The relationship between metaphysics and theology is more subtle, complex, and problematic. Under Schuon's view, a Divine Revelation is always the cradle of any orthodox religion while metaphysical insight derives from intellection. The dichotomy here is more apparent than real, Revelation taking the place of intellection for the human collectivity in question. This is a principle not easily grasped but without it the apparent antagonisms of theology and metaphysics cannot be resolved. Schuon defines the relationship between Revelation and intellection in this way:

> In normal times we learn *a priori* of divine things through Revelation, which provides for us the symbols and the indispensable data, and we have access *a posteriori* to the truth of these things through Intellection, which reveals to us their essence beyond received formulations, but not opposing them. . . . Revelation is an Intellection in the Macrocosm, while Intellection is a Revelation in the microcosm; the *Avatara* is the outward Intellect, and the Intellect is the inward *Avatara*.[55]

It might be said, then, that intellection appears in a more "subjective" mode, but with this qualification:

---

[55] *Esoterism as Principle and as Way*, "Introduction", 10. See also S.H. Nasr, *Knowledge and the Sacred*, 148-149.

It is "subjective" because empirically it is within us. The term "subjective", as applied to the intellect, is as improper as the epithet "human"; in both cases the terms are used simply in order to define the way of approach.[56]

Schuon, ever alert to the pitfalls of a reductionist psychologism, insists that the truth to which intellection gives access is beyond all spatio-temporal determinations. Biblical formulations such as "the Kingdom of Heaven is within you" certainly do not mean that Heaven, God, or Truth are of a psychological order but simply that access to these realities is to be found through the center of our being.[57]

Religion itself, flowing from the Divine, must contain within itself principial or metaphysical knowledge, but this will often be veiled by the forms in question. For instance:

> The message of Christ, like that of the Bible, is not *a priori* a teaching of metaphysical science; it is above all a message of salvation, but one that necessarily contains, in an indirect way and under cover of an appropriate symbolism, metaphysics in its entirety.[58]

The metaphysical accent varies from one tradition to another. Buddhism, for example, is primarily a spiritual therapy but one which of necessity requires metaphysical doctrines, while Hinduism is, in the first place, a metaphysics which implies, under the same necessity, a spiritual therapy.[59] "There is no science of the soul," says Schuon, "without a metaphysical basis to it and without spiritual remedies at its disposal."[60]

The relationship of theology to metaphysics is that of exoterism to esoterism. Exoterism is "unable of being conscious of the relationship which, at one and the same time, justifies it and yet limits it."[61] Theological dogmatism elevates a particular point of view, or aspect of reality under a specific formal guise, to an absolute value with exclusive claims. As we have seen already, what characterizes esoterism, on the other hand, is the discernment of the universal in the particular, of the essence in the form. This distinction

---

[56] *Understanding Islam*, "The Koran", 57n.

[57] *Light on the Ancient Worlds*, "Keys to the Bible", 116-118.

[58] *Logic and Transcendence*, "Evidence and Mystery", 86.

[59] See *Spiritual Perspectives and Human Facts*, "Contours of the Spirit", 54-56. Doubtless there are those who will asseverate that Buddhism is indifferent to metaphysics, pointing to the Buddha's refusal to answer the indeterminate questions. We need only recall Nagarjuna's statement that the Buddha taught two levels of truth and that an understanding of this distinction, not possible without a metaphysical doctrine, is a precondition for a full understanding of the *dharma*.

[60] *Logic and Transcendence*, "The Contradiction of Relativism", 14.

[61] *Treasures of Buddhism*, "Cosmological and Eschatological Viewpoints", 49n.

can be hinged on the terms "belief" and "gnosis" or, similarly, "faith" and "certitude". The difference is

> Comparable to the difference between a description of a mountain and direct vision of it; the second no more puts us on the mountain top than does the first, but it does inform us about the properties of the mountain and the route to follow. Let us not however forget that the blind man who walks without stopping advances more quickly than a normal man who stops at each step.[62]

Elsewhere Schuon refers to the theologies as taking upon themselves the contradiction of being "sentimental metaphysics":

> They are oblivious to the differentiation of things into aspects and points of view, and consequently they operate with arbitrarily rigid elements whose antinomies can be resolved only beyond this artificial rigidity; moreover, they operate with sentimental tendencies, which is described as "thinking piously".[63]

Such remarks should not be construed as an attack on the theological perspective but only as a caution about the limits of dogmatism and exclusivism. As Pallis so neatly puts it:

> What one always needs to remember is that traditional forms, including those bearing the now unpopular name of dogmas, are keys to unlock the gate of Unitive Truth; but they are also (since a key can close, as well as open a gate) possible obstacles to its profoundest knowledge.[64]

Schuon compares the religions to the beads of a rosary, gnosis being the cord on which they are strung. In other words, the religious orthodoxies, or more specifically theologies, are only able to fulfill their function when they remain attached to the principial knowledge which is preserved in the esoteric dimension of each tradition.

*   *   *

The planes on which philosophy, theology, and metaphysics are situated can be identified by comparing their respective approaches to "God". For the philosopher "God" is a "problem" to be resolved and His existence or non-existence a question to be approached rationally, as if human reason could prove no matter what!; the theologian will be less concerned with proofs—the existence and reality of God being a revealed and thus axiomatic datum—than with faith and its moral concomitances; the metaphysician

---

[62] *Understanding Islam*, "The Path", 179.

[63] *Form and Substance in the Religions*, "The Human Margin", 205.

[64] M. Pallis, Foreword to W. Perry (ed.), *A Treasury of Traditional Wisdom*, 10.

is primarily concerned neither with rational argument nor with faith/belief but with an intellectual evidence which brings certitude. To put it another way, one might say that philosophy trades in opinions and arguments, theology focuses on beliefs and moralities, and metaphysics articulates doctrines which are the fruit of intellection. Or, again, one could say that the philosopher is intent on constructing a mental system, the theologian on proclaiming and living by the "will of heaven", and the metaphysician on a transformative gnosis.

We can recapitulate some of the central points made in our discussion of philosophy, theology, and metaphysics through a passage from Schuon's *The Transcendent Unity of Religions*:

> Intellectual or metaphysical knowledge transcends the specifically theological point of view, which is itself incomparably superior to the philosophical point of view, since, like metaphysical knowledge, it emanates from God and not from man; but whereas metaphysics proceeds wholly from intellectual intuition, religion proceeds from Revelation. . . . In the case of intellectual intuition, knowledge is not possessed by the individual insofar as he is an individual, but insofar as in his innermost essence he is not distinct from the Divine Principle. . . . The theological point of view, because it is based in the minds of believers on a Revelation and not on a knowledge that is accessible to each one of them . . . will of necessity confuse the symbol or form with the naked and supraformal Truth while metaphysics . . . will be able to make use of the same symbol or form as a means of expression while at the same time being aware of its relativity. . . . Religion translates metaphysical or universal truths into dogmatic language. . . . What essentially distinguishes the metaphysical from the philosophical proposition is that the former is symbolical and descriptive . . . whereas philosophy . . . is never anything more than what it expresses. When philosophy uses reason to resolve a doubt, this proves precisely that its starting point is a doubt it is striving to overcome, whereas . . . the starting point of a metaphysical formulation is always something intellectually evident or certain, which is communicated to those able to receive it, by symbolical or dialectical means designed to awaken in them the latent knowledge that they bear unconsciously, and it may even be said, eternally within them.[65]

A Note on "Philosophy"
It is perhaps worth making a few remarks about Schuon's use of the term "philosophy". Referring to *The Transcendent Unity of Religions*, Schuon has more recently written:

---

[65] *Transcendent Unity of Religions*, xxviii-xxx.

In our first book ... we adopted the point of view of Ghazzali regarding "philosophy": that is, bearing in mind the great impoverishment of modern philosophies, we simplified the problem, as others have done before us by making "philosophy" synonymous with "rationalism".[66]

We have followed more or less the same procedure here. But, in Schuon's words, the term "philosophy", in itself, "has nothing restrictive about it". Schuon explores the issues raised by both the ancient and modern use of the term in an essay entitled "Tracing the Notion of Philosophy".[67] Secondly, it must also be admitted that the preceding discussion of the relationships of philosophy, theology, and metaphysics has entailed some necessary oversimplifications. From certain points of view the distinctions in question are not as clear-cut as our discussion has suggested. As Schuon himself writes:

In a certain respect the difference between philosophy, theology, and gnosis is total; in another respect it is relative. It is total when one understands by "philosophy" only rationalism, by "theology" only the explanation of religious teachings, and by gnosis only intuitive and intellective, thus supra-rational, knowledge; but the difference is only relative when one understands by "philosophy" the fact of thinking, by "theology" the fact of speaking dogmatically about God and religious things, and by gnosis the fact of presenting pure metaphysics, for then the categories interpenetrate.[68]

Metaphysics and Realization
The hierarchic superiority of gnosis to all other forms of knowledge and of metaphysical doctrine to all other kinds of formulations should not be allowed to obscure the inter-dependent relationship of the esoteric and the exoteric, of the metaphysical domain and the rest of any religious tradition. Three general points need to be made, concerning the ineffectiveness of intellection outside a traditional framework, the distinction between doctrinal understanding and realization, and the relationship between metaphysical discernment and the spiritual life in general.

"There are", writes Schuon,

no metaphysical or cosmological reasons why in exceptional cases direct intellection should not occur in men who have no link at all with

---

[66] *Sufism: Veil and Quintessence*, "Tracing the Notion of Philosophy", 95n10.

[67] *Sufism: Veil and Quintessence*, "Tracing the Notion of Philosophy", 89-100. See also *Transfiguration of Man*, "Thought: Light and Perversion", 3.

[68] *Sufism: Veil and Quintessence*, "Tracing the Notion of Philosophy", 97.

revealed wisdom; but an exception, though it proves the rule, certainly cannot create it.[69]

In more normal cases

> Intellection has need of tradition, of a Revelation fixed in time and adapted to a society, if it is to be awakened in us and not go astray. . . . The importance of orthodoxy, of tradition, of Revelation is that the means of realizing the Absolute must come "objectively" from the Absolute; knowledge cannot spring up "subjectively" except within the framework of an "objective" divine formulation of Knowledge.[70]

Thus, although intellection can occur as "an isolated miracle" anywhere, it will have neither authority nor efficacy outside tradition.[71] (In this context the case of Ramana Maharshi is not without interest, remembering how the sage had to cast his own mystical insight into the moulds of classical Vedanta in order to communicate it.[72])

The distinction between doctrinal understanding, and even intellection itself, on the one hand, and realization, on the other, is crucial. Contemplative intelligence and metaphysical insight alone do not save, "do not prevent titans from falling".[73] There must be a participation of the will in the intelligence; as one scholar glossed Meister Eckhart, "The intellective center is not truly known without involving the volitive circumference."[74] Here the will can be defined as "a prolongation or a complement of the intelligence"[75] while intelligence itself refers to a contemplative receptivity rather than any mental cleverness, an intelligence which, in Nasr's words, "differs as much from mental virtuosity as the soaring flight of an eagle differs from the play of a monkey".[76] Morality and the virtues, love, faith—these must be inte-

---

[69] *Spiritual Perspectives and Human Facts*, "Thought and Civilization", 10. This statement by Schuon should perhaps be balanced by another: "It is altogether erroneous to believe that religion in the ordinary sense of the term—including an esoterizing exoterism—is the indispensable condition and sole guarantee of intellectual intuition and of the practical consequences derived from it" (*Spiritual Perspectives and Human Facts*, "Appendix: Selections from Letters and Other Previously Unpublished Writings", 237).

[70] *Understanding Islam*, "The Path", 157.

[71] *Stations of Wisdom*, "The Nature and Arguments of Faith", 57.

[72] The best accounts of the life of the sage are T.M.P. Mahadevan, *Ramana Maharshi: The Sage of Arunacala* and A.R. Natarajan, *Timeless in Time: Sri Ramana Maharshi*.

[73] *Spiritual Perspectives and Human Facts* (1969), "Love and Knowledge", 138.

[74] C.F. Kelley, *Meister Eckhart on Divine Knowledge*. (Kelley's book clearly owes a great deal to Schuon, whose aphorisms are repeated almost word for word, but nowhere in the book can we find any appropriate acknowledgment.)

[75] *Light on the Ancient Worlds*, "Religio Perennis", 119. See also *Logic and Transcendence*, "Understanding and Believing", 199.

[76] S.H. Nasr, *Ideals and Realities of Islam*, 21.

grated with metaphysical insight if full realization is to occur, which is to say there must be a merging of intellectual and volitive elements in a harmonized unity. It should also be remembered that although the Intellect is

> situated beyond sentiment, imagination, memory and reason . . . it can at the same time enlighten and determine all of these since they are like its individualized ramifications, ordained as receptacles to receive the light from on high and to translate it according to their respective capacities.[77]

The spiritual life, lived in conformity with a way provided by tradition, forms both a precondition and a complement to intellection. As Aquinas put it, "By their very nature the virtues do not necessarily form part of contemplation but they are an indispensable condition for it."[78] Moreover, sanctity itself may or may not be accompanied by metaphysical discernment: one may be a saint but no metaphysician, as history repeatedly demonstrates. To expect, as a necessity, metaphysical wisdom of the saint is to confuse different modes of spiritual perfection. As Schuon reminds us:

> To say "man" is to say *bhakta*, and to say spirit is to say *jnanin;* human nature is so to speak woven of these two neighboring but incommensurable dimensions. There is certainly a *bhakti* without *jnana*, but there is no *jnana* without *bhakti*.[79]

The perspectives of Ramanuja and Shankara might be cited as illustrative examples.[80]

If metaphysical discernment is to transform one's being then intellection alone is insufficient for "Human nature contains dark elements which no intellectual certainty could, *ipso facto*, eliminate."[81] Here the role of faith is critical:

> A man may possess metaphysical certainty without possessing "faith". . . . But, if metaphysical certainty suffices on the doctrinal ground, it is far from being sufficient on the spiritual level where it must be completed and enlivened by faith. Faith is nothing other than our whole being clinging to Truth, whether we have of truth a direct intuition or

---

[77] *Transfiguration of Man*, "Reflections on Ideological Sentimentalism", 25.

[78] Quoted in *Understanding Islam*, "The Path", 161n.

[79] *Esoterism as Principle and as Way*, "Understanding Esoterism", 22.

[80] See *Spiritual Perspectives and Human Facts*, "Vedanta", 109ff. For a European example of "*bhakti* without *jnana*" one might cite St Theresa of Lisieux—but the history of Christianity furnishes many examples. (As William Stoddart notes in his Foreword to this book, Schuon "much loved" St Theresa for her "holy littleness". See also C. Schuon, "Frithjof Schuon: Memories and Anecdotes", 40.)

[81] *Spiritual Perspectives and Human Facts* (1969), "Love and Knowledge", 139.

an indirect idea. It is an abuse of language to reduce "faith" to the level of "belief".[82]

In another context Schuon emphasizes this point in even more unequivocal terms. The following passage is one of the most arresting in the whole Schuonian corpus, one made all the more so by the uncharacteristic personal reference:

> One can meditate or speculate indefinitely on transcendent truths and their applications (that is moreover what the author of this book does, but he has valid reasons for doing it, nor does he do it for himself). One can spend a whole lifetime speculating on the suprasensorial and the transcendent, but all that matters is "the leap into the void" which is the fixation of spirit and soul in an unthinkable dimension of the Real. . . . This "leap into the void" we can call . . . "faith".[83]

---

[82] *Spiritual Perspectives and Human Facts* (1969), "Love and Knowledge", 127. On the relationship of intellection and realization see also S. H. Nasr, *Knowledge and the Sacred*, 310ff.

[83] *Logic and Transcendence*, "Understanding and Believing", 202. Swami Abhishiktananda, similarly: "Faith is essentially that interior sense by which the mind penetrates obscurely into those depths of one's own being which it realizes are beyond its power to explore solely by means of thought and sense perception" (*The Further Shore*, 59-60).

III

Religious Forms
and Sacred Symbols

Forms allow a direct and "plastic" assimilation of the
truths—or realities—of the spirit.

(Frithjof Schuon, *Spiritual Perspectives and Human Facts*, 24)

7

The Cycle of Abrahamic Monotheisms

The transcendent unity of the religious forms is illustrated in a particularly instructive manner by the reciprocal relationships existing between the three great so-called "monotheistic" religions.[1]

Religions are determined by archetypes, which are so many spiritual possibilities: on the one hand every religion *a priori* manifests an archetype, but on the other hand any archetype can manifest itself *a posteriori* within every religion.[2]

Every religion has a form and a substance. . . . Substance possesses every right; it derives from the Absolute; form is relative; its rights are therefore limited.[3]

In *The Transcendent Unity of Religions*, Schuon expounded the metaphysical basis of both the formal diversity of religions and their inner unity. In "The Ternary Aspect of Monotheism", Schuon explains the "reciprocal relationships" of the three Semitic monotheisms—Judaism, Christianity, Islam—which together constitute "the integral Revelation of monotheism".[4] Schuon has many times written on these traditions. Rather than essaying a conspectus of these writings, here we shall isolate a few Schuonian themes which highlight some of the distinctive features of each tradition and illuminate their oft-misunderstood relations. Our purpose, as elsewhere in this study, is to do no more than indicate some possible points of entry into Schuon's writings and, by implication, into the unbounded spiritual universes which those writings intimate.

As we have seen earlier, perennialism affirms the principle of multiple Revelations, each one attuned to the receptivities of that human collectivity for whom it is destined. Every Revelation communicates a Divine Message and discloses Truth unqualified, but only by way of religious forms which are themselves, necessarily, limited and partial. Furthermore, each Revelation privileges a certain aspect of the Truth which is providentially shaped to the needs of a particular ethnic and cultural community. Thus the forms in which the Message springs forth will differ. In this context it is worth consid-

---

[1] *Transcendent Unity of Religions*, "The Ternary Aspect of Monotheism", 95.
[2] *Christianity/Islam*, "The Question of Protestantism", 15-16.
[3] *Form and Substance in the Religions*, "Form and Substance in the Religions", 14.
[4] *Transcendent Unity of Religions*, "The Ternary Aspect of Monotheism", 104.

ering the ways in which Schuon accents both the *formal diversity* (and hence theological antagonisms) and the *inner unity* (or mystical convergence) of the different branches of Abrahamic monotheism, without here reckoning with the various temporal exigencies and vicissitudes which helped to shape the unfolding of these traditions.

The motive force behind much of Schuon's writing in this field is revealed in the following passage:

> The antagonisms between these forms no more affect the one universal Truth than the antagonisms between opposing colors affect the transmission of the one uncolored light. . . . Just as every color, by its negation of darkness and its affirmation of light, provides the possibility of discovering the ray that makes it visible and of tracing this ray back to its luminous source, so all forms, all symbols, all religions, all dogmas, by their negation of error and their affirmation of Truth, make it possible to follow the ray of Revelation, which is none other than the ray of the Intellect, back to its Divine Source.[5]

In many respects this is a summation of Schuon's project at large: to make clear the ways in which *limited forms* communicate *limitless Truth*.

Judaism

Judaism, Christianity, and Islam are each rooted in God's primordial Revelation of Himself to the patriarch Abraham.

> Hear O Israel: The Lord our God is one Lord. And thou shalt love the Lord with all thine heart, and with all thy soul, and with all thy might. (Deuteronomy 6:4-5)

These verses, a veritable formula of monotheism repeated throughout the *Torah*, comprise the "two pillars of all human spirituality, namely metaphysical discernment . . . and contemplative concentration"[6]—doctrine and method, truth and way, intellectuality and spirituality. This affirmation (of God's Oneness) and injunction (to love God) is "the fundamental enunciation of Judaism".[7] Abraham's affirmation of monotheism continued through his sons Isaac and Ishmael, the former lineage culminating in the Mosaic Revelation, "the Sinaitic definition of God being essential, total, and definitive",[8] from whence Judaism as such originated, based on the Covenant between God and His people. Christianity itself, in turn, was a kind of culmination and "universalization" of Judaism, especially in its Messianic

---

[5] *Transcendent Unity of Religions*, "Preface", xxxiv.
[6] *Esoterism as Principle and as Way*, "The Supreme Commandment", 151.
[7] *Esoterism as Principle and as Way*, "The Supreme Commandment", 156.
[8] *Christianity/Islam*, "Alternations in Semitic Monotheism", 71.

aspect, freeing the monotheistic message from its ethnic ties to the Jews and to the land of Israel, and revivifying a spiritual way threatened by an ossified and hypocritical Pharasaism.

> Christ shattered the frontiers of ethnic Israel in order to replace it with a purely spiritual Israel; and he placed the love of God before the prescribed act.[9]

Christianity was "a return to a mystery of inwardness, holiness, and divine Life".[10] Finally, through the line of Ishmael, Abrahamic monotheism was crystallized anew in the Descent of the Koran from whence, through God's Messenger Muhammad, Islam erupted into the Arab world.

In Judaism the one, eternal God of Israel involves Himself as a partner in the sacred history and events of His people; He rescues them from bondage in Egypt, protects them against their enemies, chastises them when they stray from His ways. Schuon comments on this relationship:

> As for Judaism, it is peculiar in that it puts the whole emphasis on God as the partner of His Chosen People, the link between the two parties being the Law; one might also say that it is the latter that receives the whole emphasis since it is situated between God and Israel; if Israel is the People of God, God for His part is the God of Israel, the pact being sealed by the Sinaitic Law.[11]

In other words, the Law, symbolically speaking, is a Divine isthmus between God and His people. God's pact with Israel hinges upon obedience to this Law: "Now, if you will obey me and keep my covenant, you will be my own people. The whole earth is mine, but you will be my chosen people" (Exodus 19:5-6).

From a metaphysical viewpoint the drama of this relationship between God and his people mirrors the relationship between the Absolute and relative: "[It] reflects the drama between *Atma* and *Maya*, with all its ambiguity and all its final glory, from the double point of view of cosmic rhythms and of the Apocatastasis".[12] In its universal symbolic aspect, Judaism is, in

---

[9] *Form and Substance in the Religions*, "Form and Substance in the Religions", 20-21. An analogous process took place in the Eastern world when Buddhism repudiated an excessive and sterile literalism/ritualism within the Hindu tradition; in recasting the perennial truths enshrined in Hinduism, Buddhism universalized them. Furthermore, Schuon remarks, "Buddhism is a kind of 'Hindu Christianity', which no doubt explains the interest it has for Westerners; but it goes without saying that in other respects—precisely because it is Hindu and not Western in origin—it is much further from Christianity than are Judaism and Islam" (*Spiritual Perspectives and Human Facts*, "Knowledge and Love", 137-138n).

[10] *Form and Substance in the Religions*, "Form and Substance in the Religions", 20.

[11] Frithjof Schuon, "The Perennial Philosophy", 22.

[12] Frithjof Schuon, "The Perennial Philosophy", 22. The Apocatastasis—akin to the *pralaya*

Leo Schaya's words, "man—personified in Moses—ascending towards God while raising the fallen world with him, so as to unite everything with the One at the summit of the Mountain of Illumination".[13] Judaism reflects the journey of the soul in its return to God. David, the builder of Jerusalem, and Solomon, the builder of the Temple, dramatize the encounter of the creature with the Creator, "the mystery of man standing before his God" and "appear as two inseparable poles, or as the two sides [i.e., exoteric and esoteric respectively] of one and the same Revelation".[14] The bondage of slavery, the fall into moral decay, idolatry, the indifference to the Prophets—these are so many states of the soul in exile, turned away from God. But God's redeeming Mercy is the source of an ever-renewed hope, one which finds its distinctive Judaic inflection in Messianism.

The spiritual economy of Judaism is centered on righteous conduct, on the observance of the Law (as expressed in the *Torah*, the *Mishnah*, and the *Talmud*), and on participation in the rites and festivals of the community.[15] Thus, as Schuon observes, "Judaism, in its basic form, is a *karma-marga* [the way of action, or work] rather than a *bhakti* [the way of devotion, or love], whereas the relationship is inverse in Christianity", without forgetting that the former "necessarily comprises an element of *bhakti*, 'love', and vice versa".[16] With the Gospel introduction of the word "mind" into the Abrahamic formula (Mark 12:29-30) Christianity shifts the emphasis from "works" to the interiorized state from whence arise all external behaviors. In contrast, as Schuon explains, within Judaism mind "is in a certain fashion the inward concomitance of outward observance"[17]—and this is in conformity with the Mosaic Revelation.

In discussing Judaism's "reciprocal relationships" with the other Semitic monotheisms Schuon draws attention to the Sufic ternary of fear, love, and knowledge, these corresponding to the keynotes of Judaism, Christianity, and Islam respectively.

A paradoxical reason for this phenomenon is that the blossoming forth of the perspective of love presupposes a human milieu molded by the

---

of Hinduism—is "the reabsorption of all manifestation into the Unmanifest" (*Logic and Transcendence*, "The Symbolism of the Hourglass", 169.) The Christian doctrine of the Apocatastasis was elaborated by Clement of Alexandria, Origen, St Gregory of Nyssa, and St Gregory Nazianzus.

[13] L. Schaya, "Some Universal Aspects of Judaism", 61. (Schaya's invaluable essay provides an overview of Judaism, including its esoteric dimensions.)

[14] *In the Face of the Absolute*, "David, Shankara, Honen", 131.

[15] Under the Rabbinic view the Hebrew Scripture contains no less than 613 commandments. See H. Smith, *The World's Religions*, 286.

[16] *Esoterism as Principle and as Way*, "The Supreme Commandment", 152.

[17] *Esoterism as Principle and as Way*, "The Supreme Commandment", 151-152.

perspective of fear, and the emergence of the perspective of gnosis pre-supposes a milieu steeped in that of love. This is to say that a religion must have the time to form its humanity so that it can project, with the benefit of this ambiance, different types of spiritual accentuations.[18]

However, he also points out that this ternary unfolds itself within each tradition. In Judaism: the era of the Pentateuch, in which the people stand in fear and awe of the one, eternal, terrific, and transcendent God (fear); the flowering of the Psalms and the "Song of Songs" (love); the late blossoming of Jewish esoterism in the medieval Kabbalah (knowledge). But "fear" remains throughout, for this is integral to the Revelation itself: "the fear of God is the framework for the perspectives of love and knowledge, neither of which could be absent, love being closely bound here to hope".[19]

Christianity
In the "elliptical and audacious" formula of St Irenaeus, "God became man that man might become God".[20] Two great mysteries: the Incarnation and the Redemption. ("By 'mystery' we do not mean something incomprehensible in principle . . . but something which opens onto the Infinite".[21]) Together with the discernment between the Real and the illusory, which is at the heart of all religious wisdoms, this is the metaphysical doctrine from which flows everything else in Christianity. Christianity belongs to that religious type which is fixed not on the Absolute as such but on the Logos—"God as man" or, in specifically Christian terms, "the Word made flesh". In this respect it belongs with the bhaktic branches of Hinduism devoted to the *avataras*, and with Amida Buddhism, rather than with Platonism, Judaism, Islam, Taoism, and Vedanta.[22] (One token of the similarities and convergences in question is suggested by the especially privileged place in the former traditions of the Invocation of the Divine Name.[23])

Christianity envisages the Absolute *a priori* in relation to man, and man in relation to the Absolute: the Incarnation and the Redemption thus become the doctrinal cornerstones of the tradition. Furthermore, Christianity presents an esoterism of interiority and Love.

---

[18] *Form and Substance in the Religions*, "Form and Substance in Religions", 29.

[19] *Form and Substance in the Religions*, "Form and Substance in Religions", 30.

[20] *Christianity/Islam*, "The Idea of 'The Best' in Religions", 105.

[21] *Form and Substance in the Religions*, "The Question of Theodices", 155.

[22] See *Survey of Metaphysics and Esoterism*, "Outline of Religious Typologies", especially 103-104.

[23] The fact that Invocation is also central in the spiritual methodology of Islam only goes to accent the universality of that tradition. On the Invocation of the Name of Jesus see *Transcendent Unity of Religions*, "Universality and Particular Nature of the Christian Religion", 145-148.

Christianity transposes the prescriptive Law onto the inward plane, and along with it Messianism itself, whence the fundamental lack of understanding between the Jewish and Christian religions; nascent Christianity was opposed to legalistic and formalistic Judaism (though not to Essenism) as the "spirit" is opposed to the "letter" . . . or as essence is opposed to form. Having shattered the formal Mosaic framework in the name of essence, the message emerged as an esoterism, but it was an esoterism of love, capable of becoming in its turn an exoterism in fact, without, however, needing or being able to lose thereby its esoteric virtualities, including that of gnosis.[24]

In relation to Judaism, Christianity derives its essentially esoteric character from three elements: inwardness, a "quasi-unconditional charity" or sacrificial love, the sacraments.[25]

> Christ brought only an esoterism. . . . This results not only from the doctrine of the Gospel but also from the particular character of the rites; without this specific character, this laying bare of spiritual realities until then hidden, the coming of Christianity would be unintelligible.[26]

Within Christianity's exoteric framework, which inevitably emerged over time, the truth of the Absolute is veiled, for "its central content seems to be not God as such but Christ; that is, not so much the nature of the Divine Being as its human manifestation";[27] Christianity pivots on the mysterious truth of the Incarnation and Redemption, one not formally compatible with the implacable monotheism of either Judaism or Islam—and herein lies yet another source of various necessary theological ostracisms. Christ Himself is the Revelation, "the Way, the Truth, and the Life", the Message Itself, but one only fully intelligible within the framework of an inherited Jewish "mythology". As Schuon notes, "Christianity superimposes on man's post-Edenic misery the saving person of Christ."[28]

> The Christian perspective is founded on the fall of Adam, which requires as its complement the Messianic redemption. . . . Christianity begins with the fall of Adam and presupposes that man is the fall. . . . In other words Christianity is founded on the primordial fall of the unique man.[29]

[24] *Logic and Transcendence*, "Introduction", 2.
[25] *Fullness of God*, "Outline of the Christic Message", 3
[26] *Spiritual Perspectives and Human Facts*, "Contours of the Spirit", 83-84.
[27] *Roots of the Human Condition*, "Outline of the Christian Message", 74.
[28] *Form and Substance in the Religions*, "Form and Substance in the Religions", 17.
[29] *Spiritual Perspectives and Human Facts*, "Contours of the Spirit", 54, 57.

To repair the consequences of the primordial fall of Adam, the messianic Redemption eliminates the fall itself by restoring equilibrium through the new Adam, Christ.

In a metaphysical framework,

> Christ, "Light of the World", is the universal Intellect, as the Word is the "Wisdom of the Father". Christ is the Intellect of microcosms as well as that of the macrocosm. He is then the Intellect in us as well as the Intellect in the Universe and *a fortiori* in God; in this sense, it can be said that there is no truth nor wisdom that does not come from Christ, and this is evidently independent of all considerations of time and place.[30]

Christianity realizes the spiritual possibilities of union through love—union within the Trinity and the union of God and man. Schuon:

> In man the Spirit becomes the ego in order that the ego may become pure Spirit; the Spirit or the Intellect (*Intellectus*, not *mens* or *ratio*) becomes ego by incarnating in the mind in the form of intellection, of truth, and the ego becomes the Spirit or Intellect through uniting with It. Thus Christianity is a doctrine of union, or the doctrine of Union, rather than of Unity [as in Islam]; the Principle unites itself to Manifestation so that the latter may become united to the Principle; hence the symbolism of love and the predominance of the bhaktic Path. "God became man", says St Irenaeus, "because of the immensity of His love", and man must unite himself with God also through "love", whatever meaning—volitive, emotional, or intellectual—be given to that term. "God is Love": as Trinity He is Union and He wishes Union.[31]

The Incarnation necessarily brings into the Christian perspective both Trinitarian metaphysics and Trinitarian theology: "For Christians, to say that God is one means nothing if one does not add that God is three".[32] Schuon elucidates the *theological* Trinitarianism of Christianity by recourse to the *metaphysical* trinity of Beyond-Being, Being, and Existence. Metaphysically speaking, in the Christian vocabulary it is the "Father" who corresponds to the Divine Essence, the "Son" (the "Word Incarnate") to the Logos, and the "Holy Spirit" to Radiation. Schuon also traces the theological Trinity of Christianity to the ternary aspect within Beyond-Being:

> On the level of Being—which is that of the personal God, hence also that of theology—we shall discern the Essence, then the "Form" or the "Image", and then Radiation [corresponding to Father, Son, and Holy

---

[30] *Essential Frithjof Schuon*, "The Christian Tradition: Some Thoughts on Its Nature", 233.

[31] *Understanding Islam*, "The Path", 139-140.

[32] *From the Divine to the Human*, "The Interplay of the Hypostases", 42.

Spirit]. This Trinity is necessarily anticipated in Beyond-Being, which comprises the aspects of Absoluteness, Infinity, and All-Possibility.[33]

Although the Christian Trinity, theologically speaking, does not reach beyond Being or the ontological principle, it is a principial reflection of the metaphysical Trinity, and is implicitly contained in the Absolute Essence. Because the accent of the Revelation is on "God made man", on Incarnation, Christianity absolutizes the relative, again a cause of scandal to Jews and Muslims. For Christianity it could not be otherwise, for it "is founded on the idea and the reality of Divine Manifestation. . . . It must enclose everything within its fundamental idea of Manifestation; the Absolute must therefore be envisaged exclusively in connection therewith."[34]

Christianity is essentially an inward Message to the Heart-Intellect of man: the sapiential Message is Christ Himself, Who is "the eternal content of the Intellect". Schuon speaks of this "eternal content" in these words:

> This message or content is: love God with all your faculties and, in function of this love, love your neighbor as yourself; that is, become united—for in essence to love means to become united—with the Heart-Intellect and, in function or as a condition of this union, abandon all pride and all passion and discern the Spirit in every creature.[35]

However, since Christ's Message is for everyone, it has to find expression within the exoteric dimension too. So, by its form the Message "is addressed *a priori* to the passional element in man, to the point of fall in his nature".[36] This is a characteristic of Christianity, whereas in Islam the Message is directed *a priori* to man *qua* intelligence. However, in

> "exoteric" Christianity, man is *a priori* will, or, more exactly, he is will corrupted; clearly the intelligence is not denied, but it is taken into consideration only as an aspect of will; man is will and in man will is intelligent; when the will is corrupted, so also is the intelligence corrupted in the sense that in no way could it set the will to rights. Therefore a divine intervention is needed: the sacrament.[37]

In Christianity the divine Manifestation presents itself through the Incarnation; the reality of Divine Love personified in Manifestation—Jesus Christ, the Word made flesh, and the Virgin Mary who carried the Word.

> The Blessed Virgin is inseparable from the incarnate Word, as the lotus is inseparable from the Buddha and as the heart is the predestined seat

---

[33] *Roots of the Human Condition*, "Man in the Face of the Sovereign Good", 71.

[34] *Logic and Transcendence*, "Evidence and Mystery", 98.

[35] *Understanding Islam*, "The Path", 140.

[36] *Gnosis: Divine Wisdom*, "Some Observations", 112.

[37] *Understanding Islam*, "Islam", 2.

of immanent Wisdom. In Buddhism there is an entire mysticism of the Lotus, which communicates a celestial image of unsurpassable beauty and eloquence, a beauty analogous to the monstrance containing the Real Presence and analogous above all to that incarnation of divine Femininity which is the Virgin Mary. The Virgin, *Rosa Mystica*, is like a personification of the celestial Lotus: in a certain respect, she personifies a sense of the sacred, which is the indispensable introduction to the reception of the Sacrament.[38]

Schuon envisages the Virgin as Femininity *in divinis, Sedes Sapientiae* ("Throne of Wisdom"), divine Mercy, as "Spouse of the Holy Spirit" and "Co-Redemptress", the divine *Sophia* and *Rosa Mystica*, the archetypal personification of spiritual poverty, submission, and quintessential prayer, and in Hindu terms, Divine *Maya* and *Shakti*—to mention only a few of her modes and functions. She plays a central part in Christian spirituality and occupies a special place in the life and teachings of Schuon.[39]

Schuon's insights into Christian doctrine and Christian spirituality are more or less inexhaustible, and here we have only touched in the briefest possible fashion on a few of the motifs which pervade his writings.[40] However, perhaps enough has been said to indicate in a general way the distinctive position occupied by Christianity in the cycle of Abrahamic monotheisms. To conclude the present discussion at the same point it started: Christianity is essentially bhaktic; it "operates through love of God—a love which responds to the divine love for man, God being Himself Love".[41]

Islam

Here are the opening lines of Schuon's *Understanding Islam*:

Islam is the meeting between God as such and man as such.

[38] *Fullness of God*, "The Seat of Wisdom", 137

[39] See J-B. Aymard and P. Laude, *Frithjof Schuon: Life and Teachings*, 41-42, 74-76, and "A Spiritual Patroness" in *Frithjof Schuon: Messenger of the Perennial Philosophy*, 95-100, 208-211. Schuon's most extended writings on the Virgin include "Mysteries of Christ and the Virgin" in *Gnosis: Divine Wisdom*, and "Sedes Sapientiae" in *In the Face of the Absolute* (these essays can also be found in *Fullness of God*), and "The Virginal Doctrine" in *Form and Substance in the Religions*. (In the summer of 1969 Schuon named his spiritual way "the Path of Mary" [*Tariqah Maryamiyyah*] in honor of his spiritual patroness.) The place of the Virgin in Schuon's paintings is discussed in chapter 11.

[40] Not the least interesting of Schuon's commentaries are those on "Christian Divergences", which include the following observation on the Reformation: "In the framework of Christianity as a whole, the Reformation, while appearing logically and technically as a heresy . . . possesses in itself a justification and hence an efficacy which it draws from a spiritual archetype that was, if not entirely ignored by Rome, at least 'stifled'" (*In the Face of the Absolute*, "Christian Divergences", 116-117). See also "The Question of Protestantism" in *Christianity/Islam*.

[41] *Understanding Islam*, "The Path", 142.

God as such: that is to say God envisaged, not as He manifested Himself in a particular way at a particular time, but independently of history and inasmuch as He is what He is and also as He creates and reveals by His nature.

Man as such: that is to say man envisaged, not as a fallen being needing a miracle to save him, but as man, a theomorphic being endowed with an intelligence capable of conceiving of the Absolute and with a will capable of choosing what leads to the Absolute.[42]

In a nutshell, Islam is the religion of the Absolute. It completes the cycle of Abrahamic traditions, returning to the pure monotheism of the patriarch Abraham; Muhammad is the "Seal of the Prophets". In this sense, Islam is the first and last in the monotheistic cycle—"the alpha and the omega".[43] In another sense it attains a kind of Equilibrium, poised between Obedience (Judaism) and Interiority (Christianity).

Doctrinally, Islam rests on the affirmation of the Unity of God, as revealed to His Messenger Muhammad. The essence of this doctrine is in chapter 112:

1. Say: He is God, the One and Only;
2. God, the Eternal, Absolute;
3. He begetteth not, nor is He begotten;
4. And there is none like unto Him.

The "great argument of Islam is Unity, which becomes *ipso facto* the argument of the Prophet; it is the blinding and incontrovertible truth that justifies and guarantees its herald."[44] The two great testimonies of the *Shahadah*—*La ilaha illa 'Llah* ("There is no divinity save the sole Divinity") and *Muhammadun rasulu 'Llah* ("Muhammad is the Messenger of the Divinity")—are the bedrock of Islam which, in adamantine and sometimes combative fashion, presents a doctrine of the One. The *Shahadah* contains within itself

> two assertions, two certitudes, two levels of reality: the Absolute and the relative, Cause and effect, God and the world. Islam is the religion of certitude and equilibrium, as Christianity is the religion of love and sacrifice. . . . Islam seeks to implant certitude—its unitary faith stands forth as something manifestly clear without in any way renouncing mystery—and is based on two axiomatic certainties . . . "that God alone is" and . . . that "all things are attached to God".[45]

---

[42] *Understanding Islam*, "Islam", 1.
[43] *Christianity/Islam*, "The Idea of 'The Best' in Religions", 112.
[44] *Spiritual Perspectives and Human Facts*, "Vedanta", 67.
[45] *Understanding Islam*, "Islam", 5.

As with all religious forms, the *Shahadah* can be understood esoteri-cally as well as exoterically, for "All metaphysical truths are comprised in the first of these testimonies and all eschatological truths in the second. . . . It could also be said that the first *Shahadah* is the formula of discernment or "abstraction" while the second is the formula of integration or "analogy".[46] "The Testimony of Faith of Islam", writes Schuon,

> is both sword and shroud: on the one hand it is a lightning bolt in its ful-gurating unicity, and on the other hand a sand dune or blanket of snow in its peace-giving totality; and these two messages refer respectively, not only to the mysteries of Absoluteness and Infinitude, but also—in a certain fashion—to those of Transcendence and Immanence.[47]

In another felicitous comparison Schuon has written that the *Shahadah* is "both an *Upanishad* and a *mantra*".[48]

In several books devoted to Islam, Schuon presents a highly detailed explication of a great many aspects of Islamic doctrine and practice. Here we will confine ourselves to a sample of Schuon's observations about a few of the tradition's other salient features: the nature of the Koran; Islam as a mes-sage directed towards man's intelligence, will, and the faculty of speech; and the centrality of the remembrance of God in the spiritual way of Islam.

For Islam the Koran is "the uncreated word of God—uncreated though expressing itself through created elements such as words, sounds, and let-ters—but also the model *par excellence* of the perfection of language". It might even be said that in its well-known difficulties and ambiguities the Koran is an exemplary Scripture:

> The seeming incoherence of these texts [sacred Scriptures] . . . always has the same cause, namely the incommensurable disproportion between the Spirit on the one hand and the limited resources of human language on the other: it is as though the poor and coagulated language of mortal man would break under the formidable pressure of the Heav-enly Word into a thousand fragments, or as if God, in order to express a thousand truths, had but a dozen words at his disposal and so was compelled to make use of allusions heavy with meaning, of ellipses, abridgements, and symbolical syntheses.[49]

[46] *Understanding Islam*, "Islam", 6.
[47] *In the Face of the Absolute*, "Islam and Consciousness of the Absolute", 155.
[48] *Spiritual Perspectives and Human Facts*, "Appendix", 234. (On the *Shahadah* see also P. Samsel, "The *Shahadah* as Truth and as Way").
[49] *Understanding Islam*, "The Koran", 40-41.

Furthermore, the Koran, like any sacred Scripture, "is a totality, a diversified image of Being" but one which "has no means of expression other than the very substance of the nescience of which our soul is made".[50]

Again and again in Schuon's *oeuvre* we find formulations such as this: "Man's vocation is consciousness of the Absolute."[51] It might be said that this is the governing principle of Islam. Islam affirms transcendent intelligence as a human birthright: man is a theomorphic creature, made for the Absolute and blessed with an intelligence commensurate with this exalted vocation. Indeed, the Prophet himself declared, "God has created nothing more noble than intelligence, and His wrath is on him who despises it."[52] Islam is squarely addressed to this intelligence. Salvation is attained by the acknowledgment of and conformity to the Absolute, realized firstly through an acceptance by the "intelligence" that the transcendent Absolute alone is, secondly through submission (*islam*) to the Law of the Absolute by the "will", and thirdly through the sincerity of both of these two attitudes.[53] (It might be noted in passing that Islam reverses the Christian conception of the relation of "intelligence" and "will".[54])

Mention must also be made of another distinctive element of Islamic spirituality: the peculiar status of human "speech" as a divine endowment which distinguishes man from all other creatures, and whose most noble function is prayer—the content of which expresses the intelligence, while the act itself manifests the will.[55] So it is that

> What constitutes the originality of Islam is not the discovery of the saving function of intelligence, will, and speech—that function is . . . known to every religion—but that it has made of this, within the framework of Semitic monotheism, the point of departure in a perspective of salvation and deliverance. . . . This could also be expressed as follows: if man, being made in the image of God, is distinguished from other creatures by having transcendent intelligence, free will, and the gift of speech, then Islam is the religion of certainty, equilibrium, and prayer, to take in their order the three deiform faculties.[56]

In this way "Islam bases itself upon the axiom of the unalterable deiformity of man".[57]

---

[50] *Understanding Islam*, "The Koran", 41.

[51] *Play of Masks*, "Being Conscious of the Real", 82.

[52] *Understanding Islam*, "Islam", 35.

[53] See *Christianity/Islam*, "The Idea of 'The Best' in Religions", 95.

[54] *Understanding Islam*, "Islam", 3.

[55] *Understanding Islam*, "Islam", 3.

[56] *Understanding Islam*, "Islam", 3-4.

[57] *Form and Substance in the Religions*, "Form and Substance in the Religions", 21.

It follows from what has already been said that the remembrance of God (*dhikr*), encompassing recitation of the Koran, contemplative concentration, and, above all, the invocation of the Divine Names, must needs be the pivot of Islamic spirituality: "*Dhikr* cuts through the Gordian knot of the soul's obscurities and troubles".[58] Indeed, the Five Pillars of the Faith (the *Shahadah*, or testimony of faith; canonical prayer; the fast of Ramadan; almsgiving; and the *Hajj*) all serve to maintain that remembrance of God to which the faithful are called and which was supremely exemplified by the Prophet, the very model of all the human virtues (pre-eminently serenity, strength, and generosity but also humility, truthfulness, perseverance, patience, and piety, to mention those most frequently extolled in the Koran). As the Sufis say, the Prophet is "The synthesis of all spiritual possibilities".[59] And so, "Imitation of the Prophet implies: strength as regards oneself; generosity as regards others; serenity in God and through God. It could also be said: serenity through piety, in the most profound sense of that term".[60]

*   *   *

The three Abrahamic traditions, each in its own divinely-appointed way, furnishes a doctrine and a spiritual path sufficient to the needs of its adherents, whilst together, along with the Abrahamic Revelation from which they all flow, they comprise the full and integral Revelation of monotheism, one of the great spiritual patrimonies of humankind.

---

[58] *Sufism: Veil and Quintessence*, "Appendix: Selections from Letters and Previously Unpublished Writings", 133.

[59] *Survey of Metaphysics and Esoterism*, "Outline of Religious Typologies", 107.

[60] *Understanding Islam*, "The Prophet", 110.

8

Eastern Traditions:

Hinduism, Buddhism, and the Heritage
of the Far East

Truth is one and it would be vain to refuse to look for it except in one particular place, for the Intellect contains in its substance all that is true, and truth cannot but be manifested wherever the Intellect is deployed in the atmosphere of a Revelation.[1]

What matters in a religion is its central affirmation, its qualitative content, which is indispensable for man and of which the peripheral arguments are like a protective enclosure.[2]

The passage from one Asiatic tradition to another—Hinduism, Buddhism, Taoism—is a small thing, seeing that the metaphysical content is everywhere clearly apparent and even throws into relief the relativity of "mythological" diversities.[3]

While much of Schuon's work has been devoted to the religious forms of the Abrahamic traditions, his metaphysical expositions, like those of Guénon, are rooted in Advaita Vedanta, and this for a very simple reason: Vedanta "is the most direct possible expression of gnosis"[4] and "an intrinsic esoterism".[5] From his youthful days Schuon evinced a particular affinity with Eastern religious forms, both doctrinal and artistic. In a 1982 letter to Leo Schaya, Schuon wrote of the years following his move as a sixteen year-old to Paris:

> For about ten years I was completely spellbound by Hinduism, without however being able to be a Hindu in the literal sense. . . . I lived no other religion but that of the Vedanta and the *Bhagavad Gita*; this was my first experience of the *religio perennis*.[6]

---

[1] *Light on the Ancient Worlds*, "Religio Perennis", 121.
[2] *Spiritual Perspectives and Human Facts*, "Contours of the Spirit", 71.
[3] *In the Tracks of Buddhism*, "Science, Myth, and the Meaning of the Ancestors", 82.
[4] *Gnosis: Divine Wisdom*, "Gnosis: Language of the Self", 61n. Similarly, "The doctrine of the Vedantists is incontestably metaphysical in the highest possible sense; it transmits every essential truth" (*Light on the Ancient Worlds*, "American Indian Shamanism", 75).
[5] *Survey of Metaphysics and Esoterism*, "Two Esoterisms", 118.
[6] Frithjof Schuon, letter to Leo Schaya, August 11, 1982, quoted in J-B. Aymard and P. Laude, *Frithjof Schuon: Life and Teachings*, 10.

Soon after his arrival in Paris in 1923 he was introduced to Guénon's *Introduction to the Study of the Hindu Doctrines, Man and His Becoming According to the Vedanta,* and *East and West,* which he read with the greatest interest and enthusiasm.[7] Here is a passage from a letter written in 1929:

> I feel Hindu, like a branch of this soul or of this spirituality, which spreads from the burning *Gopurams* of the Ganges to the red-gold shadows of the silent *Gompas* . . . as far as Angkor Wat and the Shivaite harmony of Mongolia and Cambodia, and which is still alive in pious Bali. This kinship is a fact and not a voluntary monomania; it corresponds to natural laws, to an elective affinity.[8]

Think, too, of Schuon's remark that "Being *a priori* a metaphysician, I have had since my youth a particular interest in Advaita Vedanta, but also in the method of realization of which Advaita Vedanta approves."[9] It was only because of the insurmountable barrier of caste that Schuon could not embark directly on this path—hence the turn towards Sufism. He also felt a particular affinity with both Buddhism and Taoism, finding the latter "peerless and unique".[10] From his earliest years Schuon was also fascinated by the arts of the Far East. In an unusual personal reference in one of his works he tells of coming face to face, as a child, with a Buddha figure in an ethnographical museum, a traditional representation in gilded wood, flanked by statues of the Bodhisattvas Seishi and Kwannon, which seemed "to have emerged from a celestial river of golden light, silence, and mercy". Of the encounter with "this overwhelming embodiment of an infinite victory of the Spirit" Schuon writes, "*veni, vidi, victus sum*".[11]

These biographical fragments remind us, firstly, of the axial place of Vedantic metaphysics in Schuon's work, and secondly, that Schuon was a *jnanin* whose intellectuality and aesthetic sensibility were not bound by those limits normally imposed by birth, culture, and formal religious affiliation. It is for this reason, among others, that Schuon's expositions of Eastern doctrines and practices have been hailed by the most exacting authorities from within those traditions. Here we will consider four Oriental traditions,

---

[7] Schuon said of these works, "Guénon was the first European who dared to affirm in the West the superiority of the Hindu spirit over the modern Western spirit, and, in the name of Eastern spirituality and that of the ancient West, dared mercilessly to criticize modern civilization. . . . He expounded all the fundamental data that it is necessary to know in the West in order to understand India" (Quoted in J-B. Aymard and P. Laude, *Frithjof Schuon: Life and Teachings,* 142n).

[8] Frithjof Schuon, quoted in *Frithjof Schuon: Messenger of the Perennial Philosophy,* 26.

[9] Frithjof Schuon, quoted in *Frithjof Schuon: Messenger of the Perennial Philosophy,* 27.

[10] Unpublished writings, courtesy of World Wisdom..

[11] *Treasures of Buddhism,* "Treasures of Buddhism", 8. (Translation: "I came, I saw, I was conquered.")

isolating a few features which are accented in Schuon's writings, paying most attention to his account of Hinduism for reasons foreshadowed above.

The Hindu Tradition

In the context of Schuon's work as a whole, three aspects of the Hindu tradition deserve particular attention: Vedantic metaphysics; the caste system and its typology of spiritual dispositions; and the four paths or yogas. Before proceeding it might be as well to note Schuon's caution that

> Hinduism, while it is organically linked with the *Upanishads*, is nonetheless not reducible to the Shivaite and Shankarian Vedantism, although this must be considered as the essence of the Vedanta and thus of Hindu tradition.[12]

Unlike the Christian perspective, "The Hindu perspective begins with Reality, not with man; the fall is one cosmic accident among thousands of others".[13] It envisages things "primarily in relation to divine principle",[14] which is to say that Hinduism is *primarily* a metaphysic rather than a spiritual method: it starts from a gnosis which is rooted in an unwavering discernment of the distinction between the Absolute and the relative, between *Atman* (or *Brahman*) and *maya*. This knowledge was revealed through the rishis of yore in the *Vedas*, and was most systematically and lucidly articulated in the *Upanishads*—the "end of the *Vedas*", Vedanta.

> The Vedanta stands out among explicit doctrines as one of the most direct formulations possible of what constitutes the very essence of our spiritual reality.... The Vedantic perspective finds its equivalents in the great religions which regulate humanity, for truth is one.[15]

The doctrine which governs the Vedanta and which is reaffirmed throughout the *Upanishads* is the identity of the Self (*Atman*) and Ultimate Reality (*Brahman*) which, insofar as it can be said to have attributes, is *Sat-Cit-Ananda* (Being-Consciousness-Bliss). The supreme goal, for man, is the realization of the Self; the surest path to this realization is *jnana* yoga, the way of knowledge. The world of space-time relativities is *maya*—from one point of point, illusion; from another, divine play (*lila*)—which both veils and discloses the Absolute, outside of which there is nothing:

[12] *Spiritual Perspectives and Human Facts*, "Vedanta", 99.

[13] *Spiritual Perspectives and Human Facts*, "Contours of the Spirit, 55.

[14] *Spiritual Perspectives and Human Facts*, "Contours of the Spirit, 58-59.

[15] *Spiritual Perspectives and Human Facts*, "Vedanta", 99.

There is nothing unrelated to this Reality; even the "object" which is least in conformity with it is still it, but "objectified" by *Maya*, the power of illusion, resulting from the infinity of the Self.[16]

Maya is at once light and darkness: as "divine art" it is light inasmuch as it reveals the secrets of *Atma*; it is darkness inasmuch as it hides *Atma*. As darkness it is "ignorance", *avidya*.[17]

Maya encompasses the whole of the manifested realms, not only the material and animic world: she is also "affirmed already *a fortiori* 'within' the Principle; the divine Principle 'desiring to be known'—or 'desiring to know'—condescends to the unfolding of its inward infinity, an unfolding at first potential and then outward or cosmic".[18] The Intellect is the microcosmic "crystallization" of *Atma* so that man may be "integrated within the subjective and thus returned to the divine Subject".[19] *Tat tvam asi*: That art thou.

A modern Hindu saint who is the very embodiment of the timeless truth of the Vedanta is Ramana Maharshi, of whom Schuon writes in these terms:

In Sri Ramana Maharshi one meets ancient and eternal India again. Vedantic truth—that of the *Upanishads*—is reduced to its simplest expression but without any betrayal: it is the simplicity inherent in the Real, not the artificial and quite external simplification that springs from ignorance.

The spiritual function that consists in an "action of presence" found its most rigorous expression in the Maharshi. In these latter days Sri Ramana was as it were the incarnation of what is primordial and incorruptible in India in opposition to modern activism; he manifested the nobility of contemplative "non-action" in opposition to an ethic of utilitarian agitation, and he showed the implacable beauty of pure truth in opposition to passions, weaknesses, betrayals.

The great question "Who am I?" appears in his case as the concrete expression of a "lived" reality, if one may put it this way, and this authenticity gives each word of the Maharshi a perfume of inimitable freshness—the perfume of Truth, which incarnates itself in the most immediate way.

The whole Vedanta is contained in Sri Ramana's question: "Who am I?" The answer is the Inexpressible.[20]

---

[16] *Spiritual Perspectives and Human Facts*, "Vedanta", 101-102.

[17] *Spiritual Perspectives and Human Facts*, "Vedanta", 105.

[18] *Light on the Ancient Worlds*, "Tracing *Maya*", 76.

[19] *Spiritual Perspectives and Human Facts*, "Vedanta", 102.

[20] *Spiritual Perspectives and Human Facts*, "The Vedanta", 129.

A more or less infallible litmus test of the modern mentality is the attitude to the Indian caste system, almost universally misunderstood and castigated in the West. We shall have more to say on this subject in a later chapter on spiritual anthropology, but a few general remarks here will not be out of place. It is of paramount importance to understand the principles which, on the one hand, give rise to caste systems such as we find within Hinduism, and on the other, elsewhere preclude them in favor of religious egalitarianism. The four *varnas* within the Hindu caste system, sanctioned by Scripture, are based on a division of man's understanding of the Real. The caste system, Schuon insists,

> is founded on the nature of things or, to be more exact, on one aspect of that nature, and thus on a reality which in certain circumstances cannot but manifest itself; this statement is equally valid as regards the opposite aspect, that of the equality of men before God. In short, in order to justify the system of castes it is enough to put the following question: does diversity of qualifications [spiritual and intellectual] and heredity exist? If it does, then the system of castes is both possible and legitimate. In the case of an absence of castes, where this is traditionally imposed, the sole question is: are men equal, not just from the point of view of their animality which is not in question, but from the point of view of their final end? Since every man has an immortal soul this is certain; therefore in a given traditional society this consideration can take precedence over that of diversity of qualifications. The immortality of the soul is the postulate of religious "egalitarianism", just as the quasi-divine character of the intellect—and hence of the intellectual elite—is the postulate of the caste system.[21]

Schuon goes on to elucidate some of the differences between the "leveling" outlook of Islam and Christianity (and one might here add Buddhism) and the hierarchical categories of the Hindu *varnas*, which identify those fundamental tendencies which divide men. For the moment all that needs to be further said is that the four levels of the caste hierarchy, and the two groupings "outside" (i.e. the *sannyasin* and the *chandala*), correspond with differing spiritual temperaments or dispositions, determined by the law of heredity which is so little understood in the modern West.

Hinduism is a primordial tradition which embraces a diversity of spiritual possibilities, "an uncommon wealth of doctrines and methods"[22]—to an even greater extent than many other traditions. We remember that the great spiritual universes centered on each of the integral traditions will provide, in one way or another, for the needs of all human types and for the

[21] *Language of the Self,* "The Meaning of Caste", 113.
[22] *Treasures of Buddhism,* "Originality of Buddhism", 19.

exigencies of the cyclic circumstances prevailing at the time—hence such phenomena as the "theistic" Buddhism to be found in the Pure Land schools of the Far East, and, by the same token, the "non-theism" which appears within theistic esoterism.[23] But even taking this principle into account, the Hindu tradition has been able to accommodate an extraordinary diversity. Truly Hinduism is a compendium of spiritual possibilities. As Martin Lings has observed:

> An advantage of Hinduism as a basis for the exposition of universal truth is the comprehensive breadth of its structure. On the one hand, like Judaism and Islam, it depends on direct revelation and makes a rigorous distinction between what is revealed and what is merely inspired. On the other hand, like Christianity, it depends on the *Avatara*, that is, the descent of the Divinity into this world.[24]

It is no surprise, then, that Hinduism should offer its adherents several pathways to *moksha* (liberation), the most pertinent of which are those of *jnana*, *bhakti*, and *karma* yoga—the ways of knowledge, devotion, and action (or work) respectively. *Jnana* yoga is the path of plenary esoterism, directed towards full realization of the Self, which comes from intellection. The spiritual disciplines of the *jnanin* are meditation, contemplative prayer, study, and various techniques and austerities which purify the mind, free it from the distractions of the ego, and release it from the bonds of ignorance so that the veil of *maya* becomes completely transparent and only the Real remains. This is the path to be followed by Brahmins, which is to say those blessed with an intelligence attuned to the Real. The path of *bhakti* harnesses man's will and his emotions and brings about a spiritual alchemy through devotion to one of the deities "personifying" *Brahman*, pre-eminently Shiva and Vishnu, or one of the *avataras*, amongst whom Krishna is the most popular and who extols the paths of both *bhakti* and *karma* yoga in one of India's most exalted Scriptures, the *Bhagavad Gita*.[25] *Karma* yoga is the way of action or work done in a spirit of selfless detachment and without any concern for the fruits thereof. Both *bhakti* and *karma* yoga offer a way

---

[23] See *Treasures of Buddhism*, "Originality of Buddhism", 17-20. Thomas Merton speaks of this tradition: "the Christian contemplative . . . is called mainly to penetrate the wordless darkness [void] and apophatic light of an experience beyond concepts, and here he gradually becomes familiar with a God who is 'absent' and as it were 'non-existent' to all human experience" (Merton quoted in W. Shannon, *Thomas Merton's Dark Path*, 11). See also T. Merton, *Contemplation in a World of Action*, 186.

[24] M. Lings, "The World of Today in the Light of Tradition", 196.

[25] Described so memorably by Emerson as "the first of books; it was as if an empire spoke to us, nothing small or unworthy, but large, serene, consistent, the voice of an old intelligence which in another age and climate had pondered over and disposed of the same questions which exercise us" (Quoted in E. Sharpe, *The Universal Gita*, 24).

which can be practiced by anyone, no matter how modest their intellectual endowments, and is thus suited to the majority of adherents, whilst *jnana* must remain the preserve of a spiritual elite, institutionalized in India in the caste of the Brahmins. *Raja* yoga is a system of psycho-spiritual techniques through which, under the guidance of a properly qualified guru, the psyche is cleansed and one is enabled to find in the *guha*, the innermost chamber of the heart, the supreme Self, "that great Purusha, of the color of the sun, beyond all darkness" (*Svetasvatara Upanishad*).

Buddhism

Schuon opens his book on Buddhism with these salutary remarks which, if heeded, will immediately erase many outlandish notions that have accumulated around this subject in the modern West:

> Whoever sets out to define a spiritual phenomenon situated in the still quasi-heavenly era of the great Revelations has to beware of assessing it according to the impoverishing categories of a later age or, still worse, those belonging to the completely profane "free-thinking" world. Buddhism . . . has in fact nothing to do with an ideology that is purely human and thus lacking any enlightening or saving quality. To deny the celestial character of Shakyamuni and his Message is after all tantamount to saying that there can be effects without a cause.[26]

This tradition's status, so to speak, is a subject which has caused untold confusion—amongst the adherents of the other religions, amongst those who champion atheism and agnosticism, amongst many Western converts, and even, in these later times, amongst practitioners within the Buddhist homelands whose thinking has been adulterated by modern influences. No doubt these misapprehensions arise from many different sources, but four are immediately apparent: firstly, from a Hindu viewpoint Buddhism presents itself as a heterodoxy; secondly, Buddhism is problematic from the viewpoint of any exoteric theism; thirdly, the spiritual methodology of Buddhism rests on the metaphysic of the Void, misunderstood as a kind of nihilism of which, it is thought, the doctrine of no soul (*anatma*) is another scandalous instance; lastly, many Westerners attracted to Buddhism, often unaware of its close affinities with the Christian tradition which they have rejected, laud it as "rational", "empirical", "scientific", "humanistic", and the like, and disavow its religious "trappings". Such folk often assert that Buddhism is a "way of life" or a "philosophy" rather than a "religion". What does Schuon say about these matters?

---

[26] *Treasures of Buddhism*, "Originality of Buddhism", 17.

On the question of Buddhism's relation to the Hindu tradition out of which it emerged:

> The first question to be asked concerning any doctrine or tradition is that of its intrinsic orthodoxy: that is to say one must know whether that tradition is consonant, not necessarily with another given tradition-ally orthodox perspective, but simply with Truth. As far as Buddhism is concerned, we will not ask therefore whether it agrees with the letter of the Veda or if its non-theism—and not "atheism"!—is reconcilable in its expression with Semitic theism or any other, but only whether Buddhism is true in itself; which means, if the answer is affirmative, that it will agree with the Vedic spirit and that its non-theism will express the Truth, or a sufficient and efficacious aspect of the Truth, whereof theism provides another possible expression, opportune in the world it governs.[27]

No doubt, from a certain viewpoint, Buddhism might be understood as a reaction against various excesses, corruptions, and degenerations within the Hindu tradition, just as Christianity can be seen as a reaction against Judaic legalism and pharisaism. But to think of the Buddha as a "reformer" is to misunderstand him and his message.[28] The Buddha is "renunciation, peace, mercy, and mystery", the last being "the essence of truth which cannot adequately be conveyed through language".[29]

On the vexed question of Buddhism's non-theism and its "negative" metaphysic, Schuon writes this:

> "Extinction" or "Voidness" is none other than Selfhood, a word which Buddhism, however, refrains from defining or even naming; the whole doctrine of *anatma* is calculated to prevent any conceptual and there-fore restrictive attribution being applied to the Divine Suchness which, being free from all otherness, alone is wholly Itself.[30]

Likewise:

> If Buddhism denies the outward, objective, and transcendent God, this is because it puts all its emphasis on the inward, subjective, and immanent Divinity—called *Nirvana* and *Adi-Buddha* as well as other

---

[27] *Treasures of Buddhism*, "Originality of Buddhism", 18.

[28] *Treasures of Buddhism*, "Originality of Buddhism", 17-18.

[29] *Art from the Sacred to the Profane*, "Far Eastern Art", 99.

[30] *In the Tracks of Buddhism*, "Some Facts and Fallacies Concerning Buddhism", 65. Elsewhere Schuon writes this: "No doubt, the Buddhist *Nirvana* is nothing other than the Self, *Atma*; but whereas for the Hindus the starting point is that reflection of the Self which is the 'I', for the Buddhists on the contrary the starting point is entirely negative and moreover purely empiri-cal: it is the *Samsara* as the world of suffering, and this world is merely a 'void', *shunya*" (*To Have a Center*, "David, Shankara, Honen", 135-136).

names—which moreover makes it impermissible to describe Buddhism as atheistic.[31]

Then again:

> If it be admitted that "the kingdom of Heaven is within you", there is no logical cause for reproaching Buddhism with conceiving the Divine Principle in this respect alone. The "Void" or "Extinction" is God—the supra-ontological Real and Being seen "inwardly"—within ourselves; not in our thought or in our ego, of course, but starting from that "geometrical point" within us whereby we are mysteriously attached to the Infinite.[32]

Buddhism's non-theism is one expression amongst many of the Truth:

> Buddhism, inasmuch as it is a characteristic perspective and independently of its various modes, answers to a necessity: it could not but come to be, given that a non-anthropomorphic, impersonal, and "static" consideration of the Infinite is in itself a possibility; such a perspective had therefore to be manifested at a cyclic moment and in human surroundings that rendered it opportune, for wherever the receptacle is, there the content imposes itself.[33]

Furthermore, Buddhism is "a 'Hinduism universalized', just as Christianity and Islam—each in its own way—are a Judaism rendered universal, hence detached from its particular ethnic environment and made accessible to men of all manner of racial origins".[34] Whilst it be true that Buddhism rests on a metaphysic which is in no essential way different from that of the Vedanta, it would be a grave mistake to infer that thereby it "does not represent as spontaneous and autonomous a reality as do the other great Revelations".[35] Concerning the well-known polemic of Shankara against Nagarjuna, Schuon says this:

> The antagonism between Shankara and Nagarjuna is of the same order as that between Ramanuja and Shankara, with this difference, however: when Shankara rejects the Nagarjunian doctrine, it is because its form corresponds—independently of its real content and spiritual

[31] *Esoterism as Principle and as Way*, "The Problem of Sexuality", 141.

[32] *Treasures of Buddhism*, "Originality of Buddhism", 22. "Buddhist 'atheism' consists in a refusal to objectivize or to exteriorize dogmatically the 'God within'." However it is also true, as Schuon points out, that "such an objectivizing does occur on occasion in a 'provisional' sense in the merciful message of *Amitabha*, but the very possibility of such an objectivizing proves precisely that Buddhism is in no way 'atheistic' in the privative sense of the word" (*Treasures of Buddhism*, "Originality of Buddhism", 22).

[33] *Treasures of Buddhism*, "Originality of Buddhism", 19.

[34] *Treasures of Buddhism*, "Originality of Buddhism", 19-20.

[35] *Treasures of Buddhism*, "Originality of Buddhism", 19.

potential—to a more restricted perspective than that of the Vedanta. When on the other hand Ramanuja rejects the Shankarian doctrine, it is for the opposite reason: the perspective of Shankara surpasses that of Ramanuja, not merely by its form, but in its very foundation.

In order truly to understand Nagarjuna, or the Mahayana in general, it is necessary to take account of two facts before everything else: first that Buddhism presents itself essentially as a spiritual method and therefore subordinates everything to the methodic point of view and second that this method is essentially one of negation.[36]

"Buddhism does not begin with the notion of the ego as do the religions of Semitic origin but with the wholly empirical reality of suffering".[37] Dialectically and methodically, it is founded on the experience of human suffering; it is a spiritual way directed to the cessation of such suffering:

> The doctrines of the Buddha are only "celestial mirages" intended to catch, as in the golden net, the greatest possible number of creatures plunged in ignorance, suffering, and transmigration, and . . . it is therefore the benefit of creatures and not the suchness of the Universe which determines the necessarily contingent form of the Message. . . . Buddhism, within the framework of its own wisdom, goes beyond the formal "mythology" or the "letter" and ultimately transcends all possible human formulations, thus realizing an unsurpassable contemplative disinterestedness as do the Vedanta, Taoism, and analogous doctrines.[38]

It follows that the wishful claims sometimes made by Orientalists and Western converts that Buddhism is simply a "philosophy" or "natural religion" are announcements that the persons in question are seeing Buddhism refracted through modern prejudices.

*   *   *

Buddhism comprises an immense spiritual universe in which we find an encyclopedic range of religious forms and practices, as is evident in the very different inflections given to the Buddha's saving message in the Theravada, Vajrayana, Zen, and Pure Land branches of the tradition. On these great branches and the various schools and sects contained therein, Schuon has written with characteristic percipience. These writings are all the more illuminating, and sometimes startling, given that Buddhism has received comparatively little attention within the perennialist school. As is well-known, Guénon himself for many years harbored the notion that Buddhism was no more than a Hindu heterodoxy until he was set right by Ananda Cooma-

---

[36] *Spiritual Perspectives and Human Facts*, "Vedanta", 109.
[37] *Spiritual Perspectives and Human Facts*, "Contours of the Spirit", 56.
[38] *Treasures of Buddhism*, "Christianity and Buddhism", 107-108.

raswamy and Marco Pallis, both of whom, after Schuon, the two foremost perennialist authorities on this tradition. Given the scope of the present work we cannot delve further into the treasure-house of Schuon's writings on Buddhism: they are there, awaiting the discerning reader searching for an exegesis commensurate with its subject.

Notes on Taoism and Shinto
The pre-Buddhist Chinese tradition, with its Confucian and Taoist branches, belongs to the traditional family of Mongoloid shamanism, as does Shintoism, each of these resting on doctrines of

> a complementary opposition of Heaven and earth and a cult of Nature, the latter being envisaged under the aspect of its essential causality and not of its existential accidentality; they are also distinguished by a certain parsimony in their eschatology.[39]

The religious heritage of China covered the Far East and included lands beyond the present national boundaries, encompassing ancestorism, shamanism, Taoism, and Confucianism, and later assimilating Buddhism and giving it a distinctive expression through the Ch'an/Zen and Pure Land schools. Rather than untangling this skein from either an historical or a doctrinal point of view, we will here confine ourselves to noting a few of Schuon's observations about Confucianism, which has stamped so many aspects of Chinese culture, and Taoism, the most metaphysical and mystical branch of the Chinese heritage.[40] These reflections will also illuminate, sometimes obliquely, other aspects of the whole tradition which will not come within our immediate purview.

As is so often the case, Schuon is able to condense the essential and distinctive features of a tradition into a short and decisive formulation which tells us more than a whole shelf of Orientalist tomes. In the case of Confucianism he starts from the outer social framework:

> Confucianism divides men into rulers and ruled. From the former it requires a sense of duty and from the latter filial piety. Here we see that the social Law is in no wise detached from the spiritual meaning

---

[39] *Feathered Sun*, "The Shamanism of the Red Indians", 22-23. This "parsimony", Schuon explains, derives from several factors, including the fact that the eschatological element is manifested in the cult of the emperor (and of heroes and ancestors), and the emphasis in warrior traditions on deeds rather than words. In this perspective "the act, as a decisive affirmation of the immortal person, seems almost sufficient unto itself; the act is the character and the character is salvation, in a certain sense" (*Treasures of Buddhism*, "The Meaning of Ancestors", 179).

[40] It was René Guénon who first made it perfectly clear to Western readers that these, far from being two different "religions", were complementary dimensions of a single tradition. See R. Guénon, "Taoism and Confucianism".

of the whole tradition; inevitably it has concomitant spiritual elements which concern man as such, that is, man envisaged independently from society.

This, it might be noted in passing, gives the lie to one of the most threadbare Western clichés about Confucianism—that it is no more than "a system of social ethics" which, we are told, performs a "conservative" ideological function in the Chinese social formation. But to return to Schuon's remarks:

> Indeed every man rules or determines something that is placed in some way in his keeping, even if it is only his own soul, which is made up of images and desires; on the other hand every man is governed or determined by something that in some way surpasses him, even if it is only his Intellect. Thus each man bears in himself the double obligation of duty in relation to the inferior and piety in relation to the superior, and this double principle lends itself to incalculable applications: it includes even inanimate nature in the sense that anything may serve—with regard to us and according to circumstances—as a celestial principle or as a terrestrial substance.
>
> Chinese wisdom foresees an application of the universal pair "Heaven-Earth" (*Tien-Ti*) that is first of all social and then personal, and thereby a conformation to the "Ineffable" (*Wu-Ming*) from which the pair proceeds. The point of connection between Confucianism and Taoism is in the virtues: Confucianism considers their social and human value and Taoism their intrinsic and spiritual quality. Man is the place where Heaven and Earth meet. Egoism must be extinguished between devotion and duty.[41]

The "Great Triad", or ternary, of Taoism, Heaven-Man-Earth (*Tien-Ti-Jen*), provides the scaffold for Taoist metaphysics, cosmology, and spiritual practice.

The ethnic genius of both the Chinese and the Japanese peoples finds one of its most distinctive expressions in the traditional art of the Far East, one which vibrates with those spiritual mysteries which lie beyond the reach of discursive thought and verbal formulation. Mystery may be revealed "in an illuminating flash through a symbol, such as a key word, a mystic sound, or an image whose suggestive action may be scarcely graspable"—so it is with the Zen *koans* which are "verbal symbols calculated to provoke an ontological breach in our carapace of ignorance", and with the "mysterious and transparent atmosphere of Taoist and Zen landscapes" which witness the fact that "no peoples have been more successful in visualizing the mystery of things".[42]

---

[41] *Spiritual Perspectives and Human Facts*, "Contours of the Spirit", 62-63.
[42] *Art from the Sacred to the Profane*, "Far Eastern Art", 99.

Far-Eastern painting has an aerial grace, the inimitable charm of a fur-
tive and precious vision; by compensation, the terrifying presence of
dragons, genii, and demons adds to the art of the Far East a dynamic
and flamboyant element.[43]

Taoist landscape paintings "exteriorize a metaphysic and a contemplative
state: they spring, not from space, but from the 'void'", and constitute "one
of the most powerfully original forms of sacred art".[44]

It only remains to make a few fragmentary but suggestive remarks about
Shinto, the mythological and shamanistic tradition indigenous to Japan.
Firstly, it is as well to banish the common error of supposing that Shinto
ancestorism replaced the Divinity with the ancestors, which overlooks the
fact that "the Divinity itself is conceived in the Far East as a kind of Ancestor,
and one's human ancestors are like a prolongation of the Divinity".[45] It is
for this reason that "the ancestor is at once the origin and the spiritual or
moral norm":

> He is, for his descendants, the essential personality, that is to say the
> substance of which they are like the accidents; and piety consists
> precisely in viewing him thus and in seeing in him but the bridge con-
> necting them—his descendants—with the Divine. . . . Ancestors are the
> human imprints of angelic substances and, for that reason, also of divine
> Qualities; to be true to them is to be true to God.[46]

The cult of the Emperor is a particular expression of the same principle.

The spiritual affinities between Shinto and other forms of "Hyperborean
Shamanism" are evident in "many mythological, and even vestimentary similarities", in the cult of Nature, and in "their thirst for freedom, their contempt for luxury, their taciturnness and other similar characteristics"[47]—the
comparisons with the American Indians are too obvious to need laboring.
These affinities also go to explain why Shinto was so easily able to assimilate
Far Eastern forms of Buddhism (especially the ideal of the *Bodhisattva*), also
remembering that "The passage from one Asiatic tradition to another—Hinduism, Buddhism, Taoism—is a small thing, seeing that the metaphysical
content is everywhere clearly apparent".[48]

---

[43] *Art from the Sacred to the Profane*, "Far Eastern Art", 101.
[44] *Art from the Sacred to the Profane*, "Far Eastern Art", 103.
[45] *Treasures of Buddhism*, "The Meaning of Ancestors", 173.
[46] *Treasures of Buddhism*, "The Meaning of Ancestors", 176.
[47] *Treasures of Buddhism*, "The Meaning of Ancestors", 177.
[48] *In the Tracks of Buddhism*, "Science, Myth, and the Meaning of the Ancestors", 82.

9

Beauty, Symbolism, Art

Sacred art is the form of the Supra-formal, it is the image of the Uncreate, the language of Silence.[1]

The sense of the sacred is the innate consciousness of the presence of God: it is to feel this presence sacramentally in symbols and ontologically in all things.[2]

The foundations of art lie in the spirit, in metaphysical, theological, and mystical knowledge, not in knowledge of the craft alone nor yet in genius.[3]

Traditional art derives from a creativity which combines heavenly inspiration with ethnic genius, and which does so in the manner of a science endowed with rules and not by way of individual improvisation; *ars sine scientia nihil.*[4]

Schuon has elaborated the principles which inform an "integral aesthetics", that is, "a science that takes account not only of sensible beauty but also of the spiritual foundations of this beauty, these foundations explaining the frequent connection between the arts and initiatic methods".[5] Furthermore, Schuon's work on sacred art is distinguished (in both senses of the word) by an immediate and intuitive understanding of the role of beauty in the "interiorizing alchemy" of the soul. If Coomaraswamy's insights were largely the result of a prodigious scholarship, guided by the metaphysical principles transmitted by Guénon, Schuon's writings on sacred art attest to a direct and spontaneous apprehension of a very rare kind. Of Schuon's singular ability to penetrate visible forms, Titus Burckhardt has remarked:

> At the moment of sanctity a saint is given a special gift. In the case of Schuon, this gift was the "discernment of forms". He has the ability to look at a piece of clothing or an artifact from a culture and know everything about that culture. He sees the archetypes inherent in all

---

[1] *Art from the Sacred to the Profane,* "Principles and Criteria of Art", 4-5. Cf. a formulation by Walter Andrae quoted in A. Coomaraswamy, *"Ars Sine Scientia Nihil"* in *Selected Papers 1,* 231.

[2] *From the Divine to the Human,* "The Sense of the Sacred", 104.

[3] *Art from the Sacred to the Profane,* "Principles and Criteria of Art, 11.

[4] *Art from the Sacred to the Profane,* "Principles and Criteria of Art", 5.

[5] *Esoterism as Principle and as Way,* "Foundations of an Integral Aesthetics", 177.

things and immediately understands the essence of the form and the entire culture from which it came.[1]

Patrick Laude observes that "If sapiential intelligence is the directing principle of Schuon's work, beauty is its main mode of manifestation and assimilation. Beauty is the language of Truth as the Word is the language of Being. It pervades the entire spiritual universe that Schuon outlines in his books."[2] Laude points out that Beauty itself entails three dimensions, which he associates with the Vedantic ternary of *Sat-Cit-Ananda*, each readily apparent in the life, teaching, and handiwork of Schuon: "a doctrine of Beauty which pertains to the domain of metaphysical consciousness" (*Cit*); "a methodical and spiritual awareness of the beautiful as a means of grace" (*Sat*); "a creative joy, a dimension of beatitude (*Ananda*), which is expressed by [Schuon's] poetical and pictorial productions and by a contemplative receptivity to feminine beauty as a privileged mirror of the Divine".[3] In this chapter we will provide a rudimentary account of traditional understandings of sacred art and symbolism, drawing on Schuon's work but also paying some attention to the work of other perennialists.

Archetypes

In former times the doctrine of archetypes was espoused the world over. No integral tradition has been able to do without it, though the language in which it is clothed may speak not of archetypes but of "essences", "universals", "Divine Ideas" and so on. Plato gave the doctrine its definitive European expression, but there is nothing peculiarly Occidental about it as such.[4] It lies at the root of all traditional art. Consider the following sample of suggestive quotations:

> A form is made in the resigned will according to the platform or model of eternity, as it was known in the glass of God's eternal wisdom before the times of this world. (*Jacob Boehme*)[5]

[1] From an interview with Titus Burckhardt, transmitted by Michael Fitzgerald and quoted in J-B. Aymard and P. Laude, *Frithjof Schuon: Life and Teachings*, 179n.
[2] J-B. Aymard and P. Laude, *Frithjof Schuon: Life and Teachings*, 125.
[3] J-B. Aymard and P. Laude, *Frithjof Schuon: Life and Teachings*, 108. For those interested in detailed commentaries on the place of beauty, symbolism, and sacred art in Schuon's work, see chapter 4 of the work just cited and Michael Fitzgerald, "Beauty and the Sense of the Sacred: Schuon's Antidote to the Modern World". Most of Schuon's extended writings on sacred art are gathered together in *Art from the Sacred to the Profane*.
[4] "Archetypes" have come to be associated in the popular mind with the theorizations of Carl Jung. It should be noted that Jung's ideas do not constitute a metaphysical doctrine but, at best, a precarious hypothesis about certain psychic phenomena.
[5] Boehme (Christian theosophist, 1575-1624), quoted in W. Perry (ed.), *A Treasury of Traditional Wisdom*, 671.

All forms of being in this corporeal world are images of pure Lights, which exist in the spiritual world. (*Suhrawardi*)[6]

The Sages have been taught of God that this natural world is only an image and material copy of a heavenly and spiritual pattern; that the very existence of this world is based upon the reality of its celestial archetype. (*Sendivogius*)[7]

Crazy Horse dreamed and went out into the world where there is nothing but the spirits of things. That is the real world that is behind this one, and everything we see here is something like a shadow from that world. (*Black Elk*)[8]

Things in every instance involve universals. . . . If there were no universals, things could not be described as "things". (*Kung-sun Lung*)[9]

Formulations of this kind could be multiplied more or less indefinitely but their burden is clear enough. Meister Eckhart provided a concise statement of the doctrine in writing, "form is a revelation of essence".[10] Everything that exists, whatever its modality, necessarily participates in universal principles which are uncreated and immutable essences contained, in Guénon's words, in "the permanent actuality of the Divine Intellect". Consequently, all phenomena, no matter how ephemeral or contingent, "translate" or "represent" these principles in their own fashion and at their own level of existence.[11] Without participation in the immutable, they would "purely and simply be nothing".[12] Sacred art expresses the essence in the form, and "art in the broadest sense is the crystallization of archetypal values".[13] It is for this reason that Schuon writes:

---

[6] Suhrawardi (twelfth century Sufi philosopher of Aleppo), quoted in W. Perry (ed.), *A Treasury of Traditional Wisdom*, 673.

[7] Sendivogius (seventeenth century Moravian alchemist), quoted in W. Perry (ed.), *A Treasury of Traditional Wisdom*, 672.

[8] Black Elk, quoted in J. Neihardt, *Black Elk Speaks*, 67.

[9] Kung-sun Lung (third century BC Chinese philosopher), quoted in W. Perry (ed.), *A Treasury of Traditional Wisdom*, 670.

[10] Eckhart, quoted in W. Perry (ed.), *A Treasury of Traditional Wisdom*, 673. For an exposition of Eckhart's view of art, see A. Coomaraswamy, *The Transformation of Nature in Art*, 59-96.

[11] As one of Schuon's followers has written, "if a world did not cast down shadows from above, the worlds below it would vanish altogether, since each world in creation is no more than a tissue of shadows entirely dependent on the archetypes in the world above" (Abu Bakr Siraj ad-Din, *The Book of Certainty*, 50). This book gives an account of the doctrine of archetypes and of the multiple states of being from a Sufic perspective.

[12] R. Guénon, *Spiritual Authority and Temporal Power*, quoted in W. Perry (ed.), *A Treasury of Traditional Wisdom*, 302.

[13] *To Have a Center*, "To Have a Center", 30. A contemporary Buddhist stated the principle precisely: "If we look at the world with . . . the eyes of the spirit we shall discover that the simplest material object, nay anything that is formed, be it by man or by nature, is a symbol,

True aesthetics is nothing other than the science of forms; hence its aim is the objective, the real, not subjectivity as such. Forms, intellections: the whole of traditional art is founded upon this correspondence.[14]

The doctrine of archetypes implies the multiple and hierarchic states of being which have been discussed previously. Moreover, the fact that natural forms necessarily participate in the higher orders of Reality confers on them a sacred quality. Sacred art, somewhat paradoxically, brings Essence and form together:

> On the plane of spiritual values no two things are more divergent than wisdom, which is inward, and art, which is outward; between them is all the distance separating essence and form. Yet "extremes meet" and nothing is closer to wisdom and sanctity than sacred art . . . which explains the value, in no way disproportionate, that traditional civilizations attach to these disciplines.[15]

Symbolism

The analogies between the archetypes or "Divine Ideas"—which "represent uniquely perfections and totalities, and not privative and hence fragmentary manifestations"[16]—and the transitory material forms of "this dream-veil world", as Schuon calls it, give to phenomena certain *qualitative* significances which render them symbolic expressions of higher realities.[17] The world is a "fabric of theophanies":

> When perceiving a sign-proof of the divine Principle, the contemplative mentality has two spontaneous reactions, namely essentialization and interiorization, the first being objective, and the second subjective: through the first, man sees in the sign or quality that which is essential—the divine intention if one will—whereas through the second, he finds the sign or quality in his own soul; on the one hand "unto the pure all things are pure"; on the other, "the kingdom of God is within you." The first reaction refers to transcendence, and the second to immanence, although transcendence too relates to what we bear within ourselves, and although immanence also exists outside ourselves.

a glyph of a higher reality and a deeper relationship of universal and individual forces" (A. Govinda, *Creative Meditation and Multi-Dimensional Consciousness*, 102). The same idea is implicit in Mircea Eliade's claim that *homo religiosus* is also, necessarily, *homo symbolicus*; see M. Eliade, "Methodological Remarks on the Study of Religious Symbolism", 95.

[14] *Spiritual Perspectives and Human Facts*,"Aesthetics and Symbolism in Art and Nature", 23.
15 *Art from the Sacred to the Profane*, "Sacred Art", 36.

[16] *Logic and Transcendence*, "Rationalism, Real and Apparent", 54.

[17] As S.H. Nasr states, "To understand symbols is to accept the hierarchic structure of the Universe and the multiple states of being" (*Sufi Essays*, 88). See also G. Eaton, *The Richest Vein*, 186ff and M. Pallis, *A Buddhist Spectrum*, 144-163.

Thus, we live in a fabric of theophanies of which we are a part; to exist is to be a symbol; wisdom is to perceive the symbolism of things.[18]

A symbol may be defined as a reality of a lower order which participates analogically in a reality of a higher order of being. Therefore, a properly constituted symbolism rests on the inherent and objective qualities of phenomena and their relationship to spiritual realities: the symbol partakes of the reality which is its referent, allowing the direct communication of higher truths.

> Man needs beauty and he also needs symbolism. It is not enough to think about metaphysics, one wants also to see and to hear metaphysics in visible forms and this is symbolism.[19]

This is vital in any consideration of sacred art which, in a sense, is not separate from the reality to which it gives access and which it manifests on a particular plane, for "the function of every symbol is to break the shell of forgetfulness that screens the knowledge immanent in the Intellect".[20]

The science of symbolism is a rigorous discipline which can only proceed through a discernment of the *qualitative* significances of substances, colors, forms, spatial relationships and so on. Symbolism derives from "the ontological reality of things"[21] and not from any arbitrary cultural fashion or subjective impulse. Symbolic significances cannot be invented or imputed:

> It is not a question here of subjective appreciations, for cosmic qualities are ordered toward Being and are in keeping with a hierarchy that is more real than the individual; hence they are independent of our tastes.[22]

Traditional symbolism, then, is an objective language which is conceived not according to the impulses of individual or collective "taste" but in confor-

---

[18] *Roots of the Human Condition*, "Traces of Being, Proofs of God", 57-58. Schuon continues: "And perhaps we ought to recall here the distinction between a symbolism that is direct, concrete, and evident, and another that—while being traditional—is indirect and more or less arbitrary with respect to formal adequacy, which precisely it does not have in view. Direct symbolism 'manifests' the reality symbolized, whereas indirect symbolism merely 'indicates' a fragmentary, contingent, or accidental aspect of the image chosen. From another vantage point, we would say that the worship of symbols must obey sacramental rules: to worship the sun in place of God is one thing; to be aware of its spiritual emanation, and to know how to impregnate oneself with it ritually, is another."

[19] Schuon interview, cited in *Frithjof Schuon: Messenger of the Perennial Philosophy*, xxxi.

[20] *Esoterism as Principle and as Way*, "Introduction", 11. See also *Spiritual Perspectives and Human Facts*, "Aesthetics and Symbolism in Art and Nature", 39.

[21] S.H. Nasr, *Sufi Essays*, 88.

[22] *Gnosis: Divine Wisdom*, "Seeing God Everywhere", 90.

mity with the nature of things. Traditional symbolism takes account not only of "sensible beauty" but of *"the spiritual foundations of this beauty"*.[23] This means that

> the foundations of art lie in the spirit, in metaphysical, theological, and mystical knowledge, not in the knowledge of the craft alone nor yet in genius, for this may be just anything. . . . Art is an activity, an exteriorization, and thus depends on a knowledge that transcends it and gives it order; apart from such knowledge, art has no justification: it is knowledge which determines action, manifestation, form, and not the reverse.[24]

It follows that "'Truth' in art can by no means be reduced to the subjective veracity of the artist but resides first and foremost in the objective truth of forms, colors, materials."[25] It is hardly surprising that "One of the major errors of modern art is its confusion of art materials: people no longer know how to distinguish the cosmic significance of stone, iron, or wood, just as they do not know the objective qualities of forms and colors".[26]

The science of symbolism is a kind of objective analogue of the gift of "seeing God everywhere", that is, the awareness of the transparency of phenomena and of the transcendent dimension which is present in every cosmic situation.[27] Ramakrishna, who could fall into ecstasy at the sight of a lion, a bird, a dancing girl, exemplified this gift, though in his case, Schuon adds, it was not a matter of deciphering the symbolism but of "tasting the essences".[28] Mircea Eliade, approaching the whole question from a different angle, has noted how, for *homo religiosus*, everything in nature is capable of revealing itself as a "cosmic sacrality", as a hierophany. He also observes that for our secular age the cosmos has become "opaque, inert, mute; it transmits no message, it holds no cipher".[29]

The universality of certain recurrent symbols is adequately explained by the principles which have been under discussion. It is quite unnecessary to resort to fanciful diffusionist theories to explain this phenomenon.[30] In

---

[23] *Esoterism as Principle and as Way*, "Foundations of an Integral Aesthetics", 177 (italics mine). See also B. Keeble, "Tradition, Intelligence, and the Artist", 240-241.

[24] *Art from the Sacred to the Profane*, "Principles and Criteria of Art", 11.

[25] *Spiritual Perspectives and Human Facts*, "Aesthetics and Symbolism in Art and Nature", 30.

[26] *Art from the Sacred to the Profane*, "Naturalistic Art", 47.

[27] See *Gnosis: Divine Wisdom*, "Seeing God Everywhere", 87-100.

[28] *Esoterism as Principle and as Way*, "Foundations of an Integral Aesthetics", 182n.

[29] M. Eliade, *The Sacred and the Profane*, 12, 178.

[30] W.J. Perry's once-popular pan-Egyptian hypothesis, now thoroughly discredited, is a conspicuous example of looking for the key to a universal symbolism in the wrong place. Perry's principal works were *The Origin of Magic and Religion* (1923) and *The Primordial Ocean*

general, such theories do little more than unwittingly pile up material evidence of the existence of a universal symbolism.[31] The study of symbolism has also in recent times been much influenced by the work of Carl Jung. All that need be said here is that there is much that is illuminating in Jung's researches provided one is not seduced by the temptation to reduce the provenance and field of symbolism to a purely psychic level where symbols must take on something of a fugitive and phantasmic nature. Psychism of this kind is always infra-intellectual and thus anti-spiritual.[32]

Truth, Goodness, and Beauty in Sacred Art

The doctrine of archetypes and the attendant understanding of symbolism form the foundation of traditional theories of art and of the art itself. We perceive in the sacred art of normal civilizations a recurrent set of principles, functions, and characteristics which vary in their material applications and expressions, but which are everywhere fundamentally the same. Firstly there is the intimate nexus between the ideals of Truth, Goodness, and Beauty. The inter-relationships of the three are inexhaustible and there is no end to what might be said on this subject, starting with Plato's immortal declaration that "Beauty is the splendor of Truth". Marsilio Ficino, the Renaissance Platonist, defined beauty as "that ray which, parting from the visage of God, penetrates into all things".[33] Beauty, in most canons, has this divine quality. It is a manifestation of the Infinite on a finite plane and so introduces something of the Absolute into the world of relativities. Its sacred character "confers on perishable things a texture of eternity".[34]

> The archetype of Beauty, or its Divine model, is the superabundance and equilibrium of the Divine qualities, and at the same time the overflowing of the existential potentialities in pure Being. . . . Thus beauty always manifests a reality of love, of deployment, of illimitation, of equilibrium, of beatitude, of generosity.[35]

(1935). It might also be noted that even when a diffusionist theory may have some limited historical validity, tracing the spatio-temporal genealogy of a particular symbol and explaining its metaphysical and cosmological significance are two quite different matters. See M. Eliade, "Methodological Remarks on the Study of Religious Symbolism", 93.

[31] See G. Eaton, *The Richest Vein*, 187.

[32] See letter from Frithjof Schuon to Titus Burckhardt, reproduced in T. Burckhardt, "Cosmology and Modern Science" in *The Sword of Gnosis*, ed. J. Needleman, 177. See also Burckhardt's discussion of Jung in the same essay, 167-178. For other critiques, from a traditionalist point of view, see P. Sherrard: "An Introduction to the Religious Thought of C. G. Jung"; H. Oldmeadow, *Mircea Eliade and Carl Jung: "Priests Without Surplices"?*. See also P. Novak, "C.G. Jung in the Light of Asian Philosophy".

[33] Quoted in R.J. Clements, *Michelangelo's Theory of Art*, 5.

[34] *Understanding Islam*, "The Koran", 45.

[35] *Logic and Transcendence*, "Truths and Errors Concerning Beauty", 241. For some traditional

Likewise, "Beauty is a crystallization of a certain aspect of universal joy; it is a limitlessness expressed by a limit."[36] Beauty is distinct but not separate from truth and virtue. As Aquinas affirmed, beauty relates to the cognitive faculty and is thus connected with wisdom.[37] The rapport between beauty and virtue allows one to say that they are but two faces of the one reality: "goodness is internal beauty, and beauty is external goodness" or, similarly, "virtue is the beauty of the soul as beauty is the virtue of forms".[38] The relationships of beauty, truth, and goodness explain why, in the Oriental traditions, every *avatara* embodies a perfection of Beauty. It is said of the Buddhas that they save not only by their doctrine but by their superhuman beauty. As Schuon notes, "the name *Shunyamurti*—'manifestation of the void'—applied to a Buddha, is full of significance".[39]

Schuon gathers together some of these principles in the following passage:

> The earthly function of beauty is to actualize in the intelligent creature the Platonic recollection of the archetypes. . . . There is a *distinguo* to make, in the sensing of the beautiful, between the aesthetic sensation and the corresponding beauty of soul, namely such and such a virtue. Beyond every question of "sensible consolation" the message of beauty is both intellectual and moral: intellectual because it communicates to us, in the world of accidentality, aspects of Substance, without for all that having to address itself to abstract thought; and moral, because it reminds us of what we must love, and consequently be.[40]

This passage, so alien to any modern aesthetic, equips us with the conceptual tools to understand the nature of sacred art which, as Schuon reminds us, is an *indispensable* part of every religious tradition. He refers to

> The *obligatory* role played by the aesthetic quality in *every* traditional civilization: no religion is situated outside Beauty, *every* religion expresses itself through it; *every* traditional world is a world of Beauty, and this proves Beauty's interiorizing virtue.[41]

---

formulations on Beauty, see W. Perry (ed.), *A Treasury of Traditional Wisdom*, 659-670.

[36] *Spiritual Perspectives and Human Facts*, "Aesthetics and Symbolism in Art and Nature", 25.

[37] See A. Coomaraswamy, "The Mediaeval Theory of Beauty" in *Selected Papers 1*, 211-220, and two essays, "Beauty and Truth" and "Why Exhibit Works of Art?" in *Christian and Oriental Philosophy of Art*, 7-22 (esp. 16-18) and 102-109.

[38] *Logic and Transcendence*, "Truths and Errors Concerning Beauty", 245-246. See also *Esoterism as Principle and as Way*, "The Triple Nature of Man", 95.

[39] *Spiritual Perspectives and Human Facts*, "Aesthetics and Symbolism in Art and Nature", 24n. See also *Treasures of Buddhism*, "Treasures of Buddhism", 8.

[40] *Esoterism as Principle and as Way*, "Foundations of an Integral Aesthetics", 178-179.

[41] Frithjof Schuon, quoted in *Frithjof Schuon: Messenger of the Perennial Philosophy*, xxxi (ital-

Now, what does Schuon mean by "sacred art"? The question is best answered, perhaps, by one of his ruminations on the term "sacred":

> What then is the sacred in relation to the world? It is the interference of the uncreate in the created, of the eternal in time, of the infinite in space, of the supraformal in forms; it is the mysterious introduction into one realm of existence of a presence which in reality contains and transcends that realm and could cause it to burst asunder in a sort of divine explosion. The sacred is the incommensurable, the transcendent, hidden within a fragile form belonging to this world; it has its own precise rules, its fearful aspects, and its merciful qualities; moreover any violation of the sacred, even in art, has incalculable repercussions. Intrinsically the sacred is inviolable, and so much so that any attempted violation recoils on the head of the violator.[42]

So, sacred art is that which symbolically renders visible (or audible) that which is "incommensurable" and "transcendent": "sacred art is the form of the Supraformal, it is the image of the Uncreate, the language of Silence".[43] All religious art in the traditional worlds was obviously sacred in this sense: "Sacred art is first of all the visible and audible form of Revelation and then also its indispensable liturgical vesture."[44] However, as Schuon and Coomaraswamy both note, in a traditional society there can be no profane art, properly speaking, but rather what might be called "extra-liturgical" art—the making of mundane implements and utensils, for example, or the vestimentary arts.[45] Indeed, "In primordial periods art always was limited to either objects of ritual use or working tools and household objects, but even such tools and objects were, like the activities they implied, eminently symbolical and so connected with ritual and with the realm of the sacred."[46] It is only in the post-medieval world that we find an "art" which is completely profane, which is to say, altogether cut off from the sacred.

Beauty can be either an open or a closed door: when it is identified only with its earthly support it leaves man vulnerable to idolatry; it brings man closer to God when he "perceive[s] in it the vibrations of Beatitude and Infinity, which emanate from Divine Beauty".[47] The "ambiguous" nature of Beauty is precisely the ambiguity of *maya*:

---

ics mine).

[42] *Art from the Sacred to the Profane*, "Principles and Criteria of Art", 4.

[43] *Art from the Sacred to the Profane*, "Principles and Criteria of Art", 4-5.

[44] *Art from the Sacred to the Profane*, "Sacred Art", 33.

[45] See *Esoterism as Principle and as Way*, "The Degrees of Art", 183-186. On the distinction between traditional and sacred art, see also S.H. Nasr, *Knowledge and the Sacred*, 275n.

[46] *Art from the Sacred to the Profane*, "Principles and Criteria of Art", 3.

[47] *Esoterism as Principle and as Way*, "Foundations of an Integral Aesthetics", 182.

Just as the principle of manifestation and illusion both separates from the Creator and leads back to Him, so earthly beauties, including those of art, can favor worldliness as well as spirituality, which explains the diametrically opposed attitudes of the saints towards art in general or a given art in particular.[48]

As an accessory to wisdom, sacred art takes account of the fact that intellectual certitude depends not on the ability to give an exhaustive account of the external characteristics of phenomena, but on the discernment of their essences.[49] Lama Govinda, drawing on the traditional Tibetan conception of art, affirms the same principle in writing: "while using the forms of the external world, [art] does not try to imitate nature, but to reveal a higher reality by omitting all accidentals, thus raising the visible form to the value of a symbol."[50] Thomas Merton alerts us to the dangers of a naturalism which now obtrudes on the liturgy of the post-Vatican II Roman Church, and contrasts it with a properly constituted symbolism:

> Symbolism fortifies and concentrates the spirit of prayer, but illustration [i.e., naturalism] tends rather to weaken and dissipate our attention. Symbolism acts as a very efficacious spiritual medium. It opens the way to an intuitive understanding of mystery—it places us in the presence of the invisible. Illustration tends rather to become an obstacle, to divert and to amuse rather than to elevate and direct. It tends to take the place of the invisible and to obscure it.[51]

Sacred art fulfils functions of incalculable importance in a traditional civilization: it "is indispensable as a support for the intelligence of the collectivity".[52] Bypassing the pitfalls of abstract thought, traditional art is accessible to the humblest mentality in evoking a sense of the sacred. "Sacred art helps man to find his own center, that kernel whose nature is to love God".[53] This miraculous quality derives from Beauty itself:

> Beauty is like the sun: it acts without detours, without dialectical intermediaries, its ways are free, direct, incalculable; like love, to which it is closely connected, it can heal, unloose, appease, unite, or deliver through its simple radiance.[54]

---

[48] *Art from the Sacred to the Profane*, "On Beauty and the Sense of the Sacred", 21.

[49] See B. Keeble, "Tradition, Intelligence, and the Artist", 242. The attempt to give an exhaustive account of the external characteristics of phenomena is, of course, precisely the aim of modern science.

[50] A. Govinda, *Creative Meditation and Multi-Dimensional Consciousness*, 152.

[51] T. Merton, "Absurdity in Sacred Decoration", in *Disputed Questions*, 251.

[52] *Art from the Sacred to the Profane*, "Principles and Criteria of Art", 9.

[53] *Art from the Sacred to the Profane*, "Sacred Art", 37.

[54] *Treasures of Buddhism*, "Treasures of Buddhism", 7.

Through its symbolism such art addresses itself to the whole person rather than to the mind alone and thereby helps to actualize the teachings of the tradition in question. We need to remember that "The cathedral is as much an exposition of medieval Christianity as the *Summa* of Thomas Aquinas".[55] It is also worth remarking that the need for sacred art becomes more imperative as tradition "moves" further away from its origin (i.e. Revelation). Whilst "the Desert Fathers had no need of colonnades and stained glass windows",[56] man's "increasing weakness, and therewith the risk of forgetfulness and betrayal" obliged Christianity "to exteriorize and to make explicit things that were at the beginning included in an inward and implicit perfection". Likewise:

> Saint Paul needed neither Thomism nor Cathedrals, for all profundities and splendors were within himself and all around him in the sanctity of the early community. . . . More or less late epochs—the Middle Ages, for example—are faced with an imperious need for exteriorizations and developments . . . not to change that patrimony, but to transmit it as integrally and as effectively as possible.[57]

Arts and Crafts

Traditional arts are marked by their objectivity: they are constituted by elements prescribed by tradition according to a set of principles and rules. In a traditional society it matters not whether one is fashioning a water container, painting an icon or a *thanka*, or designing a stained glass window, whether one is painter, potter, or smith: in each case the artisan works under the creative constraints, if one might so express it, of tradition. These constraints are all the more exacting in the domain of religious art as such. Here we might recall the stipulation of the Second Council of Nicea:

> Art [the integral perfection of the work] alone belongs to the painter, while ordinance [the choice of subject] and disposition [the treatment of the subject from the symbolical as well as the technical and material points of view] belongs to the Fathers.[58]

Sacred art formed part of the Christian liturgy and could not therefore be left to any arbitrary impulses. Like any true religious art it had to be sacred in content, symbolic in detail, and hieratic in treatment. These "restraints" conferred qualities of depth and power such as the individual artist could

---

[55] C. Morey, *Christian Art* (1935), quoted in A. Coomaraswamy, *Christian and Oriental Philosophy of Art*, 104.

[56] *Art from the Sacred to the Profane*, "Sacred Art", 35.

[57] *Art from the Sacred to the Profane*, "Christian Art", 55.

[58] Quoted in *Transcendent Unity of Religions*, "Concerning Forms in Art", 75 (interpolations are Schuon's).

not have drawn out of purely personal resources.[59] The anonymity of the traditional artist also testifies to the subordination of individual tastes and impulses to the dictates of tradition.

The notion of "art for art's sake" is inconceivable in a traditional context where art, of whatever kind, is always directed to a use—spiritual or mundane, often both. The modern distinction between the beautiful and the useful could not flourish in a traditional climate. In the case of sacred art the uses are spiritual, realized through a symbolic language. But no traditional art is produced merely for the gratification of the senses: St. Augustine voiced the traditional view when he dismissed as a "madness" the idea that any art worthy of the name could have no other purpose than to please.[60] In the same vein Schuon writes that "the purpose of art is not *a priori* to induce aesthetic emotions, but to transmit, together with these, a more or less direct spiritual message".[61] Furthermore:

> Apart from their intrinsic qualities forms of art correspond to a strict utility. In order that spiritual influences may be able to manifest without encumbrance they have need of a formal setting which corresponds to them analogically. . . . In the soul of a holy man they can shine in spite of everything, but not everyone is a saint and a sanctuary is made to facilitate resonances of the spirit, not to impede them. Sacred art . . . is made at the same time for God, for angels, and for man; profane art on the other hand exists only for man and by that fact betrays him.[62]

If we move from sacred art as such to the arts and crafts of everyday life we can see that in traditional societies they always serve a double purpose: that of immediate physical utility, and secondly, a spiritual function (which may or may not be didactic). The relationship of utility and symbolic significance is obvious enough in much religious art—in ritual supports for example. The sacred pipe of the American Indians furnishes an instance of an apparently simple and useful artifact carrying a whole complex of ritualistic and symbolic significances.[63] So much so that one might say that the entire doctrine of the Plains Indians is condensed in the Calumet, which is the vehicle for metaphysical, cosmological, and anthropological messages. However, the symbolic vocabulary of more mundane arts and crafts often

[59] See *Language of the Self*, "Principles and Criteria of Art", 84, and *Spiritual Perspectives and Human Facts*, "Aesthetics and Symbolism in Art and Nature", 36-37. See also S.H. Nasr, *Knowledge and the Sacred*, 254.
[60] See A. Coomaraswamy, *Christian and Oriental Philosophy of Art*, 108-109.
[61] *Logic and Transcendence*, "The Saint and the Divine Image", 232.
[62] *Spiritual Perspectives and Human Facts* (1969), "Aesthetics and Symbolism in Art and Nature", 28-29.
[63] See J.E. Brown, *The Sacred Pipe* (1971), 6-9.

escapes the modern eye, jaundiced as it is in favor of narrow aesthetic and sentimental considerations to the exclusion of everything else. "The purpose of art of every kind", Schuon insists, "is to create a climate and forge a mentality. . . . In the beginning, nothing was profane: each tool was a symbol, and even decoration was symbolistic and sacral."[64] Schuon has written extensively not only about the glories of religious art but about art in its manifold forms—in habitation, dress, and furniture, for instance, or in the plastic arts of architecture and dance, in music and poetry.[65] Schuon and other perennialists have repeatedly disclosed the ways in which any and every traditional civilization, including its arts and crafts, is permeated with a sense of the sacred and with spiritual resonances.[66]

The initiatic and esoteric possibilities of traditional arts, crafts, and sciences warrant a few brief remarks. A principle often invoked by Coomaraswamy and Schuon is *ars sine scientia nihil* (art without science is nothing). These were the words of the Parisian Master, Jean Mignot, directed during the building of the Cathedral of Milan as a riposte to another view which was then just beginning to take shape—*scientia est unum et ars aliud* (science is one thing and art another).[67] The arts, crafts, and sciences all interpenetrate one another—masonry (craft), geometry (science), and architecture (art) in the building of a cathedral, for example.[68] All provided

---

[64] *Art from the Sacred to the Profane*, "Principles and Criteria of Art", 6.

[65] See, for instance, *Art from the Sacred to the Profane*, "The Art of Dress and Ambience" and "Poetry, Music, and Dance".

[66] Much of Coomaraswamy's work was given over to the deciphering of traditional symbolic languages which found their expression not only in religious iconographies but in the most unassuming crafts of everyday life. He found a symbolic density, and thus a teaching, in the most diverse productions of traditional cultures—in Shaker furniture, a Javanese puppet, Indian Gupta seals, in traditional oriental dress, to name but a few examples from amongst hundreds. For a sample of his work in this field see *Selected Papers 1*. Guénon, on the other hand, was primarily interested in the metaphysical significance of symbols, without evincing much interest in the role of arts and crafts in daily life—though he sometimes shines a light in this direction too. In *The Reign of Quantity and the Signs of the Times*, for instance, he devotes a fascinating chapter to the "degeneration of coinage" whereby coins have been robbed of the spiritual significance they once carried through their symbolism—yet another sign of the increasing "quantification" of everyday life. (See *The Reign of Quantity and the Signs of the Times*, 133-139.) Marco Pallis has shown how the daily implements of Tibetan life were charged with spiritual significance. (M. Pallis, "Introduction to Tibetan Art", 22-35.) Coomaraswamy, and scholars such as Mircea Eliade and Adrian Snodgrass, have directed attention to the symbolisms once inherent in the simplest house or dwelling-place. See "The Symbolism of the Dome" in *Selected Papers 1*, 422ff; M. Eliade, *The Sacred and the Profane*, 20-67; and A. Snodgrass, *Architecture, Time, and Eternity*.

[67] See A. Coomaraswamy, "*Ars Sine Scientia Nihil*" in *Selected Papers 1*, 229. See also letter to *Art News*, May-August 1939, *Selected Letters*, 378-380.

[68] On this subject see T. Burckhardt, "Perennial Values in Islamic Art" in *The Sword of Gnosis*, ed. J. Needleman, 313. In this light we can see how the modern distinctions between "fine"

arenas for the exploration of analogical relationships and for the application of symbolic languages. The relationships between material forms and spiritual realities provided an initiatic point of entry into many esoteric disciplines. Mention should be made of the invaluable work done on initiatic arts, sciences, and crafts by men like Guénon, Burckhardt, and Nasr.[69] This is an enigmatic field into which have intruded all manner of incompetent theorizers who have no grip on the principles involved.[70] To offer but one illustration: the common dismissal of the alchemists as "charcoal burners" and "primitive chemists".[71]

One of the tragedies of modern civilization is the desecration and mechanization of work: this is to rob man of dignified and meaningful work. A long line of commentators—Blake, Ruskin, Dickens, William Morris, Eric Gill, Coomaraswamy, Dorothy Sayers, to mention only a few English writers—have denounced the spiritual devastation caused by scientism, industrialization, and the tyranny of the machine (these three being all of a piece). But no one has stated the case more succinctly than Schuon:

> What the people need in order to find meaning in life, hence the possibility of earthly happiness, is religion and the crafts: religion because every man has need of it, and the crafts because they allow man to manifest his personality and to realize his vocation in the framework of a sapiential symbolism; every man loves intelligible work and work well done. Now, industrialism has robbed the people of both things: on the one hand of religion, denied by scientism from which industry derives, and rendered implausible by the inhuman character of the ambience of machinery; and on the other hand of the crafts, replaced precisely by machines; so much so, that . . . there is nothing left for the people which can give meaning to their life and make them happy.[72]

---

and "applied" arts, between arts and crafts, between artist and artisan, between the beautiful and the useful, make little sense in a traditional framework.

[69] Amongst their most important works, in this context, are: R Guénon, *The Reign of Quantity and the Signs of the Times;* T. Burckhardt, *Mirror of the Intellect, Mystical Astrology According to Ibn Arabi,* and *Art of Islam;* S.H. Nasr, *Science and Civilization in Islam, Man and Nature, Islamic Science: An Illustrated History,* and "The Traditional Sciences". See also Schuon, *Light on the Ancient Worlds,* "American Indian Shamanism", for an exposition of shamanic practices which activate some of the principles which govern many initiatic sciences.

[70] The occultists, who see this as one of their special provinces, are no exception. One can find all manner of absurdities in popular occultist writings in the field.

[71] The definitive study is T. Burckhardt, *Alchemy: Science of the Cosmos, Science of the Soul.* For a misunderstanding of alchemy one can consult almost any encyclopedia or history of Western science!

[72] *Art from the Sacred to the Profane,* "Man and Art", 27-28. For some more extended considerations of this theme see also D. Sayers, "Why Work?" and R. Sworder, "The Desacralization of Work", in H. Oldmeadow (ed.), *The Betrayal of Tradition,* and B. Keeble, *Every Man An Artist.*

Naturalism, Aestheticism, and Profane Art

Traditional art carries an implicit repudiation of modern art and of prevailing aesthetic theories. Modern European art, for the most part, ignores the cognitive, moral, and utilitarian functions proper to art and is governed rather by aesthetic, sensory, and subjective factors, most conspicuously in the visual arts. The perennialist arraignment of modern art has been executed primarily by Coomaraswamy and Schuon; the prosecution has been by no means lenient, the charges being serious ones. The defining characteristic of post-mediaeval art is that it is—whether consciously or inadvertently is of no account—anti-traditional, which is to say, anti-religious, anti-spiritual, bereft of any sense of the sacred. Some of the tell-tales: a rank individualism; a preoccupation with novelty and a misnamed "originality"; an aestheticism indifferent to the moral, intellectual, and spiritual functions of art; stylistic excesses veering from a pedantic naturalism on one side to a barbarous surrealism on the other. As Schuon remarks, "the ambition of artistic creation seeking to start from zero, as if man could also create *ex nihilo* . . . ends . . . in the subhuman aberrations of surrealism".[73] The critique of modern art is implicit in much that has already been said and need not be labored here.

One of the least understood aspects of traditional art is its indifference to the claims of naturalism. Confusion over the principles involved has sometimes inveigled art historians and others into talk about "the lack of sophistication" of much traditional art, evinced, for example, by a putative inability to master the demands of perspective. Needless to say the purveyors of such views usually subscribe to an evolutionary or progressivist view of art. Such views would be laughable did they not encourage a view of the past which is both impudent and condescending. Schuon reminds us that a more or less exact observation of nature may find a place in traditional art, as it does, for example, in that of Phaoronic Egypt. However, the attempt to "imitate" nature could never be an end in itself in traditional art which, generally being concerned with analogical relationships and symbolisms, will not seek to reproduce the surfaces and appearances of the material world in any "realistic" fashion. The revelation of the transparent and transcendental aspects of phenomena sits awkwardly with naturalism:

> There is a relative but not irremediable incompatibility . . . between the spiritual content or radiance of a work and an implacable and virtuosic naturalism: it is as if the science of the mechanism of things killed their spirit.[74]

---

[73] *Spiritual Perspectives and Human Facts*, "Aesthetics and Symbolism in Art and Nature", 31.

[74] *Esoterism as Principle and as Way*, "The Degrees of Art", 191.

Artistic naturalism proceeds from an exteriorizing mentality which, more often than not, also lacks "the instinct of sacrifice, sobriety, restraint",[75] and which could not be normative in any traditional civilization. Rather, a traditional art will tend to

> combine intelligent observation of nature with noble and profound styl-izations in order, first, to assimilate the work to the model created by God in nature and secondly, to separate it from physical contingency by giving it an imprint of pure spirit, of synthesis, of what is essential.[76]

Naturalism on the other hand is

> clearly luciferian in its wish to imitate the creations of God, not to men-tion its affirmation of the psychic element to the detriment of the spiri-tual, and above all, of the bare fact to the detriment of the symbol.[77]

European art since the Renaissance has not sprung from a tradition regulated by these kinds of principles but from an increasingly secular, humanistic, and individualistic view of art, one of its motive forces being the notion of "genius".[78] During the Renaissance the traditional character of European civilization in general, and Christian art in particular, was vitiated by "a sort of posthumous revenge on the part of classical antiquity".[79] This marked a triumph for the alliance of rationalism and naturalism which had shaped the art of classical Greece, evident in "the dramatic titanism, and the fleshly and vulgar delirium, of the megalomaniacs of the Renaissance and the seventeenth century, infatuated with anatomy, turmoil, marble, and gigantism".[80] Most modern art historians still fall into euphoria at the mere mention of the "Golden Age" of classical Greek art, but as Schuon makes so starkly clear,

> The whole of the so-called miracle of Greece amounts to a substitu-tion of reason for intelligence as such; apart from the rationalism which inaugurated it, artistic naturalism would have been inconceivable. Ex-treme individualism results from the cult of "form", of form envisaged as something finite and not as "symbol"; reason indeed regulates the

---

[75] *Transfiguration of Man*, "Art, Its Duties and Its Rights", 47.

[76] *Art from the Sacred to the Profane*, "Naturalistic Art", 51.

[77] *Transcendent Unity of Religions*, "Concerning Forms in Art", 77-78. For a more detailed discussion of these issues, see A. Coomaraswamy, "The Mediaeval Theory of Beauty", "Imita-tion and Expression", and "Figures of Speech or Figures of Thought?" in *Selected Papers 1*, 189-228, 276-285, 20-25.

[78] For some discussion of the changes in the prevailing European view of art in the Renais-sance, see A. Blunt, *Artistic Theory in Italy 1500-1600* and R.J. Clements, *Michelangelo's Theory of Art*.

[79] *Transcendent Unity of Religions*, "Concerning Forms in Art", 70.

[80] *Esoterism as Principle and as Way*, "The Degrees of Art", 189.

science of the finite, of limits and of order, so that it is only logical that an art which is directed by reason should share with reason itself a flatness refractory to all mystery.[81]

European art since the Renaissance, that "Caesarism of the bourgeois and bankers",[82] has been less and less illuminated by any spirituality, and placed at the mercy of the individual artist. Its source is no longer the font of tradition but the psychic resources of the individual. These may be quite prodigious as in the case of, say, a Leonardo or a Michelangelo, but a fundamental change has taken place whereby art ceases to "exteriorize either transcendent ideas or profound virtues"[83] and, instead, communicates the "unbridled subjectivism"[84] of the artist. Recall Vasari's commendation of Michelangelo's role in this change: "the craftsmen owe him an infinite and everlasting obligation, he having broken down the bonds and chains by reason of which they had always followed a beaten path in the execution of their works."[85] For Vasari this marked a liberation of individual creativity; from a traditional perspective it is the beginning of the end:

> The modern conception of art is false in so far as it puts creative imagination . . . in the place of qualitative form, or insofar as a subjective and conjectural valuation is substituted for an objective and spiritual one.[86]

A grievous error in the modern understanding of art is the belief that the anonymous artist/artisan in the traditional world was a kind of slave to the "bonds and chains" of convention. It is certainly true that traditional artists were not free to do just as they pleased, but to believe that the constraints of tradition stifled all creativity goes against the evidence and is to indulge in wishful simplifications.

> The rights of art, or more exactly of the artist, lie in the technical, spiritual, and intellectual qualities of the work: these three qualities are

---

[81] *Art from the Sacred to the Profane*, "Naturalistic Art", 48.

[82] *Spiritual Perspectives and Human Facts*, "Aesthetics and Symbolism in Art and Nature", 37.

[83] *Spiritual Perspectives and Human Facts*, "Aesthetics and Symbolism in Art and Nature", 32.

[84] *To Have a Center*, "To Have a Center", 9.

[85] G. Vasari, *Lives of the Painters*, quoted in A. Blunt, *Artistic Theory in Italy 1500-1600*, 75.

[86] *Language of the Self*, "Principles and Criteria of Art", 104. See also W. Perry (ed.), *A Treasury of Traditional Wisdom*, 660. There is a telling anecdote in Mircea Eliade's journal *No Souvenirs*, 133: "I met Henri Michaux. He talked about Padre Pio, whose mass he had attended several times. Extraordinary impression: Padre Pio speaks with God; for him God is *there*. At the end of three days he left for fear of being converted. 'My path is entirely different,' he told me. 'I'm an artist. I have my personal experiences'." No commentary needed!

so many modes of originality. In other words, the artist can be original through the aesthetic quality of his work, by the nobility or piety reflected in it, and by the intelligence or knowledge which enables him to find inexhaustible variations within the framework laid down by tradition. . . . This framework . . . does indeed restrict incapacity but not either talent or intelligence. True genius can develop without making innovations: it attains perfection, depth, and power of expression almost imperceptibly by means of the imponderables of truth and beauty ripened in that humility without which there can be no true greatness.[87]

Schuon concedes that the art of the Renaissance retained some qualities of "intelligence and grandeur" but the Baroque style which followed it "could hardly express anything but the spiritual penury and the hollow and miserable turgidity of its period".[88] Inexorably the humanistic conception of art sponsored the mania for novelty (which later came to be regarded as "originality") until today this becomes a criterion for the value and validity of any artistic creation. "Nothing is more monotonous than the illusions of originality found in men who have been inculcated from childhood with a bias for 'creative genius'."[89] The individual "genius" venerated in the post-medieval West is "all too often a man without a center, in whom this lack is replaced by a creative hypertrophy".[90] The relentless pursuit of "originality" could lead only to an anarchic art which must increasingly seek out the bizarre, the abnormal, the monstrous—thus surrealism and other kindred deformities. The "liberation" of the Renaissance ends in the grotesqueries of a Dali, not to mention the even more loathsome and diabolic productions which sometimes come under the canopy of modern "art". Nor are these profane productions harmless, for

When a man surrounds himself with the ineptitudes of a deviated art, how can he still "see" what he should "be"? He runs the risk of "being" what he "sees", of assimilating the errors suggested by the erroneous forms among which he lives.

Modern satanism is manifested—in the most external way no doubt but also in the most immediately tangible and intrusive way—in the unintelligible ugliness of forms.[91]

---

[87] *Art from the Sacred to the Profane*, "Principles and Criteria of Art", 7-9.

[88] *Spiritual Perspectives and Human Facts*, "Aesthetics and Symbolism in Art and Nature", 36.

[89] *Spiritual Perspectives and Human Facts*, "Aesthetics and Symbolism in Art and Nature", 29.

[90] *To Have a Center*, "To Have a Center", 8.

[91] *Spiritual Perspectives and Human Facts*, "Aesthetics and Symbolism in Art and Nature", 26

Plato claimed that any art directed solely towards pleasure can produce nothing but "toys".[92] Under a perennialist view this, at best, is the status of much modern art, which serves nothing but aesthetic purposes, which is to say the stimulation, if not always the pleasing, of our senses. The traditional vinculum between the ideals of Truth, Beauty, and Goodness, between the cognitive, aesthetic, and moral domains, has been sundered. Arts and crafts which were once rooted in a vocational pursuit that simultaneously served the needs of both the body and the spirit have been replaced by a dehumanizing industry on the one hand, and a sterile and pretentious aestheticism on the other. A sense of beauty has become not a matter of truths but of tastes, and the "emancipation of the artist" is nothing other than the "freedom" to ignore the claims of any ideal higher than "self-expression".

*   *   *

Beauty, Symbolism, Art: the whole body of Schuon's writings, both metaphysical and poetic, are pervaded by these three motifs, which also converge in his paintings, to which we turn in chapter 11. The elaborations and ramifications of the principles on which we have touched in this chapter are to be found everywhere in Schuon's work. Whilst it is true that he devoted comparatively few systematic essays to these subjects one cannot venture far into any of his writings before they appear. To conclude, a translation of one of Schuon's German poems on the earthly traces of Divine Beauty:

> Beauty is first and foremost in nature —
> Everywhere thou seest the trace of the Creator.
> Then there is great human art —
> In every noble work God's favor blooms.
> Beauty of language: the genius of Dante
> Braids a garland that links thee with God.
> Music: a mystery that resounds from heaven,
> And brings the inexpressible to earth.
> To the magic of music belongs the dance —
> The garland of *gopi*s circle round Krishna's flute.
> Then there is woman: the quintessence of the beautiful —
> The reconciling ray of the power of God.[93]

---

[92] Quoted in A. Coomaraswamy, "Figures of Speech or Figures of Thought?", *Selected Papers 1*, 20.
[93] Frithjof Schuon, *World Wheel*, Fifth Collection, LXXVII.

10
The Primordial Message of the Plains Indians

The Indian world represents on this earth a value that is irreplaceable; it possesses something unique and enchanting. . . . It is human greatness, and at the same time harbors within itself something mysterious and sacred, which it expresses with profound originality.[1]

The Indian world signifies first and foremost the reading of the primordial doctrine in the phenomena of Nature . . . and the experiencing of Nature as the holy, primordial Home that everywhere manifests the Great Spirit and everywhere is filled with Him; and this consciousness gives the Red Man his dignity, composed of reverence for Nature and of self-dominion; it also throws light on the singular majesty of his artistically richly-accented appearance, in which eagle and sun combine and which, in the archetypal realm, belongs to the divine prototypes.[2]

The Indian like all the yellow race—for he is a Mongoloid—stays in Nature and is never detached from it; psychologically he is like a samurai become hunter or nomad; his contemplativeness, where it is most intimate and exalted, is without doubt not unrelated to that intuitive and inarticulate method which is Zen, or in other respects, to the spiritualized Nature in Shinto.[3]

Archaic, Historical, and Modern Cultures
In *The Reign of Quantity and the Signs of the Times* René Guénon observes that it is only in these latter days, marked by the ever-accelerating "solidification" of the world, that "Cain finally and really slays Abel"[4]—which is to say that the sedentary civilizations destroy the nomadic cultures. Moreover,

It could be said in a general way that the works of sedentary peoples are works of time: these people are fixed in space within a strictly limited domain, and develop their activities in a temporal continuity which appears to them to be indefinite. On the other hand, nomadic and pastoral peoples build nothing durable, and do not work for a future which escapes them; but they have space in front of them, not facing

---

[1] *Feathered Sun*, "Excerpts from a Diary", 147.
[2] *Feathered Sun*, "Excerpts from Correspondence", 158.
[3] *Feathered Sun*, "A Metaphysic of Virgin Nature", 20.
[4] R. Guénon, *The Reign of Quantity and the Signs of the Times*, 78.

them with any limitation, but on the contrary always offering them new possibilities.[5]

No doubt it was with similar considerations in mind that Frithjof Schuon remarked that "traditions having a prehistoric origin are, symbolically speaking, made for 'space' and not for 'time'."[6] It follows from these observations that the slaying of Abel—the violent extirpation of the primordial nomadic cultures—not only constitutes a drastic contraction of human possibilities, but is actually a cosmic desecration. Recall the words of Marco Pallis on the destruction of the traditional and largely nomadic culture of Tibet:

> One can truly say that this remote land behind the snowy rampart of the Himalaya had become like the chosen sanctuary for all those things whereof the historical discarding had caused our present profane civilization, the first of its kind, to come into being. . . . The violation of this sanctuary and the dissipation of the sacred influences concentrated there became an event of properly cosmic significance, of which the ulterior consequences for a world which tacitly condoned the outrage or, in many cases, openly countenanced it on the plea that it brought "progress" to a reluctant people, have yet to ripen.[7]

Similar considerations may be applied in more or less analogous cases, whether we think of the fate of the American Indians, the Australian Aborigines, the Inuit, the Bedouin, the Gypsies, the Bushmen of the Kalahari, or any other peoples who have been trampled by the juggernaut of modernity. Since the genocidal vandalisms of the nineteenth century a great deal has been written about the destruction of the Indian cultures of North America. There have also been many attempts, with varying degrees of success, to elucidate and to reanimate at least some aspects of this ancestral way of life. Many writers on these subjects are impervious to the deeper significance of the events and processes which they seek to explain.

Much of the early literature concerning the religious life of the Indians came from anthropologists who were tyrannized both by the prejudices of the age and by the limitations of their discipline. Recent anthropologists have abandoned many of the cruder racist and progressivist assumptions of their predecessors, but all too often have succeeded only in replacing nineteenth

---

[5] R. Guénon, *The Reign of Quantity and the Signs of the Times*, 180. G. La Piana also alludes to the symbolism of the Cain and Abel story in writing, "Cain, who killed his brother, Abel, the herdsman, and built himself a city, prefigures modern civilization, one that has been described from within as a 'murderous machine, with no conscience and no ideals'" (La Piana, cited in *Feathered Sun*, "The Sacred Pipe", 70n).

[6] *Light on the Ancient Worlds*, "Light on the Ancient Worlds", 8.

[7] M. Pallis, Review of Jacob Needleman (ed.), *The New Religions*, 189-190.

century prejudices with those more characteristic of our own time whilst still retaining a childish faith in the capacity of a rationalistic and materialistic pseudo-science to grasp the mysteries of a complex spiritual tradition. Not for nothing has Mircea Eliade written of the "religious illiteracy" of so many scholars of so-called "primitive" religious traditions.[8] Whilst intellectual fashions amongst ethnologists and anthropologists have changed over the last century, the one constant has been an intransigent reductionism which refuses to treat primal traditions in their own terms or, indeed, in terms appropriate to any religious tradition. The influential theories of Freud, Durkheim, and Levy-Bruhl, and their derivatives, are all variations on the reductionist theme. As Whitall Perry once observed, "the scientific pursuit of religion puts the saddle on the wrong horse, since it is the domain of religion to evaluate science, and not vice versa".[9]

Mircea Eliade has provided a useful schema for the broad classification of worldviews: archaic, historical, and modern. "Archaic" refers to nomadic, non-literate cultures governed by an orally-transmitted mythology and a cyclic view of time; "historical" to the sedentary civilizations in which sacred texts and a strong sense of history are foregrounded; and "modern" to those cultures in which the sense of the sacred has been largely eclipsed by secular/materialist values and ideas. Using these categories we can situate the traditions of primal cultures (often called "indigenous" these days) as "archaic", the major religious traditions as "historical", and the profane and humanistic culture of the post-medieval West as "modern". Eliade's schema is in no way evolutionary; indeed, in many respects it is counter-evolutionary.

Most of Schuon's writings have been concerned with the world's major "historical" traditions—Hinduism, the Chinese tradition, Buddhism, the Abrahamic monotheisms. However we should not overlook his writings on

---

[8] M. Eliade, *Australian Religions*, xiii-xiv.

[9] W. Perry in *Studies in Comparative Religion* 7:2, 1973, 127. Of course, it must be acknowledged that some anthropologists have been acutely aware of the dangers of reductionism in the study of indigenous cultures. Here, for instance, are the words of the Australian anthropologist, W.E.H. Stanner, written over forty years ago, concerning the anthropological literature on the Australian Aborigines: "It is preposterous that something like a century of study, because of rationalism, positivism, and materialism, should have produced two options: that Aboriginal religion is either (to follow Durkheim) what someone called 'the mirage of society' or (to follow Freud) the 'neurosis of society'" (W.E.H. Stanner in *Religion in Aboriginal Australia*, ed. M. Charlesworth, 155). Nonetheless, the strictures above notwithstanding, it can be noted that anthropologists and other scholars accumulated a massive amount of information about traditional Indian life even if the data in question were often only superficially understood (if not altogether misunderstood!). It comes as no surprise that comparative religionists, less inhibited by materialistic/functionalistic assumptions and more attuned to the realm of the sacred, have sometimes been able to give us much more profound interpretations; in this context one might mention such figures as Åke Hultkrantz, Jean Servier, Mircea Eliade, Walter H. Capps, and Arthur Versluis.

Buddhists, c. 1928   Mandarins, c. 1928

Murid, 1933   Japanese woman, c. 1928

Waiting for the Enemy, 1967
Published in *The Feathered Sun*, 37

1966
Published in *Images of Primordial and Mystic Beauty*, 33

The Descent of the Sacred Pipe, 1986
Published in *The Feathered Sun*, 131

The Council, 1962
Published in *The Feathered Sun*, ii

1953
Published in *Images of Primordial and Mystic Beauty*, 35

1963
Published in *Images of Primordial and Mystic Beauty*, 121

The Creation of Woman, 1974
Published in *Images of Primordial and Mystic Beauty,* 223 and
Art from the Sacred to the Profane, 134

Virgin and Child, 1968
Published in *Images of Primordial and Mystic Beauty*, 247 and
Art from the Sacred to the Profane, 41

On his veranda, 1995

At his desk, c. 1995

primordial shamanic traditions and mythologies, most conspicuously those of the Plains Indians of North America, in whom he had a particular interest. In one vital respect such traditions constitute the purest expression of the *sophia perennis*: they express a spontaneous and intuitive understanding of the metaphysical transparency of the natural order. One might well illustrate the point through such peoples as the Bushmen of the Kalahari, the Inuit, or the Australian Aborigines, to name only a few, or to primordial traditions which, like tributaries of a great river, were later absorbed into the major historical traditions—Siberian shamanism, Tibetan Bön, Japanese Shinto, Chinese ancestorism, Scandinavian paganism, and the like. (Such phenomena form a bridge between the orally-transmitted mythologies and the "logocentric" historical religions.) However, in this chapter we will limit ourselves to Schuon's writings on the American Indians, who can here stand for all of the primal traditions which are sometimes overlooked in perennialist discourse.

As noted, Schuon's involvement with the Plains Indians of North America was one of the decisive experiences of his life. There is another reason—if one be needed—for focusing our attention on the Plains Indians, again as representatives of a primordial wisdom. Seyyed Hossein Nasr opened his 1994 Cadbury Lectures with these words: "The Earth is bleeding from wounds inflicted upon it by a humanity no longer in harmony with Heaven and therefore in constant strife with the terrestrial environment."[10] That we are now in a state of "constant strife" is widely recognized, but the root causes of this condition are rarely understood. We witness a plethora of writings on the "ecological crisis", often well-intentioned and enlivened by partial insights, but fundamentally confused because of an ignorance of those timeless cosmological principles to which the perennialists recall us. In this respect the contrast between the Indians and ourselves (as "moderns") could hardly be more dramatic. It may well be that the example of the Indians (and others like them), in their "relations" with the natural order, could have a salutary role to play in repairing that scission between Heaven and Earth of which the "ecological crisis" is but the outer symptom. As Schuon has observed,

> The Indian is predisposed towards the suprasensible and strives to penetrate the hard wall of the sensible world, seeks openings where he can, and finds them chiefly in phenomena themselves, which indeed, in their contents, are nothing other than signposts to the suprasensible. Things are hard-frozen melodies from the Beyond.[11]

[10] S.H. Nasr, *Religion and the Order of Nature*, 3.
[11] *Feathered Sun*, "Excerpts from a Diary", 154. Similarly, Seyyed Hossein Nasr: "On the highest level virgin nature can be contemplated as a theophany which possesses its own meta-

This understanding has been almost entirely lost in the modern world, with all too obvious consequences.

The Spiritual Heritage of the Indians

Frithjof Schuon's role in helping to preserve the spiritual heritage of the Plains Indians of North America has only recently come to light and must be reckoned one of the signal achievements of his life, quite aside from his writings, which include the most penetrating and authoritative account of their spiritual economy ever written by a non-Indian. In a letter written in 1947 to Chief Medicine Robe of the Assiniboine tribe, Schuon recollects that the members of his family "were educated in the love of the Indian peoples, and this was a providential disposition in the plan of the Great Spirit".[12] This family disposition dated back to his paternal grandmother's encounter with an Indian chief in Washington DC. Michael Fitzgerald, himself a contemporary expositor of Indian spirituality, has recounted the truly extraordinary story of Schuon's intimate relations with the Indians in some detail.[13] Here we will touch on only a few of the more suggestive incidents from Schuon's lifelong engagement with the Indians.

A book which, perhaps more than any other, has awakened Europeans to the spiritual density of the Plains Indians' culture is *Black Elk Speaks*, an account of the early life and visionary experiences of the great Lakota "medicine-man". At the time the book first appeared, in 1932, it had a limited impact. Interestingly, one of the few who recognized it as an extraordinary document was Carl Jung, but it was not until the counter-culture of the 60s that the book really came into its own. It is now widely recognized as one of the great spiritual testimonies of our time. So impressed was Schuon with *Black Elk Speaks* that in 1946 he suggested to a young scholar, Joseph Epes Brown, that he should find Black Elk (then living in obscurity) to learn more about the ancestral ways of the Lakota.[14] Brown spent a good deal of

---

physical message and spiritual discipline. Nature reveals the One and Its multiple qualities. It prays and invokes" (*The Need for a Sacred Science*, 124-125).

[12] *Frithjof Schuon: Messenger of the Perennial Philosophy*, 84.

[13] See M. Fitzgerald, "Frithjof Schuon's Role in Preserving the Red Indian Spirit", *Sophia* 4:2, 1998; and "Frithjof Schuon and the Native Spirit: Interview with Michael Fitzgerald", *Vincit Omnia Veritas* 3:2, July 2007. (This interview was originally conducted for the Religioperennis website, but is now available in printed form in *Vincit Omnia Veritas: Collected Essays*, ed. R. Fabbri and T. Scott, 7-33.) See also M. Fitzgerald, *Yellowtail, Crow Medicine Man and Sun Dance Chief: An Autobiography as told to Michael Oren Fitzgerald* (1991), one of the most interesting and illuminating of the many Indian "autobiographies" and personal testaments which have appeared in recent decades. Mention should also be made of two compilations, including many precious photographs, edited by Michael and Judith Fitzgerald: *Indian Spirit* (rev. ed. 2006) and *The Spirit of Indian Women* (2005).

[14] See C. Schuon, "Frithjof Schuon: Memories and Anecdotes", 41.

time, over a two year period, with Black Elk and his family. During this time Schuon wrote two letters to Black Elk, each of them, according to the holy man's son Ben, having "a tremendous impact". Black Elk also confided to Brown that he had been chosen as the one to record the sacred rites because he had been sent by a "holy man from Europe", going on to give a physical description of Schuon! He also told Brown that his imminent death (which came in 1951) did not trouble him as he knew that his own work would be continued by this "holy man". Quite remarkable![15] Another fascinating aspect of Black Elk's role was his relationship with Frithjof Schuon's elder brother, the Trappist monk, Father Gall.[16]

The result of Brown's sojourns with Black Elk was *The Sacred Pipe: Black Elk's Account of the Seven Sacred Rites of the Oglala Sioux* (1953), a book which has been through many subsequent editions. If *Black Elk Speaks* provided an enthralling narrative and recaptured something of the holy man's great visions, Brown's book provided a more coherent account of Lakota metaphysics, cosmology, and ritual life. Brown went on, partly under Schuon's influence, to write several other books which have been enormously influential in remedying the lamentable ignorance about the spiritual life of the American Indians.[17]

Another decisive episode in Schuon's encounter with the Indians was his meeting with Thomas and Susie Yellowtail in Paris in 1954, the start of an enduring friendship of kindred spirits. In the late 50s and early 60s Schuon and his wife spent a good deal of time with various Plains Indians tribes in the American West, and from these experiences emerged many of Schuon's paintings on Indian themes. Thenceforth Schuon maintained the closest relations with the Yellowtails and with many other Indians, and played no small role in their efforts to preserve their imperiled heritage. Schuon was initiated into both the Lakota and Crow tribes, remarking of the former, in a letter, "I believe it was only then that my soul was fully healed of the wounds of my youth; I also received from the Indians a special kind of spiritual blessing."[18]

Schuon's sensitivity to the metaphysical transparency of phenomena and the "symbolist outlook" of the Indians were in deepest accord. What one commentator has written of the metaphysician applies no less to the Indians

---

[15] *Frithjof Schuon: Messenger of the Perennial Philosophy*, 91-92.
[16] Excerpts from the correspondence between the two can be found in the most recent edition of J.E. Brown, *The Spiritual Legacy of the American Indians*. (One hopes this correspondence will eventually be published in full.)
[17] Brown's other works include *Animals of the Soul* (1992) and, with Emily Cousins, *Teaching Spirits* (2001).
[18] Unpublished writings, courtesy of World Wisdom.

themselves: "For Schuon, virgin nature carries a message of eternal truth and primordial reality, and to plunge oneself therein is to rediscover a dimension of the soul which in modern man has become atrophied."[19] Indeed, virgin nature, for the Indian, fulfils the role of both Temple or Sanctuary and Divine Book.[20] In what follows we will make no attempt at a systematic account of Plains Indian metaphysics, cosmology, and spiritual life—for which readers can be directed to the writings of perennialists such as Schuon, Brown, and Fitzgerald, and to those Indians whose testimonies remain rooted in traditional understandings—Black Elk, Ohiyesa (Charles Eastman), Luther Standing Bear, Yellowtail, and a few others. Rather, we will simply sample a few aspects of Schuon's matchless work on this unique tradition, taking particular note of his observations concerning the "symbolist mentality" and "metaphysic of Nature", "polysynthetic animism", and the central place of the Sacred Pipe and Sun Dance in Indian cosmology and ritual life.

The American Indians belong in the great arc of "Hyperborean Shamanism" which stretches from Mongolia and Siberia into North America, the peoples in question embodying "the heroic side of the yellow race, in the broadest sense of the word". It is not for nothing that the Indians should exhibit some affinities, in their spiritual disposition, with certain Far Eastern forms, particularly those of Shinto, Zen, and of Siberian, Mongolian, and Tibetan shamanism.

> For these peoples, it is above all Nature that is the sanctuary. . . . The North American tradition knows the cult of the great phenomena of Nature: sun, moon, rain-bearing hurricane, wind, thunder and lightning, fire, animals, rocks, trees, without forgetting the sky and earth which are their containers; above them all . . . [the] "Great Spirit".[21]

Despite the considerable diversity of the Indian cultures throughout North America,

> There is nevertheless a unity based on the symbolism of the Directions of Space and on the use of the Sacred Pipe, and above all on the idea of a Supreme Being. And this religion too, with its many forms and its many different symbols is firstly discernment and then union—discernment between this vanishing world of dreams and the everlasting Reality which lies behind it, and union with this Reality even on this earth and in this life.[22]

---

[19] B. Perry, *Frithjof Schuon: Metaphysician and Artist*.

[20] *Feathered Sun*, "The Sun Dance", 92-93.

[21] *Treasures of Buddhism*, "The Meaning of Ancestors", 177-178.

[22] *Feathered Sun*, "A Message on Indian Religion", 102.

The "discernment" to which Schuon refers is, of course, that between the Real and the illusory, the Absolute and the relative, the Immutable and the ephemeral—the discernment on which metaphysics pivots. The fact that the metaphysical understandings of the Indians were expressed primarily in myth, symbol, and ritual, and through a reading of the Book of Nature, rather than through abstruse texts and verbal explications should not blind us to their doctrinal profundity. Recall Schuon's insistence that "Wisdom does not lie in any complication of words but in the profundity of the intention".[23]

The Indian perspective is anchored in a metaphysic of Nature. All natural forms and phenomena reflect qualities or aspects of the Great Spirit, or Great Mystery (Lakota: *Wakan-Tanka*). As Brown tells us:

> The term *Wakan-Tanka*, Great Mysterious, is an all-inclusive concept that refers both to a Supreme Being and to the totality of all gods or spirits or powers of creation. Such conceptualizations embracing both unity and diversity are typical of the polysynthetic nature of the languages of these peoples, and thus of their modes of conceptualization and cognitive orientations.[24]

It is a symptom of modern confusions that it should often be supposed that the Indians were "pantheists" and thereby "nature-worshippers". It is true that they sensed a sacred presence in all phenomena (particularly animals) but they certainly did not confuse physical entities with their celestial prototypes. Schuon refers to "the symbolist vision of the cosmos [which] is *a priori* a spontaneous perspective that bases itself on the essential nature—or the metaphysical transparency—of phenomena, rather than cutting these off from their prototypes".[25] The Indians did not imagine that *Wakan-Tanka* was simply the sum of all things, nor that God was "in the world", nor that God was the sun (though they shared with Dante the belief that "No object of sense is more worthy to be made a type of God than the sun"[26]); rather, they knew that "the world is mysteriously plunged in God".[27] That *Wanka-Tanka* is, in the terms of the monotheistic theologies, both transcendent and immanent, is made perfectly clear by the Lakota sage, Black Elk:

> We should understand well that all things are the works of the Great Spirit. We should know that He is within all things: the trees, the grasses, the rivers, the mountains, and all the four-legged animals and

---

[23] *Understanding Islam*, "The Koran", 133.

[24] J.E. Brown, *Spiritual Legacy of the American Indian*, 70.

[25] *Feathered Sun*, "The Symbolist Mind", 6.

[26] Dante, quoted in G. Eaton, *The Richest Vein*, 187.

[27] *Feathered Sun*, "The Sacred Pipe", 68.

the winged peoples; and *even more important, we should understand that He is also above all these things and peoples.*[28]

Or, in similar vein, this from Luther Standing Bear:

> The Lakota loved the sun and earth, but he worshipped only *Wakan-Tanka*, or Big Holy, who was the Maker of all things of earth, sky, and water. *Wakan-Tanka* breathed life and motion into all things, both visible and invisible. He was over all, through all, and in all, and great as was the sun, and good as was the earth, the greatness and goodness of the Big Holy were not surpassed. The Lakota could look at nothing without at the same time looking at *Wakan-Tanka*, and he could not, if he wished, evade His presence, for it pervaded all things and filled all space. All the mysteries of birth, life, and death; all the wonders of lightning, thunder, wind, and rain were but the evidence of His everlasting and encompassing power.[29]

Far from being childish "nature-worshippers", the Indians see everywhere in Nature, "the translucence of the Eternal", to recall Coleridge's marvelous phrase:

> The most important manifestations of the Great Spirit are the West, the North, the East, the South, Heaven and Earth; then come forms like the Sun, the Eagle, the Buffalo, the Rock, the Morning Star.... They are prefigured in the Great Spirit Himself: although He is One, He has in Himself all these Qualities whose outer form we see in the Directions of Space and in certain phenomena of Nature.[30]

Furthermore, the Indians evince what Schuon has called a "polysynthesism", "a consciousness of the profound homogeneity of the created world and the sense of universal solidarity which results therefrom",[31] an outlook "which sees appearances in their connection with essences".[32] Again, Black Elk beautifully expressed the principle in the inimitable idiom of his people:

> Peace . . . comes within the souls of men when they realize their relationship, their oneness, with the universe and all its Powers, and when

---

[28] J.E. Brown, *The Sacred Pipe*, xx. These are Black Elk's words as recounted by Brown (italics mine).

[29] Luther Standing Bear, *Land of the Spotted Eagle*, 197.

[30] *Feathered Sun*, "A Message on Indian Religion", 105.

[31] *Feathered Sun*, "A Metaphysic of Virgin Nature", 20.

[32] *Feathered Sun*, "The Symbolist Mind", 9. (However, Schuon also points out that not "every individual belonging to a collectivity of symbolist or contemplative mentality is himself fully conscious of all that the symbols mean" [*Feathered Sun*, "The Symbolist Mind", 10].)

they realize that at the center of the universe dwells *Wakan-Tanka*, and that this center is really everywhere, it is within each of us.[33]

It is often remarked, by anthropologists and others, that the beliefs and practices of the Indians were "animistic"—but all too often we are left with the idea that the "animism" in question amounts to little more than some kind of superstitious belief in "spirits" inhabiting various natural phenomena, which is only to be expected amongst "primitives" bereft of a properly-constituted science which would disabuse them of these notions. In other words, many modern commentators announce that they have not even a glimmer of an idea of the realities to which they so glibly and complacently refer. By contrast, Schuon's relatively slender corpus of writings on the Indians contains more insights than a whole library of anthropological works for the simple reason that here is an intelligence and metaphysical discernment adequate to its subject. As Schuon himself remarks, "to be able to know the wisdom of a people we must first of all possess the keys to such wisdom, and these indispensable keys are to be found, not in any subsidiary branch of learning [such as ethnography] but in intellectuality at its purest and most universal level".[34] In a characteristic passage, Schuon goes directly to the heart of the matter of "animism":

> It means, in principle and metaphysically, that, whatever be the object envisaged, there springs from its existential center an ontological ray, made up of "being", "consciousness", and "life" whereby the object in question is attached, through its subtle or animic root, to its luminous and celestial prototype.[35]

As Schuon writes elsewhere, "It is through the animal species and the phenomena of Nature that the Indian contemplates the angelic Essences and the Divine Qualities". He goes on to quote the following passage from one of Joseph Epes Brown's letters:

> For these people, as of course for all traditional peoples, every created object is important simply because they know the metaphysical correspondence between this world and the "Real World". No object is for them what it appears to be, but it is simply the pale shadow of a Reality. It is for this reason that every created object is *wakan*, holy,

---

[33] J.E. Brown, *The Sacred Pipe*, 115.

[34] *Feathered Sun*, "The Sacred Pipe", 46.

[35] *Feathered Sun*, "The Shamanism of the Red Indians", 30. In this context we can usefully recall the following passage from another of Schuon's essays: "We do not say that the symbolist [here, the Indian] thinks 'principle' or 'idea' when he sees water, fire, or some other phenomenon of Nature; it is simply a question of our making the reader understand what the symbolist 'sees', inasmuch as 'seeing' and 'thinking' are for him synonymous" (*Feathered Sun*, "The Symbolist Mind", 9-10).

and has a power according to the loftiness of the spiritual reality that it reflects.[36]

This "polysynthetic animism" explains a great deal about the spiritual economy of the Indians—amongst other things, the so-called "magical" techniques which operate "in virtue of the analogies between symbols and their prototypes" and enable the shaman to access the "subtle and supra-sensorial roots of things", thereby to influence natural phenomena in ways which absolutely escape the ken of the modern mind. It also informs the reluctance of the Indians to detach themselves from the natural world and to engage in a "civilization" made up of "artifices and servitudes".[37]

Schuon's writings and, indeed, his paintings on Indian themes, illuminate almost every aspect of the Indian tradition: not only their "religion"—metaphysics, cosmology, mythology, value system, ritual life, and the symbolic language in which these are expressed—but also the ways in which "religion" pervades their material culture and is inseparable from their modes of subsistence, their hunting, dress and deportment, habitations, their arts and crafts, and so on.

The Sacred Pipe, or Calumet, is central to the ritual life of the Plains Indians: it constitutes "a doctrinal synthesis, both concise and complex" and to describe its symbolism is "in a certain sense, to expound the sum of Indian wisdom".[38] Schuon demonstrates the ways in which the Pipe itself embodies teachings which are *metaphysical* (i.e., concerning the Absolute and universal realities of various degree), *cosmological* (concerning the manifest worlds, including the heavenly bodies as well as the terrestrial order of nature), and *anthropological* (concerning the human situation *vis-à-vis* these metacosmic and cosmic realities).

As Schuon remarks:

> When one stands in the midst of a plain, three things strike one's vision: the immense circle of the horizon; the immense vault of the sky; the four cardinal points. It is these elements which primordially determine the spirit and soul of the Indians; it could be said that the whole of their metaphysics or cosmology is based on these initial motifs.[39]

The Calumet expresses the metaphysical and cosmological symbolism of the cross within the circle: the six directions (four horizontal and two vertical) and the Center where they meet. As Schuon explains, the circle "corresponds to the Sky, while the cross marks the Four Directions of space and all

---

[36] *Feathered Sun*, "The Sacred Pipe", 47.

[37] *Feathered Sun*, "The Shamanism of the Red Indians", 34-35, 31.

[38] *Feathered Sun*, "The Sacred Pipe", 44.

[39] *Feathered Sun*, "Symbolism of a Vestimentary Art", 71.

other quaternaries of the Universe; it also marks the vertical ternary Earth-Man-Sky, which situates the horizontal quaternary on three levels".[40] The Four Directions provide the frame for an exceptionally eloquent symbolism. Man stands at the center of the four horizontal directions of space; as well, he is the axis of the vertical ternary, thus becoming mediator between Earth and Sky. Man is thus a totality, bearing the whole universe within himself, just as does the microcosmic Calumet, as is apparent in this passage from Black Elk:

> I fill this sacred Pipe with the bark of the red willow; but before we smoke it, you must see how it is made and what it means. These four ribbons hanging here on the stem are the four quarters of the universe. The black one is for the west where the thunder beings live to send us rain; the white one for the north, whence comes the great white cleansing wind; the red one for the east, whence springs the light and where the morning star lives to give men wisdom; the yellow for the south, whence come the summer and the power to grow. But these four spirits are only one Spirit after all, and this eagle feather here is for that One, which is like a father, and also it is for the thoughts of men that should rise high as eagles do. Is not the sky a father and the earth a mother, and are not all living things with feet or wings or roots their children? And this hide upon the mouthpiece here, which should be bison hide, is for the earth, from whence we came and at whose breast we suck as babies all our lives, along with all the animals and birds and trees and grasses. And because it means all this, and more than any man can understand, the Pipe is holy.[41]

"The Sacred Pipe means prayer. With it, man prays not only for himself, but also for the whole Universe. The whole Universe prays with him."[42]

The Four Directions which play so significant a part in the cosmology, mythology, and ritual life of the Indians also correspond to the four cardinal virtues, and which together reveal much of the Indian "character", if one may so put it: Courage, which manifests itself by way of the Indian's stoic heroism in the face of combat or adversity; Patience, displayed during the hunt or in the various trials and austerities which the Indian faces in the solitude of Virgin Nature; Generosity, expressed in the Indian love of gift-giving; and Fidelity, which shows itself in the lofty sense of honor and duty

---

[40] See *Feathered Sun*, "A Metaphysic of Virgin Nature", 14. For further reading see A. Snodgrass, *Architecture, Time, and Eternity: Studies in the Stellar and Temporal Symbolism of Traditional Buildings*, Volume 2, 425-449. Snodgrass elaborates the spatio-temporal relationships of the four Winds and the directions, as well as the symbolic significances of Lakota "architecture".

[41] *Black Elk Speaks*, cited in *Feathered Sun*, "The Sacred Pipe", 52-53.

[42] *Feathered Sun*, "A Message on Indian Religion", 106.

most evident in the Indian's dealings with his fellow tribespeople. To these four virtues should be added another significant aspect of the Indian ethos to which Schuon draws attention:

> The Indian tends towards independence and so towards indifference with regard to the outward world: he surrounds himself with silence as with a magic circle, and this silence is sacred as being the vehicle of the heavenly influences. It is from this silence—of which the natural support is solitude—that the Indian draws his spiritual strength; his ordinary prayer is unvoiced: what is required is not thought but consciousness of the Spirit, and this consciousness is immediate and formless like the vault of heaven.[43]

The smoking of the Pipe is integral to nearly all of the rituals of the Indians, of which the most significant are the Sweat Lodge (*Inipi* in the Lakota dialect), "Crying for a Vision" or "Solitary Invocation" (*Hanblecheyapi*), and the Sun Dance (*Wiwanyag Wachipi*):

> The Sweat Lodge means purification. In it, man renews himself; he becomes a new being. He becomes pure before his Creator. The solitary Invocation is the highest form of prayer. It is contemplation and union. But it also benefits the whole community, in a subtle and indirect way. . . . This is the highest and most complete form of spiritual life. The Sun Dance is in a sense the prayer of the whole community. For those who dance, it is union with the Great Spirit. . . . The Sun Dance attaches us to the Great Spirit.[44]

Schuon counted the Sun Dance he observed in 1959 as "one of the most powerful things I have ever witnessed", and wrote of it in these terms:

> The Sun Dance is a cosmic drama, indeed it is the cosmos itself. It is without beginning and without end: it is the temporal fraction of a timeless and supernatural reality. . . . The Sun Dance is the remembrance of God, purification from the multiple and the outward, union with the One and the Real.[45]

> The clear symbolic significance and the elemental convincing power of the Sun Dance are all quite overwhelming. . . . The buffalo is the sacred, primordial power and fecundity of the earth, and the eagle is the light that comes from above, the Revelation; the buffalo is mountain or rock, and the eagle sky and lightning; but the buffalo is also the sun, or the earthly image thereof.[46]

---

[43] *Feathered Sun*, "The Sacred Pipe", 64.

[44] *Feathered Sun*, "A Message on Indian Religion", 106.

[45] *Feathered Sun*, "Excerpts from a Diary", section on "The Sun Dance", 128-139. These impressions are from pages 129, 135, and 134, respectively.

[46] *Feathered Sun*, "Excerpts from a Diary", 134. The "buffalo" and "eagle" each perform a

The Fate of the Indian Peoples

During the burgeoning of interest in the Indians since the 1960s, attested by the popularity of such books as *Black Elk Speaks, Bury My Heart at Wounded Knee,* and *Touch the Earth,*[47] a great deal has been written about the fate of the American Indians, often lamenting the many injustices that were perpetrated in the name of "civilization" and "progress". There have also been many more accounts of this melancholy history as seen from the Indian side, as well as an efflorescence of books about their spiritual traditions. However, many of these accounts are unsatisfactory or, at the least, partial, as they are so often marred by that "unrelieved ignorance of metaphysical principles" which Nasr identified as one of the defining characteristics of the modern outlook. No such reproach can of course be leveled at Frithjof Schuon, who has not only explicated the Indian metaphysics and cosmology with rare authority, but who has explained the deeper significance of the tragic fate of these peoples:

> In order fully to understand the abruptness of the breakup of the Red Indian race one must take account of the fact that this race had lived for thousands of years in a kind of paradise that was practically speaking without limits. . . . Theirs was a rugged paradise to be sure, but one that nevertheless provided an environment full of grandeur and of a sacred character. . . . The Indians identified themselves spiritually and humanly with this inviolate Nature. . . . But as time went on, and concordantly with the development of the "Iron Age" in which passions predominate and wisdom disappears, abuses begin to arise with increasing frequency. . . . The privileged situation of the Indians, on the fringe of "History" and of its crushing urban civilizations, had inevitably to come

symbolic role in the Sun Dance, primarily through the presence of the buffalo skull and the eagle feathers and eagle-bone whistles.

[47] Dee Brown's *Bury My Heart at Wounded Knee* (1970) gave an historical account of the European-Indian confrontation from a vantage-point sympathetic to the Indians while *Touch the Earth* (1971), edited by T.C. McLuhan, was a compilation of oral and written Indian testimonies. These books were popular in the 70s, and beyond. Dee Brown's book has now sold more than 5 million copies around the world. Whatever their shortcomings, they helped to remedy the effects of the triumphalist and often racist accounts of the "winners". They also paved the way for many books, by both Indians and Europeans, which attempted, with varying degrees of success, to give some account of the traditional culture of the Indians, and/or to give an even-handed account of their troubled relations with the "wasichus". Among the more interesting and popular one may mention Theodora Kroeber, *Ishi in Two Worlds* (1961), John Fire Lame Deer and R. Erdoes, *Lame Deer: Seeker of Visions* (1972), and Peter Matthiessen, *Indian Country* (1985). However, none of these compare to the works evincing a more fully traditional outlook—the various accounts of Black Elk, Ohiyesa (Charles Eastman), Yellowtail, and Standing Bear, and books by Schuon, Brown, and the Fitzgeralds (all mentioned earlier in this chapter).

to an end. There is nothing surprising in the fact that this disintegration of a paradise . . . coincided with modern times.

However, whilst the fate of the Indians had a certain ineluctability, this in no way excuses or extenuates "the villainies of which the Indian has been the victim during several centuries", nor mitigates the pathos of their predicament. The destruction of the Indian peoples and their traditions "remains one of the greatest crimes and most blatant cases of vandalism in all human history".[48]

Let us bring this brief discussion to a close with another profound and poignant passage from Schuon concerning the destiny of the Indians:

> The crushing of the Indian race is tragic because in its deepest and most intimate nature this noble people was opposed to "assimilation"; the red man could only conquer or die; it is the spiritual basis of this alternative that confers on the destiny of the red race an aspect of grandeur and martyrdom. . . . They embodied a character, an idea, a principle, and, being what they were, they could not be unfaithful to themselves. This great drama might be defined as the struggle, not only between a materialistic civilization and another that was chivalrous and spiritual, but also between urban civilization (in the strictly human and pejorative sense of this term, with all its implications of artifice and servility) and the kingdom of Nature considered as the majestic, pure, unlimited apparel of the Divine Spirit. And it is from this idea of the final victory of Nature (final because it is primordial) that those Indians who have remained faithful to their ancestors draw their inexhaustible patience in the face of the misfortunes of their race; Nature, of which they feel themselves to be embodiments, and which at the same time is their sanctuary, will end by conquering this artificial and sacrilegious world, for it is the Garment, the Breath, the very Hand of the Great Spirit.[49]

---

[48] *Feathered Sun*, "The Shamanism of the Red Indians", 41-42.
[49] *Feathered Sun*, "The Sacred Pipe", 70.

11

Frithjof Schuon's Paintings and Poetry

Beauty always communicates a celestial dew-drop, if only for an instant.[1]

What I seek to express in my paintings—and indeed I cannot express anything other—is the Sacred combined with Beauty; thus, spiritual attitudes and virtues of the soul. And the vibration that emanates from my paintings must lead inward.[2]

In poetry, the musicality of things, or their cosmic essentiality, erupts onto the plane of language.[3]

Why has God given us the gift of speech?
For prayer.[4]

We have seen how Frithjof Schuon was fascinated by traditional arts from his earliest days, and noted his marvelous ability to discern in their visible forms both the celestial imprint of the Revelation from which the tradition in question emerged, and the ethnic genius of the people in question—a kind of collective signature, one might say. Schuon has been acutely sensitive to the role of Beauty in the spiritual life, its "interiorizing alchemy" which brings the soul back to God. Given all this it is not surprising that Schuon himself was an artist and poet as well as a metaphysician. He enjoyed drawing and painting in his childhood years but, by his own reckoning, it was not until after his marriage that his paintings achieved a maturity of style.

Schuon himself made no claims for his art, insisting that his essential message was conveyed in his metaphysical writings: "I am not a painter with an interest in metaphysics, but a metaphysician who from time to time produces a painting."[5] When approached about the possibility of exhibiting some of his paintings—this fairly late in his life—Schuon was reluctant, but acceded because his paintings too carried a spiritual message. In 1981 a selection of Schuon's paintings on Indian themes, entitled "Scenes of Plains Indian

---

[1] *To Have a Center*, "To Have a Center", 18.

[2] From a letter by Frithjof Schuon, quoted in Michael Pollack's Editor's Introduction to *Images of Primordial and Mystic Beauty: Paintings by Frithjof Schuon*, 4.

[3] *Spiritual Perspectives and Human Facts*, "Appendix: Selections from Letters and Previously Unpublished Writings", 233.

[4] Frithjof Schuon, "Panacea", *Adastra & Stella Maris*, 211.

[5] Frithjof Schuon, quoted in Foreword to *Songs for a Spiritual Traveler*, viii.

Life", was exhibited at the Taylor Museum in the Colorado Springs Fine
Arts Center. Some of these paintings appeared as plates in *The Feathered
Sun: Plains Indians in Art and Philosophy* (1990), while a fuller collection
of Schuon's paintings and drawings, *Images of Primordial and Mystic Beauty*,
was published in 1992. While Schuon's artwork has been a secondary and
mostly private undertaking, there is no dissonance between the metaphysical
works and the paintings; they are mutually illuminating. It could not be
otherwise, for as Schuon wrote to a friend, "my paintings flow forth from
the depths of my heart".[6] Any conspectus of Schuon's work must take into
account this significant body of work—something in the order of 200 oil
paintings as well as many sketches and drawings.

As a child and in his youth Schuon often turned not only to drawing and
painting but to the writing of poetry, influenced by the lyric side of German
Romanticism. For more than two decades his poetic output was minimal
but after several visionary experiences in the mid-60s he produced a series of
poems in Arabic. However, it was not until the last few years of his life that
he produced "an unimaginably rich and unforeseen poetic cycle",[7] written
first in English and appearing as *Road to the Heart* (1995), and then in his
native German, amounting to more than three thousand poems, published in
English translation in *Songs for a Spiritual Traveler* (2001), *Adastra & Stella
Maris* (2003), *Songs Without Names I-XII* (2006), *World Wheel I-VII* (2006),
and *Autumn Leaves & the Ring* (2010). Schuon's poems have been variously
compared to those of David, Angelus Silesius, Rumi, Shankara, Milarepa,
Han Shan, and Rilke.[8] His biographer has observed that "This final poetical
opus is in many ways a synthesis of his life's written work and provides a
complement to the sage's articles."[9] Another commentator, referring to the
"incredible sharpness, profundity, comprehensiveness, and compassion" of
the poems, acclaims them as Schuon's "final gift to the world, his testament
and legacy".[10]

The Indian Paintings
As Michael Pollack observed in his Introduction to *Images of Primordial and
Mystic Beauty*, Schuon's art revolves around two great subjects:

> On the one hand, the Plains Indian, and on the other hand, the mystery
> of cosmic and human femininity; Goethe's "Eternal Feminine" or the

[6] Frithjof Schuon, letter to Leo Schaya, August 28, 1985, quoted in *Frithjof Schuon: Messenger
of the Perennial Philosophy*, 212.
[7] *Frithjof Schuon: Messenger of the Perennial Philosophy*, 132.
[8] Such comparisons may be found in the Forewords and Introductions to the collections just
mentioned.
[9] *Frithjof Schuon: Messenger of the Perennial Philosophy*, 133.
[10] W. Stoddart, Introduction to *World Wheel: Poems by Frithjof Schuon*, Vols. I-VII, ix.

Hindu *Shakti*. The first subject has its roots in his affinity with the fascinating world of Red Indian heroism and mysticism; the second subject of his art—sacred femininity—has its roots in metaphysics and cosmology; one could also say, in a more relative sense, in Schuon's affinity with Hinduism.[11]

Between 1950 and 1965 Schuon's paintings depicted almost exclusively Indian subjects and themes, whilst those from 1965 onwards most often portrayed Celestial Femininity—as the Holy Virgin, or as the White Buffalo Calf Woman of Red Indian mythology, or as a manifestation of *Shakti*, with reminiscences of Lakshmi and Durga, or other Oriental representations of the merciful and bounteous aspects of the Divine Feminine, such as the Tara of Brahmanism and Kwan-Yin. Thus these paintings draw together certain motifs from the Semitic, primordial, and Eastern mythologies in a synthetic vision which was intensely personal but which vibrated with universal resonances, if one may so put it. Schuon's general approach and style is described by Barbara Perry, in her catalogue notes for the 1981 exhibition, as

> quite simple, spontaneous, and natural, and without any affectation of didactic symbolism. Fundamentally, what he portrays are higher realities as lived through the medium of his own soul.[12]

Schuon's American Indian paintings address their primordial world in all its "sacerdotal hieratism and heroic dignity",[13] and its sacramental and polysynthetic sense of the theophanic qualities of nature. One can discern two recurrent subjects/themes, often within the same painting: the Indian sage/chief (Wisdom) and the Indian woman (Beauty), sometimes as Pté San Win, the celestial messenger, sometimes as an Indian maiden. As Patrick Laude has noted, this "encounter of Shamanic Primordiality and Celestial Femininity is far from fortuitous".[14] Schuon himself remarked of his earliest fully realized artwork:

> My first paintings portrayed two Red Indian women, one clothed and the other naked; since then I have more than once repeated this theme, as it signifies the antithesis between sacred form and sacred content, or between the veiling and the unveiling of the holy. Besides purely narrative Indian pictures I often painted the sage—or the masculine nature of wisdom—in the form of an old Indian chief; I often represented him as the center of a council. My paintings of women represented the

---

[11] M. Pollack, Editor's Introduction to *Images of Primordial and Mystic Beauty: Paintings by Frithjof Schuon*, 2.

[12] B. Perry, *Frithjof Schuon: Metaphysician and Artist* (unpaginated; later reproduced, with some modifications, in *Feathered Sun*).

[13] J-B. Aymard and P. Laude, *Frithjof Schuon: Life and Teachings*, 117.

[14] J-B. Aymard and P. Laude, *Frithjof Schuon: Life and Teachings*, 117.

complement to this, namely beauty, with all the virtues that go with it; my starting point here—in these as in other pictures—was not a deliberate symbolism, but simply a reality that flowed forth from my nature; the meaning was prefigured in my inward being, and did not lie in my conscious intention.[15]

Schuon often also returned to the sacred image of the feathered sun which was found on Indian vestments and tipis, and which he described in these words:

> The Sun is composed of concentric circles formed of stylized eagle feathers; the resulting impression is particularly evocative in that the symbol simultaneously suggests center, radiation, power, and majesty. This symbiosis between the sun and the eagle, which is to be found again in the celebrated headdress of feathers formerly worn by chiefs and great warriors, brings us back to the symbolism of the Sun Dance: here man is spiritually transformed into an eagle soaring towards Heaven and becoming identified with the rays of the Divine Sun.[16]

Over the years and without any intention on his part, the feathered sun became a symbol for Schuon's own spiritual message.[17] Whilst most of Schuon's Indian paintings center on the chief/sage and/or woman, many related motifs and a wealth of visual details pertaining to Indian life give these canvases both vibrancy and poignancy. In recapturing something of the ambience of the ancestral world they serve as an irreplaceable complement to Schuon's writings on the Indians.

Celestial Femininity
As Seyyed Hossein Nasr observes in his introduction to a compilation of Schuon's articles,

> There is certainly a strong awareness of the feminine dimension of spirituality and the spiritual significance of femininity in his writings. While dealing on the metaphysical level with the Divine Infinity as the feminine hypostasis of the One and creative act or *maya* as the feminine consort of the creating word or Logos, he has also written some of the most beautiful pages of living spirituality concerning the Virgin Mary in both Christianity and Islam and even explained the reason for the presence of a feminine element in Mahayana Buddhism, a tradition which appears to be so masculine in both its doctrine and its operative aspects.

[15] Frithjof Schuon, quoted in M. Pollack, Editor's Introduction to *Images of Primordial and Mystic Beauty: Paintings by Frithjof Schuon*, 3-4.

[16] *Feathered Sun*, "The Sun Dance", 100.

[17] Frithjof Schuon, letter to Leo Schaya, October 10, 1981, quoted in *Frithjof Schuon: Messenger of the Perennial Philosophy*, 102. (The feathered sun is also the emblem for World Wisdom, Schuon's publisher.)

His paintings are also replete with feminine American Indian figures or the Virgin who is the subject of his non-Indian paintings.[18]

Of Beauty in the feminine form Schuon has written:

> Woman, synthesizing in her substance virgin nature, the sanctuary, and spiritual company, is for man what is most lovable; in a certain respect she represents the projection of merciful Inwardness in barren out-wardness, and in this regard she assumes a sacramental or quasi-Divine function.[19]

Elsewhere he writes of "the alchemical role and the 'dissolving' power of woman's beauty" which triggers the "liquefaction of the hardened heart".[20] Metaphysically, femininity is a kind of reverberation of the "unlimitedness, virginal mystery, and maternal mercy" of the Divine Principle Itself.[21] These fragments help to explain the centrality of the Feminine in Schuon's artistic *oeuvre*, in both Indian and non-Indian paintings.

Following Schuon's visions of Mary in 1965 his paintings were largely given over to the Virgin Mother:

> Since that experience I could scarcely paint anything other than the Holy Virgin. . . . I painted her, not as she is portrayed in Christian religious art, but as I had inwardly experienced her, that is as virginal Mother or as motherly Virgin, and beyond all theological forms; as the embodiment of the Divine Mercy and at the same time of the *Religio Perennis*, somehow uniting in her person Christianity, Islam, and Hinduism, in conformity with my own nature.[22]

These paintings were "not in the style of Christian icons but in the form of the Biblical Shulamite or the Hindu *Shakti*".[23] He later wrote of these paintings, in a letter:

> These pictures have something sacramental about them and hence have by principle an interiorizing effect; and at the same time . . . they have their source in the same archetype as the sacramental images of the Buddha. The meaning of these images is the actualization of the Presence of the Sacred, then it is holy immobility, silence, and inwardness; thus the remembrance of God. Hence in my pictures of Mary there is something of the golden, earth-remote *barakah* of the Buddhist spiri-

---

[18] S.H. Nasr, Introduction to *Essential Frithjof Schuon*, 40.

[19] *Logic and Transcendence*, "Concerning the Love of God", 194.

[20] *Stations of Wisdom*, "Manifestations of the Divine Principle", 86.

[21] *From the Divine to the Human*, "The Message of the Human Body", 95.

[22] Frithjof Schuon, quoted in *Frithjof Schuon: Messenger of the Perennial Philosophy*, 102-103. It should be noted that Schuon also had a visionary dream about Pté San Win, described in a letter dated November 14, 1984; see 213.

[23] B. Perry, *Frithjof Schuon: Metaphysician and Artist*.

tual message; it is as though something of that world of the Spirit had also to be present in our spiritual way. . . . I must mention that the image of the Buddha was for me a kind of revelation even in my child-hood, and that something of it lies in my very nature.[24]

Elsewhere he wrote of sacred art and of the Holy Virgin (and, by exten-sion, of kindred manifestations of the Divine Feminine):

This is indeed the meaning of sacred art: to immobilize in the Center the human being who strays, or is tossed about, in the world; to hold him fast by means of beauty, but beauty of the holy, which is beauty of the Inward, the beauty of Paradise, of prayer; the beauty of God. And this is also represented in human form by the Holy Virgin: she is "exteriorization with a view to interiorization", visibleness of the Invis-ible; she is the merciful Inward in the outward, and hence the merciful way to the Inward; she is prayer become man, and thus also Paradise become man.[25]

Sacred Nudity

In Schuon's paintings the feminine form is often presented in a state of sacred nudity. Here we are a world away from the representations of the female nude in European oil painting, which all too often amounts to no more than a celebration of the flesh as flesh, sometimes degenerating into the lascivious. Schuon's paintings are much more akin to the ancient traditions of Hindu art, and also to Buddhist and Shinto art wherein nudity is associ-ated with primordiality. Asked about the significance of nude figures in his own paintings, Schuon made this reply:

Sacred nudity—which plays an important role not only with the Hindus but also with the Red Indians—is based on the analogical corre-spondence between the "outmost" and the "inmost": the body is then seen as the "heart exteriorized", and the heart for its part "absorbs" as it were the bodily projection; "extremes meet". It is said, in India, that nudity favors the irradiation of spiritual influences; and also that feminine nudity in particular manifests Lakshmi and consequently has a beneficial effect on the surroundings. In an altogether general way, nudity expresses—and virtually actualizes—a return to the essence, the origin, the archetype, thus to the celestial state: "And it is for this that, naked, I dance," as Lalla Yogishwari, the great Kashmiri saint, said after having found the Divine Self in her heart. To be sure, in nudity there is a *de facto* ambiguity because of the passional nature of man; but there is not only the passional nature, there is also the gift of contemplativity

[24] Frithjof Schuon, letter to Leo Schaya, August 28, 1985, quoted in *Frithjof Schuon: Messenger of the Perennial Philosophy*, 102.
[25] Frithjof Schuon, quoted in *Frithjof Schuon: Messenger of the Perennial Philosophy*, 111.

which can neutralize it, as is precisely the case with "sacred nudity"; similarly, there is not only the seduction of appearances, there is also the metaphysical transparency of phenomena which permits one to perceive the archetypal essence through the sensory experience. St. Nonnos, when he beheld St. Pelagia entering the baptismal pool naked, praised God for having put into human beauty not only an occasion of fall, but also an occasion of rising towards God.[26]

In several canvases, the White Buffalo Calf Woman, Pté San Win (who in her "celestial substance" is the goddess Wohpé), appears naked or semi-naked. At the time these paintings appeared, Europeans were unaware of several traditional accounts of the coming of the Calumet in which the heavenly envoy is described as being naked. Owing to the Christian missionaries' abhorrence of any depictions of nudity, the narratives had been somewhat doctored for European consumption, the full accounts only coming to light in a book incorporating English translations of recordings of Lakota holy men, made by James R. Walker in the twilight years of the nineteenth century.[27] Schuon had known intuitively that the White Buffalo Calf Woman would, of necessity, have appeared in a naked state: the disclosure of the traditional accounts corroborated his intuition. Michael Fitzgerald relates that he compared Pté San Win with "other manifestations of celestial femininity in Hinduism, Buddhism, and Shintoism, who are often traditionally depicted in a primordial state without clothing."[28]

Schuon's treatment of sacred nudity in his Indian paintings foreshadowed his analogous treatment of the Virgin. Needless to say, these paintings provoked some scandal amongst those who could only accept representations of the Virgin within the conventions of the Christian tradition. Such folk might usefully recall St Paul's dictum that "Unto the pure, all things are pure".[29] On the subject of nudity we might also take note of Patrick Laude's explanation of this aspect of Schuon's art:

> If nudity is frequent in Schuon's pictorial opus, it is because it is like the sacerdotal garment of esoterism. Extrinsically, it is also plausible that the manifestation of sacred nudity had a positive role to play as antidote to the trivialization and profanation—most often unconscious—of the

[26] Deborah Casey, "The Basis of Religion and Metaphysics: An Interview with Frithjof Schuon", 74-78.

[27] James R. Walker, *Lakota Belief and Ritual* (1980). Since the publication of Walker's recordings other accounts confirming the nakedness of the Buffalo Calf Woman have also come to light. For more details on this fascinating episode see *Frithjof Schuon: Messenger of the Perennial Philosophy*, 109-110, 213.

[28] *Frithjof Schuon: Messenger of the Perennial Philosophy*, 110.

[29] Barbara Perry mobilizes this Pauline maxim (Titus 1:15) in her discussion of nudity in Schuon's art in *Frithjof Schuon: Metaphysician and Artist*.

human body in the modern world. The deepest way of revealing the corruption of a phenomenon does not in fact consist of dissimulating or excluding its manifestations . . . but in exalting and explaining the sacred norm whose corruption has led astray its message.[30]

But let us give the last word to Schuon himself, in his German poem "Lalla", in honor of the fourteenth century Kashmiri saint:

> When Lalla Yogishwari found *Atma*
> Within herself, the outer world became
> Her sole garment, a web of dreams;
> Thus she went naked beneath the vault of Heaven.
> And as she entered from the outward to the Inward,
> So did the Inward enter her body's fullness;
> And thus she went naked and dancing through the land —
> In Lakshmi's ecstasy and in *Atma*'s stillness.[31]

Principles and Style in Schuon's Art

Given our extended discussion (in chapter 9) of archetypes, symbolism, and the functions of traditional art, and Schuon's explication of those principles which preclude an exteriorizing and literalistic naturalism, it is unnecessary to make more than a few passing remarks about Schuon's artistic style in his oil paintings. Most of his canvases are no more than 24 inches in height or width. They combine the principles and rules of traditional art, particularly those of icons, with some techniques of Western painting, though—obviously!—never lapsing into the sentimental humanism or opaque naturalism of post-Renaissance art. The strict application of the laws of perspective is thus precluded, as is excessive foreshadowing or shading.[32] In her catalogue notes Barbara Perry wrote that

> The fact that Schuon combines these [traditional] rules with a kind of intellectual rigor on the one hand and an adequate observation of nature on the other gives his painting a powerful originality and exceptional expressiveness. In short, he combines the positive features of Western art with the rigor and symbolism of the Egyptian wall painting or Hindu miniature. Perhaps one could say that Schuon's work, as regards its technical aspects, lies somewhere between the Hindu miniature and

---

[30] J-B. Aymard and P. Laude, *Frithjof Schuon: Life and Teachings*, 123.

[31] Frithjof Schuon, "Lalla", *Songs for a Spiritual Traveler*, 129; the German original is on page 128.

[32] For a more extended discussion of particular aspects of Schuon's art, and its relation to the metaphysical principles which he expounds in his written work, see P. Laude's "Metaphysical and Spiritual Aesthetics", in J-B. Aymard and P. Laude, *Frithjof Schuon: Life and Teachings*, 107-131.

expressionism, while at the same time being flavored with a certain influence from Japan.[33]

Michael Pollack, too, furnishes us with a succinct statement about Schuon's style:

> It is essential to understand that Schuon as a painter is not interested in originality and innovation; he is fascinated by the subject matter alone, its origin being what he observed among the Indians or an inner vision of spiritual realities. As for style, Schuon applies the general rules of traditional pictorial art, the first principle being that a painting must take into account the flatness and immobility of the surface; it should not represent three-dimensional space nor a too accidental and hence fragmentary movement. Schuon has an affinity with Hindu art and Christian icons, and also, in a more secondary way, he accepts—at least partially—the techniques of a Van Gogh, a Gauguin, a Hodler, or a Covarrubias. We should also mention that Schuon likes to repeat his subjects, which fact derives from his interest or fascination with them; it would be superficial and pedantic to reproach the painter for this kind of monotony, all the more so in that traditional art always has the tendency to repeat the same motifs, thus to unfold their potentialities.[34]

Pollack's claim here may appear to contradict Perry's reference to Schuon's "originality"; but the contradiction is more apparent than real as Pollack stresses that "originality" (understood as innovation and novelty) was no part of Schuon's intention or aspiration. The undoubted originality (in the sense of uniqueness) of Schuon's art simply derives from the fact that it was the production of an extraordinarily gifted individual, blessed with both penetrating metaphysical discernment and an exceptional aesthetic sensibility. The fact that Schuon was able to draw on many different traditional and cultural influences also testifies to the peculiar conditions in which we live in the modern era—conditions which are generally inimical but which have their compensatory aspects. Concerning Schuon's assimilation of certain post-impressionist techniques, most conspicuously from Gauguin, as well as a certain "primordial flavor and qualitative insight"[35] which a few modern painters evince in spite of all, Sharlyn Romaine has added this:

---

[33] B. Perry, *Frithjof Schuon: Metaphysician and Artist.*

[34] M. Pollack, Editor's Introduction to *Images of Primordial and Mystic Beauty: Paintings by Frithjof Schuon*, 2.

[35] J-B. Aymard and P. Laude, *Frithjof Schuon: Life and Teachings*, 116. Laude also observes that "Schuon's affinity with Gauguin doubtless results from the perfume of virginal and primordial innocence that emanates from the best of Gauguin's Tahitian paintings."

In the case of "post-impressionist" painters such as Gauguin, Van Gogh, and Hodler, one may sense the lack of an interesting choice of subjects, but one cannot deny the fascinating message of their styles. Conversely, one may reject the naturalistic style of the "academic" artists from Michelangelo to Ingres, but one must nevertheless accept those works whose content shows nobility and grandeur. . . . In these cases the aesthetic, psychological, and moral qualities of the subject excuse or even neutralize the errors of a totally naturalistic style.[36]

Schuon's work, in all its dimensions—metaphysical, artistic, poetic—is concerned not only with metaphysical principles (though these are the bedrock of all else), but with "their cosmic and human radiation".[37] This is not to say that his paintings are a didactic application or extension of his metaphysical expositions; rather, they are a complementary aspect of a thoroughly integrated spiritual and aesthetic personality. Whatever the various influences that exerted themselves on Schuon's artistic techniques and on his formal artistic vocabulary, his "pictorial genius is his own and could never be isolated from the spiritual infusion that animates it".[38]

Schuon's Poetry

Annemarie Schimmel, the distinguished Islamicist, has observed that poetry is the natural medium of the mystic, "trying to beckon to a mystery that lies beyond normal human experience".[39] Schuon himself discussed the nature and purpose of poetry in a letter of 1971, now published in part:

Poetry is the "language of the gods"; and *noblesse oblige*; what I mean by this is that the poet has certain responsibilities. In poetry, the musicality of things, or their cosmic essentiality, erupts onto the plane of language; and this process requires grandeur, hence also authenticity, of both image and of the sentiment. The poet spontaneously intuits the underlying musicality of phenomena; under the pressure of an image or an emotion—the emotion, moreover, being naturally combined with concordant images—he expresses an archetypal beauty; without this

---

[36] S. Romaine, "Intention and Style" in *Images of Primordial and Mystic Beauty: Paintings by Frithjof Schuon*, 6. (Fitzgerald notes that "Romaine is the first among several later painters whom Schuon instructed and who thereafter adopted his style of painting. Thus there are paintings that appear at first glance to be Schuon's work but which are by one or another of his students. In the parlance of art historians, one would speak of works that are of 'the school of Schuon'" (*Frithjof Schuon: Messenger of the Perennial Philosophy*, 213).

[37] M. Pollack, Editor's Introduction to *Images of Primordial and Mystic Beauty: Paintings by Frithjof Schuon*, 1.

[38] J-B. Aymard and P. Laude, *Frithjof Schuon: Life and Teachings*, 117.

[39] A. Schimmel, Foreword to *Songs without Names: Poems by Frithjof Schuon*, Vols. I-VI, vii.

pressure, there is no poetry, which means that true poetry always has an aspect of inward necessity, whence its irreplaceable perfume.[40]

He continues, in an unpublished part of the letter:

> Therefore, we must have the subjective and objective grandeur of the point of departure or of the content, then the profound musicality of the soul and of the language; now the grandeur of language must be drawn from its own resources, and this is what the whole formal art of poetry is. Dante had not only grandeur, he also knew how, on the one hand, to infuse this grandeur into language and, on the other, wield language so as to render it adequate to his inward vision.[41]

"The musicality of things"—here is one key to Schuon's poetry, which he also described as "the music of my immutable soul".[42] Another is to be found in a couplet of one of his own poems: "Why has God given us the gift of speech?/For prayer."[43] Schuon's poems: musical prayers. Schuon's poems also recapitulate his metaphysical teachings in a concise lyric form, and, in William Stoddart's words, are "a crystalline and living expression of the *religio perennis*", epitomizing "truth, beauty, and salvation".[44] Of their overt subject matter and inner themes, Stoddart has also written the following:

> In his rich profusion of references to the many and varied cultural forms of Europe and beyond—the streets of the Latin Quarter, Andalusian nights, the Virgen del Pilar, the Macarena, sages such as Dante, Shankara, Pythagoras and Plato, the Psalms of David, Arab wisdom, the graces of the Bodhisattvas, Tibetan prayer-wheels, Samurai and Shinto, the songs of love and longing of many peoples—in all of these diverse cultures, Schuon captures the timeless message of truth and beauty which each contains, and renders it present in a most joyful way. When these cultural forms happen to be ones that the reader himself has known and loved, the joy that emanates from the poems is great indeed.[45]

In the letter already cited Schuon reveals something of his view about how poetry should be composed:

---

[40] *Spiritual Perspectives and Human Facts*, "Appendix: Selections from Letters and Previously Unpublished Writings", 233.

[41] Unpublished writings, courtesy of World Wisdom.

[42] Frithjof Schuon, quoted in *Frithjof Schuon: Messenger of the Perennial Philosophy*, 132.

[43] Frithjof Schuon, "Panacea", *Adastra & Stella Maris*, 211.

[44] W. Stoddart, Introduction to *Songs without Names: Poems by Frithjof Schuon*, Vols. I-VI, xv.

[45] W. Stoddart, Introduction to *Songs without Names: Poems by Frithjof Schuon*, Vols. I-VI, xiv.

Hardly anyone knows how to write it—spiritual motives notwith-standing—and also because most true poets are the dupes of their talent and get lost in prolixity instead of letting the muse take over, for the muse is sometimes very parsimonious, which is saying something! This implies that there is an inward pressure that tolerates no vagueness or chitchat, and this pressure must be of a certain order of grandeur, whence the "musical crystallinity" of poetry, the convincing power of its inward necessity.[46]

And in his playfully entitled "By the Way":

> Poetry is a message — or else merely art,
> A play of words, before which one bows;
> I would rather be a minstrel in the streets
> Who proclaims a way to the Highest Good.[47]

In her Foreword to *Songs Without Names*, Annemarie Schimmel compares Schuon's poems to those of Rilke and discusses the difficulties of poetic translation. But, she suggests, in the end it is the content of the poems which "really matters", "the simple prayers of the longing soul", expressed in a mode far from the complex elaborations of his metaphysical expositions. In these prayerful poems, writes Schimmel,

> God is the center, the primordial ground which comprehends every-thing, manifesting Himself through the colorful play of His creations. And it is the human heart alone which can reflect the incomprehensible Being, for man's central quality is divinely inspired love, which is the axis of our life.[48]

*   *   *

> Ihr meint, ich sei der Sänger, weil ich singe —
> Weil in der Schönheit ich die Gottheit sah.
> Ich bin in einen Strom hineingestiegen —
> Der namenlose Sang war immer da.
> Das Liebeslied ist jenseits aller Zeit —
>
> Wer kann der Dichtung Zauber voll erfassen?
> O ewiger Gesang, o Himmelsstrom,
> Geboren aus dem Quell de Seligkeit —
> O Andacht, die der Seele Sein vergisst
> Und nur noch weiß, was Licht und Liebe ist.
>
> ("Der Sänger")

---

[46] *Spiritual Perspectives and Human Facts*, "Appendix: Selections from Letters and Previously Unpublished Writings", 233.

[47] Frithjof Schuon, "By the Way", *Adastra & Stella Maris: Poems by Frithjof Schuon*, 229.

[48] A. Schimmel, Foreword to *Songs without Names: Poems by Frithjof Schuon*, Vols. I-VI, vii.

Ye think I am a singer, because I sing —
Because in beauty I have seen Divinity.
I have but stepped into a river —
The nameless song was ever there.
The love song is beyond all time —
Who can fathom the magic of poetry?
O eternal song, O heavenly stream,
Born of the fountainhead of bliss —
Of devotion, that forgets the soul's existence,
And now knows only Light and Love.

("The Singer")[49]

---

[49] Frithjof Schuon, *Songs for a Spiritual Traveler*, 100-101.

IV

Signs of the Times

"Our own time" possesses no quality that makes it the measure or criterion of values in regard to that which is timeless. It is the timeless that, by its very nature, is the measure of our time.

(Frithjof Schuon, "No Activity without Truth", 36-37)

12

Cosmic Cycles and the *Kali-Yuga*

Maya is the breath of *Atma*: *Atma* "breathes" through *Maya*. . . . The Universe proceeds from God and returns to Him: these are the cosmic cycles belonging to the microcosm as well as to the macrocosm.[1]

Our age . . . marks the end of a great cyclic period of terrestrial humanity . . . and so must recapitulate or manifest again in one way or another everything that is included in the cycle, in conformity with the adage "extremes meet".[2]

The doctrine of the *Kali-Yuga* and the *Kalki-Avatara*—the "dark age" and the "universal Messiah"—[is] a doctrine whose importance is such that no Revelation can ignore it, whatever its symbolism, which is to say that it constitutes a criterion of orthodoxy and thereby of spiritual purity and wholeness. Since this truth, which is Christian as well as Hindu, being indeed found everywhere, excludes evolutionism, it is a bulwark of tradition against the most pernicious errors.[3]

The Romanian philosopher, E.M. Cioran, has written, "Out in the street, suddenly overcome by the 'mystery' of Time, I told myself that Saint Augustine was quite right to deal with such a theme by addressing himself directly to God: with whom else to discuss it?"[4] Well, one sympathizes. The modern mentality has flattened Time into nothing more than a quantitative and horizontal duration, robbing it of its internal rhythms, resonances, and qualitative determinations. Time has becomes nothing more than profane history. In order to recuperate traditional understandings of Time, Guénon turned to the ancient Indian tradition. He opens *Crisis of the Modern World* (1927) with this passage:

The Hindu doctrine teaches that a human cycle, to which it gives the name *Manvantara*, is divided into four periods marking so many stages during which the primordial spirituality gradually becomes more and more obscured; these periods correspond with the Golden, Silver, Bronze, and Iron Ages of the ancient Western traditions. We are now in the fourth age, the *Kali-Yuga* or "dark age", and have been so already, it

---

[1] *In the Face of the Absolute*, "*Atma-Maya*", 64.
[2] *Transcendent Unity of Religions*, "Preface", xxxiii.
[3] *Gnosis: Divine Wisdom*, "Vicissitudes of Spiritual Temperaments", 45.
[4] E.M. Cioran, *Anathemas and Admirations*, 122.

is said, for more than six thousand years. . . . Since that time, the truths which formerly lay within reach of all mankind have now become more and more hidden and difficult of approach. . . . It is also stated that what is thus hidden will become visible again at the end of our cycle, which, by reason of the continuity linking all things together, will coincide with the beginning of a new cycle.[5]

Time and the Doctrine of Cycles

Some of the principal themes of Guénon's later writings emerge in the light of the doctrine of cycles, which is most clearly expounded within the Indian tradition but which can be found in one form or another virtually everywhere in the traditional worlds. The doctrine provides the context for Guénon's exposure of the "solidification" and "materialization" whereby humankind becomes increasingly impervious to beneficent spiritual influences from above and, by the same token, increasingly vulnerable to infernal influences from below (psychism being a case in point). Guénon is also at pains to point out that because man and the cosmos itself are reciprocally influenced then the same process of degeneration so clearly evident in man himself is also taking place, simultaneously, in the terrestrial environment. This is all of a piece with Guénon's anatomization of the "signs of the times" and his unyielding critique of "modernity" in all its bizarre guises. Schuon assumes all this as background: it is clear that this doctrine also informs Schuon's understanding of time, his sense of terrestrial and human history as a whole, and his understanding of the "end times" in which we find ourselves.[6] It is perfectly clear from his writings that Schuon, like Guénon, is keenly aware of the imminent end of the current cycle. In *The Feathered Sun* (1990) we find this: "The writer of these lines knows that the present world will come to an end, in a future which is not far off."[7] In this chapter it is not our

---

[5] R. Guénon, *Crisis of the Modern World*, 1.

[6] One does not find in Frithjof Schuon's writings any sustained and systematic exposition of this doctrine, though there are many references to the *Kali Yuga*, and to the "latter days", the "end times", and so on. Clearly, Schuon is familiar with the Hindu sources; furthermore, he is also conversant with a range of Indian texts concerning cycles, including the *Manava Dharma Shastra* and several *Puranas*, of which Guénon himself was apparently unaware. (See *René Guénon: Some Observations*, "René Guénon: Some Observations", 11-12.) No doubt there are good reasons for Schuon's comparative reticence on this subject—amongst them his eschewal of historicism of all kinds. As he remarks in one of his essays, "it is not normally our practice to enter into the details of historical or personal phenomena" (*Esoterism as Principle and as Way*, "The True Remedy", 162).

[7] *Feathered Sun*, "A Message on Indian Religion", 107. See also J. Biès, "Frithjof Schuon: A Face of Eternal Wisdom" (interview), 8, where Schuon unequivocally states that "We are in the last phase of the *Kali-Yuga*, [though] not in the very last. . . .".

purpose to unravel this doctrine nor to consider its manifold ramifications.[8] Rather we shall touch on a few aspects of the doctrine which are especially germane to Schuon's work. However, before that, a few general remarks.

Firstly, it is perhaps useful to point out that the doctrine is both metaphysical and cosmological, which is to say that it is concerned both with those ultimate realities which lie "outside" time and space (metaphysics), and, in the light of that "science of the Real", with the various time-space relativities which comprise the universe in both its subtle and gross aspects (cosmology). It might also be said, recalling our discussion of the Five Divine Presences, that the doctrine pertains to that which lies "between" the divine Principle and the manifested world, and with the "creative rhythm emerging from the divine nature itself".[9] All this is nicely summed up in this passage from Schuon:

> Basically, metaphysical doctrine is nothing other than the science of reality and illusion, and it presents itself, from the starting-point of the terrestrial state—and thus with its cosmological extension—as the science of the existential or principial degrees, as the case may be: on the one hand, it distinguishes within the principle itself between Being and Non-Being, or in other words between the personal God and the impersonal Divinity; on the other hand, within manifestation, metaphysics—now become cosmology—distinguishes between the formless and the formal, the latter being in turn divided into two states, the one subtle or animic and the other gross or corporeal.[10]

The doctrine of cycles—which is "diverse, but nonetheless homogeneous with regard to the essential"[11]—is antithetical to the views of time and history which have so tyrannized the modern mentality, mesmerized as it is by "evolution" and "progress". It concerns the unfolding of various terrestrial and cosmic cycles without an understanding of which we are quite unable to discern the larger, transhistorical forces at work throughout human history—not to mention the awesome mysteries of time and space as they are writ on the universe at large. One Indian scholar has summarized

---

[8] Readers interested in more detailed accounts of the doctrine of cycles and traditional understandings of time are directed to the following sources: R. Guénon, *Crisis of the Modern World* and *The Reign of Quantity and the Signs of the Times*; A.K. Coomaraswamy, *Time and Eternity*, M. Lings, *Ancient Beliefs and Modern Superstitions*, chap. 1, and *The Eleventh Hour*; A. Snodgrass, *Architecture, Time, and Eternity*. Interesting commentaries are also to be found in W. Quinn, *The Only Tradition*; Joseph Campbell (ed.), *Man and Time: Papers from the Eranos Yearbooks*; Mircea Eliade, *The Myth of the Eternal Return* and "Religious Symbolism and Modern Man's Anxiety" in *Myths, Dreams, and Mysteries*.

[9] *Esoterism as Principle and as Way*, "Understanding Esoterism", 27n.

[10] *René Guénon: Some Observations*, "René Guénon: Definitions", 2.

[11] *From the Divine to the Human*, "Structure and Universality of the Conditions of Existence", 60n.

the Hindu understanding of the cosmological process this way: "manifestation from the unmanifest, gradual unfoldment, involution in the reverse sequence, and final dissolution in the original source".[12] In brief, everything "comes from" *Brahman* and everything "returns" thither. Schuon gives us a more elaborate metaphysical exposition which also makes clear that the Hindu understanding of the doctrine is but one of its expressions.

> The doctrine of Relativity or of "Illusion", or of the "Divine Magic", is joined to that of cosmic cycles: the world, or the manifested universe, the creation, therefore, is like the "breathing" of the Divinity; it is essentially subject to phases, to "divine lives", as the Hindus would say. There is firstly the *para*, which is the "life" of the demiurge itself and which lasts one hundred "years of Brahma"; the "days of Brahma"—the *kalpas*—each represent the duration of a world, hence a "historical creation", the "night of Brahma" being the "divine void" between two creations *ex nihilo*. Each *kalpa* comprises one thousand *maha-yugas*, each of which is divided into four ages or *yugas*, namely: the *krita-*, the *treta-*, the *dvapara-*, and the *kali-yuga*; these are, analogically speaking, the golden age, the silver age, the bronze age, and the iron age. Doubtless, there are variations in the different cosmological symbolisms of India, but the fundamental pattern remains identical; be that as it may, what matters essentially is to know that the world is an "optical illusion", and that this illusion necessarily comprises modes and cycles, as is shown, moreover, by the modes and cycles of nature around and within us. The universal modes and cycles are so to speak the marks of Relativity, by their very diversity and plurality; to the Principle alone belongs the glory of being simple and unique. We could also say that "creation as such"—the invariability of the existential phenomenon and the coeternal chain of the cycles—attests to the Divine Necessity, while a "particular creation"—a given mode and cycle—attests on the contrary to the Divine Freedom; although from another point of view, and quite evidently, Necessity and Freedom are everywhere combined.[13]

In *The Reign of Quantity and the Signs of the Times* Guénon alludes frequently to the Hindu formulations of the doctrine; the whole work is pervaded by a sense of the inevitable cataclysm which must close the present terrestrial cycle and bring this world to an end. Other perennialists, particularly Martin Lings, have also written about the "eleventh hour" and the "latter days" to which so many traditions allude. However, this is a domain into which one should venture with great caution; it is all too easy to get lost in endless speculations about the precise duration of the ages and in fruitless attempts to determine exactly where we might stand with regard

---

[12] N. Panda, *Cyclic Universe*, vol. 2, 742.
[13] *Survey of Metaphysics and Esoterism*, "Creation as a Divine Quality", 55-56.

to the Last Days. As Schuon cautions, "no one can know the 'moment' of the end of the world, and . . . no calculation—even one established on serious bases—can lead to an even slightly precise result".[14] Speculations in this domain often produce a jumble of traditional images and symbols, wrenched out of context and forcibly married to an historicist understanding of time and history, one quite immune to various considerations which would make the traditional doctrines more intelligible—the characteristically Indian penchant for the hyperbolic use of number, for instance, or the privileging of myth over history, or, indeed, the recondite symbolism of numbers themselves. More often than not the method of analysis and interpretation is altogether inadequate to the material at hand. This is but one of many fields where "the reign of quantity" has obscured any real understanding. It hardly need be added that when the spiritually immature are exposed to doctrines concerning the end of the world, then all manner of incongruous results may well be expected.

One of the sayings of the Prophet Muhammad: "No time cometh upon you but is followed by a worse."[15] As we have seen when considering the relationship of a religious tradition to its origin in a divine Revelation, the traditional outlook generally supposes that the best of worlds was "in the beginning", at the moment of creation, and that thereafter follows firstly an "unfolding" and then a long process of decline and degeneration—though there may also be periods of growth, of regeneration, and blossoming. In the frame of human history this process can be most clearly seen in the spiritual radiance which shines forth from the moment of a particular Revelation, inevitably followed, over time, by man's increasing indifference to the messages of Revelation vouchsafed by tradition, his neglect of those teachings and values which his ancestors held dear, his increasing ensnarement in ephemeralities and superficialities, his forgetfulness, his "descent" into matter.

In previous ages, a different spiritual and material order obtained, one quite unintelligible—indeed, impenetrable—to a scientistic mentality which, on the one hand, is more or less completely ignorant of the supra-corporeal dimensions of reality and the "multiple states of being", and, on the other, is locked into a horizontal and quantitative understanding of time and an evolutionistic view of history. To adduce one instance of a feature of earlier ages which is now beyond the grasp of both "science" and "history"— simple enough but with far-reaching implications—one need only refer to the fact that previously, in Schuon's words, "The partition between the material and

---

[14] *Treasures of Buddhism*, "Cosmological and Eschatological Viewpoints", 50n. See also J. Biès, "Frithjof Schuon: A Face of Eternal Wisdom" (interview), 9.

[15] The Prophet, quoted in W. Stoddart, *Remembering in a World of Forgetting*, 5.

animic states was not yet 'hardened' or 'congealed' as is above all the case in our own epoch".[16] And to go one step further, to demonstrate how an ignorance of metaphysical and cosmological principles plays itself out even in the reading of the "material evidence", consider the implications of the whole process of "materialization" (as mapped by Guénon) in the context of evolutionary theory. In his magisterial essay on traditional cosmology and modern science, Titus Burckhardt does just this. After surveying and juxtaposing traditional cosmogonies and Darwinian evolution, he observes that

> It is certain that the process of materialization, going from supersensory to sensory, had to be reflected within the material or corporeal state itself, so that one is on safe ground in saying that the first generations of a new species did not leave their mark in the great book of earthly layering; it is therefore useless to want to seek in sensible matter the ancestors of a species and especially those of man.[17]

Whilst on the subject of evolutionism, it is worth remarking that Schuon has affirmed that while the doctrine of the *Kali-Yuga* and the *Kalki-Avatara* is one most readily found in the Hindu and Christian traditions (the latter clothing the doctrine in a different symbolic vocabulary), its "importance is such that no Revelation can ignore it, whatever its symbolism". The doctrine manifestly excludes evolutionism as a universal principle or as an overarching explanatory theory. Schuon:

> We do not deny that evolution exists within certain limits, as is indeed evident enough, but we do deny that it is a universal principle, hence a law that affects and determines all things, including the immutable; evolution and degeneration can moreover go hand in hand, each then occurring on a different plane. Be that as it may, what has to be categorically rejected is the idea that truth evolves or that revealed doctrines are the product of an evolution.[18]

The Latter Days
It is no accident that the world's religious mythologies are replete with stories of a Fall of some kind; the dramatic allegorical narratives—myths—of peoples from around the globe testify to a more or less universal intuition of the principle that "things go downhill". The principle might most succinctly be summed up this way: creation-expansion-deterioration-dissolution. As Guénon observes, "the development of anything that is manifested will necessarily imply a gradual accelerating movement away from the principle

---

[16] *From the Divine to the Human*, "The Message of the Human Body", 98n.
[17] T. Burckhardt, "Cosmology and Modern Science" in *The Sword of Gnosis*, 148-149.
[18] *Gnosis: Divine Wisdom*, "Vicissitudes of Spiritual Temperaments", 45.

whence it originates".[19] This motif is clearly evident, for example, in the Old Testament accounts of the Creation, the Fall, the Flood, and the Tower of Babel. The principle is given rich symbolic expression in various myths about the different ages, usually four in number and most commonly associated with the metals gold, silver, bronze, and iron. Both the mythological and metaphysical expressions of the principle find their richest expressions in the Hindu tradition, though analogous narratives and doctrines are to be found everywhere (although sometimes heavily veiled, for reasons to which some allusion has already been made).

The doctrine several times surfaces in Schuon's writings about the American Indians; for instance, in "His Holiness and the Medicine Man" in *The Feathered Sun*, Schuon draws attention to the parallelism of the buffalo and the bull in the respective symbolic vocabularies of the Plains Indians and the Hindus:

> A most striking feature of the North American branch of the Primordial *Sanatana Dharma* is the doctrine of the four *yugas*: the sacred animal of the Plains Indians, the buffalo, symbolizes the *maha-yuga* [the great age or cycle], each of its legs representing a *yuga* [an age within the cycle]. At the beginning of this *maha-yuga* a buffalo was placed by the Great Spirit at the West in order to hold back the waters which menace the earth; every year this bison loses a hair, and in every *yuga* it loses a foot. When it will have lost all its hair and its feet, the waters will overwhelm the earth and the *maha-yuga* will be finished. The analogy with the bull of *Dharma* in Hinduism is very remarkable; at every *yuga*, this bull withdraws a foot, and spirituality loses its strength; and now we are near the end of the *kali-yuga*.

And lest we be in any doubt as to the authenticity of the doctrines embedded in this mythic imagery, Schuon goes on to add this:

> Like the orthodox Hindus, the traditional Red Indians have this conviction [of our proximity to the end of the *Kali-Yuga*] which is obviously true in spite of all the mundane optimism of the modern world; but let us add that the compensation of our very dark age is the Mercy of the Holy Name, as it is emphasized in the *Manava Dharma Shastra* and the *Shrimad Bhagavata* and other holy scriptures.[20]

Here is how the *Vishnu Purana*, a Hindu text dating back nearly two millennia, envisages the degenerations which can be expected in the latter days of the *Kali-Yuga*:

---

[19] R. Guénon, *Crisis of the Modern World*, 1.
[20] *Feathered Sun*, "His Holiness and the Medicine Man", 113-114.

Riches and piety will diminish daily, until the world will be completely corrupted. In those days it will be wealth that confers distinction, passion will be the sole reason for union between the sexes, lies will be the only method of success in business, and women will be the objects merely of sensual gratification. The earth will be valued only for its mineral treasures, dishonesty will be the universal means of subsistence, a simple ablution will be regarded as sufficient purification. . . . The observances of castes, laws, and institutions will no longer be in force in the Dark Age, and the ceremonies prescribed by the *Vedas* will be neglected. Women will obey only their whims and will be infatuated with pleasure . . . [while] men of all kinds will presumptuously regard themselves as equals of Brahmins. . . . The Vaishyas will abandon agriculture and commerce and will earn their living by servitude or by the exercise of mechanical professions. . . . The dominant caste will be that of the Shudras.[21.]

No one of any spiritual discernment can fail to be struck by the chilling accuracy of this passage as a description of our present circumstances. As Guénon remarked,

By all traditional data we know that we have been in the *Kali-Yuga* for a long time already; and we can say without fear of error that we are in an advanced phase, a phase whose description in the *Puranas* corresponds in the most striking fashion to the characteristics of our present epoch.[22]

As William Stoddart has noted, this Puranic account has a close parallel in the writings of the Apostle:

In the last days, perilous times shall come: men will love nothing but money and self; they will be arrogant, boastful, and abusive, with no respect for parents, no gratitude, no piety, no natural affection. . . . They will be men who put pleasure in the place of God, who preserve the outward form of religion, but are a standing denial of its reality. . . . Ever learning, but never able to come to a knowledge of the truth.[23]

No civilization is immune to the ravages of the *Kali-Yuga* but Schuon reminds us that there is a significant difference between a falling away from traditional wisdom, such as can today be observed almost anywhere in the East, and its complete repudiation—either by explicit denial or, perhaps

---

[21] *The Vishnu Purana*, quoted in W. Stoddart, *An Outline of Hinduism*, 75-76. These passages, in a different translation, can be found in *The Vishnu Purana*, vol. 2, trans. and ed. H.H. Wilson and Nag Sharan Singh, 662-663, 866-867.

[22] R. Guénon, *Traditional Forms and Cosmic Cycles*, 8.

[23] 2 Timothy 3:1-7, quoted in W. Stoddart, *Remembering in a World of Forgetting*, 64.

more commonly, by neglect—which, amongst the so-called intelligentsia at least, has been the hallmark of the modern West:

> The Oriental civilizations, in their cyclical decadence, have more or less disfigured or corrupted the principles; modern Western civilization denies them, which amounts to killing the patient in order to cure the disease; the *kali-yuga* is everywhere.[24]

Our understanding of the doctrine of cycles will be precarious if it is not also realized that there are cycles within cycles: each civilization, each tradition, will itself go through cycles which echo the greater cosmic rhythms on a smaller temporal scale. Furthermore, the appearance of an *avatara*, or even a great saint or sage, or some other divinely-initiated event, may well inaugurate a new "golden age" within the tradition which yet remains subject to those greater degenerations whose patterns can only be seen from a distant vantage-point. It is in the nature of things that any particular period in human history will necessarily exhibit both "ascents" (returning to the principle) and "descents" (falling away from the principle), both centripetal and centrifugal tendencies. In other words, there are oscillations, alternations, and modulations in Time itself, an understanding of which precludes those over-simplifications which often characterize both linear and cyclic "philosophies" of history. As Schuon writes,

> Objective time is so to speak a spiroidal movement comprising four phases, and this movement is qualitatively ascending or descending, according to what the period of the full cycle requires; this is to say that time is like a wheel that turns, this rotation being itself submitted to a greater rotation, exactly as the rotation of the earth is inscribed in the rotation of the planet around the sun.[25]

It might also be useful to remark in passing that if the doctrine of cycles is to be protected from the corrosive effects of a reductionist historicism we cannot too often repeat that it is only the relative dimensions of Reality which are in any way subject to the vicissitudes of time. One of the abiding principles of the *sophia perennis* is that of aeviternity, in Eliade's words "the eternal intemporal present".[26] A lucid statement of the principle comes from Aquinas: "there is no *before* or *after* to be reckoned with in constant changeless Reality. . . . The *now* of time is not time: the *now* of eternity is

---

[24] *Esoterism as Principle and as Way*, "The True Remedy", 162n.

[25] *From the Divine to the Human*, "Structure and Universality of the Conditions of Existence", 60.

[26] M. Eliade, "Time and Eternity in Indian Thought" in *Man and Time: Papers from the Eranos Yearbooks*, quoted in W. Quinn, *The Only Tradition*, 123.

really the same as eternity."[27] But all this is quite beyond a materialistic outlook in which Time has been flattened out into nothing more than a horizontal duration. Accompanying this "flattening" has been the rise of historicism and the more or less obsessive recording of the minutiae of our temporal existence, paralleling the relentless drive of science to accumulate ever more empirical data—as if understanding could ever be based on mere aggregation! Nor is the rise of historicism without its ironies. Mircea Eliade has suggested that modern man's almost phobic fixation on history—which from a metaphysical viewpoint is an "aspect", so to speak, of *maya*, and thus possessing no more than a contingent reality—might parallel the dying man's re-living of his life in all its particularities, and thus be a sign (seen only by the few) that we are indeed rapidly approaching the end times.[28] "History", after all, is but "the rhythm of universal decadence".[29]

Esoterism in the *Kali-Yuga*

We live in anomalous times. Nowhere is this more graphically demonstrated than in the fact that in the most irreligious and impious period in human history the esoteric wisdoms preserved by the religious traditions are more widely and easily accessible than ever before. Sapiential truths, which previously had remained extrinsically inexpressible and which had been protected by those few capable of understanding them, are now on public display, as it were. Schuon and other perennialists have played a significant role in bringing esoteric wisdoms within the purview of a greater number of people. This calls for some explanation.

The breaching of the prophylactic barriers which previously enclosed traditions has, in part, been caused by historical factors which, in a sense, are "accidental". One might cite the exposure of the Upanishadic Scriptures as a case in point; here certain historical factors— such as the introduction into India of cheap printing presses—conspired with a degree of imprudence on the part of some of the "reformers" of Hinduism to subvert the esoteric status of these Scriptures, which were made available to anyone and everyone. Also there are innumerable cases where a garbled version of half-understood secret doctrines has been thoughtlessly and carelessly put into public circulation. The Biblical verse "For there is nothing covered, that shall not be revealed" has sometimes been taken as a license for all manner of excesses in the popularizing of esoteric doctrines. The warnings about false prophets might often be more to the point.

---

[27] Aquinas, quoted in W. Quinn, *The Only Tradition*, 123.

[28] See Eliade's fascinating essay on this subject in *Myths, Dreams, and Mysteries*.

[29] *Gnosis: Divine Wisdom*, "Vicissitudes of Spiritual Temperaments", 50.

In the case of the traditionalists the unveiling of some esoteric teachings has been considered and prudent. What sorts of factors have allowed this development? Firstly, there are certain cyclic conditions now obtaining which make for an unprecedented situation. In discussing the fact that what was once hid in the darkness is now being brought into the light, Schuon writes:

> There is indeed something abnormal in this, but it lies, not in the fact of the exposition of these truths, but in the general conditions of our age, which marks the end of a great cyclic period of terrestrial humanity—the end of a *maha-yuga* according to Hindu cosmology—and so must recapitulate or manifest again in one way or another everything that is included in the cycle, in conformity with the adage "extremes meet"; thus things that are in themselves abnormal may become necessary by reason of the conditions just referred to.[30]

Secondly, from a more expedient point of view:

> It must be admitted that the spiritual confusion of our times has reached such a pitch that the harm that might in principle befall certain people from contact with the truths in question is compensated by the advantages that others will derive from the self-same truths.[31]

Schuon reminds us of the Kabbalistic adage that "it is better to divulge Wisdom than to forget it".[32] And thirdly there is the fact already mentioned: esoteric doctrines have, in recent times, been so frequently "plagiarized and deformed" that those who are in a position to speak with authority on these matters are obliged to give some account of what "true esoterism is and what it is not".[33]

From another perspective it can be said that the preservation, indeed the very survival, of the formal exoterisms may depend on the revivifying effects of an esoterism more widely understood:

> Exoterism is a precarious thing by reason of its limits or its exclusions: there arrives a moment in history when all kinds of experiences oblige it to modify its claims to exclusiveness, and it is then driven to a choice: escape from these limitations by the upward path, in esoterism, or by the downward path, in a worldly and suicidal liberalism.[34]

---

[30] *Transcendent Unity of Religions*, "Preface", xxxi.
[31] *Transcendent Unity of Religions*, "Preface", xxxi.
[32] *Transfiguration of Man*, "Thought: Light and Perversion", 10.
[33] *Transfiguration of Man*, "Thought: Light and Perversion", 10.
[34] *Esoterism as Principle and as Way*, "Understanding Esoterism", 19.

At a time when "the outward and readily exaggerated incompatibility of the different religions greatly discredits, in the minds of most of our contemporaries, all religion",[35] the exposure of the underlying unity of the religions takes on a deep urgency. This task can only be achieved through esoterism. The open confrontation of different exoterisms, the extirpation of traditional civilizations, and the tyranny of profane ideologies are symptomatic of the cyclical conditions; all play a part in determining the peculiar circumstances in which the most imperious needs of the age can only be answered by a recourse to traditional esoterisms. There is perhaps some small hope that in this climate and given a properly constituted metaphysical framework in which to affirm the "profound and eternal solidarity of all spiritual forms",[36] the different religions might yet "present a singular front against the floodtide of materialism and pseudo-spiritualism".[37]

The hazards and ambiguities attending the exposure of esoteric doctrines to an audience in many respects ill-equipped to understand them have posed the same problems for custodians of traditional esoterisms the world over. Joseph Epes Brown writes of the disclosure of traditional Lakota wisdom, to choose one example, in terms very similar to those used by Schuon:

> In these days those few old wise men still living among them say that at the approach of the end of a cycle, when men everywhere have become unfit to understand and still more to realize the truths revealed to them at the origin . . . it is then permissible and even desirable to bring this knowledge out into the light of day, for by its own nature truth protects itself against being profaned and in this way it is possible it may reach those qualified to penetrate it deeply.[38]

It is no accident that the few remaining holy men amongst the American Indians and perennialists like Schuon should see this matter in the same terms.

* * *

At a time when the forces of anti-Tradition sometimes seem overwhelming and when we feel unable to keep our hands to the plough, let us recall Schuon's reminder that no effort on behalf of the Truth is ever in vain.[39] We

---

[35] *Transcendent Unity of Religions*, "Preface", xxxi.
[36] *Transcendent Unity of Religions*, "Preface", xxxi.
[37] *Gnosis: Divine Wisdom* (1959), "The Sense of the Absolute in Religions", 12. See also W. Perry (ed.), *A Treasury of Traditional Wisdom*, 22n.
[38] J.E. Brown *The Sacred Pipe*, xii. (This passage was omitted from the Penguin edition.) See also *Sufism: Veil and Quintessence*, "Human Premises of a Religious Dilemma", 75-88.
[39] Frithjof Schuon, "No Activity Without Truth", 39.

must dispel the false charges sometimes leveled at traditionalists that they are dusty obscurantists "out of touch" with the contemporary world, that they want to "wind back the clock", that they are romantic reactionaries escaping into an idealized past. The essential message of Tradition is timeless and thus ever new, ever fresh, and always germane to both our immediate condition and to our ultimate destiny. No doubt our crepuscular era is riddled with all manner of confusion but there are always saints and sages in our midst to whom we can turn for guidance. In recent times one might mention such figures as the Algerian Sufi master, Shaykh Ahmad al-Alawi, Hindu sages such as Paramahamsa Ramakrishna, Ramana Maharshi, and Anandamayi Ma, Native American visionaries such as Black Elk and Yellowtail, the Christian mystics Padre Pio and the Benedictine monk, Henri Le Saux, who became Swami Abhishiktananda, not to mention the many wise lamas and masters of the Far Eastern world. Then, too, there is the abiding work and example of the great perennialists. Here are some words from Guénon we would do well to ponder:

> Those who might be tempted to give way to despair should realize that nothing accomplished in this order can ever be lost, that confusion, error, and darkness can win the day only apparently and in a purely ephemeral way, that all partial and transitory disequilibrium must perforce contribute towards the great equilibrium of the whole, and that nothing can ultimately prevail against the power of truth. Their device should be that used formerly by certain initiatory organizations of the West: *Vincit Omnia Veritas.*[40]

As Titus Burckhardt has reminded us, "every loss spells gain: the disappearance of forms calls for a trial and a discernment; and the confusion in the surrounding world is a summons to turn, bypassing all accidents, to the essential".[41] By way of a final observation on the cyclic conditions now obtaining we can take note of a recurrent theme in Schuon's writings on spirituality: the peculiar efficacy, in the latter days, of the Invocation of the Holy Name.[42] This is a "saving barque" to which we can cling when nearly everything else of the spiritual order has been lost to sight. "For whosoever shall call upon the Name of the Lord shall be saved."[43] These words of St. Paul take on new weight and urgency at this juncture in history.

---

[40] These are the concluding words of René Guénon's *Crisis of the Modern World* (1927). This translation is taken from the *Vincit Omnia Veritas* website.

[41] T. Burckhardt, "What is Conservatism?", *The Essential Titus Burckhardt*, 186.

[42] See "Communion and Invocation" in *Pray Without Ceasing*, ed. P. Laude, 72-78.

[43] Romans 10:13.

13

Scientism, Evolutionism, and "Progress"

Modern science is a totalitarian rationalism, which eliminates both Revelation and Intellect, and at the same time a totalitarian materialism which ignores the metaphysical relativity—and hence the impermanence—of matter and the world.[1]

The evolutionary leap from matter to intelligence is the most arbitrary, the most inconceivable, and the most foolish hypothesis possible, in comparison with which "simple faith" seems like a mathematical formula.[2]

Evolutionism is the very negation of the archetypes and consequently of the divine Intellect; it is therefore the negation of an entire dimension of the real.[3]

Guénon and Coomaraswamy detailed an unsparing critique of modernism and identified the chasm which separates normal civilizations from the anomalies of our own times. In most of Schuon's work the explication of metaphysic and the penetration of religious forms remains his central purpose; censures of modernism, tangential to this purpose, tend to be launched through a series of asides. For this reason, while keeping Schuon's work to the forefront, in this chapter we will draw on the work not only of his fellow perennialists but also a range of other commentators who share at least some ground with the traditional outlook. This will provide some background against which readers coming to Schuon's work for the first time might be able better to understand his case against modernism in all its guises.

Modernism and the Tyranny of Scientism

Modernism: this portmanteau term we may loosely define as the assumptions, values, and attitudes of a world-view fashioned by the most pervasive intellectual and moral influences of recent European history, an outlook in conformity with the spirit of the times.[4] One might classify the constituents

---

[1] *Light on the Ancient Worlds*, "Man in the Universe", 98.
[2] "Consequences Flowing from the Mystery of Subjectivity", 197-198. (This essay, in another translation, can also be found in *From the Divine to the Human*, 5.)
[3] *To Have a Center*, "Survey of Integral Anthropology", 50.
[4] It will already be clear to the reader that we are not here using "modernism" in its restricted meaning, designating various experimental movements in the arts in the early twentieth cen-

of modernism under any number of different schema. Lord Northbourne typifies modernism as "anti-traditional, progressive, humanist, rationalist, materialist, experimental, individualist, egalitarian, free-thinking, and intensely sentimental"[5] while Seyyed Hossein Nasr identifies the defining characteristics of modernity as anthropomorphism (i.e., a false humanism), evolutionist progressivism, the absence of any sense of the sacred, and an unrelieved ignorance of metaphysical principles.[6]

For the perennialists, modernism is nothing less than a spiritual disease which continues to spread like a plague across the globe, ravaging traditional cultures wherever they are still to be found. Although its historical origins are European, modernism is now tied to no specific area or civilization. Its symptoms can be detected in a wide assortment of inter-related "mind sets" and "-isms", sometimes involved in cooperative co-existence, sometimes engaged in apparent antagonism, but always united by the same under-lying principles. Scientism, rationalism, relativism, materialism, empiricism, positivism, historicism, psychologism, individualism, humanism, existentialism—some of the prime follies of modernist thought. The pedigree of this family of ideas can be traced back through a series of intellectual and cultural disruptions in European history and to certain vulnerabilities in Christian civilization which left it exposed to the subversions of a profane science.[7] The Renaissance, the Scientific Revolution, and the Enlightenment were all incubators of ideas and values which first decimated Christendom and then spread throughout the world like so many bacilli. Behind the pro-liferating ideologies of the last few centuries we can discern an ignorance of ultimate realities and an indifference, if not always an overt hostility, to the eternal verities conveyed by Tradition.

The foundations of the modern worldview are to be found in post-medieval philosophy and in the ideology of modern science. In earlier chapters we intimated some of the ways in which Western philosophy, since the time of Descartes, has been belligerently anti-traditional and the parent of that "Single Vision" which so appalled Blake and the Romantics.[8] In this chapter we turn to modern philosophy's accomplice, scientism. After some introductory remarks about scientism we will dissect one of its particularly insidious forms, evolutionism, as a kind of case-study.

tury, but in a much more wide-ranging sense.

[5] Lord Northbourne, *Religion in the Modern World*, 13.

[6] S.H. Nasr, "Reflections on Islam and Modern Thought", 119-131.

[7] For a profound analysis of this process see S.H. Nasr, *Man and Nature*, especially chaps. 1 and 2. See also W. Perry, *The Widening Breach: Evolutionism in the Mirror of Cosmology*.

[8] And how suggestive it is that the terms "Romantic" and "Romanticism" have become pejorative in scientific circles: this is hardly surprising as it was the Romantic philosophers and poets who fought a valiant rearguard action against the scientism of their day.

For several centuries now the West has trumpeted the onward march of "Science", extolling its intrepid explorers who, so the story goes, have heroically pushed back the frontiers of knowledge and banished the religiously-motivated superstitions of our credulous ancestors. The luminaries of modern science—Bacon, Descartes, Copernicus, Galileo, Newton, Darwin, Einstein et al.—form modernity's intellectual pantheon. And, indeed, our world has been shaped by the ideas and "discoveries" of such philosophers and scientists. There is no gainsaying the fact that science, through its technical applications, has conferred some benefits on the modern world, though these are often much more ambiguous than was first supposed; we are all too familiar with scientific and technological "advances" whose sinister ramifications took some time to manifest. (A short-hand sample: eugenics, DDT, thalidomide, electro-shock "therapy", Chernobyl, Bhopal.) Not without reason have some of the most disturbing and resonant literary works of the past two centuries been concerned with the unforeseen effects of a runaway science; think of *Frankenstein, Dr. Jekyll and Mr. Hyde, Brave New World*. Increasingly, many thoughtful people are questioning the modern shibboleth of an inexorable "progress", fueled by "science" and implemented by technology. In the face of ever-mounting evidence on all sides it is now dawning on even the most sanguine apostles of a progressivist science that there is something profoundly amiss with our understanding of reality, of ourselves, and our place in the natural order, and that this malady is somehow connected with the despotism of modern science. The contemporary "ecological crisis", actually rooted in a spiritual malaise of which the material disorder is a symptom, is but one token of this state of affairs. There are many others; one might mention, amongst much else, genetic engineering, cloning, cryogenics, industrial diseases, "behavior modification", drug-resistant viruses, nuclear, chemical, and biological warfare, or a projected planetary migration, all of which are cause for the gravest apprehension amongst people who have not been seduced by the materialist ideology and the rhetorical self-aggrandizement of modern science, or more precisely, of *scientism*.

The Scientific Revolution of the seventeenth century heralded the triumph of a particular philosophical outlook (rationalist, materialist) with its attendant epistemology (empiricism) and procedures and protocols (the "scientific method"). Contrary to popular assumption, modern science is *not* simply a disinterested, detached, and value-free mode of inquiry into the material world; it is a complex of disciplines and techniques anchored in culture-bound *assumptions* about and *attitudes* to the nature of reality and the proper means whereby material phenomena might be explored, explained and, perhaps most tellingly, *controlled*. It is, in fact, impossible to separate the methods of modern science from the theories and ideologies which provide its motive force, and it is to this tangled skein that the term "scientism" refers. And like any other "-ism", scientism has its own repertoire of narratives, fables, and images, its own vocabulary and conceptual arsenal, its own paradigms and modes, all these together amounting to what René Guénon called a "pseudo-mythology".[9]

Perhaps the central plank in the scientistic platform is the assumption that modern science contains within itself the necessary and sufficient means for any inquiry into the material world, and that it can and should be an autonomous and self-validating pursuit, answerable to nothing outside itself. This was a new idea in the history of human thought, at radical odds with the traditional view that any inquiry into the natural world could only properly proceed within the cadre of philosophy and religion. Shankara stated that "the world of *maya* is not inexplicable; it is only not self-explanatory". In other words, the tissue of fugitive relativities which comprise the time-space world cannot be properly understood in their own terms but only by recourse to a knowledge which surpasses them. The nature of the material universe is known only in the light of metaphysics, which sees beyond mechanical and auxiliary causes (i.e. the physical "laws", processes, properties, and appearances with which modern science is solely concerned) to the fundamental spiritual causes which underlie all phenomena and without which the chimerical material world would instantly vanish. This principle informs *sacra scientia* and, by the same token, is mocked on all sides by modern science which is a profane inquiry, governed by materialistic assumptions and by an

---

[9] In considering the material discoveries of modern science we would also do well to heed the following passage from Schuon: "In an analogous order of ideas, we should like to answer here the following question: why did Providence leave man in ignorance of certain things—on the plane of the sensible world—which he was bound to discover in the long run? Given that 'an ounce of prevention is worth a pound of cure' and that Heaven could not but foresee the disastrous repercussions—material as well as psychological—of modern discoveries and inventions, it had every interest in speaking to man about paleontology and molecular physics and situating these things in relation to the Absolute and immortality. The chief answer . . . is that it sufficed that Revelation, always preoccupied with 'the one thing needful' and conscious of the uselessness and harmfulness of a purely outward and quantitative knowledge, would not set the example of what it wished to avoid or the coming of what it wished at least to delay. But there is yet another reason to be considered, one that is doubtless less fundamental but not less plausible from our point of view: it was indeed necessary—since 'it must needs be that offences come'—that the men of the 'latter times' should find in their surroundings reasons for believing themselves superior to their ancestors and too intelligent for Revelation; consequently it was necessary to reserve a possible form of knowledge—but one that is spiritually indifferent—that would corroborate and feed the illusions of the Dark Age, the age when the Law of the Buddha shall be 'forgotten', after having been 'imitated' in the preceding age. All this refers, in short, to this saying of the Buddha, which we repeat from memory: 'And why have I taught you nothing about the world? Because this would be of no use to you for the knowledge of the causes of suffering, for the cessation of suffering, for Nirvana'" (*Treasures of Buddhism*, "The Question of Illusion", 46-47).

empirical and quantitative methodology. Not without reason did Guénon characterize modernity as "the reign of quantity". Indeed, it might be said that modern science, in its most fundamental aspect, is based on this *negation*, on the denial of all the suprasensorial dimensions of reality and of the possibilities of human knowledge thereof, vouchsafed by all integral religious and sapiential traditions. In any event, a profane science can only ever tell us about secondary and cooperative causes; it can never get to the root of things, just as it must remain mute whenever we confront questions about *meaning* and *value*. Though modern science has doubtless revealed much material information that was previously unknown, it has also supplanted a knowledge which infinitely outreaches it. As Gai Eaton has observed of the swaggering "discoveries" of modern science: "Our ignorance of the few things that matter is as prodigious as our knowledge of trivialities."[10] We see this in the complacencies and condescensions of those scientists who suppose that we have "outgrown" the "superstitions" of our ancestors.[11]

Critiques of scientism are much in vogue these days. The precarious philosophical foundations of modern science, its epistemological ambiguities, its inability to accommodate its own findings within the Cartesian-Newtonian frame, the consequences of a Faustian pursuit of knowledge and power, the diabolical applications of science in the military industry, the dehumanizing reductionisms of the behavioral "sciences"—all of these have come under fierce attack. New "discoveries" by physicists and the paradoxes of Quantum Theory throw conventional assumptions about time, space, and matter into disarray; Heisenberg's Uncertainty Principle, Chaos Theory, and the New Physics jeopardize the much-vaunted "objectivity" of science; the mechanistic conceptions of a materialistic science, the very language of science, are found to be inadequate in the face of bewildering phenomena which simply do not fit the prevailing models. Commentators as disparate as René Guénon, Kathleen Raine, Theodore Roszak, Mary Midgley, E.F. Schumacher, Philip Sherrard, Wendell Berry, Marilynne Robinson and Seyyed Hossein Nasr awaken us to the provincialism of modern science and

---

[10] *Tomorrow* 13:3, 1964, 191.

[11] Here is a random example from a prestigious Nobel-laureate: "I myself, like many scientists, believe that the soul is imaginary and that what we call our mind is simply a way of talking about the function of our brains. . . . Once one has become adjusted to the idea that we are here because we have evolved from simple chemical compounds by a process of natural selection, it is remarkable how many of the problems of the modern world take on a completely new light" (F. Crick, *Molecules and Men*, quoted in T. Roszak, *Where the Wasteland Ends*, 188). Here indeed is an "intelligence without wisdom" or what Roszak calls a "well-informed foolishness". This kind of materialism is presently "the reigning orthodoxy among philosophers of the mind" (Daniel Dennett, quoted in H. Smith, *Beyond the Post-Modern Mind*, 135-136).

the dangers of a corrosive materialism, an instrumentalist rationality, and its attendant technology. We see that rationality has become man's definition instead of his tool, a tyrannical master rather than a humble servant.

In their uncompromising critique of scientism Schuon and other perennialists do not appeal to a vague humanism nor do they entertain a vision of a "reformed" science. Their impeachment of modern science is authorized by metaphysical principles and by the truths and values enshrined in religious traditions. Much of this repudiation of modern science is predicated on the distinction rehearsed by Whitall Perry:

> Traditional learning is basically qualitative and synthetic, concerned with essences, principles, and realities behind phenomena; its fruits are integration, composition, and unity. Profane academic learning—whether in the arts or sciences—is quantitative and analytical by tendency, concerned with appearances, forces, and material properties; its nature is to criticize and to decompose; it works by fragmentation.[12]

Traditional learning proceeds within a larger framework, that provided by Revelation and Intellection. Modern science, by contrast, asserts a Promethean autonomy and scorns all other avenues of knowledge. This is the crux of the problem. Here we will consider two specific issues: the cleavage between religion and science; and the epistemological limits of a materialistic science.

The modern scientistic outlook is, *in principle*, unable to countenance God (by whatever name), who is either repudiated as an obsolete "hypothesis" or altogether ignored—which amounts to the same thing. Likewise, scientism cannot allow any *sense of the sacred*, the absence of which defines modernity as a whole. As to the much vaunted empiricism of modern science, Schuon remarks, "there is no worse confession of intellectual impotence than to boast of a line of thought because of its attachment to experiment and disdain for principles and speculations".[13]

It is nowadays a commonplace that many of the ills of our time stem from the rift between "faith" and "science", but few people have suggested any convincing means of reconciling the two. Certainly the effusions and compromises of the liberal theologians and "demythologizers" are of no help, marking little more than a thinly-disguised capitulation of religion to

---

[12] W. Perry (ed.), *A Treasury of Traditional Wisdom*, 731. Nasr makes a more explicit distinction between modern and traditional science: "Modern science studies change with respect to change, where a traditional science studies change vis-à-vis permanence through the study of symbols, which are nothing but reflections of permanence in the world of change" (*Sufi Essays*, 88).

[13] *Stations of Wisdom*, "Orthodoxy and Intellectuality", 40.

science.[14] Nor should we be seduced by those ostensibly conciliatory scientists who seem willing to allow a place for religious understandings, all the while making it clear that science will concede nothing of substance (and here we can find no better exemplar of the mentality in question than E.O. Wilson in his popular and muddle-headed work, *Consilience*[15]). However, in the light of traditional metaphysical understandings many of the apparent contradictions between "science" and "religion" simply evaporate. As Schuon remarks:

> The tragic impasse reached by the modern mind results from the fact that most men are incapable of grasping the *compatibility* between the symbolic expressions of tradition and the material discoveries established by modern science.[16]

This is a vital point. It is important to understand that Schuon's disapprobations do not fall on the findings of science as such—he is not an obscurantist—but on the absence of such principles as would situate these discoveries in a context which could preserve the incomparably more important truths incarnated in tradition. A concrete example from Schuon will give the point more weight:

> According to the observations of experimental science, the blue sky that stretches above us is not a world of beatitude, but an optical illusion due to the refraction of light by the atmosphere, and from this point of view it is obviously right to deny that the home of the blessed can be found there; but it would be a great mistake to deny that the association of ideas between the visible heavens and the celestial Paradise results from the nature of things and not from ignorance and naiveté mixed with imagination and sentimentality, for the blue sky is a direct and therefore adequate symbol of the higher—and supersensory—degrees of Existence; it is even in fact a distant reverberation of those degrees and it is necessarily so since it is truly a symbol, consecrated by the sacred Scriptures and by the unanimous intuition of peoples. . . . The fact that the symbol itself may be no more than an optical illusion in no way impairs either its precision or efficacy, for all appearances, including those of space and of the galaxies, are strictly speaking only illusions created by relativity.[17]

---

[14] If an example be required one might adduce the "postmodernist theology" of Don Cupitt.
[15] E.O. Wilson, *Consilience: The Unity of Knowledge*. This work has been subjected to the most searching criticism by Wendell Berry in *Life is a Miracle*.
[16] *Stations of Wisdom*, "Preface", 8-9 (emphasis mine). See also Lord Northbourne, *Looking Back on Progress*, 23-41.
[17] *Light on the Ancient Worlds*, "Fall and Forfeiture", 26-27.

The key to traditional understandings lies in their symbolism, a mode of knowledge quite inaccessible to the scientific mentality. No one will deny that, from one point of view, the earth is not the center of the solar system; this is no reason for jettisoning the more important truth which was carried by the geocentric picture of the universe.[18] (A heliocentric cosmology could also have been the vehicle for the selfsame truth.[19]) Indeed, without the protective truths of traditional symbolisms such material discoveries as do issue from a profane science are likely to be more or less useless or positively destructive. A materially inaccurate but symbolically rich view is always preferable to the reign of brute fact. In falling under the tyranny of a fragmentary, materialistic, and quantitative outlook modern science is irremediably limited by its epistemological base. Of spiritual realities, modern science knows and can know nothing whatever. As Schuon observes:

> Thus there can be no more desperately vain an illusion—far more naïve than is Aristotelian astronomy—than to believe that modern science will end up reaching, through its dizzying course, . . . the truths of religious and metaphysical doctrines.[20]

Furthermore, there is something alienating in science's obsessive interest in the "infinitely small" and the "infinitely great": as Schuon declares elsewhere, "the world of atoms as well as that of galaxies—to express ourselves *grosso modo*—is hostile to human beings, and comprises for them, in principle or potentially, a climate of alienation and terror."[21] Goethe was quite right to refuse to peer down the microscope!

By now it should be clear enough why it is a dangerous prejudice to believe that a materialistic science is harmless enough if it be confined to its own domain—the material world. This realm does not exist *in vacuo* and to pretend that it does only breeds trouble, as history so chillingly demonstrates: "a purely physical science, when it reaches vast proportions, can only lead to catastrophe".[22] Burckhardt exposes some of the issues involved here in writing

> Modern science displays a certain number of fissures that are not only due to the fact that the world of phenomena is indefinite and that therefore no science could come to the end of it; those fissures derive especially from a systematic ignorance of all the noncorporeal dimensions of reality. They manifest themselves right down to the foundations of modern science, and in domains as seemingly "exact" as

[18] *To Have a Center*, "Concerning a Question of Astronomy, 171-177.
[19] *Roots of the Human Condition*, "Problems of Space-Time", 27.
[20] *Form and Substance in the Religions*, "The Five Divine Presences", 65.
[21] *Roots of the Human Condition*, "The Veil of Isis", 18-19.
[22] *Form and Substance in the Religions*, "The Five Divine Presences", 63.

that of physics; they become gaping cracks when one turns to the disciplines connected with the study of the forms of life, not to mention psychology, where an empiricism that is relatively valid in the physical order encroaches strangely upon a foreign field. These fissures, which do not affect only the theoretical realm, are far from harmless; they represent, on the contrary, in their technical consequences, so many seeds of catastrophe.[23]

These fissures might be probed at some length. However, enough has been said to provide a frame within which we can examine one cancerous manifestation of the scientistic spirit, evolutionism, which has a tenacious grip on the mentality of most moderns.

Darwinism: Mega-Evolution and the Transformist Hypothesis

Darwin's hypothesis, foreshadowed in the work of many other contemporary scientists and social theorists alike and germinated in the noxious population theories of Malthus, is one of the most elegant, seductive, and pernicious of "pseudo-mythologies"—a grandiose explanatory theory rooted in metaphysical ignorance and fashioned to the prejudices of the age. In a beguiling admixture of fact, imaginative speculation, circular argumentation, and ingenious system-building Darwin seemed to produce an "objective" account of the development of species. Evolutionism may be defined as the concurrence of certain paleontological and biological facts, assumptions, and speculations wedded to a cluster of philosophical and socio-political ideas and values. Thus Darwinism has both a scientific/biological and an ideological/social dimension. Indeed, in the end, as Schuon insists,

> The deficiency of modern science is essentially related to the question of universal causality; it will no doubt be objected that science is not concerned with philosophical causality but with phenomena, but this is false, for all of evolutionism is nothing but a hypertrophy imagined as a result of denying the real causes; and this materialist negation as well as its evolutionist compensation pertains to philosophy and not to science.[24]

While the scientific and philosophical dimensions of Darwinism are two sides of the same coin, it will save some confusion if we separate them for the purposes of our discussion. Let us start with the zoological theory itself, a foundational prop of modern science but one riddled with contradictions, anomalies, absurdities, and lacunae.

---

[23] T. Burckhardt, "Cosmology and Modern Science", 131. Some of these fissures are dealt with in Guénon's *The Reign of Quantity and the Signs of the Times*, esp. chap. XXIV and following. See also P. Sherrard, *The Rape of Nature*, chap. 3, and G. Eaton, *King of the Castle*, 142-164.

[24] *Form and Substance in the Religions*, "The Human Margin", 221-222.

A preliminary caution. Evolutionism is under attack from several directions. Some critics take their stand on entirely the wrong ground and not all "critiques" carry the same authority, although many share the basic intuition that evolutionism is, in the words of one of its critics, "a hoax". Michael Negus alerts us to some of the dangers which attend this field:

> There is a need to avoid two errors: the first is the error of rejecting adequately established scientific fact, e.g. the age of the earth or the space-time dimensions of the universe. This is the trap into which the biblical fundamentalists fall. The second error is that of accepting pseudo-doctrines like evolutionary progress with all its implications and thereby subverting Tradition. This is the trap into which the followers of Teilhard de Chardin fall.[25]

The balance lies in first acknowledging the supremacy of traditional doctrines over any profane science whatsoever but at the same time accepting, within appropriate limits, such facts as scientific inquiry has uncovered even though these often have no relevance to man's spiritual destiny. The denial of such facts only taints legitimate opposition to evolutionism with the suspicion of crankiness and obscurantism. It is crucial not to confuse the metaphysical position espoused by Schuon and others with a literalist fundamentalism which goes on insisting, in the face of incontrovertible evidence, that the earth is only a few thousand years old or that all life was created in a few days.[26] No perennialist wishes to evade or cover up scientific discoveries but only to separate fact from fiction and to situate the former in a framework which allows adequate interpretation.[27]

Material and logical objections to evolutionism by no means exhaust the case but they are an important component of it. There is a growing body of literature by reputable scientists—paleontologists, botanists, zoologists, geneticists, and others—which throws many of the central tenets of the Darwinian hypothesis into very serious question. *Scientific* critiques of evolutionary theory by men like Douglas Dewar, Evan Shute, Guiseppi Sermonti, Roberto Fondi, and L. Bournoure proceed through the premises and methodologies of modern science itself; the theory is being eroded from within.[28] The debate hinges on some very complex evidence which cannot

---

[25] M. Negus, "Reactions to the Theory of Evolution", 194. See also S.H. Nasr, *Knowledge and the Sacred*, 205-214, esp. 205.

[26] Nor is it of much use to put forward counter-theories of a quasi-scientific kind which are even less credible than those of the evolutionists. See Michael Negus' review of Anthony Fides' *Man's Origins*.

[27] Rodney Blackhirst has argued that, from a certain point of view, "Darwinism is a perverted truth rather than a complete falsehood". See R. Blackhirst, "Evolutionism and Traditional Cosmology" in *Vincit Omnia Veritas: Collected Essays*, ed. R. Fabbri and T. Scott, 137-142.

[28] For some of this literature see D. Dewar, *The Transformist Illusion* (first published in 1957);

be reviewed here; rather, brief mention will be made of three lines of attack, concerning the evolutionary conception of life's beginnings, the transformist thesis of "mega-evolution" whereby one species evolves into another, and the notion of man's primate ancestry.

The conception of life's beginnings and its subsequent development as presented by the evolutionists is quite illogical and defies all common sense. A contemporary psychiatrist has this to say:

> If we present, for the sake of argument, the theory of evolution in a most scientific formulation we have to say something like this: "At a certain moment of time the temperature of the earth was such that it became most favorable for the aggregation of carbon atoms and oxygen with the nitrogen-hydrogen combination, and that from random occur- rences of large clusters molecules occurred which were most favorably structured for the coming about of life, and from that point it went on through vast stretches of time, until through processes of natural selec- tion a being finally occurred which is capable of choosing love over hate, and justice over injustice, of writing poetry like that of Dante, composing music like that of Mozart, and making drawings like those of Leonardo." Of course, such a view of cosmogenesis is crazy.[29]

In a recent work William Stoddart summons two observations which are very much to the point: "It is impossible that blind, deaf, and dumb evo- lution could have given rise to eye, ear, and voice"; and, "The miracle of consciousness did not arise from a heap of pebbles".[30]

A keystone in the evolutionary theory is the notion that one species can, over time, be transformed into another—mega-evolution. The testimony of many reputable scientists, such as Evan Shute, demands our attention. Martin Lings, drawing on Shute's work, points out that

> The only evolution that has been scientifically attested is on a very small scale and within narrow limits. To conclude from this "micro- evolution", which no one contests, that there could be such a thing as "mega-evolution"—that for example, the class of birds could have evolved from the class of reptiles—is not merely conjecture but per- verse conjecture. . . . Micro-evolution demonstrates the presence in nature of all sorts of unseen barriers that ensure the stability of the

---

L. Bournoure, *Determinisme et finalite double loi de la vie*; E. Shute, *Flaws in the Theory of Evolution*; P. Moorehead and M. Kaplan (eds.), *Mathematical Challenges to the neo-Darwinian Interpretation of Evolution*; G. Fremondi and R. Fondi, *Dopo Darwin*; Michael Denton, *Evolu- tion: A Theory in Crisis*. For a lawyer's critique of evolutionism see Phillip E. Johnson, *Darwin on Trial*. Some of the scientific criticisms of Darwinism are discussed in my *Traditionalism* (chap. 10) in more detail than is allowed here.

[29] Karl Stern quoted in E.F. Schumacher, *A Guide for the Perplexed*, 127-128.

[30] W. Stoddart, *Remembering in a World of Forgetting*, 34.

various classes and orders of animals and plants and that invariably cause transformation, when it has run its little course, to come to a dead-end.[31]

Lemoine and other European scientists have shown how the fossil record on which the evolutionists base their arguments displays the abrupt appearances of whole new species and thus contradicts the transformist hypothesis.[32] All these theories involve so much hocus-pocus concealed by the technical jargon which insulates these speculations from the inquiries of any lay person trying to follow the logic of the argument.

The mega-evolution and transformist thesis is, of course, the platform for the idea that there is an essential continuity between man and the animals and that *homo sapiens* is a highly-evolved primate. The debate about the "missing link" between man and the other primates now takes on the characteristics of farce. The spectacle of evolutionists falling over each other in their attempts to find this link shows no sign of ending. Nor is another vexing question any closer to solution: What precisely are the criteria which distinguish humans from apes? Why are scientists unable to answer these questions? In this context we might also note the words of an American paleontologist:

> You can, with equal facility, model on the Neanderthaloid skull the features of a chimpanzee or the lineaments of a philosopher. These alleged restorations of ancient types of man have very little, if any, scientific value, and are likely only to mislead the public.[33]

That there are certain similarities between men and apes no one will deny: what is at issue is the significance of these similarities (an issue to which we will return presently).

---

[31] M. Lings, "Signs of the Times", 113. Likewise, Jean Rostand, the French biologist: "The world postulated by transformism is a fairy world, phantasmagoric, surrealistic. . . . We have never been present at one authentic phenomenon of evolution" (J. Rostand, *Le Figaro Littéraire*, quoted in T. Burckhardt, "Cosmology and Modern Science", 143).

[32] See S.H. Nasr, *Man and Nature*, 125ff and S.H. Nasr, *Knowledge and the Sacred*, 238ff. Not all evolutionists have been able to turn a blind eye to this evidence but rather than questioning the whole theory they have developed new hypotheses which are somehow assimilated into the Darwinian framework. Having scorned the idea of the Creator some evolutionists now find themselves endowing nature itself with powers of instantaneous creation—thus we have, for example, Schindewolf's theory of "explosive evolution" or Severtzoff and Zeuner's theory of "aramorphosis", or again the theory of "quanta of evolution" or "tachygenesis" (see M. Lings, *Ancient Beliefs and Modern Superstitions*, 78-80) or recent "neo-Darwinian" speculations about "punctuated equilibrium" and "organicistic revolutions" (see S.H. Nasr, *Religion and the Order of Nature*, 146).

[33] E.A. Hooton, quoted in M. Lings, "Signs of the Times", 113n.

Here is yet another embarrassment to evolutionism's portrayal of man as a "superior ape": man's ability to create an extraordinary number of artifacts. Now, according to the Darwinian theory of natural selection and adaptation this skill must evolve in response to environmental pressures; it represents an adaptation necessary for survival. In most species we find that an animal has only "evolved" the skills necessary to manufacture one artifact—say, a nest in the case of a bird.[34] In the case of man we are asked to swallow the same explanation for the fact that he is capable of making not one nor even half a dozen different artifacts but hundreds of thousands if not millions. Wherein is the explanation of this singularity? Howbeit that man alone can evolve these skills in what, from a geological point of view, must have been a minuscule period of time in his prehistory? The massive disjunction between man's unprecedented cultural achievements and the theory of adaptation and natural selection is one that no evolutionist has been able to explain in terms which have the slightest plausibility.

Darwin and his epigones offer us a spectacular instance of the truth of René Guénon's observation that

> When profane science leaves the domain of the mere observation of facts, and tries to get something out of an indefinite accumulation of separate details which is its sole immediate result, it retains as one of its chief characteristics the more or less laborious construction of purely hypothetical theories. These theories can necessarily never be more than hypothetical, for facts in themselves are always susceptible of diverse explanations and so never have been and never will be able to guarantee the truth of any theory. . . . And besides, such theories are not really inspired by the results of experience to nearly the same extent as by certain preconceived ideas and by some of the predominant tendencies of modern thought.[35]

The Metaphysical Argument

The perennialists, Titus Burckhardt and S.H. Nasr pre-eminently, have made some forays into the scientific debate about evolutionary theory. However, this is really only a side-show. The most fundamental grounds for a rejection of evolutionism are metaphysical. Schuon:

> Transformist evolution is accepted as a useful and provisional postulate, as one will accept no matter what, provided no obligation is felt to

---

[34] We will leave aside for now the awkward fact that where evidence is available it suggests that the species in question appeared with this skill ready-made: spiders, for example, were, as far as we can tell, always able to spin webs. There is not an iota of evidence to suggest that this was an "adaptation", "evolved" over a period of time. See T. Burckhardt, "Cosmology and Modern Science", 144-146.

[35] R. Guénon, *The Reign of Quantity and the Signs of the Times*, 149.

accept the primacy of the Immaterial, since the latter escapes the control of our senses. And yet, starting from the recognition of the immediately tangible mystery that is subjectivity or intelligence, it is easy to understand that the origin of the Universe is, not inert and unconscious matter, but a spiritual Substance which, from coagulation to coagulation and from segmentation to segmentation—and other projections both manifesting and limiting—finally produces matter by causing it to emerge from a more subtle substance, but one which is already remote from principial Substance.[36]

Evolutionism is "a compensation 'on a plane surface' for the missing dimensions" of Reality.[37] Thus,

> Transformist evolution is but a materialist substitute for the ancient concept of the solidifying and segmenting "materialization" of a subtle and suprasensorial primordial substance, in which were prefigured all the diverse possibilities of the *a posteriori* material world. The answer to evolutionism is to be found in the doctrine of archetypes and "ideas", the latter pertaining to pure Being—or to the Divine Intellect—and the former pertaining to the primordial substance in which the archetypes became "incarnated" as it were by reverberation.[38]

Transformist evolutionism flatly contradicts certain axiomatic metaphysical/cosmological principles. At the heart of the Darwinian schema lies a preposterous inversion of traditional understandings. In the opening passage of St John's Gospel, one of the most exalted mystical texts, we are told that "In the beginning was the Word, and the Word was with God, and the Word was God . . . and the Word became flesh" (John 1:1, 14). Darwin proposes precisely the opposite: "In the beginning was the Flesh (that is, matter), which became Word (consciousness, or Spirit). . .". The whole evolutionary conception rests on the metaphysically absurd notion that the greater can emerge from the lesser. In brief, the microscopic organisms from the prehistoric algal slime—organisms whose origins Darwin is utterly unable to explain—turn into Man. Or, to put it even more tersely, the primeval amoeba turns into a St. Francis, a Rumi, a Lao Tzu!

Darwin's thesis hinges on the proposition that one species can transform itself into another. Whatever localized insights Darwin's work might yield,

---

[36] *From the Divine to the Human*, "Consequences Flowing from the Mystery of Subjectivity", 5-6. See also S.H. Nasr, *Knowledge and the Sacred*, 235.

[37] *Form and Substance in the Religions*, "The Five Divine Presences", 63. Similarly: "Transformist evolutionism offers a patent example of 'horizontality' in the domain of the natural sciences, owing to the fact that it puts a biological evolution of 'ascending' degrees in place of a cosmogonic emanation of 'descending' degrees" (*Roots of the Human Condition*, "On Intelligence", 5).

[38] *Logic and Transcendence*, "The Contradiction of Relativism", 13n.

this central theme is an absurdity which flies in the face of all traditional wisdom as well as common sense. The notion of organic transformation, of mega-evolution, is from the outset quite incompatible with the doctrine of archetypes, which finds one of its applications in the animal kingdom. Metaphysically, each species "is an archetype, and if it is only manifested by the individuals belonging to it, it is nonetheless as real and indeed incomparably more real than they are".[39] Burckhardt concludes his discussion of this issue by reminding us that

> A species in itself is an immutable "form"; it could not evolve and become transformed into another species, although it can include variants, all these being "projections" of a single essential form from which they will never become detached.[40]

Darwinism postulates such variants to be "buds" of new species, a quite illegitimate assimilation and one that does nothing to hide either the gaps in the paleontological "succession" of species or the fact that whole new species appeared suddenly. The facts which paleontology has uncovered, some of them indisputable, are amenable to a quite different interpretation, as Burckhardt demonstrates.

> All that paleontology proves to us is that the various animal forms such as are shown by fossils preserved in successive layers of the earth made their appearance in a vaguely ascending order, going from relatively undifferentiated organisms—but not simple ones—to ever more complex forms, without this ascension representing, however, a univocal and continuous line. It seems to move in jumps; that is to say, whole categories of animals appear at once, without real predecessors. What means this order, then? Simply that on the material plane, the simple or relatively undifferentiated always precedes the complex and differentiated. All "matter" is like a mirror that reflects the activity of the essences by inverting it; that is why the seed comes before the tree, and the leaf bud before the flower, whereas in the principial order perfect "forms" pre-exist. The successive appearance of animal forms according to an ascending hierarchy therefore in no wise proves their continual and cumulative genesis.[41]

---

[39] T. Burckhardt, "Cosmology and Modern Science", 141. See also M. Pallis, *A Buddhist Spectrum*, 150.

[40] T. Burckhardt, "Cosmology and Modern Science", 141. See also S.H. Nasr, *Man and Nature*, 124.

[41] T. Burckhardt, "Cosmology and Modern Science", 143-144. One might add that the evolutionary hypothesis also depends on a linear and one-dimensional view of time. Nasr has discussed the effects of neglecting the doctrine of cosmic cycles. See S.H. Nasr, *Knowledge and the Sacred*, 209ff.

All traditional teachings affirm that there is a radical discontinuity between humankind and other life forms.[42] The privileged and axial position of man in the cosmos is completely ignored by evolutionism, which would have it that man is a "more evolved" ape. As Kathleen Raine has observed, "If the naive materialist supposes that 'nature' can produce man, that man is a product of nature, sacred tradition sees, on the contrary, 'nature' as the domain of man."[43]

How can the similarities between man and the primates be explained without resort to evolutionary speculations? The anatomical similarities between men and apes are always explained tendentiously by evolutionists. However, if we start from the doctrine of archetypes and the multiple states of being, these physical correspondences appear in a completely different light.

> However paradoxical this may seem, the anatomical resemblance between man and the anthropoid apes is precisely explainable by the difference, not gradual but essential, separating man from all other animals. Since the anthropoid form is able to exist without that "central" element that characterizes man—and that moreover is manifested anatomically by his vertical position, among other things—that form must exist; in other words there cannot but be found, at the purely animal level, a form that realizes in its own way—that is to say, according to the laws of its own level—the very plan of the human anatomy. It is in this sense that the monkey is a prefiguration of man, not as an evolutionary phase, but in virtue of that law that decrees that at every level of existence analogous possibilities will be found.[44]

It is, of course, for this very reason that it is impossible to define the differences between the apes and man in purely physiological terms. Man's especial estate is not due to the fact "that he has two hands which he manipulates or that he can make planes that fly or calculating machines that perform difficult mathematical operations in a short time. These and other abilities are no more than accidental to his real nature".[45] About this real nature a materialistic science can tell us nothing.[46]

---

[42] The fact that some oriental exoterisms understand this distinction in terms of *karma* rather than ontologically in no wise affects the principle itself.

[43] K. Raine, "The Underlying Order: Nature and the Imagination", 208.

[44] T. Burckhardt, "Cosmology and Modern Science", 149-150.

[45] S.H. Nasr, *Ideals and Realities of Islam*, 23.

[46] By way of an aside it is also worth noting that even today when more people are sensitive to the pitfalls of extrapolating from the biological to the social plane, there are still a host of "naked ape" theories, supported by the bastard science of "ethology", which flout any scientific prudence; the repugnant theories of Konrad Lorenz, Robert Ardrey, Desmond Morris and their successors are of this ilk. For a sample from this disturbing genre of pseudo-scientific

There are plenty of other puzzles concerning early man which embarrass evolutionary science. To think clearly about these matters involves balancing the modern scientific preoccupation with time, matter, and change with traditional conceptions of space, Substance, and Eternity. One then has a more comprehensive framework within which to work and all sorts of new possibilities present themselves. To give but one example: it is possible that the first humans in this particular terrestrial cycle left no solid traces, either because their bodies were not yet so materialized or because the spiritual state normal in those times, together with the cosmic and cyclic conditions then obtaining, made possible a resorption of the physical into the subtle body at the moment of death.[47] On man's origins Schuon has written this:

> Original man was not a simian being barely capable of speaking and standing upright: he was a quasi-immaterial being enclosed in an aura still celestial, but deposited on earth; an aura similar to the "chariot of fire" of Elijah or the "cloud" that enveloped Christ's ascension. That is to say, our conception of the origin of mankind is based on the doctrine of the projection of the archetypes *ab intra;* thus our position is that of classical emanationism. . . . Evolutionism is the very negation of the archetypes and consequently of the divine Intellect; it is therefore the negation of an entire dimension of the real.[48]

After summarizing the two ideas that predominate in the current debate about man's origins, namely the "evolutionist hypothesis" and the idea of a sudden creation *ex nihilo*, Schuon remarks:

> In reality, the evolutionist hypothesis is unnecessary because the creationist concept is so as well; for the creature appears on earth, not by falling from heaven, but by progressively passing—starting from the archetype—from the subtle to the material world, materialization being brought about within a kind of visible aura quite comparable to the "spheres of light" which, according to many accounts, introduce and terminate celestial apparitions.[49]

"research", especially popular in the 1960s and 70s, see Konrad Lorenz's *On Aggression*, Robert Ardrey's *African Genesis*, and *The Naked Ape*, by Desmond Morris.

[47] See T. Burckhardt, "Cosmology and Modern Science", 150.

[48] *To Have a Center*, "Survey of Integral Anthropology", 50. Schuon's view here echoes the account of primordial men in the Pali text, the *Agganna Sutta*, where we are told that these beings "used to shine like stars, glide through the air, and feed on Beatitude" (*Treasures of Buddhism*, "Cosmological and Eschatological Viewpoints", 64n).

[49] *From the Divine to the Human*, "The Message of the Human Body", 88. In a footnote Schuon adds: "One will recall the 'chariot of fire' that lifted up Elijah, and the 'cloud' which veiled the Christ during the Ascension."

Social Darwinism and the Gospel of "Progress"

Darwin's biological hypothesis became a Pandora's Box for nineteenth century social theory. His work was pillaged for new tools of social and historical analysis and for new categories of thought. The evolutionist schema and its methodology soon came to be applied to non-biological categories such as classes, races, and nations, even religions. The first authors of what came to be known as "Social Darwinism" were E.B. Tylor and Herbert Spencer. The earliest formulation of their ideas actually preceded Darwin's *The Origin of Species*; indeed, it was Spencer rather than Darwin who coined the term "survival of the fittest", a slogan under which all manner of social, racial, and imperial brutalities were to be justified. The ideology of Social Darwinism was to be harnessed to a wide range of purposes: the assertion of Anglo-Saxon racial and cultural superiority; the colonial exploitation of other countries and peoples; the justification, in pseudo-scientific terms, of a rapacious capitalism and of various policies of social and economic *laissez-faire*; the shoring up of nationalist and racist ideologies, not only in Britain but in Europe and America as well.

> More than most theories, Darwinism lent itself to such stratagems of persuasion, enjoying not only the prestige and authority attached to science, but also the faculty of being readily translated into social terms. That this translation was rather free and loose was an added advantage, since it gave license to a variety of social gospels.[50]

Darwinism was a "grand narrative" perfectly suited to the temper of the age—an account of the beginnings and the development of life which erased the Creator, now replaced by a clutch of more or less inexorable "laws", an account, moreover, which looked to an inevitable *advance* or *progression*. Evolutionism lent itself to social ideologies in which the remorseless imperatives of competition, self-interest, "survival", and racial "hygiene" were all valorized as "natural" and assimilated into the idea of Progress.[51] Consider the chilling implications of a passage such as the following, from Darwin's *The Descent of Man*:

> At some future period, not very distant as measured by centuries, the civilized races of man will almost certainly exterminate and replace the savage races throughout the world. At the same time the anthropomorphous apes ... will no doubt be exterminated. The break between man and his nearest allies will then be wider, for it will intervene between

[50] G. Himmelfarb, *Darwin and the Darwinian Revolution*, 340.
[51] On the social effects of Darwinist ideas see Marilynne Robinson's essay, "Darwinism", in *The Death of Adam: Essays on Modern Thought*, 28-75. For the historical development of social Darwinism see J.W. Burrow, *Evolution and Society: A Study in Victorian Social Theory* and R. Hofstadter, *Social Darwinism in American Thought*.

man in a more civilized state, as we may hope, even than the Caucasian, and some ape as low as a baboon, instead of as now between the negro or Australian and the gorilla.[52]

Through its connections with a false gospel of Progress, evolutionism has seeped into our way of looking at history and has subverted the whole idea of tradition. Although social Darwinism has been thoroughly discredited on a theoretical level, the average mentality is still very much under its sway. Progress, after all, is one of the most comfortable of illusions. It is still not uncommon to find formulations such as this one from a very well-known anthropological theorist: "Man has made objective progress in improving his society and . . . we in the West seem at this stage to have the best society in recorded history."[53] This is a staggering claim. It is a measure of the influence of the idea of progress, buttressed by evolutionism, that this kind of statement will be swallowed without demur by many people today. Indeed, one could catalogue a more or less endless list of the tokens of evolutionist assumptions in almost every aspect of contemporary thought.

The ideal of progress is by now looking very tawdry to those who see our present situation clear-eyed. Writing some years ago—our global circumstances have since deteriorated even further—Theodore Roszak wrote this:

> The Last Days were announced to St. John by a voice like the sound of many waters. But the voice that comes in our day summoning us to play out the dark myth of the reckoning is our meager own, making casual conversation about the varieties of annihilation . . . the thermonuclear Armageddon, the death of the seas, the vanishing atmosphere, the massacre of the innocents, the universal famine to come. . . . Such horrors should be the stuff of nightmare. . . . They aren't. They are the news of the day. . . . We have not stumbled into the arms of Gog and Magog; we have *progressed* there.[54]

Evolutionism as Pseudo-Religion
Evolutionism has become a kind of pseudo-religion, with its own inviolable dogmas, a fact which explains the zealotry with which many scientists remain willfully blind to the mounting scientific evidence against the Darwinian scheme. Over seventy years ago the distinguished entomologist F.R.S. Thompson remarked:

---

[52] Quoted in M. Robinson, "Darwinism", 35.

[53] I.C. Jarvie, *The Revolution in Anthropology*, 14.

[54] T. Roszak, *Where the Wasteland Ends*, ix. As Gai Eaton observes, "A superstitious faith in progress endures even when the dogma of progress has been exposed as an illusion" (*King of the Castle*, 10).

The concept of organic Evolution is very highly prized by biologists, for many of whom it is an object of genuinely religious devotion, because they regard it as a supreme integrative principle. This is probably the reason why the severe methodological criticism employed in other departments of biology has not yet been brought to bear against evolutionary speculation.[55]

Rather than discarding a hypothesis with which the facts do not conform, the evolutionists go on endlessly modifying, qualifying, and hedging their theories with ever more subtlety and ingenuity whilst all the time clinging to the basic premises on which the whole edifice of evolutionism rests. As Murray Eden observes, "Neo-Darwinian evolutionary theory has been modified to the point that virtually every formulation of the principles of evolution is a tautology."[56] It may be that the tide is now turning. Certainly evolutionary theory has been subjected to more stringent criticism in the last half century and increasing numbers of people, scientific and lay, are no longer prepared to accept the evolutionary account of life.

The perennialists have been concerned, in the main, with the effects of evolutionism on attitudes to religion, to the past, to tradition; in all these areas they find evolutionism's bequeathals to be malign. As Schuon has remarked:

> One of the effects, among others, of modern science has been that of mortally wounding religion by posing in concrete terms problems which esoterism alone can resolve and which remain unresolved because esoterism is not heeded. . . . Faced by these new problems, religion is disarmed, and it borrows clumsily and gropingly the arguments of the enemy, and this obliges it to falsify imperceptibly its own perspective and more and more to disavow itself.[57]

The enervating effects of both biological and social Darwinism on attitudes to the Christian faith are well-known. E.F. Schumacher echoes the traditionalist position in writing:

> Evolutionism is not a science; it is a science fiction, even a kind of hoax . . . that has imprisoned modern man in what looks like an irreconcilable conflict between "science" and "religion". It has destroyed all faiths that pull mankind upward and has substituted a faith that pulls

---

[55] F.R.S. Thompson, *Science and Common Sense*, quoted in S.H. Nasr, *Man and Nature*, 139n. See also S.H. Nasr, *Knowledge and the Sacred*, 234-235.

[56] M. Eden, "Inadequacies of neo-Darwinian Evolution as Scientific Theory", 109. See also S.H. Nasr, *Knowledge and the Sacred*, 237.

[57] *Light on the Ancient Worlds*, "Fall and Forfeiture", 27.

mankind down. . . . It is the most extreme product of the materialistic utilitarianism of the nineteenth century.[58]

As we have seen in our discussion of the doctrine of cycles, the idea of progress and of evolution finds not a whit of support in any of the traditional doctrines concerning man and time, nor in terms of any spiritual criteria— quite the contrary. As Schuon affirms:

All the traditional doctrines agree in this: From a strictly spiritual point of view, though not necessarily from other much more relative and therefore less important points of view, mankind is becoming more and more corrupted; the ideas of "evolution", of "progress", and of a single "civilization" are in effect the most pernicious pseudo-dogmas.

Further:

We say not that evolution is non-existent but that it has a partial and most often quite external applicability; if there be evolution on the one hand, there are degenerations on the other, and it is in any case radically false to suppose that our ancestors were intellectually, spiritually, or morally our inferiors. To suppose this is the most childish of "optical delusions"; human weakness alters its style in the course of history, but not its nature.[59]

It is a sign of the times that an anti-traditional, evolutionist Utopianism should find its way into domains where it should not for a moment have been countenanced. The work of Teilhard de Chardin is a conspicuous example of what results when one tries to reconcile the platitudes of evolutionist ideology with a traditional theology. Kurt Almqvist has rightly pilloried it as a "pseudo-metaphysical synthesis of neo-modernism, where evolutionist and pantheist materialism substitutes itself for religion by means of subversion and parody."[60] As Schuon observes:

The speculations of Teilhard de Chardin provide a striking example of a theology that has succumbed to microscopes and telescopes, to machines and to their philosophical and social consequences, a "fall" that would have been unthinkable had there been here the slightest

[58] E. F. Schumacher, *A Guide for the Perplexed*, 129-130.

[59] Frithjof Schuon, "No Activity Without Truth", 38-39.

[60] K. Almqvist, "Aspects of Teilhardian Idolatry", 195. For traditionalist commentary on Teilhard see also S.H. Nasr, *Knowledge and the Sacred*, 240-244; T. Burckhardt, "Cosmology and Modern Science", 150-153; P. Sherrard, "Teilhard and Christian Vision", 150-175; and W. Smith, *Teilhardism and the New Religion*. On the plight of the Roman Church since Vatican II see Rama P. Coomaraswamy, *The Destruction of the Christian Tradition*, and M. Pallis, "The Catholic Church in Crisis", 57-80. See also *Esoterism as Principle and as Way*, "The Role of Appearances", 201-204.

direct intellective knowledge of immaterial realities. The inhuman side of the doctrine in question is highly significant.[61]

---

[61] *Understanding Islam*, "Islam", 25n. No doubt Chardin's work is ingenious, even subtle if somewhat opaque, but the result is none the less dangerous for that. That the Catholic hierarchy should, however uneasily, allow this to be passed off as "Catholic" thought in any sense whatsoever is in itself a sad commentary. Would that we could still confidently accede to G.K. Chesterton's remark that "the Church is the only thing that saves us from the degrading slavery of becoming children of our times" (quoted in a review by W. Perry in *Studies in Comparative Religion*, 12:3-4, 1978, 247).

14

Humanism, Psychologism, Culturism

If Rousseau and other "idealists" had foreseen all the outcomes of their inane philanthropy they would have become Carthusian monks.[1]

Humanism is the reign of horizontality, either naïve or perfidious: and since it is also—and by that very fact—the negation of the Absolute, it is a door open to a multitude of sham absolutes.[2]

Psychoanalysts have arrogated to themselves a monopoly in all that concerns the "inner life", where they mix together the most diverse and irreconcilable things in a common process of leveling and relativization.[3]

Genius is nothing unless determined by a spiritual perspective.[4]

There is a fundamental crisis in the modern world; its root causes are spiritual. The crisis itself can hardly be disputed. Some of the symptoms: ecological catastrophe, a material sign of the rupture between Heaven and Earth; a rampant materialism and consumerism, signifying a surrender to the illusion that man can live by bread alone; the genocidal extirpation of traditional cultures by the careering juggernauts of "modernization"; political barbarities on an almost unimaginable scale; social discord, endemic violence, and dislocations of unprecedented proportions; widespread alienation, ennui, and a sense of spiritual sterility amidst the frenetic confusion and din of modern life; a religious landscape dominated by internecine and inter-religious strife and by the emergence of aggressive fundamentalisms in both East and West; the loss of any sense of the sacred, even among those who remain committed to religious forms, many of whom have retreated into a simplistic and credulous religious literalism or into a vacuous liberalism where "anything goes".[5] These "signs of the times"—and the inventory is

---

[1] *Stations of Wisdom*, "Complexity of the Idea of Charity", 111n.
[2] *To Have a Center*, "To Have a Center", 29.
[3] *Understanding Islam*, "The Path", 139n.
[4] *Art from the Sacred to the Profane*, "Sacred Art", 41.
[5] Some fifty years ago the English writer Dorothy Sayers offered a diagnosis of the contemporary condition: "Futility; lack of a living faith; the drift into loose morality, greedy consumption, financial irresponsibility, and uncontrolled bad temper; a self-opinionated and obstinate individualism; violence, sterility, and lack of reverence for life and property ... the exploitation of sex, the debasing of language ... the commercializing of religion ... mass hysteria and

by no means exhaustive—are plain enough to those with eyes to see. No amount of gilded rhetoric about "progress", the "miracles of modern science and technology", or the "triumphs of democracy" (to mention just three shibboleths of modernity) can hide the fact that our age is tyrannized by an outlook inimical to our most fundamental needs, our deepest yearnings, our most noble aspirations. As Schuon observed in a diary entry:

> It is the great error of modern Western culture that it should confuse living conditions with the meaning of life and take them to be life's only content. What do modern states do? They engage in trade, industry, and politics—not because they could not live without them, but because they do not know what to do with life.[6]

No one will deny that modernity has its compensations, though these are often of a quite different order from the boisterously applauded "benefits" of science and technology—some of which are indubitable but many of which issue in consequences far worse than the ills which they are apparently repairing. Furthermore, many so-called "advances" must be seen as the poisoned fruits of a Faustian bargain which one day must come to its bitter conclusion. What indeed is a man profited if he gain the whole world but lose his own soul?

No doubt one might approach the spiritual crises of modernity from many different angles—as is done in other parts of this work. In this chapter, in the context of Schuon's work, we will simply analyze three "-isms" which are altogether characteristic of modernity: humanism, psychologism, and culturism. Whilst it would be foolish to imagine that a brief analysis of this kind could "explain" the confusions and disorders of the modern world, there is no doubt that these representative "thought-forms" are deeply implicated in the anti-traditional temper of our times.

Humanism: The Betrayal of Man

Humanism is not, of course, a single-head monster but an ideological hydra. The "humanisms" of such representative figures as, let us say, Karl Marx, Bertrand Russell, Julian Huxley, Simone de Beauvoir, and Christopher Hitchens, present different philosophical countenances, some more unattractive than others.[7] However, we can isolate a defining characteristic in all these secu-

---

"spell-binding", venality, and string-pulling in public affairs . . . the fomenting of discord . . . the exploitation of the lowest and stupidest mass-emotions" (D. Sayers, *Introductory Papers on Dante* (1954), quoted in E.F. Schumacher, *A Guide for the Perplexed*, 151-152). Who could deny that such symptoms of a deep-seated spiritual malaise are even more acute today?

[6] Frithjof Schuon, quoted in *Frithjof Schuon: Messenger of the Perennial Philosophy*, 16.

[7] For a sample of humanist writings see J. Huxley (ed.), *The Humanist Frame*. See especially Huxley's own introductory essay, 13-48.

larist humanisms be they atheistic or agnostic, "optimistic" or "pessimistic", Marxist or existentialist or "scientific": the insistence that man's nature and purpose is to be defined and understood purely in terms of his terrestrial existence. This is a first principle of humanism wherein man is seen as an autonomous, self-sufficient being who need look no further than himself in "explaining" the meaning of life and who need pay homage to nothing beyond himself. "Man is free only if he owes his existence to himself"; we may take Marx's dictum as a "dogma" of secular humanism.[8] Indeed, many of the prejudices which have huddled behind the banner of "humanism" are on full display in this well-known passage from Marx:

> Man, who looked for a superman in the fantastic reality of heaven and found nothing there but the *reflexion* of himself, will no longer be disposed to find but the *semblance* of himself, the non-human (*Unmensch*) where he seeks and must seek his true reality. . . . *Man makes religion,* religion does not make man. In other words, religion is the self-consciousness and self-feeling of man who has either not yet found himself or has already lost himself again. . . . The struggle against religion is therefore . . . the struggle against *the other world*, of which religion is the spiritual *aroma*. . . . Religion is the sigh of the oppressed creature, the heart of a heartless world, just as it is the spirit of a spiritless situation. It is the *opium* of the people. The abolition of religion as the *illusory* happiness of the people is required for their *real* happiness. . . . The criticism of religion disillusions man and makes him think and act and shape his reality like a man who has been disillusioned and has come to reason, so that he will revolve round himself and therefore round his true sun. Religion is only the illusory sun which revolves round man as long as he does not revolve round himself.[9]

Following Feuerbach, Marx's collaborator Friedrich Engels asserted that "All religion . . . is nothing but the fantastic reflection in men's minds of those external forces which control their daily life, a reflection in which the terrestrial forces assume the form of supernatural forces."[10] God is a fiction which played our ancestors false. This threadbare idea has become the very calling-card of the modern intellectual. In his doctoral thesis Marx had written,

> Philosophy makes no secret of it. Prometheus' confession "in a word, I detest all Gods", is its own confession, its own slogan against all Gods

---

[8] Quoted by S. Radhakrishnan in P.A. Schilpp (ed.), *The Philosophy of Sarvepalli Radhakrishnan,* 50.

[9] *Contribution to the Critique of Hegel's Philosophy of Right* in Karl Marx and Friedrich Engels, *On Religion,* 37-38 (italics mine).

[10] *Anti-Dühring,* in Marx and Engels, *On Religion,* 131.

in heaven and earth who do not recognize man's self-consciousness as the highest divinity.[11]

It is no surprise that Marx should hark back to the Greeks of the so-called Golden Age. "Of all things the measure is man": so said the ancient sophist Protagoras. Such a principle brazenly contradicts the teachings of all the religious traditions without exception and is the most fundamental point at issue between humanism and perennialism. Schuon states the traditional position plainly enough:

> To say that man is the measure of all things is meaningless unless one starts from the idea that God is the measure of man. . . . Nothing is fully human that is not determined by the Divine, and therefore centered on it. Once man makes of himself a measure, while refusing to be measured in turn . . . all human landmarks disappear; once cut off from the Divine, the human collapses.[12]

More succinctly, "to find man, one must aspire to God".[13] As one commentator has observed, "If anything characterizes 'modernity', it is a loss of faith in transcendence, in a reality that encompasses but surpasses our quotidian affairs."[14] Humanism is both the cause and result of this loss of faith.

Humanism often goes hand-in-hand with an evolutionist perspective on the past which suggests that we have "progressed" beyond the superstitions and obscurations which blinkered our ancestors.

> Opinions now current prove that people think themselves incomparably more "realistic" than anyone has ever been, even in the recent past; "our time" or "the twentieth century" or "the atomic age" seems to hover, like an uprooted island or a fabulously "clear-headed" monad, above millennia of childishness and blundering. The contemporary world is like a man ashamed of having had parents and wanting to create himself, and to recreate space, time, and all the physical laws, or seeking to extract from nothingness a world objectively perfect and subjectively comfortable, and all this by means of a creative activity independent of God or opposed to God; the unfortunate thing is that attempts to create a new order of Being can only end in self-destruction.[15]

---

[11] Preface to Marx's doctoral thesis, quoted in David McLellan, *Marx*, 26.

[12] *Stations of Wisdom*, "Orthodoxy and Intellectuality", 47.

[13] *Play of Masks*, "Prerogatives of the Human State", 16.

[14] An anonymous reviewer cited in H. Smith, "Excluded Knowledge: A Critique of the Western Mind Set", 432n.

[15] *Light on the Ancient Worlds*, "Naiveté", 84.

So much does the humanist philosophy depend on this condescension to the past that it is difficult to imagine any contemporary humanism divorced from the progressivism which supports it.

The humanist denial of the transcendent dimension in human life and the indifference or hostility to the very idea of God has all manner of ramifications: it impoverishes our view of reality, breeds all kinds of false definitions of man, and produces a chimerical "humanitarianism", as well as encouraging negative attitudes to the past and to tradition itself. Humanists, by definition, are skeptical about the claims of the great religious teachings. The humanist outlook is seen, by its exponents, as "open-minded", "sane", unfettered by "prejudices" and "superstitions". It seems not to occur to humanists that their own attitudes may simply be the prejudices of our period, nor that skepticism may be a function of ignorance rather than knowledge.[16] As Schuon remarks:

> Men think they have "solid earth" under their feet and that they possess a real power; they feel perfectly "at home" on earth and attach much importance to themselves, whereas they know neither whence they came nor whither they are going and are drawn through life as by an invisible cord.[17]

The denial of God and of the transcendent leads to a debased understanding of human nature and to corrupting definitions of "man". Pressed to define "man", the humanist will more often than not resort to some evasive evolutionist tactic. Man, we might be told, is a large-brained and exceptionally intelligent animal, or a tool-making or game-playing or language-using or self-conscious or rational or political animal. To the traditional ear such definitions simply sound inane: as Schumacher remarks, one might just as well define a dog as a "barking plant" or a "running cabbage".[18]

> Nothing is more conducive to the brutalization of the modern world than the launching, in the name of science, of wrongful and degraded definitions of man, such as "the naked ape". What could one expect of such a creature. . . ?[19]

The fabrication of dehumanizing social forms on the external plane depends on our assent to thought-forms which deny or distort our real nature. Humanism is a large part of the problem.[20] We cannot too often remind ourselves, in the words of Seyyed Hossein Nasr, that

---

[16] *Stations of Wisdom*, "Orthodoxy and Intellectuality", 19-20.

[17] *Light on the Ancient Worlds*, "Man in the Universe", 94.

[18] E.F. Schumacher, *A Guide for the Perplexed*, 31.

[19] E.F. Schumacher, *A Guide for the Perplexed*, 31.

[20] See P. Sherrard, "Modern Science and the Dehumanization of Man", 79.

Man's central position in the world is not due to his cleverness or his inventive genius but because of the possibility of attaining sanctity and becoming a channel of grace for the world around him. . . . The very grandeur of the human condition is precisely that he has the possibility of reaching a state "higher than the angels" and at the same time of denying God.[21]

It is the latter choice which gives modernism its essential character.

The social idealism and "humanitarianism" on which humanists pride themselves is a sentimental illusion which is fed by an ignorance concerning man's true nature and his ultimate ends. The humanists would have us forget the first of Christ's two great commandments to pursue the second as a kind of social principle or ideal. But, as Schuon points out:

> Love of God could not defraud creatures: we may forget men in loving God without thereby lacking charity towards them, but we cannot, without defrauding both men and ourselves, forget God while loving men.[22]

In this context it might be noted that humanist values have played a part in perforating the fabric of Christianity and in denaturing it into a kind of sentimental humanitarianism which envisages the Kingdom of God as an earthly super Welfare State.[23]

Humanism, which finds antecedents in the thought of Enlightenment thinkers such as Rousseau, is often susceptible to various strains of Utopianism. Utopian scenarios certainly pre-date Darwin but they received a new fillip when the theory of evolution was wedded to Enlightenment theories about the perfectibility of man and nineteenth century optimism about the inexorability of progress. The admixture of evolutionism and humanism was a heady brew. Again, the case of Marx is instructive. He anticipates a world in which all the social iniquities and inequalities, all the class oppressions of the past, are devoured in revolutionary violence, ushering in an era in which the state, the classes and the private property which is their basis, will all "wither away", to be replaced by an idyllic existence wherein a man might "hunt in the morning, fish in the afternoon, rear cattle in the

---

[21] S.H. Nasr, *Ideals and Realities of Islam*, 24-25. See also *Esoterism as Principle and as Way*, "Understanding Esoterism", 34.

[22] *Stations of Wisdom*, "Complexity of the Idea of Charity", 109, 111n. See also: *Esoterism as Principle and as Way*, "The Virtues in the Way", 104, "The Supreme Commandment", 154, and "The True Remedy", 162; and *Logic and Transcendence*, "Concerning the Love of God", 192-193.

[23] See Lord Northbourne, *Religion in the Modern World*, 16 and Gai Eaton, *King of the Castle*, 16ff.

evening" and philosophize at night.[24] A charming prospect, one might say, but quite fantastic and ominous: once men's minds are gripped by the delusion that a perfect world is within reach, then everything is permitted and no price is too high to pay. At this point in history one hardly need observe that Marx's apocalyptic Utopianism fuelled abuses so many and so monstrous that we can hardly grasp their magnitude—a case not of attaining Utopia but of making hell on earth, as the Russian novelist Dostoevsky so presciently predicted in his own dark masterpiece, *Notes from Underground* (1864). One might have thought that twentieth century history would have immunized us once and for all against the seductions of Utopianism but no, they still abound.[25] Furthermore, as Schuon tersely remarks, we know from experience that "megalomaniacal idealism and moral pettiness get along well together among those who are standard-bearers of integral humanism, especially on the political plane."[26] The worldly Utopia—so often a grotesque parody of Augustine's "City of God" but now a "City of Man"—is dangled before the credulous in many guises: the classless society of the Marxist fantasy; the anarchist dream of the "free" society; the pseudo-spiritual anticipations of a "New Age"; the quasi-theological aberrations of a Teilhard de Chardin. Each of these Utopianisms, by definition, is a form of profane humanism envisaging a human destiny which leaves no room for the transcendent, the divine, the sacred, the traditional—in a word, no room for God. As one representative of Russian Orthodoxy put it, "All the tragedy of man is in one word, 'godlessness'."[27]

The Psychological Imposture

Psychologism is another view of man built on the sands of a profane science, and as such, another symptom of modernism. Its intrusion into the religious realm has been attended by consequences no less disturbing than those coming in the train of evolutionism. As Coomaraswamy, following Guénon, observed, "While nineteenth century materialism closed the mind of man to what is above him, twentieth century psychology opened it to what is below him."[28] Psychologism, as Schuon notes, is both an end-point and a cause,

---

[24] From *The German Ideology*, quoted in Francis Wheen, *Karl Marx*, 96.
[25] Utopianism: "impossible ideal schemes for the perfection of social conditions" (Oxford English Dictionary).
[26] *To Have a Center*, "To Have a Center", 21. Utopianism of the kind under discussion also well fits Schuon's definition of stupidity: "the lack of discernment between the essential and the secondary and, as a result, that moral ugliness which is pettiness; it is also the lack of sense of proportions, hence of priorities" (from Schuon's unpublished writings, courtesy of World Wisdom).
[27] Metropolitan Anthony of Sourzah, *God and Man*, 68.
[28] Quoted in W. Perry, "Drug-Induced Mysticism", 196.

being a "logical and fatal ramification and natural ally" of other profane and materialistic ideologies such as evolutionism.[29]

Before rehearsing some of Schuon's general observations about psychologism, a few remarks about Sigmund Freud, the undisputed progenitor of modern psychology, will not be out of place. Freud remarked in a letter, "The moment a man questions the meaning and value of life he is sick, since objectively neither has any existence."[30] One need hardly do more than adduce this extraordinary claim to throw Freud's theorizing out of court altogether! As is well-known, Freud himself harbored an animus towards religion which, in his own terms, could only be described as pathological. The key-note is his insistence that, to state the matter as briefly as possible, religious beliefs were a camouflaged prolongation of childhood traumas and pathologies.[31] He identified "three powers which may dispute the basic position of science": art, philosophy, and religion, of which, he said, "religion alone is to be taken seriously as an enemy". Philosophy, he suggested, is basically harmless because, despite its ambitious pretensions, it "has no direct influence on the great mass of mankind: it is of interest to only a small number even of top-layer intellectuals and is scarcely intelligible to anyone else." Art "is almost always harmless and beneficent; it does not seek to be anything but an illusion".[32] This leaves religion as "an immense power" and an imposing obstacle to the scientific enlightenment of mankind, the project in which Freud understood himself to be engaged.

Freud identified three fatal blows against what he called man's "narcissism", by which he meant the belief that man was made in the image of God: Copernican cosmology, Darwinian biology, and psychoanalytical psychology.[33] The drift of much of Freud's thought can be signaled by a small sample of quotations, the tenebrous implications of which are readily apparent:

> [The *Weltanschauung* of science] asserts that there are no sources of knowledge of the universe other than the intellectual working-over of

[29] *Survey of Metaphysics and Esoterism*, "The Psychological Imposture", 195.

[30] Letter to Maria Bonaparte, from *Letters of Sigmund Freud*, quoted in Philip Rieff, *The Triumph of the Therapeutic*, 9.

[31] Thus, for example: "The last contribution to the criticism of the religious *Weltanschauung* [he wrote], was effected by psychoanalysis, by showing how religion originated from the helplessness of children and by tracing its contents to the survival into maturity of the wishes and needs of childhood." Likewise, "[Religion is] a counterpart to the neurosis which individual civilized men have to go through in their passage from childhood to maturity" (Sigmund Freud, *New Introductory Lectures on Psychoanalysis*, 167, 168).

[32] S. Freud, *New Introductory Lectures on Psychoanalysis*, 160-161.

[33] S. Freud, *Collected Papers*, vol. 1, cited in Whitall Perry, "The Revolt Against Moses: A New Look at Psychoanalysis", in *Challenges to a Secular Society*, 17-38.

carefully scrutinized observations . . . and alongside of it *no knowledge derived from revelation, intuition, or divination.*[34]

I should like to insist . . . that the beginnings of religion, morals, society, and art converge in the Oedipus complex.[35]

[Religious ideas] are illusions, fulfillments of the oldest, strongest, and most urgent wishes of mankind.[36]

And this, on the nature of the id, which Freud referred to as "the core of our being":

It is the dark, inaccessible part of our personality. . . . We call it a chaos, a cauldron of seething excitations. . . . It is filled with energy reaching it from the instincts, but it has no organization, produces no collective will, but only a striving to bring about the satisfaction of the instinctual needs subject to the observance of the pleasure principle. . . . The id of course knows no judgments of value. . . . The quantitative factor, which is intimately linked to the pleasure principle, dominates all its processes. Instinctual cathexes seeking discharge—*that, in our view, is all there is in the id.*[37]

Freud's bizarre theories about the "psychogenesis" of religion and his grotesque speculations about the early history of mankind, bear an unmistakably evolutionist cast. Here is a representative passage:

While the different religions wrangle with one another as to which of them is in possession of the truth, our view is that the truth of religion may be left altogether on one side. Religion is an attempt to master the sensory world, in which we are situated by means of the wishful world, which we have developed within us as a result of biological and psychological necessities. But it cannot achieve this. Its doctrines bear the imprint of the times in which they arose, the ignorant times of the childhood of humanity.[38]

As Guénon and others have noted, Freud's agenda might well be summed up in one of his favorite lines from Virgil, and one which he inscribed on the title page of his first major work: "If I cannot bend the gods, I will stir up hell."[39] In *The Reign of Quantity and the Signs of the Times*, the French

---

[34] S. Freud, *New Introductory Lectures on Psychoanalysis*, 159 (italics mine).

[35] S. Freud, *Totem and Taboo*, 156.

[36] S. Freud, *The Future of an Illusion* (1927), in *The Complete Psychological Works of Sigmund Freud*, vol. XXI, 30.

[37] S. Freud, *New Introductory Lectures on Psychoanalysis*, 74-75 (italics mine).

[38] S. Freud, *New Introductory Lectures on Psychoanalysis*, 168.

[39] From Virgil, inscribed in *Die Traumdeutung*, noted in René Guénon, *The Reign of Quantity and the Signs of the Times*, note 139, 355. For some commentary on Freud's ideas about

metaphysician drew attention to some of the infernal influences unleashed by Freudian psychoanalysis.

In more general terms psychologism can be described as the assumption that man's nature and behavior are to be explained by psychological factors which can be laid bare by a scientific and empirical psychology—which is to say that psychologism denies or ignores "data which are beyond the reach of those methods of investigation now declared to be normal, and which are arbitrarily extended to cover every conceivable kind of knowledge".[40] Moreover,

> If the Freudian psychology declares that rationality is but a hypocritical cloak for a repressed animality, this statement, evidently of a rational nature, falls under the same verdict; Freudianism, were it right, would itself be nothing else but a symbolistic denaturing of psychophysical instincts.[41]

Before proceeding further an important distinction must be made between modern psychology and traditional pneumatologies with which it shares some superficial similarities. The latter derived from radically different principles, applied different therapies, and pursued different ends. Just as it is misleading to talk about modern European philosophy and traditional metaphysic in the same breath and under the same terms, so too with modern psychology and traditional pneumatology. A good deal of confusion would be averted if people would resist such terms as "Buddhist psychology" or "Zen psychotherapy". It would also help clarify the issues at stake if many of the self-styled "experts" in this field would abandon the preposterous notion that the techniques of Western psychology can lead to the liberation spoken of in the Eastern traditions.[42] This is to confuse two quite different planes of experience.

Schuon on the "psychological imposture":

> Psychoanalysis doubly deserves to be classed as an imposture, firstly because it pretends to have discovered facts which have always been known . . . and secondly and chiefly because it arrogates to itself functions that in reality are spiritual, and thus poses practically as a religion.[43]

---

religion see W. Smith, *Cosmos and Transcendence*, 109 and Alister McGrath, *The Twilight of Atheism*, 66-77.

[40] *Logic and Transcendence*, "The Contradiction of Relativism", 10.

[41] *Logic and Transcendence*, "The Contradiction of Relativism", 10.

[42] On this issue see P. Novak, "C.G. Jung in the Light of Asian Philosophy" and J.M. Reynolds, *Self-Liberation Through Seeing with Naked Awareness*, Appendix 1.

[43] *Survey of Metaphysics and Esoterism*, "The Psychological Imposture", 195.

Furthermore:

> What we term "psychological imposture" is the tendency to reduce everything to psychological factors and to call into question not only what is intellectual or spiritual—the first being related to truth and the second to life in and by truth—but also the human mind as such, and thereby its capacity of adequation and, still more evidently, its inward illimitation and transcendence. The same belittling and truly subversive tendency rages in all the domains that "scientism" claims to embrace, but its most acute expression is beyond all doubt to be found in psychoanalysis. Psychoanalysis is at once an end-point and a cause, as is always the case with profane ideologies, like materialism and evolutionism, of which it is really a logical and fatal ramification and a natural ally.[44]

As Guénon so powerfully demonstrated in *The Reign of Quantity and the Signs of the Times*, materialism, evolutionism, and psychologism are not in fact three distinct theories but only variations on a theme.

Psychology of the modern kind defines itself by its inability to distinguish between the psychic plane, the arena in which the more or less accidental subjectivities of the individual ego come into play in the depths of the subconscious, and the infinite realm of the spirit which, in terms of the human individual, is signaled by the capacity for the plenary experience and which is thus marked by an "inward" illimitation and transcendence. The muddling of the psychic realm of the subconscious with the mystical potentialities of the human soul and the infinite reaches of the Intellect has given birth to all manner of mystifications. There is indeed a science which reveals the way in which the play of the psyche can communicate universal realities; this is one of the fields of the traditional pneumatologies. But—the proviso is crucial—such a science cannot flourish outside a properly-constituted metaphysic and cosmology. In this context the following passage from Burckhardt deserves the closest attention:

> The connection with the metaphysical order provides spiritual psychology with qualitative criteria such as are wholly lacking in profane psychology, which studies only the dynamic character of phenomena of the psyche and their proximate causes. When modern psychology makes pretensions to a sort of science of the hidden contents of the soul it is still for all that restricted to an individual perspective because it has no real means for distinguishing psychic forms which translate universal realities from forms which appear symbolical but are only vehicles for individual impulses. Its "collective subconscious" [as theorized by Jung] has most assuredly nothing to do with the true source of symbols;

---

[44] *Survey of Metaphysics and Esoterism*, "The Psychological Imposture", 195.

at most it is a chaotic depository of psychic residues somewhat like the mud of the ocean bed which retains traces of past epochs.[45]

The confusion of the psychic and the spiritual, which in part stems from the artificial Cartesian dualism of "body" and "mind",

> appears in two contrary forms: in the first, the spiritual is brought down to the level of the psychic; in the second, the psychic is . . . mistaken for the spiritual; of this the most popular example is spiritualism.[46]

The first form of the confusion thus licenses a degrading reductionism and relativism, often as impertinent as it is inadequate. The "sinister originality" of psychologism lies in its "determination to attribute every reflex and every disposition of the soul to mean causes and to exclude spiritual factors; hence its notorious tendency to see health in what is commonplace and vulgar, and neurosis in what is noble and profound".[47] This tendency is often an accomplice to a relativism whereby everything becomes, in Schuon's words,

> The fruit of a contingent elaboration: Revelation becomes poetry, religions are inventions, sages are "thinkers" and "researchers" . . . infallibility and inspiration no longer exist; error becomes an "interesting" and quantitative "contribution" to "culture". . . . If every mental phenomenon is not reduced to material causes, there is at least a denial of any supernatural, or even simply supra-sensory cause and, by the same token, the negation of any principial truth.[48]

Like evolutionism, psychologism attempts to explain the greater in terms of the lesser and excludes all that goes beyond its own boundaries. In this sense, historicism, relativism, and psychologism are all cut from the same cloth. As Schuon observes:

> The mentality of today seeks in fact to reduce everything to temporal categories: a work of art, a thought, a truth have no value in themselves and independently of any historical classification. . . . Everything is considered the expression of a "period", not of a timeless and intrinsic

---

[45] T. Burckhardt, *An Introduction to Sufi Doctrine*, 37. See also S.H. Nasr, *Sufi Essays*, 46ff, and A. Coomaraswamy, "On the Indian and Traditional Psychology, or Rather Pneumatology" in *Selected Papers 2*, 333-378. Coomaraswamy: "The health envisaged by the empirical psychotherapy is a freedom from particular pathological conditions; that envisaged by the other is a freedom from all conditions and predicaments, a freedom from the infection of mortality. . . . Furthermore, the pursuit of the greater freedom necessarily entails the attainment of the lesser" (*Selected Papers 2*, 335).

[46] R. Guénon, *The Reign of Quantity and the Signs of the Times*, 286. See chapters XXXIV-XXXV, "The Misdeeds of Psychoanalysis" and "The Confusion of the Psychic and the Spiritual", 273-290.

[47] *Survey of Metaphysics and Esoterism*, "The Psychological Imposture", 196.

[48] *Form and Substance in the Religions*, "The Five Divine Presences", 64.

value; and this is entirely in conformity with modern relativism and with a psychologism or biologism that destroys essential values.

And so:

> In order to "situate" the doctrine of a Scholastic, for example, or even of a Prophet, a "psychoanalysis" is prepared—it is needless to emphasize the monstrous pride implicit in such an attitude—and with an entirely mechanical and perfectly unreal logic, the "influences" to which this doctrine has been subject are laid bare; . . . There is no hesitation in attributing to saints all kinds of artificial and even fraudulent conduct, but it is obviously forgotten, with satanic inconsequentiality, to apply the same principle to oneself, and to explain one's own—supposedly "objective"—position by psychoanalytic considerations: in short, sages are treated as sick men, and one takes oneself for a god. . . . It is a case of expressing a maximum of absurdity with a maximum of subtlety.[49]

As Schuon remarks elsewhere, relativism sets about reducing "every element of absoluteness to a relativity, while making a quite illogical exception in favor of this reduction itself".[50] Clearly these strictures do not apply with the same force to each and every attempt by scholars to detect and explain historical and psychological factors relating to particular religious phenomena. It is possible, for example, to take these kinds of considerations into account in a sensitive way without falling prey to a reductionist relativism. Nevertheless, Schuon's general point remains valid. It can hardly be denied that a kind of iconoclastic psychologism runs through a good deal of the scholarly literature on religion.

A psychologism unrestrained by any values transcending those of a profane science corrodes religious forms by infiltrating the religious sphere itself. Schuon notes, by way of an example, the part psychologism has played in discrediting the cult of the Holy Virgin:

> Only a barbarous mentality that wants to be "adult" at all costs and no longer believes in anything but the trivial could be embarrassed by this cult. The answer to the reproach of "gynecolatry" or the "Oedipus complex" is that, like every other psychoanalytic argument, it bypasses the problem; for the real question is not one of knowing what the psychological conditioning of an attitude may be, but on the contrary, what its results are.[51]

The practice of dragging spiritual realities down to the psychological plane can everywhere be seen when religion is reduced to some kind of psycho-

---

[49] *Light on the Ancient Worlds*, "Fall and Forfeiture", 23.
[50] *Logic and Transcendence*, "The Contradiction of Relativism", 7.
[51] *Survey of Metaphysics and Esoterism*, "The Psychological Imposture", 199.

logical regimen. Many of the neo-yogic, meditation, "self-realization", and "New Age" movements are of this kind.

> One of the most insidious and destructive illusions is the belief that depth- psychology . . . has the slightest connection with spiritual life, which these teachings persistently falsify by confusing inferior elements [psychic] with superior [spiritual]. We cannot be too wary of all these attempts to reduce the values vehicled by tradition to the level of phenomena supposed to be scientifically controllable. The spirit escapes the hold of profane science in an absolute fashion.[52]

Psychologistic reductionism has unhappy consequences on both the practical and the theoretical level: on the one hand we have the notion that psychological techniques and therapies can take the place of authentic spiritual disciplines; on the other, the pretension that psychological science can "explain" religious phenomena. Both of these are related to the first form of the confusion of the psychic and the spiritual.[53] Schuon:

> That which calls for suspicion and for an implacable vigilance is the reducing of the spiritual to the psychic, a practice which has become a commonplace, to the point of characterizing Western interpretations of traditional doctrines. This so-called "psychology of spirituality"—or this "psychoanalysis of the sacred"—is the breach through which the mortal poison of modern relativism infiltrates the still living Oriental traditions.

None of this is to deny that

> spirituality, though essentially determined by supra-individual factors, comprises secondary modalities of a psychic order owing to the fact that it necessarily sets in motion all that we are. But a "psychology of the spiritual" is a contradictory notion that can only end up in the falsification and negation of the spirit; one might just as well speak of a "biology of the truth" and indeed one can be certain that someone has already done so.[54]

Let us turn briefly to the obverse side, that of falsely elevating the psychic to the spiritual. There is a vast spiritual wasteland here which we cannot presently explore, but Whitall Perry identifies some of its inhabitants in writing of those occultist, psychic, spiritualistic, and "esoteric" groups who concern themselves with

> spirits, elementals, materializations, etheric states, auric eggs, astral bodies, ids, ods, and egos, ectoplasmic apparitions, wraiths and visions,

[52] Frithjof Schuon, "No Activity Without Truth", 37.
[53] See D.M. Matheson, "Psychoanalysis and Spirituality".
[54] *Treasures of Buddhism*, "A Defense of Zen", 69.

subliminal consciousness and collective unconsciousness, doublings, disassociations, functional disintegrations, communications, obsessions and possessions, psychasthenia, animal magnetism, hypnoidal therapeutics, vibrations, thought-forces, mind-waves and radiations, clairvoyances and audiences and levitations, telepathic dreams, premonitions, death lights, trance writings, Rochester knockings, Buddhic bodies, and sundry other emergences and extravagances of hideous nomenclature.[55]

—all the while imagining that these are the stuff of the spiritual life.

Of course the perennialists are not alone in unmasking "the misdeeds of psychoanalysis". Thomas Merton, for instance:

Nothing is more repellent than a pseudo-scientific definition of the contemplative experience. . . . He who attempts such a definition is tempted to proceed psychologically, and there is really no adequate "psychology" of contemplation.[56]

Lama Govinda, more alert to this danger than some of his colleagues now in the West, warns of the "shallow-mindedness" of those who teach a kind of "pseudo-scientific spirituality".[57] Mircea Eliade makes a more general point in writing:

Psychoanalysis justifies its importance by asserting that it forces you to look at and accept reality. But what sort of reality? A reality conditioned by the materialistic and scientific ideology of psychoanalysis, that is, a historical product: we see a thing in which certain scholars and thinkers of the nineteenth century believed.[58]

Much of Guénon's work was directed to reasserting the proper distinctions between psychic phenomena and spiritual realities and to sounding a warning about the infernal forces to which the psychic occultists unwittingly expose themselves. As Schuon remarks, "modern occultism is by and large no more than the study of extrasensory phenomena, one of the most hazardous pursuits by reason of its wholly empirical character and its lack of any doctrinal basis".[59] Without the shield of traditional doctrines and disciplines, such as those which shielded the shamans, any incursions into these

---

[55] W. Perry (ed.), *A Treasury of Traditional Wisdom*, 437. What Coomaraswamy said of the individual subconscious can be applied to the psychic realm as a whole: it is "a sink of psychic residues, a sort of garbage pit or compost heap, fitted only for the roots of 'plants', and far removed from the light that erects them" (cited by Perry, 437).

[56] T. Merton, *New Seeds of Contemplation*, 6-7.

[57] A. Govinda, *Creative Meditation and Multi-Dimensional Consciousness*, 70.

[58] M. Eliade, *No Souvenirs*, 269.

[59] *Logic and Transcendence*, "Introduction", 1. See also R. Guénon, "Explanation of Spiritist Phenomena" and S.H. Nasr, *Sufi Essays*, 40-41.

realms are fraught with perils of the gravest kind. In a traditional discipline the psychic can be reintegrated with the spiritual, but without the necessary metaphysical framework and religious supports psychism all too easily becomes infra-intellectual and anti-spiritual.

Culturism and the Cult of Genius

One telling offshoot of humanism, a manifestation of the anti-traditional outlook, is the cult of genius to which some reference was made in our discussion of art in the modern era. Whilst Schuon, in the main, did not devote detailed attention to the cultural aberrations of modernity, he did produce one arresting essay on the culture of the nineteenth century. After a brief overview of the normative spiritual anthropology of India (a subject to which we will return in chapter 16) Schuon articulates his governing theme:

> We live in a world which on the one hand tends to deprive men of their center, and on the other hand offers them—in place of the saint and the hero—the cult of the "genius". Now a genius is all too often a man without a center, in whom this lack is replaced by a creative hypertrophy. To be sure, there is a genius proper to normal, hence balanced and virtuous, man; but the world of "culture" and "art for art's sake" accepts with the same enthusiasm normal and abnormal men, the latter being particularly numerous . . . in that world of dreams or nightmares that was the nineteenth century.[60]

That many of these geniuses led unhappy and desperate lives only adds to their prestige and strengthens the "seduction, indeed the fascination, which emanates from their siren songs and tragic destinies". The "unbridled subjectivism" and the "split and heteroclite psychism"[61] of many of the century's geniuses often induced melancholy and despair, sometimes psychopathology and insanity. Now, Schuon readily concedes that profane genius can, "in any human climate", be "the medium of a cosmic quality, of an archetype of beauty or greatness", in which case we can respect at least some of its productions even though they lie outside tradition. As he writes elsewhere:

> Modern art—starting from the Renaissance—does include some more or less isolated works which, though they fit into the style of their period, are in a deeper sense opposed to it and neutralize its errors by their own qualities.[62]

---

[60] *To Have a Center*, "To Have a Center", 8. (A Virgil, a Dante, a Fra Angelico furnish examples of normal men blessed with a creative genius.)

[61] *To Have a Center*, "To Have a Center", 9.

[62] *Art from the Sacred to the Profane*, "Principles and Criteria of Art", 15.

However, what we witness so often in the last few centuries is a "useless profusion of talents and geniuses" driven by a "humanistic narcissism with its mania for individualistic and unlimited production".[63] Humanism promotes a certain dynamism and a "fruitless moral idealism" which "depends entirely on a human ideology".

Schuon goes on to illustrate his theme with reference to the lives and productions of a whole gallery of nineteenth century artists, among them Beethoven, Wagner, Rodin, Nietzsche, Wilde, Gauguin, Van Gogh, Ibsen, Bizet, Balzac, Dickens, Tolstoy, and Dostoevsky—all figures whose prodigious talents were turned astray by an impoverished environment, which is not to deny the traces of incidental beauty and grandeur which can be found in many of their works. Let us briefly consider Schuon's remarks on a few representative cases. Firstly Beethoven:

> Despite the fact that Beethoven was a believer, he was inevitably situated on the plane of humanism, hence of "horizontality". And though there was nothing morbid about him, we note the characteristic disproportion between the artistic work and the spiritual personality; characteristic, precisely, for genius arising from the cult of man, thus from the Renaissance and its consequences. There is no denying what is powerful and profound about many of Beethoven's musical motifs, but, all things considered, a music of this sort should not exist; it exteriorizes and hence exhausts possibilities which ought to remain inward and contribute in their own way to the contemplative scope of the soul. In this sense, Beethoven's art is both an indiscretion and a dilapidation, as is the case with most post-Renaissance artistic manifestations.[64]

And all this despite the fact that Beethoven, compared to other geniuses, was "a homogeneous man, hence 'normal', if we disregard his demiurgic passion for musical exteriorization". Schuon also notes that

> Whereas in Bach or Mozart musicality still manifests itself with faultless crystallinity, in Beethoven there is something like the rupture of a dam or an explosion; and this climate of cataclysm is precisely what people appreciate.[65]

Rodin provides an instance of another "powerful and quasi-volcanic" genius, "direct heir to the Renaissance" in his titanesque "carnal and tormented" productions, reminiscent of ancient naturalism and the "sensual cult of the human body".[66] Victor Hugo, on the other hand, is no more

---

[63] *To Have a Center*, "To Have a Center", 10.
[64] *To Have a Center*, "To Have a Center", 12-13.
[65] *To Have a Center*, "To Have a Center", 13n.
[66] *To Have a Center*, "To Have a Center", 13-14. In some sense Rodin is heir to the "blustering and carnal paintings of a Rubens" (*Art from the Sacred to the Profane*, "Sacred Art", 39).

than a "bombastic and long-winded spokesman of French romanticism" who "puffs himself up and finally becomes hardened in the passionate projection of himself"[67] (a story repeated many times in modern "culture"!). There are others, like Ibsen and Strindberg, who become spokesmen for "a thesis that is excessive, revolutionary, subversive, and in the highest degree individualistic and anarchic":

> This kind of talent—or of genius, as the case may be—makes one think of children who play with fire, or of Goethe's sorcerer's apprentice: these people play with everything, with religion, with the social order, with mental equilibrium, provided they can safeguard their originality; an originality which, retrospectively, shows itself to be a perfect banality, because there is nothing more banal than fashion, no matter how clamorous.[68]

To turn to one of the more formidable figures of the century, Nietzsche was yet another "volcanic genius":

> Here, too, there is a passionate exteriorization of an inward fire, but in a manner that is both deviated and demented; we have in mind here, not the Nietzschean philosophy, which taken literally is without interest, but his poetical work, whose most intense expression is in part his *Zarathustra*. What this highly uneven book manifests above all is the violent reaction of an *a priori* profound soul against a mediocre and paralyzing cultural environment; Nietzsche's fault was to have only a sense of grandeur in the absence of all intellectual discernment. *Zarathustra* is basically the cry of a grandeur trodden underfoot, whence comes the heart-rending authenticity—grandeur precisely—of certain passages; not all of them, to be sure, and above all not those which express a half-Machiavellian, half-Darwinian philosophy, or minor literary cleverness. Be that as it may, Nietzsche's misfortune, like that of other men of genius, such as Napoleon, was to be born after the Renaissance and not before it; which indicates evidently an aspect of their nature, for there is no such thing as chance.[69]

Goethe, a well-balanced man with a "lofty and generous" mind, was another victim of the epoch "owing to the fact that humanism in general and Kantianism in particular had vitiated his tendency towards a vast and finely-shaded wisdom" and made him, paradoxically, "the spokesman of a perfectly bourgeois 'horizontality'".[70]

---

[67] *To Have a Center*, "To Have a Center", 20.
[68] *To Have a Center*, "To Have a Center", 20.
[69] *To Have a Center*, "To Have a Center", 15.
[70] *To Have a Center*, "To Have a Center", 16.

The nineteenth century novelists furnish many instances of "a problematic type of talent led astray from its true vocation": whereas in medieval times novels were inspired by myths, legends, and religious and chivalrous ideals, in the modern era they become "more and more profane, even garrulous and insignificant". Their authors lived only a vicarious existence through their characters: "A Balzac, a Dickens, a Tolstoy, a Dostoevsky lived on the fringe of themselves, they gave their blood to phantoms, and they incited their readers to do the same . . . with the aggravating circumstance that these others were neither heroes nor saints and, besides, never existed." Furthermore:

> These remarks can be applied to the whole of that universe of dreams which is called "culture": flooded by literary opium, siren songs, vampirizing, and—to say the least—useless production, people live on the fringe of the natural world and its exigencies, and consequently on the fringe—or at the antipodes—of the "one thing needful". The nineteenth century—with its garrulous and irresponsible novelists, its *poètes maudits*, its creators of pernicious operas, its unhappy artists, in short with all its superfluous idolatries and all of its blind allies leading to despair—was bound to crash against a wall, the fruit of its own absurdity; thus the First World War was for the *belle époque* what the sinking of the Titanic was for the elegant and decadent society that happened to be on board, or what Reading Gaol was for Oscar Wilde, analogically speaking.[71]

Then, too, there are the "unhappy painters", such as Van Gogh and Gauguin, both "bearers of certain incontestable values" but whose work, "despite the prestige of the style", is marred by "the lack of discernment and spirituality". They also dramatize the tragedy of "normally intelligent men who sell their souls to a creative activity which no one asks of them . . . who make a religion of their profane and individualistic art and who, so to speak, die martyrs for a cause not worth the trouble".[72] (Gauguin is a particularly interesting case, given the fact that Schuon's own paintings are somewhat reminiscent, in both subject matter and style, of Gauguin's.) In another essay Schuon alludes to artworks which, to some degree, escape the limitations and distortions of the age:

> Of famous or well-known painters the elder Brueghel's snow scenes may be quoted and, nearer to our day, Gauguin, some of whose canvases are almost perfect, Van Gogh's flower paintings, Douanier Rousseau with his exotic forests akin to folk painting, and, among our contemporaries, Covarrubias with his Mexican and Balinese subjects.

[71] *To Have a Center*, "To Have a Center", 17.
[72] *To Have a Center*, "To Have a Center", 19.

We might perhaps also allude to certain American Indian painters whose work shows, through a naturalistic influence, a vision close to that of the ancient pictography. Conversely, equivalents of the positive experiments of modern art can be found in the most varied of traditional art, which proves not only that these experiments are compatible with the universal principles of art, but also that—once again—"there is nothing new under the sun."[73]

Returning to "To Have a Center": Schuon goes on to describe the depredations of humanism and the cult of genius in several other fields of "cultural production", including the theatre, philosophy, and the darker recesses of Romanticism, as well as discussing the ostensible lack of "culture" (as it is understood in the modern West) amongst non-literate peoples. Our earlier discussion of metaphysics, theology, and (modern) philosophy obviates any necessity to recapitulate the argument here, but it is worth taking note of the following remark in the essay at hand:

A particularly problematic sector of culture with a humanist background is philosophical production, where naïve pretension and impious ambition become involved in the affairs of universal truth, which is an extremely serious matter; on this plane, the desire for originality is one of the least pardonable sins. . . . The most serious reproach we can make concerning the general run of these "thinkers" is their lack of intuition of the real and consequently their lack of a sense of proportion; or the short-sightedness and lack of respect with which they handle the weightiest questions human intelligence can conceive, and to which centuries or millennia of spiritual consciousness have provided the answer.[74]

The brief account above perhaps suggests that Schuon makes a blanket condemnation of modern culture; this is not quite the case. What *is* unequivocally condemned is a kind of humanistic ideology of "culturism"—but Schuon remains acutely sensitive to those qualities of intelligence and beauty which still appear in various artworks, despite the mediocre and spiritually stifling cultural milieu in which they appear, and which bear witness to the artist's nobility of soul even when this is compromised by the false idol of "art for art's sake". Readers who turn to the essay in full will find there a carefully nuanced treatment of the subject. However, if "it is not easy to have completely unmixed feelings on the subject of profane 'cultural' genius", Schuon's general case against humanistic culture is implacable:

Humanistic culture, insofar as it functions as an ideology and therefore as a religion, consists essentially in being unaware of three things: firstly,

[73] *Art from the Sacred to the Profane*, "Principles and Criteria of Art", 15.
[74] *To Have a Center*, "To Have a Center", 21-22.

of what God is, because it does not grant primacy to Him; secondly, of what man is, because it puts him in the place of God; thirdly, of what the meaning of life is, because this culture limits itself to playing with evanescent things and to plunging into them with criminal unconsciousness. In a word, there is nothing more inhuman than humanism, by the fact that it, so to speak, decapitates man.[75]

* * *

All of the "-isms" that have been under discussion in this chapter, as well as countless other modernist ideologies with which they consort, amount to bogus philosophies because they betray our real nature. And these ideologies are everywhere in the contemporary world. It is for this reason that Schuon writes, "It is necessary to reject the modern world, its errors, its tendencies, its trivialities".[76] Of the countless passages in his writings which refute these degraded views of the human condition and which affirm our real nature, here is one with which to conclude:

> Man is spirit incarnate; if he were only matter, he would be identified with the feet; if he were only spirit, he would be the head, that is, the Sky; he would be the Great Spirit. But the object of his existence is to be in the middle: it is to transcend matter while being situated there, and to realize the light, the Sky, starting from this intermediary level. It is true that the other creatures also participate in life, but man synthesizes them: he carries all life within himself and thus becomes the spokesman for all life, the vertical axis where life opens onto the spirit and where it becomes spirit. In all terrestrial creatures the cold inertia of matter becomes heat, but in man alone does heat become light.[77]

---

[75] *To Have a Center*, "To Have a Center", 37.
[76] Frithjof Schuon, unpublished writings, courtesy of World Wisdom.
[77] *Feathered Sun*, "A Metaphysic of Virgin Nature", 16.

15

Counterfeits of the Wisdom of the Ages

Truth does not deny forms from the outside but transcends them from within.[1]

The worst of these false idealisms are, in certain respects, those which annex and adulterate religion.[2]

Syncretism is never an affair of substance: it is an assembling of heterogeneous elements into a false unity.[3]

Over the last half-century there has been a good deal of talk about a "spiritual revolution" in the West, one which "promises to transform everything modern man has thought about God and human possibility". Writing of the so-called "new religions" in the 1970s, Jacob Needleman referred to a "spiritual explosion", a proliferation of movements which turn "toward the religions of the East and toward the mystical core of all religion".[4] Amongst the movements surveyed in Needleman's *The New Religions* were "American Zen", Transcendental Meditation, neo-Vedanta, Subud, "Humanistic Mysticism", and groups devoted to the teachings of figures such as Meher Baba, Gurdjieff, and Krishnamurti. The "revolution" took place all over the Western world. "Pop gurus" like Yogananda, Alan Watts, Rajneesh, Mahesh Yogi[5] and Bubba Free John (a representative sample from a gallery including more than a few rogues and charlatans) attracted the loyalties of millions of people. More recently we have had the burgeoning "New Age" movement. Then too, there is the veritable plague of occultist and "esoteric" movements ranging from theosophy, Lobsang-Rampaism, and "tantra" to black witchcraft and Scientology.[6] What are we to make of all this in the light of Schuon's work? This is one question addressed in this chapter.

---

[1] *Spiritual Perspectives and Human Facts*, "Vedanta", 119.

[2] *To Have a Center*, "To Have a Center", 30.

[3] *Light on the Ancient Worlds* (1965), "The Universality of Monasticism", 123.

[4] J. Needleman, *The New Religions*, 1.

[5] For Schuon's view of Mahesh Yogi see *Spiritual Perspectives and Human Facts*, "Appendix: Selections from Letters and Previously Unpublished Writings", 238-239.

[6] On the "new religions" see also a later collection edited by Jacob Needleman et al., *Understanding the New Religions*; T. Roszak, *The Making of the Counter Culture*, chap. 4; Mark Hayes, "The New Consciousness Movement", 43-48; A. Bancroft, *Twentieth Century Mystics and Sages* (includes chapters on Huxley, Watts, Teilhard, Krishnamurti, Gurdjieff, Subud,

Another landmark in the contemporary landscape is the confusion sponsored by the notion that all those thinkers and groups which ostensibly espouse some kind of "perennial philosophy" can be gathered together under this insignia: theosophists, anthroposophists, Gurdjieffians, neo-Hindu universalists, pseudo-mystical romantics, syncretists, neo-Deists, New Age "Aquarians", "cosmic consciousness" enthusiasts and occultists are herded together with traditionalists. One scholar, for instance, groups together Aldous Huxley, Radhakrishnan, Gerald Heard, Herman Hesse, Christopher Isherwood, Ramakrishna, Coomaraswamy, Vivekananda, and Aurobindo, amongst others.[7] However, even a modest inquiry will reveal that the similarities between such thinkers are superficial, the differences quite profound. While these figures may indeed affirm some kind of timeless, universal wisdom they do so from different vantage points, elaborate quite divergent conceptions of what it comprises, and educe varying "programs" from it. We remember Guénon's misgivings about the pseudo-traditionalists of his day—how much more appalled he would have been to find the ideas to which he gave expression lumped together with some of the bizarre claims made under the aegis of "perennial philosophy"! So, another purpose of this chapter is to restate what the *sophia perennis* is and is not by exposing some of its counterfeits.

In order to affirm the truths safeguarded by tradition Schuon has perforce occasionally had to expose those modern modes of "thought" and pseudo-forms of "spirituality" which stand like road-blocks on the path to any real understanding of the Wisdom of the Ages. A fair portion of *Logic and Transcendence* is given over to this task. In general, however, he has been concerned with principles rather than personalities, and with the underlying tendencies of the age rather than with its myriad expressions. If, in this chapter, we must sometimes move some distance from Schuon's own writings, this is for two reasons: firstly, to consider particular phenomena about which Schuon himself said little or nothing (though he supplied us with the tools for a proper consideration thereof); and secondly, to throw into

---

Mahesh Yogi, and Rudolf Steiner). On occultism and pseudo-spiritual "esoteric" movements see C.R. Evans, *Cults of Unreason* (includes sections on Scientology, Gurdjieff, "black box" cults, UFO-ism, Lobsang Rampa), Whitall Perry's review of Evans in *Studies in Comparative Religion*, 9:3, 1975, 185, and M. Eliade, *Occultism, Witchcraft, and Cultural Fashion*, 47-68. See also Whitall Perry's *Gurdjieff in the Light of Tradition* and "Drug-Induced Mysticism" in *Challenges to a Secular Society*. On Alan Watts, Krishnamurti, Radhakrishnan, and Gurdjieff, considered from a traditionalist point of view, see K. Oldmeadow, *Traditionalism*, chap. 11. For a discussion of Swami Yogananda, Lobsang Rampa, Aurobindo, Mahesh Yogi, Bubba Free John, Carlos Castaneda, Ken Wilber, and Deepak Chopra (amongst many other teachers and so-called gurus), see H. Oldmeadow, *Journeys East, passim.*

[7] See P.J. Saher, *Eastern Wisdom and Western Thought*, 123-162.

sharp relief some of the divergences between, on the one side, the outlook espoused by Schuon, and on the other, a welter of viewpoints which are symptoms of the confusion and spiritual sterility of the times.

Perennialism, Syncretism, "New Consciousness", and "Universalism"

Schuon's position is demarcated by his unambiguous stance vis-à-vis religious forms, syncretism, and the possibilities of a universal religion. This should be apparent from our earlier discussion but some reiteration might be helpful. It is impossible both in principle and in fact to construct a new, universal religion. Schuon is intent on demonstrating the universal content of each religious tradition and on situating the formal antagonisms between different exoterisms in a perspective which allows those capable of doing so to perceive "the transcendent unity of religions"—the use of the qualifying adjective is crucial. At the same time, like all perennialists-proper, Schuon seeks to preserve the formal embodiments of each religious tradition, these being self-sufficient and entirely adequate in providing all things needful to the civilizations in which they have appeared. He envisages no universal religion but a gnosis which resolves the formal antinomies of the exoteric domain. This is in no way an attempt to dispense with or bypass the exoterisms as such or to downplay the importance of the religious orthodoxies which have providentially been manifested in response to the differing needs of human collectivities. Rather, it seeks to discern the universal content of each religion and thereby demonstrate both its sufficiency and its essential unity with all other orthodox traditions. In this sense it might be called synthetic, which is to say that it "starts from principles . . . from that which is innermost; it goes, one might say, from the center to the circumference".[8] This could not provide the platform for a new or universal religion; the use of either adjective with the word "religion" is a contradiction in terms. The single unitive Truth at the heart of each religious tradition implies no syncretistic possibility whatsoever. Syncretism, in Guénon's words, is

> The juxtaposition of elements of diverse origin, assembled "from the outside" . . . without any principle of a more profound order to unify them. . . . Such a conglomeration cannot constitute a doctrine, any more than a pile of stones can constitute a building.[9]

Such syncretism, says Schuon, is "never an affair of substance", and should not be confused with a legitimate and synthetic eclecticism whereby

---

[8] R. Guénon, quoted in G. Eaton, *The Richest Vein*, 181.
[9] R. Guénon, quoted in G. Eaton, *The Richest Vein*, 181. See also R. Guénon, *The Reign of Quantity and the Signs of the Times*, 296-297 and *Logic and Transcendence*, "Introduction", 3-4.

ideas and principles hitherto foreign are assimilated into a tradition to illuminate and corroborate the spiritual perspective in question. Schuon:

> What is important in such a case is that the original perspective remain faithful to itself and accept foreign concepts only to the extent they corroborate its faithfulness by helping to elucidate the fundamental intentions of its own perspective; Christians had no reason not to be inspired by Greek wisdom since it was at hand, just as Muslims could not prevent themselves from using Neoplatonic concepts in their mystical doctrine—at least to a certain extent—as soon as they became aware of them; but it would be a serious error to speak of syncretism in these cases by mistakenly recalling the example of such artificial doctrines as those of modern theosophy. There have never been borrowings between two living religions of essential elements affecting their fundamental structures, as it is imagined when Amidism is attributed to the Nestorians.[10]

Syncretism of the kind which attempts to fashion a "universal religion" is bound to issue, as Coomaraswamy remarked, in nothing but "a mechanical and life-less monstrosity" and "a sort of religious Esperanto".[11] Nasr on such enterprises:

> Not only do they not succeed in transcending forms but they fall beneath them, opening the door to all kinds of evil forces affecting those who are unfortunate enough to be duped by their so-called universalism.[12]

This censure can be directed not only against syncretists, but against all those who imagine they can depart from traditional forms with impunity. Indeed the question of religious forms provides an acid test for separating the traditionalists from most of the other so-called perennial philosophers whose hackles are likely to rise at the mere mention of words like "tradition", "dogma", or "orthodoxy"!

---

[10] *Light on the Ancient Worlds*, "The Universality and Timeliness of Monasticism", 104-105.
[11] "Sri Ramakrishna and Religious Tolerance" in Coomaraswamy, *Selected Papers 2*, 39-40. See also R. Lipsey, *Coomaraswamy: His Life and Work*, 277.
[12] S.H. Nasr, *Sufi Essays*, 147n. Elsewhere Nasr spells out some of the principles which render any syncretistic universalism illegitimate: "The relation between man and God, or the relative and the Absolute, is central in every religion. Only each religion emphasizes a certain aspect of this relationship, while inwardly it contains the Truth as such in its teachings whatever the limitations of its forms might be. That is why to have lived any religion fully is to have lived all religions and there is nothing more meaningless or even pernicious than to create a syncretism from various religions with a claim to universality while in reality one is doing nothing less than destroying the revealed forms which alone make the attachment of the relative to the Absolute, of man to God, possible" (*Ideals and Realities of Islam*, 16).

We have already seen how the perennialists deny the possibility of any new religion whatsoever: a religion finds its source in a divine Revelation; in the present cycle the age of such Revelations has long since passed. This disqualifies any claims to a new dispensation. Movements like Mormonism, Baha'ism, or Subud, to name a few, are "signs of the times", symptoms of a spiritual hunger which looks for nourishment in all sorts of arid places. They could not be authentic and integral religions as such. However, a greater menace to the teachings of tradition comes from idiosyncratic "adaptations" of traditional teachings and from those who would overthrow tradition itself.

> Nothing is more misleading than to pretend, as is so glibly done in our day, that the religions have compromised themselves hopelessly in the course of centuries or that they are now played out. If one knows what a religion really consists of one knows . . . that they are independent of human doings; in fact, nothing men do is able to affect the traditional doctrines, symbols, or rites.[13]

Similarly:

> One of the great errors of our time is to speak of the "bankruptcy" of religion or the religions: this is to lay blame on truth for our failure to admit it.[14]

*   *   *

In a caustic but considered essay, Whitall Perry, following the teachings of Schuon, elaborated a perennialist critique of some of the characteristics shared by the "prophets" of a "new consciousness". Amongst the people he mentions as representing "the tip of the iceberg" are Aldous Huxley, Gerald Heard, R.C. Zaehner, Teilhard de Chardin, Aurobindo, Gopi Krishna, Alan Watts, and Krishnamurti—the list is obviously not exhaustive.[15] Clearly Perry has to deal in this essay with generalities which will apply to varying degrees, according to the case at hand, but the tendencies to which he takes exception are these:

> A patent individualism, a scientific and moralistic humanism, evolutionism, a relativistic "intuitionism", inability to grasp metaphysical and cosmological principles and the realities of the Universal Domain, a mockery (latent or overt) of the sacred, a prodigal dearth of spiritual

---

[13] Frithjof Schuon, "No Activity Without Truth", 29.

[14] *Stations of Wisdom*, "Preface", xi.

[15] W. Perry, "Anti-Theology and the Riddles of Alcyone", 176-192. For material on Teilhard see references provided in the previous chapter.

imagination, no eschatological understanding, a pseudo-mysticism in the form of a "cosmic consciousness".[16]

The "patent individualism" of people like Watts and Krishnamurti is attested by their refusal to submit to any traditional doctrine or spiritual discipline. Watts' flirtation with Zen can hardly pass muster while Krishnamurti was an unabashed iconoclast. Instead of conforming themselves and their ideas to an orthodoxy which would take them past the limitations of individualism, they remained locked into various intellectual and existential stalemates which stem from the conflict between an aspiration to "selflessness" and the absence of any traditional doctrine or method. As Perry remarks,

> Freedom from self requires a method . . . and recourse to cosmic principles that transcend the limitations of the human individuality. . . . And yet there are those who would vanquish the ego while obstinately refusing submission to a legitimate traditional form. . . . Autodetermination in spiritual matters amounts to intellectual anarchy.[17]

In the case of Watts this is plain enough in his later writings, which are marked by an ambivalent attitude to the status of the ego. His self-professed "spiritual materialism" (his own term) ends, and can only end, in an affirmation of the human ego.[18] No amount of Watts' literary wizardry nor his amiable wit could camouflage the fact. What we find in Watts' later work is indeed what Schuon calls "the disordered subjectivism of a personal mysticism".[19] Many people would endorse the claim that Watts "[did] more perhaps than any other writer to open the eyes of the West to the spiritual significance of Eastern religions and philosophies and to show that Truth is not the monopoly of any one school".[20] He indeed affirmed that "the Paths are many but their end is One".[21] Insofar as this principle governed Watts' enterprise we can applaud it. But the real question is whether he was qualified to convey traditional doctrines. His interpretations were too idiosyncratic to carry any authority. The title of his autobiography, *In My Own Way*, is a more fitting epitaph than he realized.[22]

The Krishnamurti fiasco is a well-known chapter in the history of the Theosophical movement. Despite his disavowal of the Messianic role

---

[16] W. Perry, "Anti-Theology and the Riddles of Alcyone", 186.

[17] W. Perry (ed.), *A Treasury of Traditional Wisdom*, 271.

[18] See L. Nordstrom and R. Pilgrim, "The Wayward Mysticism of Alan Watts", 381-399.

[19] Frithjof Schuon, "Nature and Function of the Spiritual Master", 54.

[20] L. Watts, "Foreword" to A. Watts, *In My Own Way*, vii-viii.

[21] L. Watts, "Foreword" to A. Watts, *In My Own Way*, vii-viii.

[22] See H. Oldmeadow, *Journeys East*, 261-264 for a fuller critique of Watts.

envisaged for him, Krishnamurti did "nothing to dispel the illusion that he [had] a crucial message for mankind about the inner transformation of the individual with its consequent outward transformation of society".[23] Perry exposed some of the central contradictions which hide behind a "smoke screen of sophistries" in Krishnamurti's work. We shall not rehearse the case here. Suffice it to note that Krishnamurti's wholesale rejection of "dogma, religion, church, and all that immature nonsense" stamp him as an inveterate anti-traditionalist.[24] It is worth noting Perry's condign remark that

> The man is in fact a victim of the very thought conditioning he would reject, being a product of the Brahmanic heritage from which he has deviated. The violence of his reaction to religion is a manifestation of exactly the sort of antagonism, resistance, opposition, and conflict which he pretends to be rejecting.[25]

The subjective orientation of the thinkers targeted in Perry's essay goes hand-in-hand with what he calls a "prodigal dearth of spiritual imagination", which signals another anti-traditional tendency:

> For a few very bright gentlemen of our century . . . to speak as if they have discovered spiritual truths of which the entire humanity of the world has hitherto been in ignorance— . . . surely the politest explanation one can give is lack of imagination.[26]

This attitude is also often supported with a "spiritual evolutionism", which suggests that man is now on the brink of a "new consciousness". The "scientific and moralistic humanism" to which Perry refers exposes itself in the Utopian fantasy of a science and technology wedded to a "new consciousness" towards which we have "evolved". It was the Canadian R.M. Bucke who, through a book of the same name, brought the term "cosmic consciousness" into popular parlance. Bucke spoke of "an intelligent enlightenment which alone would place the individual on a new plane of existence—would make him almost a member of a new species".[27] The evolutionist bias of this kind of thinking is plain enough and contrasts sharply with the perennial truth that "the ontological situation of man in the total scheme of things is always

---

[23] W. Perry, "Anti-Theology and the Riddles of Alcyone", 182.
[24] Krishnamurti in *Talks and Dialogues, Saanen, 1967*, quoted in W. Perry, "Anti-Theology and the Riddles of Alcyone", 183.
[25] W. Perry, "Anti-Theology and the Riddles of Alcyone", 184. See also P.T. Raju, *Idealistic Thought of India*, 399-400. (This sort of comment has also been made, with some justice, about Freud's attitude to religion.)
[26] W. Perry, "Anti-Theology and the Riddles of Alcyone", 191. See also *Light on the Ancient Worlds*, "Naiveté", 83-92.
[27] Quoted in M. Hayes, "The New Consciousness Movements", 45.

the same".[28] For most of these self-styled anti-dogmatists, evolutionism is actually a "dogma" of the most inviolable and inflexible kind: they remain unaware of the irony!

"Cosmic consciousness" has become a catch-all wherein a vague and sentimental "mysticism" consorts with a pseudo-scientific evolutionism. The working premise behind many of the "cosmic consciousness" outpourings, of which Watts' *The Book of the Taboo Against Knowing Who You Are* (1973) is an exemplary case, is that the self and the universe are identical and that when the self perceives the identity there is "enlightenment" or "cosmic consciousness". There is, of course, an echo of the Upanishadic *Atman-Brahman* formula here but usually in prostituted guise, wrapped up in quasi-psychological jargon, unsupported by any metaphysical rigor, and unverified by authentic gnosis. One might also point out a fact frequently overlooked: in the Vedantic metaphysic, *Brahman* is by no means identical with the universe and the very term "cosmic consciousness" implies a view still entrapped in *maya*.[29] Three decades ago Theodore Roszak issued a timely warning about the need for spiritual discrimination amidst the plethora of "consciousness" movements:

> The power to tell the greater from the lesser reality, the sacred paradigm from its copies and secular counterfeits . . . without it, the consciousness circuit will surely become a lethal swamp of paranormal entertainments, facile therapeutic tricks, authoritarian guru trips, demonic subversions.[30]

Today these words serve better not as a warning but as an epitaph.

Neo-Hinduism, Ramakrishna, and Vivekananda

As Arvind Sharma has noted, a distinctive approach to religious pluralism has been associated with Hinduism, going back at least to the appearance of Swami Vivekananda at the World Parliament of Religions in Chicago in 1893. This approach has variously been described as "accommodating, catholic, universal, open, assimilative, synthetic, hospitable, liberal, syncretistic, and above all tolerant".[31] The neo-Hindu renaissance associated with such figures as Ram Mohan Roy, Keshab Chandra Sen, Swami Vivekananda, the Tagores, Aurobindo Ghose and Sarvepalli Radhakrishnan, has exhibited a strong universalist strain which, at certain points, coincides with traditionalism. It is not our present purpose to explicate Hindu approaches

[28] S.H. Nasr, *Sufi Essays*, 93.
[29] See M. Hiriyana, *Essentials of Indian Philosophy*, 15ff.
[30] T. Roszak, *Unfinished Animal*, 13.
[31] A. Sharma, "All Religions are—Equal? One? True? Same?: A Critical Examination of Some Formulations of the Neo-Hindu Position", 59.

to religious pluralism,[32] nor to address any questions concerning its philo-sophical, historical, or social sources.[33] Rather we shall address a general question, given specificity through a discussion of Vivekananda: what are some of the characteristic attitudes and values of neo-Hinduism which are most sharply at odds with perennialism, as espoused by Schuon?

A shaping factor in the emergence of neo-Hinduism was the Western education to which most of its architects were exposed.[34] Inevitably they assimilated many of the prevailing European prejudices of the day, including: the over-valuation of a barren rationality and the potentialities of science; the belief in progress and the evolutionist assumptions which col-ored nearly every aspect of late nineteenth century European thought; the notion that religious traditions were "outmoded"; the preoccupation with the social and ethical aspects of religion to the neglect of the doctrinal and metaphysical. All of these were stock-in-trade for the Hindu reformers. It is, of course, no accident that the two figures who most profoundly exemplify the Hindu tradition in recent times, Ramakrishna and Ramana Maharshi, were innocent of these Western assumptions and played no part whatever in the reform movements. Western education did not necessarily disqualify one from either an orthodox Hindu or a traditional outlook, as the case of Coomaraswamy proves. Generally, however, the exposure to Western ideas, allied with certain abuses in contemporary Hinduism, produced in the reformers an attitude to tradition that was at best ambivalent. Move-ments like the Brahmo-Samaj were aggressively iconoclastic and served to erode the belief in Vedic authority, the *sine qua non* of Hindu orthodoxy, and to elevate the role of a sterile rationalism and arbitrary individual judgment. The whole idea of the supra-human origin and authority of tra-dition was thus jeopardized. Many of the neo-Hindus did affirm a kind of perennial philosophy. Indeed, Agehananda Bharati sees "all religions are one" as the key notion of the Hindu Renaissance.[35] Nonetheless, without any firm commitment to the principles of Revelation and orthodoxy, the similarities to perennialism remain more apparent than real.

[32] See A. Sharma, "All Religions are—Equal?", *passim*.

[33] See A. Sharma, "Some Misunderstandings of the Hindu Approach to Religious Plurality", 133ff.

[34] On neo-Hinduism see V.S. Naravane, *Modern Indian Thought*, V.S. Naravane and R. McDer-mott (eds.), *The Spirit of Modern India*, A.K. Saran, "The Crisis of Hinduism", and *Language of the Self*, chapters 1-4.

[35] A. Bharati, "The Hindu Renaissance and Its Apologetic Patterns", 278. For some discussion of "tradition" and "modernity" in India see: M. Chatterjee, "Tradition and Modernity with Respect to Religion in India"; F. Streng, "'Sacred' and 'Secular' as Terms for Interpreting Modernization in India"; A.K. Saran, "The Meaning and Forms of Secularism: A Note"—all in *Religious Traditions* 2:1, 1979, 14-20, 21-29 and 38-51 respectively.

Universalism, of course, is entirely proper when it stems from metaphysical discernment and when it remains on the intellectual plane, but more often the "accommodating" position of the neo-Hindus is a vapid form of religious liberalism. Consider, for instance, the implications of a formulation such as this, from Radhakrishnan: "We may measure true spiritual culture by the comprehension and veneration we are able to give to forms of thought and feeling which have influenced masses of mankind."[36] At first sight this looks like an estimable attitude. However, a little reflection reveals it as a woolly platitude. Which "forms of thought and feeling"? Do we include such aggressively anti-spiritual movements as Nazism and communism? Should we "venerate" the avaricious materialism which presently influences "masses of mankind"? If Radhakrishnan is talking of the different religions, how adequate a description is "forms of thought and feeling"? The vagueness of this kind of "open-mindedness" is characteristic. Furthermore, let us not forget that

> To tolerate the opinions of other people does not necessarily imply respect; it can also go hand in hand with a neutrality not untinged with contempt; the emphasis here is subjective, the supposed right to hold whatever opinions one pleases; an objective appreciation of those opinions as such hardly enters in.[37]

There is also in neo-Hinduism, as the term implies, a suspicion of tradition as such, of its religious and social forms. Doubtless some of the reforms advocated by the neo-Hindus could be justified as a return to traditional norms or as an attempt to cleanse Indian society of abuses which had no traditional legitimacy. More often, however, the reforming impulse was impelled not by traditional principles but by social and political values imported from the West.[38] In this context the terms "Westernization" and "modernization", the one implying an imitation of a spatially located culture and the other an adherence to a temporally restricted mentality, are both appropriate.

In the writings of people like Vivekananda and Radhakrishnan we repeatedly find the idea that traditional religious and social forms (dogmas, rites, myths, institutions) can be abandoned in the name of some apparently higher ideal—"truth", "social justice", "reason", "science", "progress" and such. Vivekananda's assertion that "Temples and churches, books and forms are simply the kindergarten of religion" is typical: it is justified in the name

[36] S. Radhakrishnan, "Fragments of a Confession" in P.A. Schilpp (ed.) *The Philosophy of Sarvapelli Radhakrishnan*, 72.

[37] M. Pallis, *A Buddhist Spectrum*, 111.

[38] See A.K. Coomaraswamy, "The Bugbear of Literacy" and "The Bugbear of Democracy, Freedom, and Equality" in *The Bugbear of Literacy*.

of "realization".[39] The perennialists would agree, of course, that realization takes precedence over all other claims—realization, properly speaking, is, after all, an "inner" actualization of the Truth and could not be opposed to it. But this is no reason to capitulate to the "mystical prejudice" that nothing counts in the spiritual life except "states"—a prejudice widespread in India.[40] What Vivekananda does not add, as any traditionalist would, is the necessity and value of forms which must remain inviolate for the vast majority of believers. Schuon's cautionary words could not be more pertinent:

> When a man seeks to escape from "dogmatic narrowness" it is essential that it should be "upwards" and not "downwards": dogmatic form is transcended by fathoming its depths and contemplating its universal content, and not by denying it in the name of a pretentious and iconoclastic "ideal" of "pure truth".[41]

Vivekananda, to be sure, did not deny forms altogether, but his attitude to them is often condescending and irreverent. In view of the fact that many "modern Hindus derive their knowledge of Hinduism from Vivekananda",[42] one can only wonder at the possible consequences of such an attitude.

It has often been remarked that Hinduism is a remarkably hospitable tradition, finding a place within its ample embrace for a wide diversity of doctrinal forms and spiritual practices. The negative side of this elasticity, if one may so express it, is that it is peculiarly vulnerable to all manner of heterodoxies, especially once Hinduism is severed from its normal and protective social context. Schuon contrasts this aspect of Hinduism with the much maligned "dogmatism" of the Occidental traditions:

> Monotheistic religions, with their invariable dogmatism and formal homogeneity, have a real advantage here in the sense that their very structure opposes the deviation to which *bhakti* is liable. The structure of Hinduism is too primordial not to be terribly vulnerable at such a period as our own. It is almost impossible for contemporary *bhakta*s to remain fully orthodox.[43]

As Louis Renou once remarked, modern-day India is an El Dorado for charlatans. All these things considered, it is not surprising that Western adoptions of Hinduism have been plagued with difficulties. It is also easy to understand how the various corruptions and compromises which entered

---

[39] Vivekananda quoted in A.R. Wadia, "Swami Vivekananda's Philosophy of Religion" in R.C. Majumdar (ed.), *Swami Vivekananda's Memorial Volume*, 257.

[40] See *Transfiguration of Man*, "Thought: Light and Perversion", 9.

[41] *Stations of Wisdom*, "Orthodoxy and Intellectuality", 16.

[42] A. Bharati, "The Hindu Renaissance", 278.

[43] *Spiritual Perspectives and Human Facts*, "Vedanta", 125n.

Hinduism by way of the neo-Hindu "reform" movements, themselves a product of Western colonialism, should be magnified in Western assimilations of Hinduism. And here one is thinking primarily not only of spurious claims to a universalism "beyond" all religion,[44] but also of the application of evolutionism to the spiritual domain itself—evident in varying degree in such disparate figures as Vivekananda, Aurobindo, Radhakrishnan, and Mahesh Yogi as well as in many Western Vedanta enthusiasts.

A final general point before turning to Vivekananda in more detail: Schuon affirms a *sophia perennis* at the heart of each integral tradition, without bias towards any particular tradition and without any wish to distil any "universal" or "new" religion; some of the neo-Hindus tend to the view that almost anything which claims to be "religious" or "spiritual" (no matter what the criteria!) has something to offer, but that Advaita Vedanta (as understood by themselves) provides a platform on which can be mounted a new universal religion. This, for example, from Vivekananda: "Vedanta, and Vedanta alone can become the universal religion of man. . . . No other is fitted for that role."[45] Now, Schuon himself is the first to affirm that Shankara's perspective is "one of the most adequate expressions possible of the *philosophia perennis* or sapiential esoterism".[46] But we will certainly not find him indulging in loose talk about a "universal religion", nor claiming that Vedanta is the sole possible expression of what it expresses. In any case, "Vedanta for the masses" is a self-evident absurdity!

Schuon's assessment of Vivekananda—from which we may infer a great deal about neo-Hinduism generally—hinges on his relationship with Ramakrishna. Of the Paramahamsa and his mission Schuon writes:

> There is something in Ramakrishna that seems to defy every category: he was like the living symbol of the inward unity of religions; he was in fact the first saint to wish to enter into foreign spiritual forms, and in this consisted his exceptional and in a sense universal mission. . . . In our times of confusion, distress, and doubt, he was the saintly "verifier" of forms and the "revealer" as it were of their single truth. . . . [His] spiritual plasticity was of a miraculous order.[47]

---

[44] An example: Mahesh Yogi's extraordinary claim that he offers "the *summum bonum* of all that Christ and Krishna, Buddha, and Muhammad taught" (quoted in *Spiritual Perspectives and Human Facts*, "Appendix: Selections from Letters and Previously Unpublished Writings", 238).

[45] Quoted in P. Atmaprana, "Swami Vivekananda on Harmony of Religions and Religious Sects" in R.C. Majumdar (ed.), *Swami Vivekananda's Memorial Volume*, 311.

[46] *Esoterism as Principle and as Way*, "Understanding Esoterism", 21.

[47] *Spiritual Perspectives and Human Facts*, "Vedanta", 122, 127.

While leaving no doubt as to Ramakrishna's sanctity and the spiritual radiance which emanated from his person, Schuon notes several vulnerabilities in his position vis-à-vis an emergent neo-Hinduism: a *jnana* extrinsically ill-supported because of his almost exclusive faith in the spiritual omnipotence of love, whence "an inadequate integration of the mind in his perspective"; a universalism "too facile because purely bhaktic"; an absence of safeguards against the dissolving influences of a modernism which left the saint himself untouched, but which permeated the milieu in which he found himself and which, in a sense, took a posthumous revenge through the influence of Vivekananda.[48] Ramakrishna, although instinctively suspicious of movements like the Brahmo-Samaj, was not altogether cognizant of the dangers posed by modernism. Furthermore, he attributed to his disciple Narendra "a genius for ontologically metamorphic transformation he neither possessed nor could have possessed",[49] Narendra (later Swami Vivekananda) being a person in the grip of certain "dynamic" mental tendencies which precluded any kind of realization comparable to that of the Master himself.

In a traditional framework which was "entire, closed, and without fissures" the potentialities for heterodoxy which lurked in Vivekananda's makeup might well have been "rectified, neutralized, and compensated". As it was, Vivekananda's development was shaped not only by the Paramahamsa but by an Occidentalism which was "unknown and incomprehensible to Ramakrishna but which stimulated in the disciple exactly those tendencies whose development had at times been feared by the master".[50] One such development was the founding of a sect or order, a function which Ramakrishna explicitly rejected as being outside Vivekananda's proper vocation.[51] It might also be noted that Ramakrishna could not have foreseen the consequences of causes which he himself had not conceived—the fact, for instance, that Vivekananda's interpretation of Vedanta was to be filtered through a screen of misconceptions and prejudices which derived not only from his own disposition but from modernist influences.

Schuon concedes that the enigma of Vivekananda can perhaps be explained in terms of the fact that Hindu-Indian nationalism was inevitable and that the Swami was its predestined champion. In order to fulfill such

---

[48] *Spiritual Perspectives and Human Facts*, "Vedanta", 125-129.

[49] *Spiritual Perspectives and Human Facts*, "Vedanta", 128.

[50] *Spiritual Perspectives and Human Facts*, "Vedanta", 125.

[51] See Swami Vireswarananda's *Life of Shri Ramakrishna*, cited by Schuon in *Spiritual Perspectives and Human Facts*, "Vedanta", 188-189fn. Incidentally, Schuon does point out that "there are contemplatives of the line of Ramakrishna whose spirituality is impeccable" and who transmit "a perfectly regular doctrine . . . whatever may be their feelings on the subject of Vivekananda." Swami Brahmananda is one such. See *Spiritual Perspectives and Human Facts*, "Vedanta", 127n.

a role Vivekananda had need of a certain anti-traditional mental dynamism and of some of the ideological premises of the modern West:

> In "modernizing" Hinduism Vivekananda at the same time "Hinduized" modernism, if one may put it this way, and by this means he neutralized some of its destructive impetus. . . . If it was inevitable that India would become a "nation", it was preferable for it to do so in some way under the distant auspices of a Ramakrishna rather than under the sign of a modernism that would brutally deny everything India had stood for throughout the millennia.[52]

Nonetheless, the fact remains that much of Vivekananda's teaching was anti-traditional, both intrinsically and extrinsically. It is as clear as the day in his own writings that his conception of tradition was nebulous, that he had scant understanding of the reciprocal relationships of the exoteric and esoteric dimensions of religion, that he was less than vigilant in preserving "the incalculable values of orthodoxy", that much of his talk about "universal religion" is of the sentimental variety, that his understanding of Vedanta is compromised by modern ideas, and that he had none of his master's genius for penetrating foreign religious forms. In brief, there is no common measure between Ramakrishna and Vivekananda.[53] None of this is to gainsay the Swami's prodigious talents, his personal charisma, or his effectiveness as a spearhead for the Hindu Renaissance: such considerations are not germane to our present purposes.

Vivekananda's penchant for the facile formulation and his disregard for traditional proprieties is suggested by his equation of Jesus, the Buddha, and Ramakrishna. It is worth rehearsing Schuon's objections to this "trinity":

> It is unacceptable, first because it is impossible in a truly Hindu perspective to put the Buddha and Christ in a trinity to the exclusion of Rama and Krishna; secondly because Christ is foreign to India; thirdly, because, if non-Hindu worlds are taken into account, there is no reason for taking only Christ into consideration still of course from the point of view of Hinduism; fourthly because there is no common measure between the river Ramakrishna and the oceans that were Jesus and Shakyamuni; fifthly, because Ramakrishna lived at a cyclic period which could in any case no longer contain a plenary incarnation of the amplitude of the great Revealers; sixthly because in the Hindu system there is no room for another plenary and "solar" incarnation of Divinity between the ninth and the tenth *Avatara*s of Vishnu—the Buddha and the future *Kalki-Avatara*. "A single Prophet", such is the teaching

---

[52] *Spiritual Perspectives and Human Facts*, "Vedanta", 128.
[53] On this question see F. Matchett, "The Teaching of Ramakrishna in Relation to the Hindu Tradition and as Interpreted by Vivekananda", 171-184.

of At-Tahawi, "is more excellent than all the friends of God taken together" (the saints).[54]

This reproach is made in a footnote to a discussion of the Prophet Muhammad, more or less as an aside. However, this is an illuminating passage in several respects: it demonstrates the principial rigor which always shapes Schuon's work; it alerts us to the fact that Schuon is more conversant than Vivekananda with the claims and proprieties of Hindu tradition; that recourse to another tradition to corroborate a point is typical of Schuon's *modus operandi*; and the passage reminds us again of the dangers of a "hospitality" offered at the expense of doctrinal rigor and metaphysical discrimination.

A small sample of quotes will be sufficient to expose the absurdities scattered through Vivekananda's writings. No perennialist would be capable, in any circumstances whatever, of giving voice to anything like the following:

> The visions of Moses are more likely to be false than our own because we have more knowledge at our disposal and are less subject to illusion. (from *Inspired Talks*)[55]

A whole chain of prejudices lies behind this kind of formulation. Another example:

> The Buddhas and Christs we know are heroes of second grade compared with those greater ones of which the world knows nothing. (from *Karma Yoga*)

—as if the perfections of Christ and the Buddha were a matter of degree which could be surpassed, and leaving aside the humanistic implications of "heroes". This sort of thing one might expect from a humanist, but hardly from a man of Vivekananda's pretensions. Such an utterance is inconceivable in the mouth of Ramakrishna. And yet another statement even more astonishing, if that be possible:

> We have seen that the theory of a personal God who created the world cannot be proved. Is there today a single child who could believe in it? . . . Your personal God, Creator of this world, has he ever succored you? This is the challenge flung down by modern science. (from *Conference on the Vedanta*)

One hardly knows where to start in excavating the prejudices buried in this: the importing of considerations ("proof") into a domain where they do not

---

[54] *Understanding Islam* (1994), "The Prophet", 103n.

[55] This passage and the two following are cited without comment by Schuon, *Spiritual Perspectives and Human Facts* (1969), "Vedanta", 124-125. They speak for themselves!

apply, the brutal insolence of such condescension to countless millions of theists, both in India and elsewhere, the utterly irrelevant appeal to modern science—all this from a man whose effusive apologists do not hesitate to compare him to Shankara!

Lest the reader imagine that such statements are unrepresentative we can only direct them to Vivekananda's writings about other religions. For a quite extraordinary agglomeration of self-contradictions, half-baked ideas, and extravagant assertions one need look no further than the essay "Buddhistic India".[56] However, a scrutiny of almost any of Vivekananda's writings will expose the Trojan Horse of modernism, one which is likely to discharge its unattractive occupants at any turn. One can only sympathize with Mircea Eliade's reaction to Vivekananda's work: "I was later to receive Vivekananda's books. But they didn't win me over. I was already immune to spiritualistic rhetoric, to popularized neo-Vedantic fervor; all that seemed shoddy to me."[57] Quite so!

Aldous Huxley's "Perennial Philosophy"

In the West the term "perennial philosophy" is most often associated with Aldous Huxley. It is not without irony that Huxley should open his 1944 anthology of that name with an error of fact: the term itself was certainly not coined by Leibniz, being used at least as early as the mid-sixteenth century by Augustinus Steuchius.[58] Huxley's exposition of the perennial philosophy is marred by more than errors of fact. Whilst Schuon himself never commented explicitly on Huxley or his book, other traditionalists have done so, often in the light of principles expounded by Schuon himself. Because the perennial philosophy has in recent times so often been associated with Huxley, and because Huxley's understanding of the timeless wisdom has been confounded with Schuon's teachings, it is of paramount importance to dispel the confusions which have thus arisen.[59] Gai Eaton suggested that Huxley's celebrated work had, in fact, "given a dangerously misleading

---

[56] Reproduced in R.C. Majumdar, xxi-xliv.

[57] M. Eliade, *No Souvenirs*, 134.

[58] See A. Huxley *The Perennial Philosophy*, viii. *De perenni philosophia* appeared in 1540. See also S.H. Nasr, Preface to *Islam and the Perennial Philosophy*, vii; C.B. Schmitt, "Perennial Philosophy: From Agostino Steuco to Leibniz"; S.H. Nasr, *Knowledge and the Sacred*, 69-70.

[59] See E.J. Sharpe, *Comparative Religion*, 262-263, where we find a misleading association of the traditionalists with neo-deists, neo-Hindus, and the Huxleyian vision of the perennial philosophy. For a similar confusion see G. Parrinder, *Comparative Religion*, 79-91 and R.S. Ellwood, book review in *Journal of the American Academy of Religion* 45, 1977, 256. Another reviewer confounds traditionalism with theosophy; see F. H. Heinemann's otherwise intelligent review of *Transcendent Unity of Religions* in *Journal of Theological Studies* VI, 1955, 338. These are only a few examples from amongst many.

impression of the traditional religious and metaphysical teaching" and dispar-
ages its spirit as "Western through and through"—that is, modernist.[60] This
imputation would doubtless be supported by other traditionalists. Without
questioning the "sincerity, intelligence, and learning" which Huxley brought
to his work, Peter Moore finds that a "moralism and scientific humanism"
distort his vision of the perennial philosophy.[61] What evidence might be
adduced to sustain such charges?

Firstly, Huxley's approach to different religious teachings, forms, and
doctrines is both partial and idiosyncratic. As Eaton notes, he approves of
Rumi but cannot fathom the doctrine of *jihad*; he acclaims Shankara but
has little time for "popular" Hinduism; he frequently invokes Eckhart but is
deeply suspicious of St. Augustine. Not without reason did Coomaraswamy
write to Huxley saying "I do not approach the great traditions, as you seem
to do, to pick and choose in them what seems to me to be right."[62] Of course
some elements of subjectivity must enter into the shaping of any anthology,
but the drift of these few examples is clear enough: Huxley has not grasped
the relationship between the esoteric and exoteric domains of religion and,
like a good many would-be mystics, wants to bypass the claims of orthodoxy
in search of the "Highest Common Factor" (his own words).[63] He is suspicious of dogmas, rituals, and sacraments—of religious forms in general. He
asseverates that Christ and the Buddha both disapproved of "ceremonies,
vain repetitions, and sacramental rites" and that the traditions issuing from
their teachings have gone their "all too human way" in developing such
forms.[64]

Huxley was one of the prime movers behind a Western hybrid of
"neo-Vedanta" in the West, one which attracted other literary figures such
as Gerald Heard and Christopher Isherwood. We can safely assume that
Huxley would have shared Heard's ideas when the latter wrote:

> A new religion has come into history—that is Western Vedanta. . . . The
> appearance of Vedanta in the West as a living religion . . . is inevitable
> just because the religious heredity of the West has now outgrown the
> tight Hebrew pot of cosmology. . . . A faith that taught hell for those
> who did not get themselves saved in this life was suited enough to put
> the fear of God into barbarians or men too busy to do much more than
> make a dash with their last breath for a deathbed repentance. But for

---

[60] G. Eaton, *The Richest Vein*, 167, 180.

[61] P. Moore, review of W. Perry (ed.), *A Treasury of Traditional Wisdom*, in *Studies in Comparative Religion*, 6:1, 1972, 63.

[62] Coomaraswamy to Huxley, 28th September, 1944, quoted in R. Lipsey, *Coomaraswamy:
His Life and Work*, 220.

[63] A. Huxley, *The Perennial Philosophy*, vii.

[64] A. Huxley, *The Perennial Philosophy*, 262-272.

people really interested in the spiritual world . . . such doctrines were
. . . a terrible obstacle.[65]

The prejudices with which this is laced are obvious enough and are characteristic of the "Western Vedanta" movement in America and elsewhere. The
complacencies of such an outlook are quite repellent to anyone with a
traditional outlook. No doubt it was the kind of thinking evinced by the
"California Vedantists" and their latter-day epigones which drew forth the
following rebuke from Schuon:

> It must be said that India is very dangerous terrain for most Westerners;
> they become imbued there with irremediable prejudices and preten-
> sions. It goes without saying that I prefer the most narrow-minded of
> Catholics—if he is pious—to these pseudo-Hinduists, arrogant and
> permanently damaged as they are. They scorn the religious point of
> view, which they do not understand in the least and which alone could
> save them.[66]

Huxley was also entranced by quasi-scientific models which he believed
shed light on spiritual matters, but which in fact tell us much more about
the time which produced them. Given his background and temperament it
is no surprise that we should find in Huxley the same evolutionist bias which
so characterizes modernism.[67] It is true that Huxley had a keen eye for some
of the more absurd pretensions of modern science, and for some of its most
sinister applications.[68] However, he was by no means immune to the seductions of pseudo-scientific models which cannot illumine but only obscure
the traditional doctrines with which he is dealing. His lengthy recapitulation
of Sheldon's typology of human personalities is a case in point.[69] He gives the
game away completely in a piece of foolishness as blatant as the following:

> In one way or another, all our experiences are chemically conditioned. .
> . . Knowing as he does . . . what are the chemical conditions of transcen-
> dental experience, the aspiring mystic should turn for technical help to
> the specialists—in pharmacology, in biochemistry.[70]

[65] G. Heard, "Vedanta and Western History" in C. Isherwood (ed.), *Vedanta for the Western
World*. Anyone who has read Coomaraswamy's "Vedanta and Western Tradition" cannot but
be struck by the contrast between this commanding essay and the conglomeration of prejudices paraded in Heard's piece.

[66] *Spiritual Perspectives and Human Facts*, "Appendix: Selections from Letters and Previously
Unpublished Writings", 239.

[67] See, for instance, A. Huxley, *The Perennial Philosophy*, vii.

[68] See his "Origins and Consequences of Some Contemporary Thought Patterns" in C. Isherwood (ed.), *Vedanta for the Western World*, 359-363.

[69] See A. Huxley, *The Perennial Philosophy*, 149ff. See also H. Bridges, "Aldous Huxley: Exponent of Mysticism in America".

[70] A. Huxley, *The Doors of Perception and Heaven and Hell*, 121-122.

Perry and others have anatomized the confusions which run rampant through this kind of literature and there is no point in treading the same ground again. Suffice to say that the formulation above would be worthy of the most categorical materialist.[71]

Huxley was also unduly preoccupied with morality and moralism: the almost obsessional concern with ideas about guilt and sin, the "ambivalent and tortuous attitude to sexuality", the exaggerated antithesis between "spirit" and "matter" in one place and their confounding in another—all these are hallmarks of Huxley's work in general. Eaton has mapped out the development of these themes in Huxley's novels, an analysis with which we are not here concerned but which does shed some light on his eccentric vision of the perennial philosophy.[72]

*   *   *

The business of comparing the views of various contemporary philosophers, "universalists", "gurus", occultists and the like with perennialism could be pursued more or less indefinitely. However, enough has now been said to clarify some of the principles which define the perennialist position mapped out by Schuon and to differentiate it from other outlooks with which it might be confused.

---

[71] See W. Perry, "Drug-Induced Mysticism: The Mescalin Hypothesis", 192-198. This in an authoritative statement on a subject on which any amount of nonsense has been written in the last four decades.

[72] G. Eaton, *The Richest Vein*, 166-180.

V

The Spiritual Life

Knowledge saves only on condition that it engages all that
we are: only when it constitutes a path which works and
transforms, and which wounds our nature as the plough
wounds the soil.

(Frithjof Schuon, *Prayer Fashions Man*, 24)

16

Spiritual Anthropology

Types, Caste, Race, and the Human Body

The reality of God and of our final ends determine all that we are.[1]

The quasi-divine character of the intellect—and hence of the intellectual elite—is the postulate of the caste system.[2]

God wishes to be worshipped by every man according to the nature He gave him.[3]

A man of another race . . . is like a forgotten aspect of ourselves and thus also like a rediscovered mirror of God.[4]

As symbols the masculine body indicates a victory of the Spirit over chaos, and the feminine body, a deliverance of form by Essence.[5]

"Spiritual anthropology", Schuon tells us, is a pleonasm because "to say man is to say spirit"[6]—but justified in circumstances where man has forgotten or denied God and so lost sight of his own nature: any proper "anthropology" must depend on a "theology" because of man's deiformity. The term "spiritual anthropology" itself might encompass all manner of significations—indeed, Schuon's boundless writings concerning the nature of man, his "relationship" with the Absolute, and the many modalities of the spiritual life might come under this canopy. Let us firstly consider the way in which Schuon understands man's essential nature, as expressed through fundamental spiritual types, before turning to three more particular themes in Schuon's *oeuvre*: caste; race and the diversity of human groups; sexuality and the message of the human body. This will take us through a descending hierarchy of human differentiations—spiritual (the different spiritual types or dispositions), psychological (the castes which are universal, whether or not institutionalized), and physical (the different races). Even these delimited themes cannot be

---

[1] *From the Divine to the Human*, "Outline of a Spiritual Anthropology", 77.
[2] *Language of the Self*, "The Meaning of Caste", 113.
[3] Letter to Benjamin Black Elk, October 7, 1947, in J-B. Aymard and P. Laude, *Frithjof Schuon: Life and Teachings*, 62.
[4] *Language of the Self*, "The Meaning of Race", 175.
[5] *Stations of Wisdom*, "Manifestations of the Divine Principle", 87.
[6] *From the Divine to the Human*, "Outline of a Spiritual Anthropology", 76.

given more than brief treatment: we shall simply throw up a few signposts which might help readers to find their way out of the thickets of confusion which characterize modern writings on these subjects.

Rudiments of a Spiritual Anthropology

As we have already seen, over the last few centuries there has been a plethora of "definitions" of man and of the human condition which have reduced him, variously, to a biological organism, a "trousered ape" (Darwin), a social being determined by his material circumstances (Marx), a puppet of illicit desires and "seething excitations" buried in the sub-conscious (Freud), a cowardly herd animal redeemed only by the "will to power" of the *Über-mensch* (Nietzsche) . . . and so on, *ad nauseam*. These modern understandings of man, whatever their superficial differences, are but variations on a theme, the repudiation of man's spiritual nature, and at the same time, necessarily, a denial of God. These notions infect our perceptions of the human form itself. In a climate in which our self-understanding oscillates between the Promethean and hubristic on one side, and the demeaning and reductionistic on the other, it has been the task of perennial philosophers such as Schuon to reaffirm the theomorphic nature of man and to reassert his timeless vocation.

As is apparent from much that has gone before, Schuon has returned again and again in his writings to those aspects of the human being which distinguish him from all other creatures and which confer the peculiar privileges and responsibilities of the human condition—his mysterious subjectivity hand-in-hand with his capacity for objectivity, "his" quasi-divine Intellect, his intelligence and will, the faculty of speech, his freedom and capacity for self-transformation. At the same time Schuon harbors no illusions concerning the depths to which man can fall when he loses sight of his true nature. "The ambiguity of the human state is that we are as it were suspended between God—our Essence—and the human form, which is 'made of clay'; we are so to speak a mixture of divinity and dust."[7] No other contemporary writer is so sensitively attuned to both the grandeur and the pathos of the human estate. No doubt there are many artists of various kind and, indeed, a handful of "philosophers" and "thinkers", who have understood something of man's modern predicament and who have graphi-cally portrayed the spiritual sterility of our times—but often these portrayals are marked by the very perplexities which they anatomize. In a climate in which we are confronted with ever more bizarre and confused "definitions" of man, Schuon's understanding of the human situation stands like a beacon in the night.

---

[7] *Stations of Wisdom*, "Manifestations of the Divine Principle", 82-83.

As all traditions testify, man comprises a body (*corpus*), soul (*anima*), and Spirit/Intellect (*spiritus*). The interplay of these elements and the predominance of one or the other, gives rise to ternaries such as *hylikos-psychikos-pneumatikos* or Fear-Love-Knowledge which, in turn, signal three spiritual types or dispositions and the corresponding spiritual paths—*karma-bhakti-jnana* (roughly, activity-devotion-knowledge; in Islam *makhafah, mahabbah, marifah*). As Schuon insists, "every science of man must prolong a science of God",[8] which is to say that man is deiform, made in the image and likeness of God. "God is 'pure Spirit': which is to say, implicitly, that He is at once Knowledge, Love, and Power."[9] This points to a concise formulation of man's essential nature, one frequently deployed by Schuon: intelligence-soul-will (or, similarly, knowledge-love-will, or, truth-virtue-freedom). There is in man, as in God, a single spirit which is knowledge and love; these are prolonged by the will, inspired by one or the other, and polarized into intention and activity:

> In our heart, the elements knowledge, love, and power—or intelligence, sentiment, and will—are combined as so many dimensions of one and the same deiform subjectivity. Outside our heart, these faculties become disassociated in the sense that intelligence seems to reside in the brain or the mind, and sentiment or affectivity in the soul, the *psyche*; the will, and with it the capacity to act, is then combined with each of these regions—for we have need of will in order to think as well as to practice the virtues.[10]

The ways in which the spiritual life engages these three faculties will be taken up in the next chapter. For now let us note that intelligence, soul, and will are pre-eminently manifested, respectively, in the jnanic, bhaktic, and karmic spiritual types. However, this threefold division is only one of several possible schemas; depending on the vantage point in question, one can also speak, as Schuon sometimes does, of four basic spiritual temperaments whilst elsewhere he alludes to five types, each corresponding with one of the elements. To keep the present discussion relatively simple we will not here delve further into this complex subject.[11] Generally speaking, the immediately intelligible jnanic–bhaktic-karmic typology provides us with the necessary framework. It must also be noted that, strictly speaking,

[8] *From the Divine to the Human*, "Outline of a Spiritual Anthropology", 76.
[9] *From the Divine to the Human*, "Outline of a Spiritual Anthropology", 76.
[10] *From the Divine to the Human*, "Outline of a Spiritual Anthropology", 79.
[11] Interested readers should turn to "Human Premises of a Religious Dilemma" in *Sufism: Veil and Quintessence*, "Vicissitudes of Spiritual Temperaments" in *Gnosis: Divine Wisdom*, and "The Three Dimensions of Sufism" in *Studies in Comparative Religion*, 10:1, 1976 (this last is one of the very few Schuon essays that has not appeared in any of his books).

castes do not correspond to spiritual temperaments: caste differentiations are vertical whilst those of temperament are horizontal; thus, these different temperaments will be found within each caste. This typology is integral to any human anthropology for differences of spiritual temperament are more fundamental than other more secondary differentiations, such as those of caste and race.

Caste

Amongst the Western "intelligentsia" caste is a subject which almost invariably stirs up a snake-pit of prejudices, the modern mentality being so spectacularly ill-equipped to understand it. Not the least of our problems here is the intensely sentimental egalitarianism which pervades the modern outlook. It is a "sign of the times" that even in India, where *Varnashrama-dharma* (the order of castes and stages of life as prescribed by Vedic norms) was given its most coherent expression, there is now a widespread hostility amongst the "educated" classes towards this scripturally sanctioned institution. (By way of an aside it might be remarked that most of the neo-Hindu "reformers"—Vivekananda, Ram Mohan Roy, Dayananda and the like—wanted to hack away from tradition whatever was not in conformity with modern prejudices; hence their opposition to the institution of caste.) It should also be noted that the misapprehension that caste is a peculiarly Indian or Hindu phenomenon generates yet more confusion. In fact, as Schuon reminds us, caste "is an ever present factor in any human collectivity",[12] even where it is not in any way institutionalized. As Mahatma Gandhi himself—so often wrongly enlisted as an opponent of caste—remarked, "*Varnashrama* is . . . inherent in human nature, and Hinduism has simply reduced it to a science."[13] The water is further muddied by the common Western assimilation of caste and class: the former pertains to a fundamental differentiation of human types and is something quite different from the socio-economic stratifications which so preoccupy sociologists. This reduction strips caste of its spiritual significance. An even more fundamental source of confusion, rarely acknowledged, is that most Western commentaries on caste are rooted in the competitive and materialistic ethos of modern industrialized societies. As Ananda Coomaraswamy so rightly observed:

> The caste system cannot be judged by concepts of success that govern life in a society organized for over-production and profit at any price, and where it is everyone's ambition to rise on the social ladder, rather than to realize his own perfection.[14]

[12] *Castes and Races*, "The Meaning of Caste", 7.
[13] E. Sharpe, "To Hinduism through Gandhi", 61.
[14] A. Coomaraswamy, *The Bugbear of Literacy*, 148.

The scriptural foundations of the Hindu caste system, the metaphysical principles which inform it, and the ways in which *varnashrama* was applied in the traditional social order of India, have all been treated in considerable detail in Coomaraswamy's masterly essay, "The Bugbear of Democracy, Freedom, and Equality".[15] Schuon, on the other hand, has been primarily concerned not with the social ramifications of caste but with explaining caste as a spiritual typology—and it is to this aspect of the subject that we now turn.

The caste system cannot but manifest itself in certain circumstances because it is "founded on the very nature of things", in particular the diversity of human endowments and qualifications. True, this principle stands at odds to another principle which is foregrounded in some religious traditions: the equality of men before God. As Schuon remarks:

> The immortality of the soul is the postulate of religious egalitarianism, just as the quasi-divine character of the intellect—and hence of the intellectual elite—is the postulate of the caste system.[16]

So it is that Hinduism accentuates those hierarchical categories which differentiate men whilst the "leveling outlook of Islam" insists that every man is a priest, though in each case there is a kind of compensating counter-balance—in Hinduism the *sannyasin* who is beyond all castes (but who "does not dream of preaching their abolition"[17]) and in Islam the existence of a religious nobility of a sort, the descendants of the Prophet. However, Schuon is less interested in the various more or less approximate institutionalizations of caste in different cultures than in the natural castes themselves, "those based on the intrinsic nature of individuals", or what he sometimes refers to as "typological" rather than social castes.[18] It should also be noted that "institutional castes are more often symbolical rather than effective as regards the real potentialities of persons, above all in later times".[19]

The Hindu caste system, which finds a Western echo in Plato's *Republic*, distinguished four basic spiritual outlooks, each determined by a certain mode of consciousness, a certain degree of perception of the Real.

> For the *brahmana*—the purely intellectual, contemplative, and sacerdotal type—it is the changeless, the transcendent which is real; in his innermost heart he does not "believe" either in "life" or in "earth". . . .

---

[15] This essay can be found in *The Bugbear of Literacy* and is reproduced in H. Oldmeadow (ed.), *The Betrayal of Tradition.*
[16] *Language of the Self*, "The Meaning of Caste", 113.
[17] *Gnosis: Divine Wisdom*, "Vicissitudes of Spiritual Temperaments", 46.
[18] *Sufism: Veil and Quintessence*, "Human Premises of a Religious Dilemma", 83.
[19] *To Have a Center*, "Survey of Integral Anthropology", 42.

The *kshatriya*—the "knightly" type—has a keen intelligence, but it is turned towards action and analysis rather than towards contemplation and synthesis; his strength lies especially in his character; he makes up for the aggressiveness of his energy by his generosity and for his passionate nature by his nobility, self-control, and greatness of soul. For this human type it is action that is "real". . . . Just as for the *brahmana* all is in motion and unreal except the Eternal and whatever is attached to It—truth, knowledge, contemplation, ritual, the Path—so for the *kshatriya* all is uncertain and peripheral except the constants of his *dharma*—action, honor, virtue, glory, nobility—on which for him all other values depend.[20]

Whilst the *kshatriya* is an idealist oriented towards action, he "readily turns poet or aesthete", and in any case "lays very little stress on matter as such".[21] The *brahmanas* (or Brahmins as they are sometimes called) and the *kshatriyas* form a nobility, determined by heredity. It should also be noted that the various dispositions identified by the caste system may exist within a single caste: there are, for instance, *brahmanas* of the *kshatriya* type, and vice versa.[22]

What the two higher castes have in common . . . is acuity of intelligence, the capacity for spontaneously placing oneself above oneself, hence the predominance of the qualitative over the quantitative and, in spirituality, the accentuation of inwardness and verticality, whether it is a question of wisdom or heroism.[23]

The consciousness of the third caste, the *vaishyas* (merchants, artisans, farmers), is governed by material considerations, most obviously expressed in the pursuit of "riches, security, prosperity, and well-being". If the *brahmana* does not altogether "believe" in this world, the *vaishya* does not altogether "believe" in the other; nor does he exhibit intellectual or chivalrous virtues. The *vaishya*'s more modest virtues include honesty, common sense, and piety.

The characteristics of the *vaishya* are *grosso modo* the following: love of work well done . . . and of wages honestly earned; an emotional accent on the fear of God and on meritorious works conscientiously and piously accomplished . . . coupled with a possible tendency to platitude

---

[20] *Language of the Self*, "The Meaning of Caste", 115.

[21] *Language of the Self*, "The Meaning of Caste", 117.

[22] See *Form and Substance in the Religions*, "The Mystery of the Two Natures", 147n. (Schuon cites Ramanuja as an example of the former.) See also *Esoterism as Principle and as Way*, "The Degrees of Art", 188 and *Spiritual Perspectives and Human Facts*, "Contours of the Spirit", 65n.

[23] *Sufism: Veil and Quintessence*, "Human Premises of a Religious Dilemma", 83.

and pedantry; an intelligence solid enough in its own way, but modest, practical, and above all circumspect.[24]

The *shudras*, the fourth caste, are "properly qualified only for manual work" and are dominated by "the satisfaction of immediate physical needs", the bodily appetites and their "psychological concomitances"; beyond this the *shudra* is passive and dependent on a will other than his own, but he is diligent; "his virtue is fidelity or a kind of massive uprightness, no doubt opaque but simple and intelligible".[25]

Finally there is also the "untouchable", the *chandala*, the man without caste, and again this is a basic human type, one with a chaotic and unruly "personality" and "a tendency to realize those psychological possibilities which are excluded for others: hence his proneness to transgression".[26] The pariah or fringe-dweller "often appears equivocal, unbalanced, sometimes simian, and protean if he is gifted; often he appears as a chimney-sweep, comedian, or executioner, not to mention illicit occupations."[27]

Schuon summarizes some of the essential distinctions in the caste system this way:

> The *brahmana* is "objective" and centered in spirit; the *kshatriya* tends towards "spirit", but in a "subjective" way; the *vaishya* is "objective" on the plane of "matter"; the *shudra* is "subjective" on that same plane.[28]

whilst the *chandala* is marked by a "decentralized subjectivity, centrifugal and without recognized limits".[29] In the Hindu system, caste is determined by heredity (which in turn is subject to the laws of *karma*); profession, or more strictly vocation, is determined by caste. To summarize the caste types in non-Hindu terms one might refer to: the sage/philosopher/priest; the hero/knight/king; the merchant/artisan/farmer (the "average" and "reasonable" man); and the laborer—remembering, though, that these terms are encrusted with associations not necessarily pertinent to natural castes.[30]

There are many aspects of caste which cannot be canvassed here—the importance of the ideal of "purity" for instance, or the law of heredity—but a few more general observations, derived from Schuon's writings, will per-

---

[24] *Sufism: Veil and Quintessence*, "Human Premises of a Religious Dilemma", 78.

[25] *Language of the Self*, "The Meaning of Caste", 117-118.

[26] *Language of the Self*, "The Meaning of Caste", 118-119.

[27] *Language of the Self*, "The Meaning of Caste", 120. (Here Schuon evidently has in mind the medieval world, the last period in which Western civilization was "normal" or traditional in the full sense.) See also *To Have a Center*, "Survey of Integral Anthropology", 42.

[28] *Language of the Self*, "The Meaning of Caste", 122-123.

[29] *Language of the Self*, "The Meaning of Caste", 122.

[30] See *To Have a Center*, "Survey of Integral Anthropology", 42-43.

haps make the subject more intelligible to Western readers. Firstly, there is the fact that "the traditional system creates—or helps to create—those very factors of which it is itself an application".[31] That is to say, the system accentuates certain human differences and thereby reinforces them. Secondly, in trying to grasp the Indian nexus between heredity and vocation, we must take account of the fact that in the modern West industrialization—remembering that "machines are in themselves inhuman and anti-spiritual"[32]—has rendered the law of heredity, if not altogether "inoperative" then at least highly "precarious and unstable", the situation being further confused by "the virtual elimination of the nobility" and the creation of new "elites". Herein lies one of the factors which enabled "the most disparate and 'opaque' elements" to present themselves as "intellectuals", "with the result that, as Guénon would have said, hardly anyone is any longer 'in his proper place'". For the same reason metaphysical knowledge (the preserve of the *brahmana*) "has now come to be envisaged in accordance with the perspective of *vaishyas* and *shudras*, a change which no amount of clap-trap about 'culture' can conceal".[33]

If the processes of modernization have meant the disappearance in the West of the intellectual elite (properly speaking), the consequences have been no less disastrous for the "common man" who is now forced into the subhuman mould of "the proletarian".

> The machine kills not only the soul of the worker, but the soul as such and so also the soul of the exploiter: the pair exploiter-worker is inseparable from mechanization, whereas the crafts by their human and spiritual quality prevent this gross alternative. The universe of the machine means, in short, the triumph of ponderous and treacherous iron-mongery; it is the victory of metal over wood, of matter over man, of cunning over intelligence . . . a world more proper to insects than to humans. . . . The "workers' world", with its mechanico-scientific and materialistic psychology, is particularly impermeable to spiritual realities, for it presupposes a "surrounding reality" which is quite artificial: it requires machinery and therefore metal, din, hidden and treacherous forces, a nightmare environment, incomprehensible comings and goings, in a word an insect-like existence carried on in the midst of ugliness and triviality. In such a world, or rather in such a "stage-set", spiritual reality comes to be regarded as an all too obvious illusion or a luxury to be despised.[34]

---

[31] *Language of the Self*, "The Meaning of Caste", 123.
[32] *Language of the Self*, "The Meaning of Caste", 125.
[33] *Language of the Self*, "The Meaning of Caste", 124-125.
[34] *Language of the Self*, "The Meaning of Caste", 125-126.

A third general point, as a corollary to the observations just made about industrialization and mechanization: the caste system is inextricably bound up with the preservation of the ancient crafts which ensured that work always retained a spiritual dimension and thus remained proportioned to human dignity and intelligence. As Schuon expresses it, "The ancient crafts were eminently intelligible and did not deprive man of his human quality, which by definition implies the faculty to think of God".[35]

Finally, and perhaps most importantly, before leaving this subject we must accent another fact which is rarely taken into account by the noisy critics of the Indian caste system. Schuon speaks directly to the issue at hand:

> The advantage of the Hindu system is that it greatly favors the purity of esoteric spirituality; in the absence of such a system esoterism becomes too closely linked with the average collective mentality, which cannot be proportionate to the demands of a disinterested perspective or, in other words, cannot be entirely free from denominational narcissism.[36]

Elsewhere:

> The pure and direct character of Vedantic metaphysics would be inconceivable apart from the caste system; in India the most transcendent intellectuality enjoys complete liberty, whereas in other traditions this same intellectuality has to accommodate itself to an esoterism that is more or less sibylline or even tortuous in its formulations and often also to certain sentimental restraints; this is the price paid for simplification of the social order.[37]

In considering any traditional social order we must take account of both its advantages and its inevitable limits and disadvantages. No one will deny that the caste system was open to certain abuses, just as more egalitarian orders—and here we are thinking of the traditional worlds of Islam, Buddhism, and Christianity in particular, and certainly not modern liberal "democracies"—had their own advantages which also entailed certain vulnerabilities and more or less inevitable abuses. The following observation, made by Schuon about religious dogmas, might also apply to traditional institutions such as caste:

> It is not enough to know that dogmas have a limitative character; it is necessary to understand as well that they have a positive value, not only through their metaphysical and mystical contents, but also

---

[35] *Language of the Self*, "The Meaning of Caste", 126.
[36] *Sufism: Veil and Quintessence*, "Human Premises of a Religious Dilemma", 75.
[37] *Language of the Self*, "The Meaning of Caste", 130.

through their purely human opportuneness—social, psychological, and so forth.[38]

The question is this: all things considered, and on balance, what might be said for and against caste, or indeed this or that social order as a whole? In any such reckoning of caste we must put on the positive side of the ledger—and it has not been our purpose here to canvas the deficiencies and weaknesses of the system, though these undoubtedly exist[39]—achievements of the most sublime and beneficent kind, namely, the preservation through millennia of a spiritual aristocracy and, concomitantly, the elaboration of the most exhaustive, authoritative, and profound metaphysics to be found anywhere, anytime. Leaving aside the very substantial social benefits brought by *varnashrama*, the attainments of India's spiritual elite count as an irrefutable argument in its favor.

Race and Human Diversity
In one of Schuon's essays we find the following passage:

> There is not only a personal God—who is so to speak the "human" or "humanized Face" of the suprapersonal Divinity—but . . . there is also, "below" and resulting from this first hypostatic degree, what we may term the "confessional Face" of God: it is the Face that God turns towards a particular religion, the Gaze He casts upon it, and without which it could not even exist. In other words: the "human" or "personal Face" of God takes on diverse modes corresponding to so many religious, confessional, or spiritual perspectives, so that it could be said that each religion has its God, without thereby denying that God is One and that this Unity can at any time pierce the veil of diversity. . . . The Divine Being contains all the spiritual possibilities and consequently all the religious and mystical archetypes; having projected them into existence, He looks upon each of them with a particular and appropriate Gaze.[40]

—a characteristically pregnant passage in which metaphysics, cosmology, and anthropology all interpenetrate. For the moment let us simply isolate a key idea pertaining to our immediate subject: religious diversity arises out of the "all-possibility" of the Divine Being and reflects the diversity of the archetypes; thus religious pluralism is a matter of divine appointment, and cannot be "explained" through any manner of historicism. Now, let us add

---

[38] *Gnosis: Divine Wisdom*, "Vicissitudes of Spiritual Temperaments", 46.

[39] On the possible abolition of such abuses see *Eye of the Heart*, "Modes of Spiritual Realization", 130-131.

[40] *Survey of Metaphysics and Esoterism*, "The Mystery of the Hypostatic Face", 91-92.

to the passage above, another, this time concerning the differentiation of the various human collectivities:

> For thousands of years humanity has been divided into several fundamentally different branches constituting as many complete humanities, more or less closed in on themselves. . . . This is not always a question of race, but more often of human groups, very diverse perhaps, but nonetheless subject to mental conditions which, taken as a whole, make of them sufficiently homogeneous spiritual recipients.[41]

Recalling our earlier discussion (in chapter 5) of the formal diversity and essential unity of the different religious traditions, it will be remembered that religious diversity betokens diversity amongst the human recipients of the providential Revelations from which the religions themselves issue forth. In this sense religious diversity answers human needs. However, it might also be said that religious diversity arises from the Divine Nature, as does human diversity, each deriving from divine archetypes which reverberate through the multiple levels of Reality. Put another way: ethnic diversity and religious pluralism are really two aspects of a single reality. It might be said that to understand human diversity is to understand religious pluralism—but it might just as easily be said that to understand the different traditions is to understand human diversity. In any event, our immediate purpose is to show how these two apparently distinct phenomena are actually inseparable.

Having explored religious diversity earlier, the question to which we now turn is this: what distinguishes the different branches of humanity, and to what extent can these branches be assimilated with races? Before addressing this question it is necessary to issue a caveat: the word "race" is fraught with hazards and no one will need reminding that racism in its various guises has been a source of much evil in the modern world. On the other hand we cannot simply evade the issue by pretending that "race" (or some more or less synonymous term) is entirely empty of meaning. As Schuon remarks, "Caste takes precedence over race because spirit has priority over form; race is a form while caste is a spirit",[42] or, it might be said, caste is "vertical", race "horizontal". Whilst there is nothing absolute about races (as there is nothing absolute about any form), nonetheless they have their own sufficient reason and "must correspond to human differences of another order [from those of caste], rather as differences of style may express equivalence in the spiritual order whilst also marking divergences of mode."[43]

---

[41] *Gnosis: Divine Wisdom*, "Diversity of Revelation", 17.
[42] *Language of the Self*, "The Meaning of Race", 147.
[43] *Language of the Self*, "The Meaning of Race", 147.

It cannot be too heavily emphasized that Schuon's schema of human races does not impute "superiority" or "inferiority" to any racial or ethnic group. It is a matter of recognizing differences in the psychic make-up of these divergent groups and of celebrating the differing endowments through which they contribute to the tapestry of human life, particularly in its spiritual aspects. This is an altogether different matter from the scientistic theories of race which have been turned to such diabolical ends in the last two centuries. Furthermore, it bears repeating that "there is a greater qualitative difference between the psychic heredity of different natural castes—even if the race be the same—than between that of members of the same caste of different races; fundamental and personal tendencies have more importance than racial modes".[44] We can turn now, admittedly in only a perfunctory fashion, to the most salient characteristics of the major human groups.

The white man exhibits certain dynamic qualities which are reflected in his "thinking" which, like his facial features and his idioms, is animated and incisive, and given to "mental arabesques" as well as to "exteriorizations", which make it prone to disequilibrium. The white race is also the most internally differentiated of the major human groupings, producing people as different as Europeans and Hindus, the former amongst the least contemplative of peoples, the latter "the most contemplative of all".[45] Coupled with the "creative rootlessness" of the white peoples, this explains the fact that the white race (which includes the Semites and the Indo-Europeans) has "given birth to a number of profoundly different civilizations".[46] The thinking of the yellow man, on the other hand, is more "visual" than "auditory" and "works by discontinuous strokes". "The spirit of the Far East may be called both static and aerial; its conciseness is compensated by its symbolical quality and its dryness by intuitive delicacy" whilst the mode of expression is "sober and elliptical" and its beauty "lyrical" rather than "dramatic".[47] While the white man lives primarily in the world of "the human and the temporal", the yellow man lives in nature; "his poetry is anchored in virgin nature and has no Promethean quality".[48] The black race, in contrast with both the white and yellow peoples, "bears within itself the substance of an 'existential wisdom'; it asks for few symbols; it needs only a homogeneous system: God, prayer, sacrifice, and dancing". The black man exhibits a "heavy contemplativity" which is earthy rather than "aerial" but, like the yellow man, his disposition is less "mental" (but by no means less spiritual)

---

[44] *Language of the Self*, "The Meaning of Race", 150.
[45] *Language of the Self*, "The Meaning of Race", 153.
[46] *Language of the Self*, "The Meaning of Race", 157.
[47] *Language of the Self*, "The Meaning of Race", 148.
[48] *Language of the Self*, "The Meaning of Race", 148.

than his white counterpart. He exhibits both the "innocent massiveness" of the earthly element as well as "the explosive force of volcanoes".[49]

Readers are urged to explore for themselves Schuon's carefully nuanced treatment of this volatile and complex subject in "The Meaning of Race". However, it is worth quoting a few particularly illuminating passages:

> The yellow and black people taken together are distinct from the whites in respect of their vitality and their lesser mental exteriorization, the yellow race in a manner that is dry and light and the black in one that is heavy and humid. . . . What distinguishes the yellow man from both the white and the black is his intuitive delicacy, his artistic faculty of expressing imponderables, his passionlessness without inertia, and his effortless equilibrium. . . . Perhaps it might also be said that the white man is essentially a "poet"; his soul is at the same time animated and "furrowed". The yellow man is first of all a "painter", an intuitive who visualizes things. . . . As for the black man, he is neither a "cerebral" nor a "visual" type but "vital", and so a born dancer; he is "profoundly vital" as the yellow man is "delicately visual", both races being existential rather than mental as compared to the white race.[50]

These observations are attended by the following qualification: "All these expressions can be no more than approximations, for everything is relative, especially in an order of things as complex as race. A race may be compared to a whole style of art with many forms rather than to one exclusive form."[51] Extending his comparison of the yellow and black races Schuon goes on to write,

> We are almost tempted to say that the yellow man thinks in pictures, even abstract ones, rather than by speculations, while the black man thinks through forces. The black man's wisdom is dynamic, it is a metaphysic of "forces". Note the very great importance amongst black peoples of tom-toms, the function of which is central and quasi-sacred: they are the vehicle for rhythms which, when communicated to human bodies, bring the whole being into contact with cosmic essences. . . . The roll of tom-toms marks, like heaven's thunder, the voice of Divinity: by its very nature and by its sacred origin it is a "remembrance of God", an "invocation" of the Power both creator and destroyer and thus also liberator, through which human art canalizes the divine manifestation and in which man participates through dancing; he thus participates with all his being in order to regain the heavenly fluidity through the "analogical

---

[49] *Language of the Self*, "The Meaning of Race", 157.
[50] *Language of the Self*, "The Meaning of Race", 154-155.
[51] *Language of the Self*, "The Meaning of Race", 155.

vibrations" between matter and the Spirit. The drum is the altar, its roll marks the descent of God, and the dance the ascent of man.[52]

After remarking that each of the three great races and their intermediate branches (the Red Indians, for instance, the Malayo-Polynesians, and the Dravidians) produce an incomparable and irreplaceable beauty, each type being "an aspect of the human norm", Schuon goes on to elaborate some of the differences between different ethnic groups within these broad categories, paying particular attention to the variegations within the European branch of the white race, and discusses the existence of various inter-racial and marginal ethnic groups. He also shows how the peculiar genius of each race manifests in its language and art, and indeed in all aspects of its intellectual and spiritual life. He also exposes the complexities and hazards of broad-brush generalizations about "East" and "West", particularly in view of the confusions and prejudices sown by the modern outlook. Schuon brings this magisterial essay to its conclusion with these words:

> A man of another race, supposing he corresponds to us by analogy or by complementarism, is like a forgotten aspect of ourselves and thus also like a rediscovered mirror of God.[53]

The Message of the Human Body

Following this brief conspectus of Schuon's writings on spiritual types, caste, and race, we now turn to another facet of Schuon's exposition of spiritual anthropology—the significance of the human form and of its sexual differentiation. By way of a prefatory aside it might also be noted that Schuon's elucidation of the symbolism of the human body is to be found as much in his paintings as in his written opus, though it is the latter which commands our attention here. More generally it might be remarked that traditional understandings of the human body are often most eloquently expressed in dance, sculpture, and painting rather than in words, for "the heaviness of language requires almost endless prolixities"—especially in the elaboration of metaphysical truths—whilst a visual symbolism "exhibits all aspects of a problem at once, but without thereby furnishing the keys allowing everything to be deciphered".[54]

The symbolism of the human body and its sexual differentiation can only be understood in the light of metaphysical principles which can be formulated in any number of ways, starting from various vantage points. In Schuon's writings we find the same fundamental truths about man expressed

---

[52] *Language of the Self*, "The Meaning of Race", 155-156.
[53] *Language of the Self*, "The Meaning of Race", 175.
[54] *In the Face of the Absolute*, "The Problems of Evil and Predestination", 37n.

and inflected in different ways, according to the needs of the moment. As a starting point let us choose this passage:

> Man is a divine manifestation, not in his accidentality and fallen state, but in his theomorphism and his primordial and principial perfection. He is the "field of manifestation" of the intellect, which reflects the universal Spirit and thereby the divine Intellect; man as such reflects the cosmic totality, the Creation, and thereby the Being of God. The divine Intelligence confers on man intellect, reason, and free will; it is by these features—and speech which manifests them—that the human being is distinguished from animals in a "relatively absolute" fashion.[55]

Man is distinguished from the animals by his "centrality" in the horizontal terrestrial plane and by his "verticality" whereby he transcends his earthly limitations and participates directly in the divine Subject. The human body is theomorphic and thereby theophanic: "man being *imago Dei*, his body necessarily symbolizes a liberating return to the divine origin and in this sense it is 'remembrance of God' . . . it is a sacrament, whether it be masculine or feminine".[56]

The differentiation of the sexes "marks a complementarity of mode and not, quite clearly, a divergence of principle".[57] The message of both human bodies, the masculine and feminine, is one of

> ascending and unitive verticality in both cases, certainly, but in rigorous, transcendent, objective, abstract, rational, and mathematical mode in the first case, and in gentle, immanent, concrete, emotional, and musical mode in the second. On the one hand, a path centered on a metaphysical Idea and Rigor, and on the other hand, a way centered on the sacramental Symbol and Gentleness.[58]

Furthermore:

> As symbols the masculine body indicates a victory of the Spirit over chaos, and the feminine body, a deliverance of form by Essence; the first is like a magic sign which would subjugate the blind forces of the Universe, and the second like celestial music which would give back to fallen matter its paradisiac transparency, or which, to use the language of Taoism, would make trees flower beneath the snow.[59]

---

[55] *Stations of Wisdom*, "Manifestations of the Divine Principle", 81.
[56] *Play of Masks*, "Man in the Cosmogonic Projection", 21-22.
[57] *Play of Masks*, "Man in the Cosmogonic Projection", 22.
[58] *From the Divine to the Human*, "The Message of the Human Body", 100.
[59] *Stations of Wisdom*, "Manifestations of the Divine Principle", 87.

And so it is that "the feminine body is far too perfect and spiritually too eloquent to be no more than a kind of transitory accident".[60]

The applications and ramifications of these principles are manifold, and have been unfolded in Schuon's many expositions concerning such matters as the feminine as a mirror of the Divine, virginity and nudity (discussed in chapter 11), the symbolism of the sexual act, the significance of the human gait and carriage, and of human physiognomy, the symbolic significance of animals, the spiritual function of clothing, and so on.[61] Schuon's paintings are also rich in these themes.

---

[60] *From the Divine to the Human*, "The Message of the Human Body", 91.

[61] The scope of the present work precludes any further discussion of these subjects here but various perennialist authors have provided helpful commentaries on Schuon's writings on these and related subjects. See, for instance: J. Cutsinger, "Femininity, Hierarchy, and God" and "The Virgin"; T. Scott, "'Made in the Image': Schuon's Theomorphic Anthropology"; P. Laude, "Metaphysical and Spiritual Aesthetics" in J-B Aymard and P. Laude, *Frithjof Schuon: Life and Teachings*; R. Fabbri, "The Milk of the Virgin: The Prophet, the Saint, and the Sage".

17

The Way: Virtue and Prayer

This is spirituality—the knowledge of divine Reality and of the means of realizing It, in some degree or other, in oneself.[1]

A spiritual virtue is nothing other than consciousness of a reality.[2]

To give oneself to God is to give God to the world.[3]

Prayer—in the widest sense—triumphs over the four accidents of our existence: the world, life, the body, the soul; or we might also say: space, time, matter, desire.[4]

Earlier it was suggested that Schuon's work, like Guénon's, does not "evolve". In a sense it was complete from the beginning: the principles, from which all else flowed, were firmly in place at the outset. There were, to be sure, elaborations and applications of these principles, brought to bear on sundry religious forms and phenomena. There was also a mellowing in Schuon's work, marked by a more lyrical and synthetic mode of expression in his metaphysical works, and by a burgeoning poetic output. It can also be said that Schuon's work comes full circle, returning to those fundamental principles and values which he had so eloquently and forcefully expressed in early works such as *The Transcendent Unity of Religions* and *Spiritual Perspectives and Human Facts*. In the light of these remarks it is altogether appropriate that, in this concluding chapter, we should draw heavily on the latter work for a framework within which to sketch out some governing themes in Schuon's treatment of the spiritual life itself. After some prefatory remarks about spirituality we will turn to two particular subjects central to Schuon's message: the virtues and the life of prayer.

Spirituality

"Spirituality" has become a fashionable catch-word, recently appropriated by all manner of people, many of whom are disillusioned with the etiolated paradigms of the mechanistic, hyper-rationalistic, materialistic, and utilitarian worldview which characterizes modernity, but who are also often

---

[1] *Feathered Sun*, "The Sacred Pipe", 45.

[2] *Spiritual Perspectives and Human Facts*, "The Spiritual Virtues", 185.

[3] *Echoes of Perennial Wisdom*, 16.

[4] *Spiritual Perspectives and Human Facts*, "The Spiritual Virtues", 228.

hostile to traditional religious forms which might provide the necessary antidotes. "Spirituality" stands as a banner under which some of the richness and complexity of human consciousness and experience can be rescued from various psychologistic strait-jackets. While one might well sympathize with these efforts to combat the intransigent horizontality of scientism it must be said that much of the present-day discussion of "spirituality" really amounts to a sentimental indulgence in which the word itself can be made to mean almost anything—more often than not referring to some kind of nebulous inner life or experience.

Spirituality might properly be conceptualized in many ways. Here is one: spirituality is both a mode of *understanding* Reality, one in which we recognize "the immortal spark of God's Being, eternally living in the depths of man's soul",[5] and a mode of *being* wherein we conform ourselves to that Reality. Further, one might say that spirituality is the domain of human experience in which a transmutation of the soul leads, depending on the vocabulary at hand, to God, to the Self, to *Nirvana*. In this context we might recall the words of Swami Abhishiktananda: "Spiritual experience . . . is the meeting place of the known and the not-known, the seen and the not-seen, the relative and the absolute."[6] Another teacher asked to sum up the message of Hinduism, replied this way: "God Is; God can be realized; to realize God is the supreme end of human life; God can be realized in many ways."[7] Whilst this formulation poses problems for some religious perspectives it might here stand as a signpost to the spiritual life in general.

Implicit in the idea that spirituality concerns both *understanding* and *being* are the attendant notions of a *doctrine* (an account of Reality in both its absolute and relative "dimensions") and a *path* (a spiritual method, provided by religious forms, whereby one might live in accordance with the Will of Heaven). Doctrine, we might say, directs us towards Truth, and the path takes us towards Virtue which actualizes the Truth in our souls. So it is that Schuon observes that "spirituality stands in a sense between metaphysical truth and human virtue": it has "an absolute need" of both but can be reduced to neither. Spiritual life "revolves around truth and the will; the one must penetrate the other".[8] Likewise: "To each metaphysical truth is attached a spiritual attitude, and to each spiritual attitude is attached a moral quality."[9]

---

[5] B. McDonald in *Seeing God Everywhere*, ix.
[6] Abhishiktananda, *Hindu-Christian Meeting Point*, 112.
[7] Swami Prabhavananda, *The Spiritual Heritage of India*, 354-355.
[8] *Spiritual Perspectives and Human Facts*, "The Spiritual Virtues", 183.
[9] Frithjof Schuon, unpublished writings, courtesy of World Wisdom.

In some contemporary understandings of "spirituality" the doctrine of the Absolute (by whatever name) and the spiritual method attuned to our relationship therewith, are left out of the picture altogether! What we are offered instead is a notion of "spirituality" as an ill-defined inner state, a kind of "warm fuzzy glow"—sometimes harnessed to formulations such as "the kingdom of Heaven is within you", as if by these words Christ meant that the kingdom of Heaven is of a psychological order! This is all of a piece with the notion that "spirituality" is a private affair, and that the spiritual life can be fashioned out of the subjective resources of the individual in question. As we have seen earlier, some of the factors which, over several centuries, have conspired to create a climate in which such ideas could take root include the rebellion against all authority, the cult of the individual, the humanistic prejudice that "man is the measure of all things", the triumph—even in the religious domain itself—of sentimentalism over intellectuality, the shibboleths of "egalitarianism" and "democracy", and the emergence of a rampant psychologism which usurps functions which properly belong to religion. The perennialists, not least Schuon himself, have not been reticent in exposing the corruptions and degradations to which such developments have inevitably led.

Traditional peoples everywhere, whatever their religious commitments, start from very different premises. To state them succinctly, and without privileging any particular theology: man is an "amphibious" or "axial" creature who lives between two worlds—on the one hand, the evanescent fabric of relativities which comprise the time-space world of multiplicity and contingency, and on the other, the infinite domain of the Divine from whence come various Revelations which provide us, in our terrestrial condition, with all things needful for our spiritual welfare. In this context one may speak of "spirituality" as a disciplined practice, within the framework of an integral doctrine (derived from a Revelation), whereby we seek to realize the "infinite potentiality and actuality" of Ultimate Reality within ourselves, thus becoming conduits through which Divine Grace may be radiated into the world around us.

It might also be suggested that all spiritual experience is in some sense an adumbration, no matter how faint, of the mystical experience proper. One mode of spirituality is the awareness of the metaphysical transparency of every cosmic situation, awakened by what are variously called epiphanies, theophanies, hierophanies, and mystical illuminations. In the theistic traditions this mode of experience is sometimes called the gift of "seeing God everywhere"—but it is a universal phenomenon and one dramatically exemplified by those many saints and sages who with the Eye of the Heart perceive the transcendent dimension which is "hidden" in all natural phenomena. One may cite as representative examples such figures as St. Francis of Assisi, St. Seraphim of Sarov, Ramakrishna, and Black Elk.

Spirituality, engaging both the intelligence and the will, "has for its object not man but God",[10] and governs the alchemical transformation of the soul whereby we realize our highest vocation. Now, whilst the metaphysical principles informing the spiritual life are everywhere the same, given the diversity of the human collectivity and the corresponding diversity of religions, the spiritual life will be envisaged in different ways according to the tradition in question. The understanding of "spirituality" which emerges within a particular religious economy will bear the signature, so to speak, of the Revelation from which it issued. We might also remind ourselves that all religious forms are limits which, somewhat paradoxically, "contain" the Limitless. As Abhishiktananda observed, "The mystery to which [religion] points overflows its limits in every direction."[11]

In a private letter Schuon made the following general remarks about spirituality. They will provide a frame for the brief exposition which follows.

> The first criterion of spirituality is that man demonstrate his *consciousness* of the incommensurability between the real and the illusory, the Absolute and the relative, *Atma* and *Maya*, God and the world.
>
> The second criterion is that man demonstrate his *choice* of the Real: that he understand the imperious necessity for active attachment to the real, hence for a concrete, operative, and salvific relationship with God.
>
> The third criterion is that man, knowing that the Real is the Sovereign Good and that it thus contains and projects all beauty, *conform* himself to it with all his soul; for what he knows to be perfect and what he wishes to attain, he must also be, and this he is through the virtues and not otherwise.[12]

Elsewhere, Schuon summarizes spirituality as the "love of God" which "is first attachment of the intelligence to the Truth, then the attachment of the will to the Good, and finally the attachment of the soul to Peace which is given by Truth and the Good."[13] In this context it is worth recalling Schuon's insistence that metaphysics carries its own moral imperatives. A "wisdom" without virtue, evinced by some self-styled "esoterists", "is in fact imposture and hypocrisy"; a purely cerebral knowledge is not only fragmentary but

---

[10] *Spiritual Perspectives and Human Facts*, "The Spiritual Virtues", 198.

[11] Abhishiktananda, *The Further Shore*, 26.

[12] *Gnosis: Divine Wisdom*, "Appendix: Selections from Letters and Previously Unpublished Writings", 143 (italics mine).

[13] *Echoes of Perennial Wisdom*, 7.

likely to produce psychic disorders and temptations such as self-sufficiency, narcissism, and pride.[14]

> The moral exigency of metaphysical discernment means that virtue is a part of wisdom. . . . Plenary knowledge of Divine Reality presupposes or demands moral conformity to this Reality, as the eye necessarily conforms to light.[15]

As Schuon states elsewhere, "A will directed towards the Good and a love directed towards the Beautiful are the *necessary* concomitants of knowledge of the True".[16]

In his remarkable essay, "The Spiritual Virtues", Schuon draws attention to the spiritual life as envisaged by St. Basil. Although St. Basil's formulation naturally has a distinctly Christian fragrance, it might well serve as a capsule statement about the spiritual life in general. Here is Schuon's gloss:

> Basilian spirituality includes four principal elements: separation from the world, purification, meditation on the sacred Scriptures, and continual prayer. The first element cuts man off from the current of profane life; the second empties the soul of illusory contents; the third infuses the discursive intelligence with divine Light; the fourth essentially brings about deification. This could be formulated as follows: in *renunciation* the soul leaves the world; in *purification* the world leaves the soul; in *meditation* God enters the soul; in continual *prayer* the soul enters God.[17]

Renunciation, purification, meditation, prayer: considered in their most universal senses, these are the hallmarks of the spiritual life in all traditions. These are all underpinned by faith: "What God requires above all from man is faith: an attachment with the very depths of our being to the Truth that transcends us".[18] Faith is a kind of catalyst in the soul as well as a shield against intellectual hubris:

> Faith as a quality of the soul is the stabilizing complement of the discerning and as it were explosive intelligence; without this complement, intellectual activity lets itself be carried away by its own movement and is like a devouring fire; it loses its balance and ends either by devouring itself in a restlessness without issue or else by simply wearing itself out to the point of sclerosis. Faith implies all the gentle and static qualities such as patience, gratitude, confidence, generosity; it offers the mercu-

---

[14] *Roots of the Human Condition*, "Pillars of Wisdom", 86.

[15] *Roots of the Human Condition*, "Pillars of Wisdom", 86.

[16] *Echoes of Perennial Wisdom*, 8 (italics mine).

[17] *Spiritual Perspectives and Human Facts*, "The Spiritual Virtues", 212 (italics mine).

[18] *Prayer Fashions Man*, "Spiritual Perspectives I", 7.

rial intelligence a fixative element and thus realizes, together with discernment, an equilibrium which is like an anticipation of sainthood.[19]

St Basil's spiritual quaternary is only one amongst many possible ways of mapping out the contours of the spiritual way. Schuon himself has had recourse to many different images and analogies in his descriptions of quintessential spirituality. Here is but one of them, by no means incompatible with the Basilian schema, but turning on the trinity of discernment-action-being, or expressed otherwise, intelligence-will-soul (in turn corresponding to the Hindu yogas of *jnana*, *karma*, and *bhakti*):

> Man possesses an intelligence, a will, and a soul: a capacity for understanding, a capacity for willing, and a capacity for loving. Each of these three faculties contains an essential and supreme function . . . a function determined by the Real and contributing to salvation. Total knowledge, free will, and disinterested love; intelligence capable of absoluteness, will capable of sacrifice, soul capable of generosity. All the dogmas, all the prescriptions, and all the means of a religion have their sufficient reason in the three fundamental vocations of man: in discernment, in practice, and in virtue.[20]

In yet another place Schuon summons four Sanskrit terms which "evoke the four principal dimensions of our Way", and thus gives us another "formula"—discernment-concentration-virtue-interiorization—of the spiritual life:

> *Vedanta*: Discernment between the Real and illusory, which implies all subsequent discernments.
> *Japa*: Invocation; essentially, methodic Concentration on the Real.
> *Dharma*: Virtue, the virtues; Conformity to the nature of the Real; beauty of soul, of character.
> *Tantra*: Spiritualization—or Interiorization—of beauty as well as of the natural pleasures, in harmony with the metaphysical transparency of phenomena.[21]

Virtue and the Virtues
We have already considered the spiritual life as a bridge between Truth and Virtue. Schuon articulates the relationship between these two poles this way:

---

[19] *Logic and Transcendence*, "Understanding and Believing", 201.

[20] *Gnosis: Divine Wisdom*, "Appendix: Selections from Letters and Previously Unpublished Writings", 143.

[21] *Spiritual Perspectives and Human Facts*, "Appendix: Selections from Letters and Previously Unpublished Writings", 240.

Truths make us understand virtues, giving them all their cosmic ampli-
tude and their efficacy. Virtues for their part lead us to truths and transform them for us into realities that are concrete, seen, and lived.[22]

As Schuon writes in another passage:

> The intellective center of a being is not reached without involving his
> volitional circumference: he who wants the center must realize the
> whole; in other words, he who wants to know with the heart-intellect
> must "know" with the whole soul, and this entails the purification of
> the soul and therefore the virtues.[23]

More pithily: "If we want truth to live in us we must live in it",[24] and,
"Without virtue there is no Way".[25]

Returning to St Basil's four elements of spirituality, the virtues can be
associated with the purification of the soul, a removal of the obscurations
arising out of egoism: virtue, in a nutshell, is "the abolition of egoism",
manifesting as veracity, charity, and humility, the three fundamental virtues.
However, from another perspective this is to take rather too narrow a view
of the virtues precisely because they are operationally indivisible from both
Knowledge and Love—themselves inseparable because "To know God is to
love him, and not to love Him is not to know Him"[26]—wherein the spiritual
life finds its fulfillment: "When virtue reaches the innermost regions of the
soul, it gives rise to illumination. . . . Complete virtue is the elimination of
everything that constitutes an obstacle to *gnosis* and love."[27] In this respect
one cannot "acquire" the virtues, which reside primordially in our own
substance:

> God has put into our substance all the virtues; they derive from the
> nature of our substance, and this nature is primordial worship. This is
> why, and we repeat it, a virtue is never an acquisition or a property,
> it always belongs to God, and through Him to the Logos; our concern
> must be to eliminate whatever is opposed to the virtues, not to gain
> virtues for ourselves; we must give free passage to the qualities of the
> sovereign Good.[28]

---

[22] *Spiritual Perspectives and Human Facts*, "The Spiritual Virtues", 183.

[23] *Spiritual Perspectives and Human Facts*, "The Spiritual Virtues", 196.

[24] *Echoes of Perennial Wisdom*, 31.

[25] *Roots of the Human Condition*, "Virtue and Way", 113.

[26] *Echoes of Perennial Wisdom*, 8.

[27] *Spiritual Perspectives and Human Facts*, "The Spiritual Virtues", 197.

[28] *Esoterism as Principle and as Way*, "The Virtues in the Way", 114. "Virtue is not a merit in
itself, it is a gift; but it is nonetheless a merit to the extent that we exert ourselves towards it"
(*Roots of the Human Condition*, "Virtue and Way", 113).

So it is that "Virtue in itself is the worship that attaches us to God and attracts us to Him, while radiating around us; the primordial and quasi-existential worship which declares itself above all else by the sense of the sacred".[29] Similarly:

> The synthesis and the substance of the moral qualities or of the virtues is devotion: the integral attitude of man before God, made of reverential fear and confident love, and also of patience and fervor.[30]

One might also characterize the spiritual path as the harmonizing of the intelligence and the will: "Truth illumines the will, which, when illumined, vivifies the truth."[31] By the same token, if intelligence is nothing without truth, will is nothing without virtue. Furthermore, as Schuon affirms, "A spiritual virtue is nothing other than consciousness of a reality",[32] or similarly, "the virtuous man is such because his intelligence and sensibility perceive the very being of things".[33] This means that a virtue is far from being merely a sentimentalism, though it is "natural" that it should be accompanied by feeling. In his unpublished writings on the spiritual path Schuon foregrounds "Six Themes of Meditation" which provide us with yet another possible schema of the spiritual life. The six themes entail the bifurcation into passive and active modes of the three spiritual paths of *karma*, *bhakti*, and *jnana* (which themselves reflect the Fear-Love-Knowledge ternary). William Stoddart has provided us with a useful diagram of this spiritual teaching.

The Six Themes of Meditation		
	passive mode	*active mode*
	1	2
Fear	renunciation, abstention	act, perseverance
	3	4
Love	resignation, gratitude	fervor, trust, generosity
	5	6
Knowledge	extinction, truth	union

These six stations, or virtues, are both successive and simultaneous.[34]

It is perhaps as well to dispel the confusion of virtue and morality which envelops so many discussions of these aspects of the spiritual life. In the

---

[29] *Esoterism as Principle and as Way*, "The Virtues in the Way", 114.

[30] Frithjof Schuon, unpublished writings, courtesy of World Wisdom.

[31] *Spiritual Perspectives and Human Facts*, "The Spiritual Virtues", 183.

[32] *Spiritual Perspectives and Human Facts*, "The Spiritual Virtues", 185.

[33] *Esoterism as Principle and as Way*, "The Virtues in the Way", 112.

[34] See *Stations of Wisdom*, "Stations of Wisdom", 148-157, and *Eye of the Heart*, "Modes of Spiritual Realization", 121-133, and "On Meditation", 167-176.

domain of religious exoterism, especially in the Occidental monotheisms, we often witness an impoverishment whence comes "a predominance of moral injunctions over considerations of spiritual alchemy: the dynamism of the will is preached, and the good residing in the very nature of things is neglected; the 'duty of doing' is insisted on, and 'being' is forgotten". This is but one consequence of the neglect of true intellectuality which "goes straight to the existential roots of the virtues; it finds the virtues again, beyond moral effort, in the nature of things."[35] The proper relation of virtue and morality is made clear in this passage from *Understanding Islam*:

> [Moralities] are styles of action conforming to particular spiritual perspectives and to particular material and mental conditions, while the virtues on the contrary represent intrinsic beauties fitted into these styles and finding through them their realization. Every virtue and every morality is a mode of equilibrium. . . . Morality is a way of acting, whereas virtue is a way of being—a way of being wholly oneself, beyond the ego, or of being simply That which is. . . . Moralities are diverse, but virtue, as it has been here defined, is everywhere the same, for everywhere man is man.[36]

As this passage intimates, each religious tradition will extol a certain moral code and thereby foreground certain virtues which are most consonant with the Revelation from which it derives and with the make-up of the human collectivity to whom the Revelation is addressed. As well as shaping behavior the "various moralities are at the same time frameworks for the virtues and their application to collectivities". To cite an example taken from our discussion of the spiritual heritage of the American Indians: amongst the Plains Indians the moral economy places a premium on courage, patience, generosity, and fidelity,[37] these in turn being assimilated to virtues as "ways of being". Or again, the fact that Buddhism is founded on the human experience of suffering makes it inevitable that compassion should hold a privileged place in that framework. Similarly one might mention the place of righteousness, love, and remembrance in the three Abrahamic traditions. However, considering the virtues from a metaphysical point of view—one which transcends particular mythological and theological perspectives—Schuon reduces the virtues to three fundamentals: veracity, charity, humility.

> Humility means looking at oneself in the limiting state of individuation; it means turning one's gaze on the ego, limitation, nothingness. Charity means looking around oneself: it means seeing God in one's neighbor

[35] *Spiritual Perspectives and Human Facts*, "The Spiritual Virtues", 199.
[36] *Understanding Islam*, "The Path", 160-161.
[37] See *Feathered Sun*, "The Sacred Pipe", 67.

and also seeing oneself there, though this time not as limitation but as a creature of God made in His image. Veracity means looking toward Truth, submitting and attaching oneself to it, and becoming penetrated by its implacable light. Each of the three virtues must be found again in the others; they are the criteria of one another.[38]

Humility, charity, veracity: "effacement of the ego, gift of self, realization of truth. . . . These attitudes correspond respectively to the stages—or states—of purification, expansion, union. They are the three 'dimensions' of perfect gnosis."[39]

The virtues can, depending on the point of view at hand, be categorized in any number of ways. As we have just seen, in his early work, *Spiritual Perspectives and Human Facts*, Schuon identifies three fundamental virtues. In other works he offers us a different schema. In *Esoterism as Principle and as Way*, for instance, Schuon, echoing the Gospels, states that "The moral substance of man is love of God and generosity towards his neighbor." He then goes on to elaborate a quaternity of virtues:

> Detachment, generosity, vigilance, gratitude: these virtues relate to four principles that we could characterize by the following terms: purity, goodness, strength, beauty; or coldness, warmth, activity, rest; or death, life, combat, peace, or again, applying them to spiritual alchemy: abstention, confidence [i.e., trust in God], accomplishment, contentment. Purity and beauty are static; strength and goodness are dynamic; from another point of view, purity and strength relate to rigor; beauty and goodness to gentleness.[40]

Detachment means "not loving anything outside of God . . . to love God *ex toto corde*"; generosity arises out of a consciousness of the divine Mercy and divine Plenitude and is "the opposite of egoism, avarice, and meanness"; vigilance is "the affirmative and combative virtue that prevents us from forgetting or betraying 'the one thing needful' . . . which ceaselessly calls us back to the remembrance of God", and which generates "discipline, domination of self, and rectitude in all things"; the grateful man "never loses sight of the symbol, the spiritual gift of things, the sign of God" and embodies "a gratitude that is both ascending and radiating".[41] These four virtues have their metaphysical and cosmological correspondences—being associated, for example, with the four cardinal points, while sapiential discernment and unitive concentration correspond to the zenith and nadir respectively.

[38] *Spiritual Perspectives and Human Facts*, "The Spiritual Virtues", 184.
[39] *Spiritual Perspectives and Human Facts*, "The Spiritual Virtues", 185.
[40] *Esoterism as Principle and as Way*, "The Virtues in the Way", 106.
[41] Quoted phrases from *Esoterism as Principle and as Way*, "The Virtues in the Way", 106-110.

Schuon's writings show how it is possible to approach a discussion of virtue and the virtues from many starting points. In another essay he organizes such a discussion around "sincerity" which is "the absence of falsehood in inward and outward behavior" and which is rooted in "sincerity towards God" which will necessarily express itself in the aspiration towards perfection.[42] In yet another piece Schuon writes that

> The first of the virtues is veracity, for without truth we can do nothing. The second virtue is sincerity, which consists in drawing the consequences of what we know to be true, and which implies all the other virtues. . . . To the virtues of veracity and sincerity are added those of temperance and fervor, or of purity and vigilance, and also, even more fundamentally, those of humility and charity.[43]

Prayer

In a rare interview in 1996, when asked about his message for people in general, Schuon replied, "Prayer. To be a human means to be connected with God. Life has no meaning without this. Prayer, and also beauty, of course; for we live among forms and not in a cloud. Beauty of soul first and then beauty of symbols around us."[44] Schuon frequently recalls St. Paul's injunction "to pray without ceasing".[45] Man has been endowed with intelligence, will, and speech: these are actualized in his encounter with God. Schuon distinguishes three kinds of prayer, each integral to the spiritual life: personal, canonical, and invocatory.

Personal prayer is subjective—the individual speaking directly and sincerely, out of his or her subjective situation, to God; it may include, but is not restricted to, petitions. Such prayer is active in the purification of the soul for

> it loosens psychic knots . . . dissolves subconscious coagulations and drains away many secret poisons; it sets forth before God the difficulties, failures, and tensions of the soul, which presupposes that the soul be humble and truthful, and this disclosure, carried out in the face of the Absolute, has the virtue of reestablishing equilibrium and restoring peace—in a word, of opening us to grace.[46]

---

[42] *Esoterism as Principle and as Way*, "Sincerity: What It Is and What It Is Not", 123-127. Quotes from 127, 125.

[43] *Roots of the Human Condition*, "Virtue and Way", 113.

[44] Deborah Casey, "The Basis of Religion and Metaphysics: An Interview with Frithjof Schuon", 77-78.

[45] I Thessalonians 5:17.

[46] *Prayer Fashions Man*, "Modes of Prayer", 57-58.

Whilst personal prayer is shaped by the existential situation of the individual, it must nevertheless follow certain rules, "for the human soul—as the Psalms admirably show—is always the same in its miseries and joys, and therefore in its duties to God".[47] It entails *gratitude*, thanksgiving for the blessings God has conferred on us; *resignation*, the acceptance that our petitions may not be answered; *regret* or contrition which expresses our awareness of those failings which separate us from God; *resolution* that we will seek to remedy our shortcomings and transgressions; and *praise* which relates every value back to God.[48]

Canonical prayers are those prescribed by tradition, couched in a liturgical and therefore "symbolically universal language", and are obligatory for all adherents; this form of prayer entails not such and such an individual but man as such, the human collectivity, addressing God. It is for this reason that such prayers are often articulated in the first person plural—"*Our* Father. . .", to give but one example. Man prays to God, in canonical prayer, with and for all. Canonical prayers "tirelessly recall truths which man needs if he is not to become lost".[49] As canonical prayer stems from a Revelation it "is not only a human discourse; it is also divine, which means that besides its literal value it has a sacramental import. It is on our level, yet at the same time beyond us."[50]

Invocatory prayer, or Prayer of the Heart, joins man to the revealed Name of God, invoked by man but pronounced by God Himself: "human invocation is only the 'outward' effect of an eternal and 'inward' invocation by the Divinity."[51] Meister Eckhart: "God is the Word which pronounces itself."[52] Likewise Ramakrishna: "God and His Name are identical".[53] The Divine Name, ritually pronounced, is "mysteriously identified with the Divinity".[54] As Schuon explained in his first major work:

> It is in the Divine Name that there takes place the mysterious meeting of the created and the Uncreate, the contingent and the Absolute, the finite and the Infinite. The Divine Name is thus a manifestation of the

---

[47] *Prayer Fashions Man*, "Modes of Prayer", 58.

[48] *Prayer Fashions Man*, "Modes of Prayer", 57-58.

[49] Frithjof Schuon, quoted in *Frithjof Schuon: Messenger of the Perennial Philosophy*, xxvi.

[50] *Prayer Fashions Man*, "Appendix: A Sampling of Letters and Previously Unpublished Materials", 197. (This passage comes from a letter by Frithjof Schuon to a Hindu admirer. Part of the letter was first published in "Invocation of the Divine Name", *Kalyana-Kalpataru*, 25:10, October 1961.)

[51] *Prayer Fashions Man*, "Modes of Prayer", 61.

[52] Eckhart, cited in W. Perry (ed.), *A Treasury of Traditional Wisdom*, 1005.

[53] Ramakrishna, quoted in *Prayer Fashions Man*, "Modes of Prayer", 60.

[54] *Transcendent Unity of Religions*, "Universality and Particular Nature of the Christian Religion", 145.

Supreme Principle, or to speak still more plainly, it is the Supreme Principle manifesting Itself.[55]

The "actualization of the consciousness of the Absolute", the "remembrance of God" which constitutes prayer in its deepest sense, is

> already a death and a meeting with God and it places us already in Eternity; it is already something of Paradise and even, in its mysterious and "uncreated" quintessence, something of God. Quintessential prayer brings about an escape from the world and from life, and thereby confers a new and Divine sap upon the veil of appearances and the current of forms.[56]

The remembrance of the Divine Name brings an illumination whereby "things become transparent and transmit to us rays of their immutable and blessed archetypes".[57]

The invocation of the Divine Name is to be found in the spiritual method of all the great traditions, most notably in the Catholic cult of the Holy Name (taught by St. Bernardino of Siena), in the Orthodox "Jesus-Prayer", in the *japa* of the Hindus, the *nembutsu* of the Far Eastern Buddhist schools, the *dhikr* of Islam. Invocatory prayer actualizes and expresses our consciousness of the Absolute and thereby "perpetuates it in the soul and fixes it in the heart, so that it penetrates the whole being and at the same time transmutes and absorbs it."[58] This is the highest and most noble form of prayer. As James Cutsinger has observed, this quintessential mode of prayer "is the capstone of the spiritual method [Schuon] taught and the form of prayer he accentuated in all his published and unpublished writings".[59]

Schuon poetically expresses the saving power of the Divine Name in these words:

> One must enclose oneself in the divine Name as in a shelter during a tempest. One must also invoke it as if the Name were a miraculous sword during a battle, and thus vanquish the enemies we carry within ourselves. At other moments it is necessary to rest in the divine Name and be perfectly content with it and to give oneself up to it with profound recollectedness, as if in a marvelously beautiful sanctuary full of blessings. And at still other times, one must cling to the divine Name

---

[55] *Transcendent Unity of Religions*, "Universality and Particular Nature of the Christian Religion", 145. In similar vein, Gershom Scholem, considering the Kabbalism of Abraham Abulafia, writes that the Name of God is "something absolute, because it reflects the hidden meaning and the totality of existence" (*Major Trends in Jewish Mysticism*, 133).

[56] *Logic and Transcendence*, "Man and Certainty", 265.

[57] *Gnosis: Divine Wisdom*, "Gnosis: Language of the Self", 71.

[58] *Prayer Fashions Man*, "Modes of Prayer", 62.

[59] Introduction to *Prayer Fashions Man*, xxi.

as if it were a rope thrown to a drowning man; it is necessary to call upon God so that He hears us and may save us; we must be aware of our distress and of God's infinite Mercy.[60]

These brief reflections on the place of prayer in Schuon's understanding of the spiritual life culminate in another lyrical passage concerning prayer in general:

Prayer—in the widest sense—triumphs over the four accidents of our existence: the world, life, the body and the soul; or we might also say: space, time, matter, desire. It is situated in existence like a shelter, like an islet. In it alone we are perfectly ourselves because it puts us in the presence of God. It is like a diamond, which nothing can tarnish and nothing can resist.

Man prays, and prayer fashions man. The saint has himself become prayer, the meeting-place of earth and Heaven; he thereby contains the universe, and the universe prays with him. He is everywhere where nature prays, and he prays with her and in her: in the peaks, which touch the void and eternity; in a flower, which scatters its scent; in the carefree song of a bird.

He who lives in prayer has not lived in vain.[61]

---

[60] *Prayer Fashions Man*, "A Sampling of Letters and Other Previously Unpublished Materials", 188.
[61] *Spiritual Perspectives and Human Facts*, "The Spiritual Virtues", 228.

Appendix

Poetic Fragments

Frithjof Schuon

Zuerst die Wahrheit, die uns alles klärt;
Dann unser Werden, was die Wahrheit kündet.
Und dann der Name, der mit Licht uns nährt —
Dann auch die Schönheit, die ins Eine mündet.

(Adastra, "Veritas")

Wahrheit und Tugend; Schönheit und Liebe;
Wenn mir nur dieses erhalten bliebe,
Könnte die Welt in den Wassern versinken —
Lasst mich vom Wahren, vom Schönen nur trinken.

(Weltrad V, IX)

Ein Ende nimmt das Buch, doch nicht das Singen;
Es liegt in Raum und Zeit und in den Dingen
Und ist doch raum- und zeitlos, ohn Gestalt —
Es ist des Daseins Strahlen und Gehalt.

(Stella Maris, "Endwort")

Zeit kann es nicht im Gotteswesen geben;
Auch nicht in der Begegnung mit dem Herrn.
Ewigkeit ist des Betens Augenblick —
Er steht am Himmel wie der Morgenstern;
In Jetzt des Herzens liegt dein ganzes Leben.

(Lieder ohne Namen VII, CX)

First the Truth, that clarifies all things;
Then our becoming what the Truth proclaims.
And then the Name that nourishes with Light —
Then Beauty, flowing back into the One.

(Adastra, "Veritas")

Truth and virtue; beauty and love;
If these alone remained to me,
The world could sink into the waters —
Let me drink only from the beautiful and the true.

(World Wheel, Fifth Collection, IX)

The book comes to an end, but not the singing;
It lies in space and time and in all things,
And yet is spaceless, timeless, beyond form —
It is the content and radiance of our existence.

(Stella Maris, "Last Word")

There is no time in the nature of God;
Nor in the encounter with the Lord.
The moment of prayer is eternity —
It stands in the sky like the morning star;
In the now of the heart lies thy whole life.

(Songs without Names, Seventh Collection, CX)

The Perennial Philosophy

Frithjof Schuon

The term *philosophia perennis*, which has been current since the time of the Renaissance and of which neo-scholasticism made much use, signifies the totality of the primordial and universal truths—and therefore of the metaphysical axioms—whose formulation does not belong to any particular system. One could speak in the same sense of a *religio perennis*, designating by this term the essence of every religion; this means the essence of every form of worship, every form of prayer, and every system of morality, just as the *sophia perennis* is the essence of all dogmas and all expressions of wisdom. We prefer the term *sophia* to that of *philosophia*, for the simple reason that the second term is less direct and because it evokes in addition associations of ideas with a completely profane and all too often aberrant system of thought.

The key to the eternal *sophia* is pure intellection or in other words metaphysical discernment. To "discern" is to "separate": to separate the Real and the illusory, the Absolute and the contingent, the Necessary and the possible, *Atma* and *Maya*. Accompanying discernment, by way of complement and operatively, is concentration, which unites: this means becoming fully aware—from the starting point of earthly and human *Maya*—of *Atma*, which is both absolute and infinite.

According to certain Fathers of the Church, "God became man so that man might become God"; an audacious and elliptical formula which we might paraphrase in a Vedantic fashion by saying that the Real became illusory so that the illusory might become real; *Atma* became *Maya* so that *Maya* might realize *Atma*. This is the very definition of Revelation and of the Revealer; of *Dharma* and of the *Avatara*.

* * *

The decisive error of materialism and agnosticism is the failure to see that the daily experiences of our lives are immeasurably below the stature of our human intelligence. If the materialists were right, this intelligence would be an inexplicable luxury; without the Absolute, the capacity to conceive it would have no cause. The truth of the Absolute coincides with the very substance of our spirit; the various religions actualize objectively what is contained in our deepest subjectivity. Revelation is in the macrocosm what intellection is in the microcosm; the Transcendent is immanent in the world, otherwise the world would not exist, and the Immanent is transcendent in relation to the individual, otherwise It would not surpass him.

What we have said about the scope of human intelligence also applies to the will, in the sense that free-will proves the transcendence of its essential end, for which man was created and because of which man is man; the human will is proportioned to God, and it is only in God and through Him that it is totally free.

One could make an analogous observation in the case of the human soul: our soul proves God because it is proportioned to the divine nature, and it is so by compassion, disinterested love, generosity—and therefore, in the last analysis, by objectivity, the capacity to transcend itself; it is this, precisely, that characterizes the intelligence and the will of man.

And it is in these foundations of human nature—image of the divine nature—that the *religio perennis* has its root.

* * *

The most direct doctrinal expression of the *sophia perennis* is undoubtedly *Advaita Vedanta*, with its notions of *Atma*, of *Maya*, and of *Tat tvam asi*; but this doctrine is also found, in one form or another, even if only sporadically in some cases, in the sapiential esoterisms of all the great religions, and this must necessarily be so in that every normal—and thus intrinsically orthodox—religion is itself an indirect and symbolic expression of the eternal *sophia*.

We quoted above the patristic formula which summarizes Christianity and at the same time expresses the *religio perennis*: "God became man so that man might become God." In Islam, the accent is not on the mystery of Divine Manifestation; it is put on that of Divine Oneness, and so on Divine Reality along with the consequences which this essentially comprises; the fundamental expression of this is the testimony of faith: "There is no divinity (= reality) except the (sole) Divinity (= Reality)." In Islam, what saves is not in the first place the Divine Manifestation; it is the acceptance, by the intelligence, of the Divine Oneness, then the fact of drawing from this all the consequences.

To discern the Real; to concentrate on it, or, more precisely, on so much of it as is accessible to us; then to conform morally to its nature; such is the Way, the only one there is. In Christianity, the Real is as if absorbed—with a view to the salvation of man—by its human Manifestation, Christ; concentration is realized through union with Him and through all the forms of prayer and ascesis that contribute thereto, without forgetting the sacraments which confer the corresponding graces; moral conformity demands humility and charity, and on this point Christianity cannot be distinguished from any other spiritual perspective, except by the specific sentimental coloration that it gives to these virtues.[1]

As for Judaism, it is peculiar in that it puts the whole emphasis on God as the partner of His Chosen People, the link between the two parties being the Law; one might also say that it is the latter that receives the whole emphasis since it is situated between God and Israel; if Israel is the People of God, God for His part is the God of Israel, the pact being sealed by the Sinaitic Law. The drama between God and His People reflects the drama between *Atma* and *Maya*, with all its ambiguity and all its final glory, from the double point of view of cosmic rhythms and of the Apocatastasis.

Completely different from the Semitic religions, and even from the Aryan religions, is Buddhism, although it itself arose in an Aryan and theistic climate: in this perspective, the Absolute-Infinite does not take the form of an objective divinity that is at the same time transcendent, immanent, and omnipotent, but appears uniquely—at least *a priori*—under the aspect of an inward state which in reality is beyond all imaginable states, being, precisely, the absolute and infinite State. The concept of *Nirvana*, though it is clearly non-theistic, is not for all that "atheistic" since it implies the notion of Absolute, Infinite, and Perfect Reality, which could not be nothingness, except in appearance and in comparison with the world of forms and passions. From another standpoint, *Nirvana* is objectivized in the form of the Buddha, which brings us back to the patristic formula already quoted, and which we might here paraphrase in the following terms: *Nirvana* (the "Divine State") became *Samsara* (= the world) so that *Samsara* might become *Nirvana*; now *Nirvana* become *Samsara* is none other than the Buddha, who is in practice God as Logos or *Avatara*.

* * *

The very expression *philosophia perennis*, and the fact that those who have used it were mostly Thomists, and so Aristotelians, raises the question as

---

[1] The sacraments, apostolic succession, oral tradition, and the decisions of the first seven councils are essential to Christianity; by more or less rejecting or attenuating these elements, as the case may be, Protestantism seems to have placed itself in a formal position of heterodoxy. But one must not overlook the fact that this movement is the providential result of what we may call a "spiritual archetype", whose laws do not necessarily coincide with outward tradition. Baptism and a fervent piety based on the Bible, on faith, prayer, and morality may suffice for salvation, at least where there are no worldly dissipations; this reservation of course applies to Catholics as well. In any case, one must not accuse original Lutheranism or Calvinism with the faults of the "liberal" Protestantism which followed later, and it is important not to lose sight of the fact that a certain Christian esoterism, namely of Boehme and his line—not forgetting Rosicrucianism—flowered in the climate of Lutheran piety.

to what, in this context, is the value of Greek wisdom, all the more so since it is generally presented as a merely human system of thought. In the first place, by Greek wisdom we mean, not just any philosophy of Classical Antiquity, but essentially Platonism with its Pythagorean root and its Plotinian prolongation; on this basis, one can even accept Aristotelianism, but on the express condition that it is combined—as in the spirit of the Muslim philosophers—with Platonism in the widest sense, of which it is then like a particular and more or less secondary dimension.[2] Then one must take account of the following, which is essential: Greek wisdom presupposes, on the one hand, initiation into the Mysteries and on the other hand the practice of the virtues; basically it pertains to gnosis—to the *jnana* of the Hindus—even when it deals with things that have no connection with knowledge; admittedly, Aristotelianism is not a *jnana*, but it nevertheless derives from a perspective which specifically pertains to this order. Aristotelianism is a metaphysics which made the mistake of opening itself towards the world, towards the sciences, towards experience, but which is no less logically valid for all that, whereas Platonism contemplates Heaven, the archetypes, the eternal values.

If on the one hand the Greek spirit—through Aristotelianism but also and above all through the sophists and the skeptics—gave rise to the aberration of profane and rationalistic philosophy, it also provided—especially through Platonism—elements that were highly useful not only for the various theologies of Semitic origin, but also for the esoteric speculations that accompany them and are superimposed upon them; we should not forget that for certain Sufis, Plato enjoys the prestige of a kind of prophet, and Meister Eckhart calls him "that great priest" who "found the way ere ever Christ was born".

* * *

Situated in a sense at the antipodes of Greek philosophy—and some will doubtless be surprised that we should mention them—are the disparate and highly unequal traditions that can be classed under the epithet shamanism. On the one hand, this traditional current, belated witness of the Primordial Tradition, gave birth to the ancient Chinese religion, then to its two complementary crystallizations, Confucianism and Taoism; it is to this current moreover that all the ancient Mongol religions belong, Shintoism as well as Bön, and the religion of Genghis Khan. On the other hand, this same current

---

[2] As for Stoicism, one hesitates to bring it into this synthesis, in spite of the interest of its moral idealism, and in spite of the influence that it exerted for this very reason. Its pantheistic immanentism can be viewed either as an intentionally fragmentary perspective exclusively aimed at a heroic morality, or as a heterodoxy pure and simple.

is manifested in the shamanism of the Indians of America, although in very different forms from those it assumes in Asia; but American shamanism has this feature in common with the Asiatic—and it is a feature moreover that characterizes all Hyperborean shamanism—namely that it is founded on the cult of the phenomena of nature and thus on a sort of immanent "pantheism",[3] in other words it envisages virgin nature as the Manifestation of the Divine Principle, and not otherwise.[4]

Obviously, the interest of shamanism does not lie in its abuse of magic and of oracles; it lies in its having its root in virgin nature and in its primordial sense of the sacred, and so in the "primordiality" of its cultic expressions, including the characteristic phenomenon of "autoprophetism", from which, moreover, the function of the shaman derives by exteriorization. The sacred Scripture of shamanism is contained, not in a book, but in the symbols of nature on the one hand and in the substance of the soul on the other, the soul moreover reflecting, and prolonging, the external world; from this it results that if on the one hand the dogmas of this religion are expressed by the signs of surrounding nature, on the other hand the soul has access to the mysteries to the extent that it is capable, morally and ritually, of detaching itself from appearances and entering into contact with its own supernatural essence.[5] All this is true in principle and virtually, and must not make us forget the degeneration of vast sectors of shamanism; but it is not the accidental human facts that matter here, it is the principle envisaged and its fundamental reality.

These survivals of the Primordial Tradition contain a message that is addressed to every man conscious of the human vocation, and this is a con-

---

[3] We would recall here that "pantheism"—like "polytheism"—is only an error when it is interpreted in a narrowly literal fashion, in accordance with the *Deus sive natura* of Spinoza, but not when the aspect of Manifestation presupposes and includes that of Transcendence.

[4] It is difficult to know for certain—and we have no intention of pursuing this simple question of fact—whether the traditions of the peoples who possess no writing, those of the Africans for example, also pertain to shamanism—not Mongolian of course—or whether they constitute different branches of the primordial current; this is independent of the question of their present-day level.

[5] "Our Sacred Book is Nature", an American Indian told us, "and our reading is Inspiration." It is unnecessary to add that this religion is not a matter of improvisation and is not accessible—integrally and *a priori*—to every man, even if he be Indian especially in the conditions of the present-day world. We may add that Zen rests on the same principle as shamanistic autoprophetism, while on the other hand this principle gives rise in our time to the most pernicious falsifications, in contempt of the most elementary traditional rules. "Look for everything within yourselves", the false prophets tell us, without explaining how, and above all while accepting or creating conditions, which go in exactly the opposite direction; all this despite the warnings of the Logos: "Whoso gathereth not with Me scattereth", and likewise, "Without Me ye can do nothing."

sciousness of the sacred character of the universal sanctuary constituted by virgin nature, which includes the most modest flower as well as the stars; it is also the consciousness of the immanence, in the depths of the heart, of the one and total Revelation. But this truth would in practice be nothing without the following one, which shamanism cannot give us, namely that the *religio perennis*, as integral Doctrine and saving Way, is inherent in the great and intrinsically orthodox traditions of humanity, and that it is in them that one must seek and not elsewhere.

SELECT SCHUON BIBLIOGRAPHY

I THE WRITINGS OF FRITHJOF SCHUON

The Works of Frithjof Schuon in English Translation

For more extensive Schuon bibliographies see the biographies by Jean-Baptiste Aymard & Patrick Laude and Michael Fitzgerald (listed below), and the website at: http://www.worldwisdom.com. Schuon's books are listed chronologically by date of first appearance in English, indicated in parenthesis after the title, followed by details of the edition which has most frequently been cited in this work.

Metaphysical Works

The Transcendent Unity of Religions (1953). Wheaton: Quest, 1993.

Spiritual Perspectives and Human Facts (1954). Bloomington: World Wisdom, 2007.

Language of the Self (1959). Bloomington: World Wisdom, 1999.

Gnosis: Divine Wisdom (1959). Bloomington: World Wisdom, 2006.

Castes and Races (1959). London: Perennial Books, 1982.

Stations of Wisdom (1961). London: Perennial Books/John Murray, 1961.

Understanding Islam (1963). Bloomington: World Wisdom, 1998.

Light on the Ancient Worlds (1965). Bloomington: World Wisdom, 2006.

In the Tracks of Buddhism (1968). London: Allen & Unwin, 1968.

Dimensions of Islam (1969). London: Allen & Unwin, 1969.

Logic and Transcendence (1975). Bloomington: World Wisdom, 1984.

Islam and the Perennial Philosophy (1976). London: World of Islam Festival, 1976.

Esoterism as Principle and as Way (1981). London: Perennial Books, 1981.

Sufism: Veil and Quintessence (1981). Bloomington: World Wisdom, 2007.

From the Divine to the Human (1982). Bloomington: World Wisdom, 1982.

Christianity/Islam: Perspectives on Esoteric Ecumenism (1985). Bloomington: World Wisdom, 2008.

Survey of Metaphysics and Esoterism (1986). Bloomington: World Wisdom, 2000.

In the Face of the Absolute (1989). Bloomington: World Wisdom, 1994.

The Feathered Sun: Plains Indians in Art and Philosophy (1990). Bloomington: World Wisdom, 1990.

To Have a Center (1990). Bloomington: World Wisdom, 1990.

Roots of the Human Condition (1991). Bloomington: World Wisdom, 2002.

The Play of Masks (1992). Bloomington: World Wisdom, 1992.

Images of Primordial and Mystic Beauty: Paintings by Frithjof Schuon (1992). Bloomington: Abodes, 1992.

Echoes of Perennial Wisdom (1992). Bloomington: World Wisdom, 1992.

Treasures of Buddhism (revised and expanded edition of *In the Tracks of Buddhism*) (1993). Bloomington: World Wisdom, 1993.

The Transfiguration of Man (1995). Bloomington: World Wisdom, 1995.

The Eye of the Heart (1997). Bloomington: World Wisdom, 1997.

Form and Substance in the Religions (2002). Bloomington: World Wisdom, 2002.

Primordial Meditation: Contemplating the Real (2007). *Sacred Web*, 20, 2007, 19-120 (originally published in German in 1935).

Poetical Works

The Garland. Bloomington: Abodes, 1994.

Road to the Heart: Poems. Bloomington: World Wisdom, 1995.

Songs for a Spiritual Traveler: Selected Poems. German-English edition. Bloomington: World Wisdom, 2002.

Adastra & Stella Maris: Poems by Frithjof Schuon. German-English edition. Bloomington: World Wisdom, 2003.

World Wheel: Poems by Frithjof Schuon, Volumes I-III. Bloomington: World Wisdom, 2006.

World Wheel: Poems by Frithjof Schuon, Volumes IV-VII. Bloomington: World Wisdom, 2006.

Songs without Names: Poems by Frithjof Schuon, Volumes I-VI. Bloomington: World Wisdom, 2006.

Songs without Names: Poems by Frithjof Schuon, Volumes VII-XII. Bloomington: World Wisdom, 2006.

Autumn Leaves & The Ring: Poems by Frithjof Schuon. German-English edition. Bloomington: World Wisdom, 2010.

Edited Works

The Essential Frithjof Schuon (1986), ed. S.H. Nasr. Bloomington: World Wisdom, 2005.

René Guénon: Some Observations, ed. William Stoddart. Hillsdale: Sophia Perennis, 2004.

The Fullness of God: Frithjof Schuon on Christianity, ed. J. Cutsinger. Bloomington: World Wisdom, 2004.

Prayer Fashions Man: Frithjof Schuon on the Spiritual Life, ed. J. Cutsinger. Bloomington: World Wisdom, 2005.

Art from the Sacred to the Profane: East and West, ed. C. Schuon. Bloomington: World Wisdom, 2007.

Articles Cited from Journals and Anthologies

"Nature and Function of the Spiritual Master". *Studies in Comparative Religion*, 1:2, 1967, 41-47.

"The Three Dimensions of Sufism". *Studies in Comparative Religion*, 10:1, 1976, 5-12.

"Consequences Flowing from the Mystery of Subjectivity". *Studies in Comparative Religion*, 11:4, 1977, 197-204.

"No Activity Without Truth". In J. Needleman (ed.), *The Sword of Gnosis*. Baltimore: Penguin, 1972, 27-39.

"The Perennial Philosophy". In R. Fernando (ed.), *The Unanimous Tradition.* Colombo: Sri Lanka Institute of Traditional Studies, 1991, 21-24.

"Communion and Invocation". In P. Laude (ed.), *Pray Without Ceasing: The Way of the Invocation in World Religions.* Bloomington: World Wisdom, 2006, 72-78.

II   SELECTED WORKS ON FRITHJOF SCHUON

Adrichem, Patricia. *Frithjof Schuon and the Problem of Religious Diversity.* La Trobe University Bendigo: unpublished doctoral thesis, 2005.

Aymard, Jean-Baptiste & Patrick Laude. *Frithjof Schuon: Life and Teachings.* Albany: SUNY, 2004.

────── (eds.). *Frithjof Schuon.* Paris: L'Age d'Homme, 2002.

Azevedo, Mateus Soares de. "Frithjof Schuon and Shri Ramana Maharshi". *Sacred Web*, 10, 2003, 185-195.

Biès, Jean. "Frithjof Schuon: A Face of Eternal Wisdom" (interview). *Sophia*, 4:1, 1998, 5-20.

Casey, Deborah. "The Basis of Religion and Metaphysics: An Interview with Frithjof Schuon". *The Quest*, 9:2, 1996, 74-78.

Chevilliat, Bernard (ed.). *Frithjof Schuon: Connaissance et Voie d'Intériorité, Biographie études et témoignages.* Paris: Connaissance des Religions, 1999.

Cutsinger, James. *Advice to the Serious Seeker: Meditations on the Teaching of Frithjof Schuon.* Albany: SUNY, 1996.

──────. "'A Knowledge that Wounds Our Nature': The Message of Frithjof Schuon". http://www.cutsinger.net.

──────. "The Mystery of the Two Natures". *Sophia*, 4:2, 1998, 111-170.

──────. "The Virgin". *Sophia*, 6:2, 2000, 115-194. (Also entitled: "Colorless Light and Pure Air: The Virgin in the Thought of Frithjof Schuon". http://www.cutsinger.net.

Fabbri, Renaud. "The Milk of the Virgin: The Prophet, the Saint, and the Sage". *Sacred Web*, 20, 2007, 225-265.

──────. "Frithjof Schuon: The Shining Realm of the Pure Intellect" (Master's Thesis). Oxford, Ohio: Miami University, 2007.

Fitzgerald, Michael. *Frithjof Schuon: Messenger of the Perennial Philosophy.* Bloomington: World Wisdom, 2010.

──────. "Frithjof Schuon's Role in Preserving the Red Indian Spirit". *Sophia*, 4:2, 1998, 220-232.

──────. "Frithjof Schuon and the Native Spirit: Interview with Michael Fitzgerald". *Vincit Omnia Veritas* 3:2, July 2007. (Also in R. Fabbri & T. Scott (eds.). *Vincit Omnia Veritas: Collected Essays,* 7-33.)

──────. "Beauty and the Sense of the Sacred: Schuon's Antidote to the Modern World". *Sacred Web*, 20, 2007, 129-154.

Keeble, Brian. "Some Thoughts on Reading Frithjof Schuon's Writings on Art". *Sophia*, 4: 2, 1998, 246-252.

Lakhani, Ali. "'Standing Unshakably in the True': A Commentary on the Teachings of Frithjof Schuon". *Sacred Web*, 20, 2007, 9-18.

Laude, Patrick. "Remarks on Esoterism in the Works of Frithjof Schuon". *Sacred Web*, 4, 1999, 57-65.

———. "*Nigra sum sed Formosa*, 'I am Black but Beautiful': Death and the Spiritual Life in Frithjof Schuon". *Sacred Web*, 19, 2007, 107-120.

———. "Quintessential Esoterism and the Wisdom of Forms: Reflections on Frithjof Schuon's Intellectual and Spiritual Legacy". *Sacred Web*, 20, 2007, 159-192.

Lindbom, Tage. "Frithjof Schuon and Our Times". *Sophia*, 4:2, 1998, 78-90.

Lings, Martin. "Frithjof Schuon: An Autobiographical Approach". *Sophia*, 4:2, 1998, 15-28.

———. "Frithjof Schuon and René Guénon". *Sophia*, 5:2, 1999, 9-24.

———. "How Did I Come To Put First Things First?". In Martin Lings, *A Return to the Spirit: Questions and Answers*. Louisville, KY: Fons Vitae, 2005, 1-16.

Michon, Jean-Louis. "The True Man: A Myth or Reality?". *Sacred Web*, 19, 2007, 57-77.

Nasr, Seyyed Hossein. "Introduction". In S.H. Nasr (ed.), *The Essential Writings of Frithjof Schuon*. New York: Amity House, 1986, 1-64.

———. "The Biography of Frithjof Schuon". In S.H. Nasr & W. Stoddart (eds.), *Religion of the Heart*, 1-6.

———. "Frithjof Schuon, 1907-1998". *Sacred Web*, 1, 1998, 15-17.

———. (ed.). Memorial Issue on Frithjof Schuon, *Sophia* 4:2, 1998. (Includes tributes and reminiscences by Martin Lings, Huston Smith, Whitall Perry, Reza Shah-Kazemi, Michael Fitzgerald, William Stoddart and others.)

Nasr, S.H. & W. Stoddart (eds.). *Religion of the Heart: Essays Presented to Frithjof Schuon on His Eightieth Birthday*. Washington DC: Foundation of Traditional Studies, 1991.

Oldmeadow, Kenneth (Harry). *Traditionalism: Religion in the Light of the Perennial Philosophy*. Colombo: Sri Lanka Institute of Traditional Studies, 2000.

Oldmeadow, Harry. *Mediations: Essays on Religious Pluralism and the Perennial Philosophy*. San Raphael: Sophia Perennis, 2008.

———. "Globalization, the Convergence of Religions, and the Perennial Philosophy". In C. Cusack & P. Oldmeadow (eds.), *The End of Religions? Religion in an Age of Globalisation*. Sydney: Sydney University, 2001, 35-51.

———. "The Heart of the *Religio Perennis*: Frithjof Schuon on Esotericism". In Edward Crangle (ed.), *Esotericism and the Control of Knowledge*. Sydney: Sydney University, 2004, 146-179.

———. "Frithjof Schuon: A Sage for the Times". *Sophia*, 4:2, 1998, 56-77.

———. "Formal Diversity, Essential Unity: Frithjof Schuon on the Convergence of Religions". *Sacred Web*, 5, 2000, 95-105.

———. "'Signposts to the Suprasensible': Notes on Frithjof Schuon's Understanding of 'Nature'". *Sacred Web*, 6, 2000, 47-58.

———. Review of Aymard, Jean-Baptiste & Patrick Laude, *Frithjof Schuon: Life and Teachings*. *Sophia*, 11:1, 2005, 197-204.

Perry, Barbara. *Frithjof Schuon: Metaphysician and Artist.* Bloomington: World Wisdom, 1981.

———. "Introduction". In Catherine Schuon (ed.), *Art from the Sacred to the Profane: East and West*, xiii-xv.

Perry, Mark. "Frithjof Schuon Seen through his Handwriting". *Sophia*, 6:1, 2001, 107-152.

Perry, Whitall. "The Revival of Interest in Tradition". In Ranjit Fernando (ed.), *The Unanimous Tradition*, 3-16.

———. "Perspectives". *Sophia*, 4:2, 1998, 32-46.

Pollack, Michael. "Editor's Introduction". In *Images of Primordial and Mystic Beauty: Paintings by Frithjof Schuon*, 1-4.

Prats, Josep & Esteve Serra (eds). *Frithjof Schuon (1907-1998): Notas biográficas, estudios, homenajes.* Palma de Mallorca: Sophia Perennis, 2004.

Raghavan, V. "Foreword". In *Language of the Self* (1959), ix-xx.

Ramachandran, Mudambai. "Frithjof Schuon: A Small Word of Homage and Celebration". *Sophia*, 4:2, 1998, 47-55.

Romaine, Sharlyn. "Intention and Style". In *Images of Primordial and Mystic Beauty: Paintings by Frithjof Schuon*, 5-6.

Schimmel, Annemarie. "Foreword". In *Understanding Islam*, v-vii.

———. "Foreword". In *Adastra & Stella Maris: Poems by Frithjof Schuon*, vii-viii.

Scott, Timothy. "Concerning Religious Forms". *Sacred Web*, 8, 2001, 73-98.

———. "'Made in the Image': Schuon's Theomorphic Anthropology". *Sacred Web*, 20, 2007, 193-224.

Schuon, Catherine. "Frithjof Schuon: Memories and Anecdotes". *Sacred Web*, 8, 2001, 35-60.

Shah-Kazemi, Reza. "Frithjof Schuon and Prayer". *Sophia* 4:2, 1998, 180-193.

Smith, Huston. "Frithjof Schuon's *The Transcendent Unity of Religions*, Pro". *Journal of the American Academy of Religion*, 154:4, 1976, 721-724.

———. "Introduction". In *The Transcendent Unity of Religions* (1984), ix-xxvii.

———. "Providence Perceived: In Memory of Frithjof Schuon". *Sophia*, 4:2, 1998, 29-31.

Stoddart, William. "The German Poems of Frithjof Schuon". *Sophia*, 4:2, 1998, 233-245.

———. "Introduction". In *World Wheel: Poems by Frithjof Schuon, Volumes I-III*, ix-xv.

———. "Frithjof Schuon and the Perennialist School". In *Remembering in a World of Forgetting: Thoughts on Tradition and Postmodernism*, 51-66.

Valodia, Deon. *Compass for the Journey: Terms Used by Frithjof Schuon.* Cape Town: privately published, 2006.

LIST OF SOURCES

In the case of multiple entries by a single author items are ordered chronologically within each of the following sub-sections: books, journal articles, reviews, contributions to multi-author works, co-authored items, works edited. Publication dates refer to the editions consulted. Occasionally the original date of publication has been indicated immediately following the title, within parentheses. When an article is cited from a book edited by a different author only limited details are provided: the full details can be found under the editor's name. All journal volume and issue numbers have been standardized. Website addresses have only been provided where there might be some difficulty in tracing the site through the name of the journal, author, or organization in question. All references to *Sophia* are to *Sophia: The Journal of Traditional Studies* (Washington DC), not to be confused with *Sophia: International Journal for Philosophy of Religion, Metaphysical Theology and Ethics* (Melbourne).

Abhishiktananda. *The Further Shore*. Delhi: ISPCK, 1975.

———. *Hindu-Christian Meeting Point*. Delhi: ISPCK, 1976.

Abu Bakr Siraj ad-Din. *The Book of Certainty*. New York: Samuel Weiser, 1974.

———. "The Spiritual Function of Civilization". In J. Needleman (ed.), *The Sword of Gnosis*, 104-108.

Almond, Philip. "Rudolf Otto and Buddhism". In P. Masefield & D. Wiebe (eds.), *Aspects of Religion*, 59-72.

Almqvist, Kurt. "Aspects of Teilhardian Idolatry". *Studies in Comparative Religion*, 12:3-4, 1978, 195-202.

Anthony (Bloom), Metropolitan. *God and Man*. London: Hodder & Stoughton, 1974.

Atmaprana, P. "Swami Vivekananda on Harmony of Religions and Religious Sects". In R.C. Majumdar (ed.), *Swami Vivekananda's Memorial Volume*.

Bâ, Amadou Hampaté. *A Spirit of Tolerance: The Inspiring Life of Tierno Bokar*. Bloomington: World Wisdom, 2008.

Baistrocchi, Marco. "The Last Pillars of Wisdom". In S.D.R. Singam (ed.), *Ananda Coomaraswamy: Remembering and Remembering Again and Again*, 350-359.

Bakhtiar, Laleh. *Sufi: Expressions of the Mystical Quest*. London: Thames & Hudson, 1976.

Bancroft, Ann. *Twentieth Century Mystics and Sages*. London: Heinemann, 1976.

Berry, Wendell. *Life is a Miracle: An Essay against Modern Superstition*. Washington DC: Counterpoint, 2000.

Bharati, Agehananda. "The Hindu Renaissance and Its Apologetic Patterns". *Journal of Asian Studies*, 29, 2, 1970, 267-287.

Blackhirst, Rodney. "Evolutionism and Traditional Cosmology". In R. Fabbri & T. Scott (eds.), *Vincit Omnia Veritas: Collected Essays*, 137-142.

Blunt, Anthony. *Artistic Theory in Italy 1500-1600*. Oxford: Clarendon Press, 1962.

Borella, Jean. "René Guénon and the Traditionalist School". In A. Faivre & J. Needleman (eds.), *Modern Esoteric Spirituality*, 330-358.

Bremer, E.S. "Some Implications for Literary Criticism from the Aesthetic Theory of Ananda Coomaraswamy". In S.D.R. Singam (ed.), *Ananda Coomaraswamy: Remembering and Remembering Again and Again*, 33-42.

Bridges, H. "Aldous Huxley: Exponent of Mysticism in America". *Journal of the American Academy of Religion*, 37:2, 1969, 341-352.

Brown, Dee. *Bury My Heart at Wounded Knee*. London: Pan, 1971.

Brown , Joseph Epes. *The Sacred Pipe*. Norman: University of Oklahoma, 1953. (Some reference is also made to the 1971 Penguin edition, as indicated.)

―――. *The Spiritual Legacy of the American Indians*. New York: Crossroad, 1972. (Some reference is also made to the 2006 World Wisdom Commemorative Edition, as indicated.)

―――. *Animals of the Soul*. Rockport: Element, 1993.

――― & Emily Cousins. *Teaching Spirits: Understanding Native American Religious Traditions*. New York: Oxford University Press, 2001.

―――. "Modes of Contemplation through Actions: North American Indians". In Y. Ibish & P.L. Wilson (eds.), *Traditional Modes of Contemplation and Action*, 233-245.

Buber, Martin. *A Believing Humanism*. Simon & Schuster, New York, 1967.

Burckhardt, Titus. *Sacred Art in East and West*. Bedfont: Perennial Books, 1967.

―――. *Alchemy: Science of the Cosmos, Science of the Soul*. Baltimore: Penguin, 1972.

―――. *Art of Islam*. London: World of Islam Festival, 1976.

―――. *Mystical Astrology According to Ibn Arabi*. Sherbourne: Beshara Publications, 1977.

―――. *Mirror of the Intellect: Essays on Traditional Science and Sacred Art*, ed. William Stoddart. Cambridge: Quinta Essentia, 1987.

―――. "Cosmology and Modern Science". In J. Needleman (ed.), *The Sword of Gnosis*, 122-178.

―――. "Perennial Values in Islamic Art". In J. Needleman (ed.), *The Sword of Gnosis*, 304-316.

Burrow, J.W. *Evolution and Society: A Study in Victorian Social Theory*. Cambridge: Cambridge University Press, 1966.

Campbell, Joseph (ed.). *Man and Time: Papers from the Eranos Yearbooks*. Princeton: Bollingen Series, 1973.

Case, Margaret (ed.). *Heinrich Zimmer: Coming Into His Own*. Princeton: Princeton University Press, 1994.

Casewit, Fatima Jane. "Islamic Cosmological Concepts of Femininity and the Modern Feminist Movement". *Sacred Web*, 7, 2001, 81-92. (Also in H. Oldmeadow, *The Betrayal of Tradition*, 171-181.)

Castleman, Graeme. "Golgotha, Athens, and Jerusalem: Patristic intimations of the *Religio Perennis*". *Eye of the Heart*, 1, 2008, 47-79.

Charcornac, Paul. *The Simple Life of René Guénon* (1958), trans. Bernard Bethell. Perth: privately published, 1991.

Charlesworth, Max et al. (eds.). *Religion in Aboriginal Australia*. St Lucia: University of Queensland, 1984.

Chittick, William C. Introduction. In W. C. Chittick (ed.), *The Essential Seyyed Hossein Nasr*. Bloomington: World Wisdom, 2005, ix-xiv.

Cioran, E.M. *Anathemas and Admirations*. New York: Arcade, 1991.

Clements, R.J. *Michelangelo's Theory of Art*. New York: New York University, 1971.

Coomaraswamy, Ananda. *Hinduism and Buddhism*. New York: Philosophical Library, 1945.

———. *Figures of Speech or Figures of Thought: Collected Essays on the Traditional or "Normal" View of Art*. London: Luzac, 1946.

———. *Time and Eternity*. Ascona: Artibus Asiae, 1947.

———. *Christian and Oriental Philosophy of Art*. New York: Dover, 1956.

———. *The Transformation of Nature in Art*. New York: Dover, 1956.

———. *Coomaraswamy 1: Selected Papers, Traditional Art and Symbolism*, ed. Roger Lipsey. Princeton: Princeton University, 1977.

———. *Coomaraswamy 2: Selected Papers, Metaphysics*, ed. Roger Lipsey. Princeton: Princeton University, 1977.

———. *The Bugbear of Literacy*. London: Perennial Books, 1979.

———. *Selected Letters of Ananda Coomaraswamy*, ed. R.P. Coomaraswamy & Alvin Moore Jr. New Delhi: Indira Gandhi National Center for the Arts, 1988.

———. *What is Civilization? and Other Essays*. Ipswich: Golgonooza, 1989.

———. "The Pertinence of Philosophy". In S. Radhakrishnan & J.H. Muirhead (eds.), *Contemporary Indian Philosophy*. London: Allen & Unwin, 1952, rev. ed.

———. "The Bugbear of Democracy, Freedom, and Equality". *Studies in Comparative Religion*, 11:3, 1977, 133-158. (Also in H. Oldmeadow (ed.), *The Betrayal of Tradition*, 121-149.)

———. Review of a book by Radhakrishnan. *The Review of Religion*, 6, January 1942.

Coomaraswamy, Rama P. *The Destruction of the Christian Tradition*. London: Perennial Books, 1981.

———. "Who Speaks for the East?" *Studies in Comparative Religion*, 11:2, 1977, 85-91.

———. "The Desacralisation of Hinduism for Western Consumption". *Sophia*, 4:2, 1998, 194-219.

———. Review of M. Eliade, *No Souvenirs*. *Studies in Comparative Religion*, 12:1-2, 1978, 123.

———. & Alvin Moore Jr. (eds.), *Selected Letters of Ananda Coomaraswamy*. New Delhi: Indira Gandhi National Center, 1988.

Cragg, Kenneth. *The Mind of the Quran*. London: Allen & Unwin, 1973.

Cusack, Carol & Peter Oldmeadow (eds.). *This Immense Panorama*. Sydney: University of Sydney, 2001.

———. (eds.). *The End of Religions? Religion in an Age of Globalisation*. Sydney: University of Sydney, 2001.

Cutsinger, James. "Femininity, Hierarchy, and God". In S.H. Nasr & W. Stoddart, *The Religion of the Heart*, 110-131.

———. "On Earth as It Is in Heaven: A Metaphysical Cosmogony". *Dialogue & Alliance*, 4:4, 1990-91, 45-68.

Daniélou, Alain. "René Guénon et la tradition hindoue". In Pierre-Marie Sigaud (ed.), *Dossier H René Guénon*. L'Age d'Homme: Lausanne-Paris, 1984.

Denton, Michael. *Evolution: A Theory in Crisis*. London: Burnett, 1985.

Desjardins, Arnaud. *The Message of the Tibetans*. London: Stuart & Watkins, 1969.

Dewar, Douglas. *The Transformist Illusion*. Hillsdale, NY: Sophia Perennis et Universalis, 2005.

Eaton, Gai. *The Richest Vein*. London: Faber & Faber, 1949.

———. *King of the Castle: Choice and Responsibility in the Modern World*. London: Bodley Head, 1977.

———. *Islam and the Destiny of Man*. Cambridge: Islamic Texts Society, 1986.

Eden, Murray. "Inadequacies of neo-Darwinian Evolution as Scientific Theory". In P. Moorehead & M. Kaplan (eds.), *Mathematical Challenges to the neo-Darwinian Interpretation of Evolution*.

Eliade, Mircea. *The Sacred and the Profane*. New York: Harcourt Brace Jovanovich, 1959.

———. *Myths, Dreams, and Mysteries*. New York: Harper & Row, 1960.

———. *Australian Religions*. Ithaca: Cornell University, 1973.

———. *The Myth of the Eternal Return*. Princeton: Princeton University, 1975.

———. *Occultism, Witchcraft, and Cultural Fashions*. Chicago: University of Chicago, 1976.

———. *No Souvenirs*. New York: Harper & Row, 1977.

———. "Methodological Remarks on the Study of Religious Symbolism". In M. Eliade & J. Kitagawa (eds.), *The History of Religions: Essays in Methodology*, 86-107.

———. "Time and Eternity in Indian Thought". In J. Campbell (ed.), *Man and Time: Papers from the Eranos Yearbooks*, 173-200.

Eliade, M. & J. Kitagawa (eds.). *The History of Religions: Essays in Methodology*. Chicago: University of Chicago Press, 1959.

Ellwood, Robert. Review. *Journal of the American Academy of Religion*, 45.

Études Traditionnelles. Le Sort de l'Occident (Special Issue), November, 1951.

Evans, Christopher. *Cults of Unreason*. London: Harrap, 1973.

Fabbri, Renaud & Timothy Scott (eds.). *Vincit Omnia Veritas: Collected Essays*. Bendigo: La Trobe University, 2008.

Faivre, Antoine & Jacob Needleman (eds.). *Modern Esoteric Spirituality*. New York: Crossroad, 1995.

Fernando, Ranjit (ed.). *The Unanimous Tradition*. Colombo: Sri Lanka Institute of Traditional Studies, 1991.

Fitzgerald, Joseph. "From Marco Pallis to Thubden Tendzin: A Son of Tibet Returns". *Sacred Web*, 22, 2009, 39-61.

Fitzgerald, Michael. *Yellowtail: Crow Medicine Man and Sun Dance Chief*. Norman: University of Oklahoma Press, 1991.

————. "In Memoriam: Dr. Martin Lings". *Sacred Web*, 15, 2005, 144-153.

Fitzgerald, Michael & Judith Fitzgerald (eds.). *Indian Spirit*. Bloomington: World Wisdom, 2006, rev. ed.

————. *The Spirit of Indian Women*. Bloomington: World Wisdom, 2005.

Fremondi, G. & R. Fondi. *Dopo Darwin*. Milan: Rusconi, 1980.

Freud, Sigmund. *Totem and Taboo*. London: Routledge & Kegan Paul, 1950.

————. *The Complete Psychological Works of Sigmund Freud*, ed. James Strachey. London: Hogarth Press, 1964.

————. *New Introductory Lectures on Psychoanalysis*. London: Hogarth Press, 1974.

Goble, Paul. "Appreciation: Remembering Marco Pallis". In M. Pallis, *The Way and the Mountain*. Bloomington: World Wisdom, 2008, xxxiii-xxvi.

Govinda, Anagarika. *Foundations of Tibetan Mysticism*. London: Rider, 1969.

————. *The Way of the White Clouds*. Boulder: Shambhala, 1970.

————. *Creative Meditation and Multi-Dimensional Consciousness*. Wheaton: Quest, 1976.

Guénon, René. *Introduction to the Study of the Hindu Doctrines*. London: Luzac, 1945.

————. *Initiation and the Crafts*. Ipswich: Golgonooza, 1974.

————. *The Crisis of the Modern World*. London: Luzac, 1975.

————. *The Symbolism of the Cross*. London: Luzac, 1975.

————. *Man and His Becoming According to the Vedanta*. New Delhi: Oriental Books Reprint Co., 1981.

————. *The Multiple States of Being*. New York: Larson, 1984.

————. *The Great Triad*. Cambridge: Quinta Essentia, 1991.

————. *East and West*. Ghent: Sophia Perennis et Universalis, 1995.

————. *The Reign of Quantity & the Signs of the Times*. Ghent: Sophia Perennis et Universalis, 1995.

————. *Fundamental Symbols: The Universal Language of Sacred Science*. Cambridge: Quinta Essentia, 1995.

————. *Traditional Forms and Cosmic Cycles*. Ghent: Sophia Perennis et Universalis, 2001.

————. "Explanation of Spiritist Phenomena". *Tomorrow*, 14:1, 1966, 69-86.

————. "Taoism and Confucianism". *Studies in Comparative Religion*, 6:4, 1972, 239-250.

————. "Oriental Metaphysics". In J. Needleman (ed.), *The Sword of Gnosis*, 40-56.

Hayes, Mark. "The New Consciousness Movement". *Religious Traditions*, 1:1, 1978, 43-49.

Heard, Gerald. "Vedanta and Western History". In C. Isherwood (ed.), *Vedanta for Modern Man*, 17-27.

Heinemann, F.H. Review of Frithjof Schuon, *The Transcendent Unity of Religions*. *Journal of Theological Studies*, 6, 1955.

Himmelfarb, Gertrude. *Darwin and the Darwinian Revolution*. London: Chatto & Windus, 1959.

Hiriyana, M. *Essentials of Indian Philosophy*. London: Allen & Unwin, 1978.

Hofstadter, Richard. *Social Darwinism in American Thought*. Philadelphia: University of Philadelphia, 1945.

Huxley, Aldous. *The Doors of Perception and Heaven and Hell*. Harmondsworth: Penguin, 1959.

———. *The Perennial Philosophy* (1944). New York: Harper & Row, 1970.

———. "Origins and Consequences of Some Contemporary Thought Patterns". In C. Isherwood (ed.), *Vedanta for Modern Man*, 359-363.

Huxley, Julian (ed.). *The Humanist Frame*. London: Allen & Unwin, 1961.

Hyde, L. "Radhakrishnan's Contribution to Universal Religion". In P.A. Schilpp, *The Philosophy of Sarvapelli Radhakrishnan*, 367-382.

Ibish, Yusuf & Peter Lamborn Wilson (eds.). *Traditional Modes of Contemplation and Action*. Tehran: Imperial Academy of Philosophy, 1977.

Isherwood, Christopher. *Ramakrishna and His Disciples*. Calcutta: Advaita Ashram, 1974.

Isherwood, Christopher (ed.). *Vedanta for Modern Man*. New York: New American Library, 1963.

———(ed.). *Vedanta for the Western World*. New American Library, New York, 1972.

Izutsu, Toshihiko. *A Comparative Study of the Key Philosophical Concepts in Taoism and Sufism*. Berkeley: University of California, 1983.

Jarvie, I.C. *The Revolution in Anthropology*. Chicago: Henry Regnery, 1969.

Johnson, Phillip E. *Darwin on Trial*. Washington DC: Henry Regnery, 1991.

Keeble, Brian. *Every Man an Artist*. Bloomington: World Wisdom, 2005.

———. "Tradition, Intelligence, and the Artist". *Studies in Comparative Religion*, 11:4, 1977, 235-250.

———. "Perennial Values against Modern Decadence". *Studies in Comparative Religion*, 13:1-2, 1979, 56-64.

Kelley, C.F. *Meister Eckhart on Divine Knowledge*. New Haven: Yale University, 1977.

Kelly, Bernard. "Notes on the Light of the Eastern Religions". In S.H. Nasr & W. Stoddart (eds.), *Religion of the Heart*, 155-176.

Krishnamurti, Jiddu. *Talks and Dialogues, Saanen, 1967*. Wassenaar: Sevire, 1969.

Kroeber, Theodora. *Ishi in Two Worlds*. Berkeley: University of California, 1961.

Krsnamurti, N.S. "Ananda Coomaraswamy". In S.D.R. Singam (ed.), *Ananda Coomaraswamy: Remembering and Remembering Again and Again*, 171-176.

Lakhani, Ali. "What Thirst is For" (Editorial). *Sacred Web*, 4, 1999, 13-16.

Laude, Patrick (ed.). *Pray Without Ceasing: The Way of the Invocation in World Religions*. Bloomington: World Wisdom, 2006.

Laurant, Jean-Pierre. *Le Sens Caché Selon René Guénon*. Lausanne: L'Age d'Homme, 1975.

———. "Le problème de René Guénon". *Revue de l'histoire des religions*, 179:1, 1971, 41-70.

Lings, Martin. *A Sufi Saint of the Twentieth Century*. Berkeley: University of California, 1971.

———. *What is Sufism?* Allen & Unwin: London, 1975.

————. *Ancient Beliefs and Modern Superstitions*. London: Allen & Unwin, 1980.

————. *The Eleventh Hour: The Spiritual Crisis of the Modern World in the Light of Tradition and Prophecy*. Cambridge: Quinta Essentia, 1987.

————. "Signs of the Times". In J. Needleman (ed.), *The Sword of Gnosis*, 109-121.

————. "The World of Today in the Light of Tradition". In S.H. Nasr & K. O'Brien (eds.), *In Quest of the Sacred*, 191-201.

Lipsey, Roger. *Coomaraswamy: His Life and Work*. Bollingen Series, Princeton: Princeton University, 1977.

Mahadevan, T.M.P. *Ramana Maharshi: The Sage of Arunacala*. London: Allen & Unwin, 1977.

Mails, Thomas. *Fools Crow*. Lincoln: University of Nebraska, 1979.

Majumdar, R.C. (ed.). *Swami Vivekananda's Memorial Volume*. Calcutta: Swami Vivekananda Centenary, 1963.

Marx, Karl & Friedrich Engels. *On Religion*. Moscow: Progress Publishers, 1957.

Masefield, Peter & Donald Wiebe (eds.). *Aspects of Religion: Essays in Honor of Ninian Smart*. New York: Peter Lang, 1994.

Matchett, Fred. "The Teaching of Ramakrishna in Relation to the Hindu Tradition and as Interpreted by Vivekananda". *Religion*, 11, 1981, 171-184.

Matheson, D.M. "Psychoanalysis and Spirituality". *Tomorrow*, 13:2, 1965, 103-108.

Matthiessen, Peter. *Indian Country*. London: Collins/Havrill, 1986.

McGrath, Alister. *The Twilight of Atheism*. London: Rider, 2004.

McGuire, William. "Zimmer and the Mellens". In M. Case (ed.), *Heinrich Zimmer: Coming Into His Own*, 31-42.

McLellan, David. *Marx*. Glasgow: Fontana/Collins, 1975.

McLuhan, T.C. (ed.). *Touch the Earth*. London: Abacus, 1971.

Merton, Thomas. *New Seeds of Contemplation*. New York: New Directions, 1972.

————. *The Asian Journal of Thomas Merton*, eds. Naomi Burton, Patrick Hart & James Laughlin. New York: New Directions, 1972.

————. *Contemplation in a World of Action*. New York: Doubleday, 1973.

————. *Disputed Questions*. New York: Noonday Press, 1977.

Michon, Jean-Louis. "The Vocation of Man According to the Koran". In A. Sharma (ed.), *Fragments of Infinity: Essays in Religion and Philosophy*, 135-152.

Moore, Jr., Alvin. "Nature, Man, and God". *Sacred Web*, 2, 1998, 51-64.

Moore, Peter. Review of Whitall Perry (ed.), *A Treasury of Traditional Wisdom*. *Studies in Comparative Religion*, 6:1, 1972, 61-65.

Moorehead, P. & M. Kaplan (eds.). *Mathematical Challenges to the neo-Darwinian Interpretation of Evolution*. Philadelphia: Wistar Institute Press, 1967.

Murti, T.R.V. "Radhakrishnan and Buddhism". In P.A. Schilpp (ed.), *The Philosophy of Sarvapelli Radhakrishnan*, 565-606.

Naravarne, V.S. "Ananda Coomaraswamy: A Critical Appreciation". In S.D.R. Singam (ed.), *Ananda Coomaraswamy: Remembering and Remembering Again and Again*, 204-209.

Naqavi, Sayyid Ali Raza. "Babism and Baha'ism: A Study of their History and Doctrine". *Islamic Studies*, 14:3, 1975, 185-217.

Nasr, Seyyed Hossein. *Ideals and Realities of Islam.* London: Allen & Unwin, 1966.

———. *Man and Nature: The Spiritual Crisis of Modern Man.* London: Allen & Unwin, 1968.

———. *Sufi Essays.* London: Allen & Unwin, 1972.

———. *Knowledge and the Sacred.* New York: Crossroad, 1981.

———. *The Need for a Sacred Science.* Albany: SUNY, 1993.

———. *Religion and the Order of Nature.* New York: Oxford University, 1996.

———. *The Spiritual and Religious Dimensions of the Environmental Crisis.* London: Temenos Academy, 1999.

———. *The Essential Seyyed Hossein Nasr,* ed. William Chittick. Bloomington: World Wisdom, 2007.

———. "Conditions for a Meaningful Comparative Philosophy". *Philosophy East and West,* 22:1, 1972, 53-61.

———. "Reflections on Islam and Modern Thought". *The Islamic Quarterly,* 23:3, 1979, 119-131.

———. "The Traditional Sciences". In Ranjit Fernando (ed.), *The Unanimous Tradition,* 129-144.

——— & K. O'Brien (eds.). *In Quest of the Sacred: The Modern World in the Light of Tradition.* Oakton: Foundation of Traditional Studies, 1994.

Natarajan, A.R. *Timeless in Time: Sri Ramana Maharshi.* Bloomington: World Wisdom, 2006.

Needleman, Jacob. *The New Religions.* New York: Pocket Books, 1972.

———. *A Sense of the Cosmos.* New York: Doubleday, 1975.

———(ed.). *The Sword of Gnosis.* Baltimore: Penguin, 1974.

Negus, Michael. "Reactions to the Theory of Evolution". *Studies in Comparative Religion,* 12:3-4, 1978, 188-194.

———. Review of Anthony Fides' *Man's Origins. Studies in Comparative Religion,* 13:1-2, 1979, 126-127.

Neihardt, John. *Black Elk Speaks.* London: Abacus, 1974.

Nietzsche, Friedrich. *A Nietzsche Reader,* ed. R.J. Hollingdale. Harmondsworth: Penguin, 1977.

Nordstrom, Louis & Richard Pilgrim. "The Wayward Mysticism of Alan Watts". *Philosophy East and West,* 30:3, 1980, 381-399.

Northbourne, Lord W.E. *Religion in the Modern World.* London: J.M. Dent/Perennial Books, 1963.

———. *Looking Back on Progress.* London: Perennial Books, 1970.

———. *Of the Land and the Spirit: The Essential Lord Northbourne on Ecology and Religion,* ed. J. Fitzgerald & C. James. Bloomington: World Wisdom, 2008.

———. "A Note on Truth, Goodness, and Beauty". *Studies in Comparative Religion,* 7:2, 1973, 107-112.

Nott, C.S. *Journey through This World.* London: Routledge & Kegan Paul, 1969.

Oldmeadow, Harry. *Mircea Eliade and Carl Jung: "Priests Without Surplices"?* Bendigo: Department of Arts, La Trobe University, 1995.

———. *Journeys East: 20th Century Western Encounters with Eastern Religious Traditions.* Bloomington: World Wisdom, 2004.

————. *A Christian Pilgrim in India: The Spiritual Journey of Swami Abhishiktananda (Henri Le Saux)*. Bloomington: World Wisdom, 2008.

————. *Mediations: Essays on Religious Pluralism and the Perennial Philosophy*. San Raphael: Sophia Perennis, 2008.

————. "Sankara's Doctrine of *Maya*". *Asian Philosophy*, 2:2, 1992, 131-146.

————. "Biographical Sketch". In R. Guénon, *The Reign of Quantity & the Signs of the Times*. Ghent: Sophia Perennis, 1995, vi-xxxvii.

————. Review of Joseph Epes Brown, *The Spiritual Legacy of the American Indian* (Commemorative Edition). *Sophia*, 12:2, 2006, 189-194.

————(ed.). *The Betrayal of Tradition: Essays on the Spiritual Crisis of Modernity*. Bloomington: World Wisdom, 2005.

————(ed.). *Light from the East: Eastern Wisdom for the Modern West*. Bloomington: World Wisdom, 2007.

Oldmeadow, Peter. *Zen: An Ancient Path to Enlightenment*. Sydney: Lansdowne, 2001.

Pallis, Marco. *Peaks and Lamas*. London: Readers Union/Cassell, 1948.

————. *The Way and the Mountain*. London: Peter Owen, 1960. (Reference also made to the 2008 World Wisdom edition, as indicated).

————. *A Buddhist Spectrum*. London: Allen & Unwin, 1980.

————. "The Catholic Church in Crisis". In J. Needleman (ed.), *The Sword of Gnosis*, 57-80.

————. "Introduction to Tibetan Art". *Studies in Comparative Religion*, 1:1, 1967, 22-35.

————. "Thomas Merton, 1915-1968". *Studies in Comparative Religion*, 3:3, 1969, 138-146.

————. "A Fateful Meeting of Minds: A.K. Coomaraswamy and René Guénon". *Studies in Comparative Religion*, 12:2-4, 1978, 175-188.

————. Review of Jacob Needleman, *The New Religions*. *Studies in Comparative Religion*, 5:3, 1971, 189-190.

Panda, Nrsimhacarana. *Cyclic Universe*, 2 vols. New Delhi: D.K. Printworld, 2002.

Parrinder, Geoffrey. *Comparative Religion*. London: Allen & Unwin, 1962.

Perry, Whitall. *Gurdjieff in the Light of Tradition*. London: Perennial Books, 1979.

————. *The Widening Breach: Evolutionism in the Mirror of Cosmology*. Cambridge: Quinta Essentia, 1995.

————. *Challenges to a Secular Society*. Washington DC: Foundation of Traditional Studies, 1996.

————. "Drug-Induced Mysticism: The Mescalin Hypothesis". *Tomorrow*, 12:3, 1964, 192-198.

————. "Gurdjieff in the Light of Tradition". *Studies in Comparative Religion*, 8:4, 1974, 211-238 and 9:1-2, 1975, 20-35.

————. "Coomaraswamy: The Man, Myth, and History", *Studies in Comparative Religion*, 11:3, 1977, 159-165.

————. "The Bollingen Coomaraswamy Papers and Biography". *Studies in Comparative Religion*, 11:4. 1977, 197-204.

————. Review of C. Evans, *Cults of Unreason*. *Studies in Comparative Religion*, 9:3, 1975, 183-185.

————. Review of Frithjof Schuon, *Logic and Transcendence*. *Studies in Comparative Religion*, 9:4, 1975, 250-253.

————. "The Man and His Witness". In S.D.R. Singam (ed.), *Ananda Coomaraswamy: Remembering and Remembering Again and Again*, 3-7.

————. "The Revival of Interest in Tradition". In R. Fernando (ed.), *The Unanimous Tradition*, 3-16.

————(ed.). *A Treasury of Traditional Wisdom*. London: Allen & Unwin, 1971.

Perry, W.J. *The Origin of Magic and Religion*. London: Methuen, 1923.

————. *The Primordial Ocean*. London: Methuen, 1935.

Prabhavananda, Swami. *The Spiritual Heritage of India*. Madras: Sri Ramakrishna Math, 1981.

———— & Christopher Isherwood (eds.), *Shankara's Crest Jewel of Discrimination* New York: Mentor, 1970.

Quinn Jr., William W. *The Only Tradition*. Albany: SUNY, 1997.

Radhakrishnan, Sarvapelli. *Indian Philosophy*, vol. 1. London: Allen & Unwin, 1931.

————. "Fragments of a Confession". In P.A. Schilpp (ed.), *The Philosophy of Sarvepalli Radhakrishnan*, 1-82.

Raine, Kathleen. *Defending Ancient Springs*. Ipswich: Golgonooza, 1985.

————. "The Underlying Order: Nature and the Imagination". In A. Sharma (ed.), *Fragments of Infinity*, 198-216.

Raju, P.T. *Idealistic Thought of India*. London: Allen & Unwin, 1953.

Reynolds, J.M. *Self-Liberation Through Seeing with Naked Awareness*. Barrymore: Station Hill Press, 1989.

Reynolds, P.L. *René Guénon: His Life and Work* (unpublished paper). Montreal, c. 1979.

Rieff, Philip. *The Triumph of the Therapeutic*. Harmondsworth: Penguin, 1973.

Robinson, Marilynne. *The Death of Adam: Essays on Modern Thought*. New York: Picador, 2005.

Roszak, Theodore. *The Making of the Counter Culture*. London: Faber & Faber, 1970.

————. *Where the Wasteland Ends*. New York: Doubleday, 1972.

————. *Unfinished Animal*. New York: Harper & Row, 1977.

Saher, P.J. *Eastern Wisdom and Western Thought*. London: Allen & Unwin, 1969.

Samsel, Peter. "The *Shahadah* as Truth and as Way". *Sophia*, 9:2, 2003-04, 77-114.

Saran, A.K. "The Crisis of Hinduism". *Studies in Comparative Religion*, 5:2, 1971, 92-109.

————. "The Meaning and Forms of Secularism: A Note". *Religious Traditions*, 2:1, 1979, 38-51.

Schaya, Leo. *The Universal Meaning of the Kabbalah*. London: Allen & Unwin, 1971.

————. "Some Universal Aspects of Judaism". In R. Fernando (ed.), *The Unanimous Tradition*, 57-75.

Schilpp, P.A. (ed.). *The Philosophy of Sarvapelli Radhakrishnan.* New York: Tudor, 1952.

Schmitt, C.B. "Perennial Philosophy: From Agostino Steuco to Leibniz". *Journal of the History of Ideas,* 27, 1966, 505-532.

Scholem, Gershom. *Major Trends in Jewish Mysticism.* New York: Schocken Books, 1995.

———. "Tradition and Commentary as Religious Categories in Judaism". *Studies in Comparative Religion,* 3:3, 1969, 147-163.

Schumacher, E.F. *A Guide for the Perplexed.* London: Jonathan Cape, 1977.

Shankara's Crest Jewel of Discrimination, trans. Swami Prabhavananda & C. Isherwood. New York: Mentor, 1970.

Shannon, William. *Thomas Merton's Dark Path.* New York: Farrar Strauss Giroux, 1988.

Sharma, Arvind, (ed.). *Fragments of Infinity: Essays in Religion and Philosophy* (a *festschrift* in honor of Huston Smith). Bridport: Prism, 1991.

Sharma, Arvind. "Some Misunderstandings of the Hindu Approach to Religious Plurality". *Religion,* 8, 1978, 133-154.

———. "All Religions are—Equal? One? True? Same?: A Critical Examination of Some Formulations of the Neo-Hindu Position". *Philosophy East and West,* 29:1, 1979, 59-72.

Sharpe, Eric J. *Comparative Religion.* London: Duckworth, 1975.

———. *The Universal Gita: Western Images of the Bhagavadgita.* London: Duckworth, 1985.

Sherrard, Philip. *The Rape of Man and Nature.* Colombo: Sri Lanka Institute of Traditional Studies, 1987. (Also published as *The Eclipse of Nature.*)

———. *Human Image: World Image.* Cambridge: Golgonooza Press, 1992.

———. *Christianity: Lineaments of a Sacred Tradition.* Brookline: Holy Cross Orthodox Press, 1998.

———. "An Introduction to the Religious Thought of C. G. Jung". *Studies in Comparative Religion,* 3:1, 1969, 33-49.

———. "Teilhard and Christian Vision". *Studies in Comparative Religion.* 4:3, 1970, 150-175.

———. "The Sexual Relationship in Christian Thought". *Studies in Comparative Religion,* 5:3, Summer 1971, 151-172.

———. "Science and the Dehumanization of Man". *Studies in Comparative Religion,* 10:2, 1976, 74-92.

Shute, Evan. *Flaws in the Theory of Evolution.* New Jersey: Craig Press, 1961.

Singam, S.D.R. (ed.). *Ananda Coomaraswamy: Remembering and Remembering Again and Again.* Kuala Lumpur: privately published, 1974.

Sigaud, Pierre-Marie (ed.). *Dossier H René Guénon.* Lausanne-Paris: L'Age d'Homme, 1984.

Smith, Huston. *Beyond the Post-Modern Mind.* Wheaton: Theosophical Publishing House, 1982.

———. *The World's Religions: Our Great Wisdom Traditions.* San Francisco: Harper, 1991.

————. "Excluded Knowledge: A Critique of the Western Mind Set". *Teachers College Record*, 80:3, 1979, 419-445.

————. "What They Have That We Lack: A Tribute to the Native Americans via Joseph Epes Brown". In S.H. Nasr & K. O'Brien (eds.), *The Essential Sophia*, 85-95.

————. Introduction. In Frithjof Schuon, *The Transcendent Unity of Religions*, 1993, ix-xxvii.

————. Foreword. In William C. Chittick (ed.), *The Essential Seyyed Hossein Nasr*, vii.

Smith, Wolfgang. *Cosmos and Transcendence: Breaking Through the Barrier of Scientistic Belief*. La Salle: Sherwood Sugden & Co, 1984.

————. *Teilhardism and the New Religion*. Rockford: Tan, 1988.

Snodgrass, Adrian. *Architecture, Time, and Eternity: Studies in the Stellar and Temporal Symbolism of Traditional Buildings*, 2 vols. New Delhi: P.K. Goel/Aditya Prakashan, 1990.

————. *The Symbolism of the Stupa*. Delhi: Motilal Banarsidass, 1992.

Standing Bear, Luther. *My People the Sioux*. Lincoln: University of Nebraska Press, 1975.

————. *Land of the Spotted Eagle*. Lincoln: University of Nebraska Press, 1978.

Stanner, W.E.H. "Religion, Totemism, and Symbolism". In M. Charlesworth et al. (eds.), *Religion in Aboriginal Australia*, 137-172.

Stoddart, William. *Outline of Hinduism*. Washington DC: Foundation for Traditional Studies, 1993.

————. *Remembering in a World of Forgetting: Thoughts on Tradition and Postmodernism*, Mateus

Soares de Azevedo & Alberto Vasconcellos Queiroz (eds.). Bloomington: World Wisdom, 2008.

————. "Right Hand of Truth". *Studies in Comparative Religion* (Titus Burckhardt Memorial Issue), 16:1-2, 1984, 3-8.

————. "In Memoriam: Whitall Perry". *Sacred Web*, 16, 2006, 189.

———— & Mateus Soares de Azevedo. "Rama P. Coomaraswamy (1929-2006): In Memoriam". *Sacred Web*, 18, 2007, 185-190.

————. "Mysticism". In R. Fernando (ed.), *The Unanimous Tradition*, 89-95.

Stunkel, Kenneth. "The Meeting of East and West in Coomaraswamy and Radhakrishnan". *Philosophy East and West*, 23:4. 1973, 517-524.

Sworder, Roger. *Mining, Metallurgy, and the Meaning of Life*. Quakers Hill: Quakers Hill Press, 1995.

————. "The Desacralization of Work". In H. Oldmeadow (ed.), *The Betrayal of Tradition*, 183-216.

Tamas, Mircea. *The Wrath of Gods: Esoteric and Occult in the Modern World*. Toronto: Rose Cross Books, 2004.

Tourniac, J. *Propos sur René Guénon*. Paris: Dervy Livres, 1973.

Valsan, Michel. "Notes on the Shaikh al-'Alawi, 1869-1934". *Studies in Comparative Religion*, 5:1, 1971, 145-150.

Vasquez, Juan A. "A Metaphysics of Culture". In S.D.R. Singam (ed.), *Ananda Coomaraswamy: Remembering and Remembering Again and Again,* 225-237.

Vishnu Purana, The, 2 vols., trans. & ed. H.H. Wilson & Nag Sharan Singh. Delhi: Nag Publishers, 1980.

Wach, Joachim. *The Comparative Study of Religions.* New York: Columbia University, 1958.

————. "Radhakrishnan and the Comparative Study of Religion". In P.A. Schilpp (ed.), *The Philosophy of Sarvapelli Radhakrishnan,* 445-458.

Wadia, A.R. "Swami Vivekananda's Philosophy of Religion". In R.C. Majumdar (ed.), *Swami Vivekananda's Memorial Volume.*

Walker, James R. *Lakota Belief and Ritual,* ed. Raymond DeMallie and Ellen Jahner. Lincoln: University of Nebraska, 1980.

Walker, Julia. *Where Time Ends: An Explication of Guénon's View of Time.* unpublished BA Honors thesis: La Trobe University Bendigo, 2006.

Waterfield, Robin. *René Guénon and the Future of the West.* London: Crucible, 1987.

Watts, Alan. *In My Own Way.* New York: Random House, 1972.

Wheen, Francis. *Karl Marx.* London: Fourth Estate, 1999.

Wilson, E.O. *Consilience: The Unity of Knowledge.* New York: Vintage, 1999.

ACKNOWLEDGMENTS

Michael Fitzgerald first suggested that I write this book. From the outset he encouraged and supported me, in many different ways. Joseph Fitzgerald, Patrick Laude, Clinton Minnaar, and William Stoddart made many helpful suggestions and corrections. I also make special mention of Ranjit Fernando, Director of the Sri Lanka Institute of Traditional Studies, who published my earlier book, *Traditionalism: Religion in the Light of the Perennial Philosophy* (2000). I thank World Wisdom for making available the latest editions and translations of Schuon's works.

It is impossible to mention all the other people who have helped along the way. They may be assured of my gratitude. As well as acknowledging my family, especially my wife Rose, I would like specifically to thank the following:

Patricia Adrichem
Rodney Blackhirst
James Cutsinger
Renaud Fabbri
Judith Fitzgerald
Paul Goble
Ali Lakhani
Barry McDonald
Seyyed Hossein Nasr
Linda Oliveira
Kathryn Paul
Catherine Schuon
Timothy Scott
Aminah Smith
Huston Smith
Mary-Kathryne Steele
Roger Sworder
Chief James Trosper
James Wetmore
Stephen Williams

INDEX

Abdel Wahed Yahya, 23. *See also* Guénon, René
Abhishiktananda, Swami, 91, 122, 213, 296, 298. *See also* Le Saux, Henri
Aborigines of Australia, 171-173
Abraham, 69, 126, 134, 307
Abu Bakr Siraj ad-Din, 38, 80, 153. *See also* Lings, Martin
Adam, 130-131, 231
Advaita Vedanta, 5, 15, 17, 51, 109, 138-139, 268, 313
Alawi, Shaykh Ahmad al-, xii, 5, 38, 213
Allah, 64
All-Possibility, 52, 132, 288
American Indians, xvi, xvii, 4, 18, 150, 162, 171, 173, 175, 176, 183, 207, 212, 303. *See also* Native Americans; Plains Indians
Amida, 102, 129, 146, 343
Amidism, 102, 129, 260. *See also* Pure Land Schools
Anandamayi Ma, xii, 213
Angels, 17, 54, 66, 162, 241
Angkor Wat, 139
Anthony of Sourzah, Metropolitan. *See* Bloom, Archbishop Anthony
Apocatastasis, 127, 314
Archetype(s), 38, 86, 125, 133, 151-154, 157-158, 189-190, 192, 214, 227-230, 251, 288-290, 314-315
Aristotelianism, 315
Aristotle, 61, 70
Atma, Atman, 54, 60, 62, 64, 88, 105, 111, 127, 140, 141, 145, 192, 201, 298, 312-314
Augustine, Saint, 29, 60, 62, 69, 162, 201, 242, 273
Aurobindo Ghose, 257-258, 261, 264, 268
Avatara(s), 64-65, 115, 143, 158, 209, 270, 312, 314

Bach, Johann Sebastian, 252
Bacon, Francis, 216
Balzac, Honoré de, 252, 254
Basil, Saint, 299-301
Beethoven, Ludwig van, 252
Being-Consciousness-Bliss, 140
Bernardino of Siena, Saint, 307
Berry, Wendell, 218, 220
Beyond-Being, 54-55, 57, 59, 64-65, 74, 131-132. *See also* Godhead; Non-Being
Bhagavad Gita, 3-4, 69, 138, 143
Bible, 76, 116, 314
Biès, Jean, 44, 202, 205
Bizet, Georges, 252
Black Elk (Hehaka Sapa), xii, 8, 153, 174-178, 181, 183, 213, 298
Black Elk, Benjamin, 279
Blackhirst, Rodney, 44, 223
Blake, William, 66, 109, 164, 215
Bloom, Archbishop Anthony, 8, 242
Bodhisattva(s), 16, 53, 139, 150, 195
Boehme, Jacob, 152, 314
Bokar, Tierno, 101-102
Bön, 173, 315
Borella, Jean, 31, 42, 44
Brahma, 52, 204
Brahman, 60, 107, 111, 140, 143-144, 204, 208, 264, 284
Brahmananda, Swami, 269
Brahmo-samaj, 92, 265, 269

For a glossary of all key foreign words used in books published by World Wisdom, including metaphysical terms in English, consult: www.DictionaryofSpiritualTerms.org.
This on-line Dictionary of Spiritual Terms provides extensive definitions, examples, and related terms in other languages.

BIOGRAPHICAL NOTES

Harry Oldmeadow is Coordinator of Religious Studies in the Department of Arts, La Trobe University, Bendigo, Australia. He studied history, politics, and literature at the Australian National University, obtaining a First Class Honors degree in history. In 1971 a Commonwealth Overseas Research Scholarship led to further studies at Oxford University. In 1980 Oldmeadow completed a Masters dissertation on the "perennialist" or "traditionalist" school of comparative religious thought. This study was awarded the University of Sydney Medal for excellence in research and was later published under the title, *Traditionalism: Religion in the Light of the Perennial Philosophy* (2000). Oldmeadow's principal intellectual interests include the perennialist school of thinkers, on whom he has written extensively during the last two decades, and the mystical and esoteric dimensions of the major religious traditions, especially Christianity, Hinduism, and Buddhism. He also has an abiding interest in the primal traditions of the Plains Indians of North America and the Aborigines of Australia.

His latest works include *Journeys East: 20th Century Western Encounters with Eastern Religious Traditions* (2004), *The Betrayal of Tradition: Essays on the Spiritual Crisis of Modernity* (2005), *Light from the East: Eastern Wisdom for the Modern West* (2007), *A Christian Pilgrim in India: The Spiritual Journey of Abhishiktananda (Henri Le Saux)* (2008), all published by World Wisdom, and *Mediations: Essays on Religious Pluralism and the Perennial Philosophy* (2008). He has published extensively in such journals as *Sophia, Sacred Web, Vincit Omnia Veritas, Eye of the Heart,* and *Studies in Comparative Religion.* He currently resides with his wife on a small property outside Bendigo.

William Stoddart was born in Carstairs, Scotland, lived most of his life in London, England, and now lives in Windsor, Ontario. He studied modern languages, and later medicine, at the universities of Glasgow, Edinburgh, and Dublin. He was a close associate of both Frithjof Schuon and Titus Burckhardt during the lives of these leading perennialists and translated several of their works into English. For many years Stoddart was assistant editor of the British journal *Studies in Comparative Religion.* Pursuing his interests in comparative religion, he has traveled widely in Europe, North Africa, India, Ceylon, and Japan. Stoddart's works include *Sufism: The Mystical Doctrines and Methods of Islam* (1976), *Outline of Hinduism* (1993), *Outline of Buddhism* (1998), *Invincible Wisdom: Quotations from the Scriptures, Saints, and Sages of All Times and Places* (2008), and *What Do the Religions Say About Each Other?* (2008). His essential writings were recently published by World Wisdom as *Remembering in a World of Forgetting: Thoughts on Tradition and Postmodernism* (2008).

Other Titles in the Perennial Philosophy
Series by World Wisdom

Light From the East: Eastern Wisdom for the Modern West,
edited by Harry Oldmeadow, 2007

Living in Amida's Universal Vow: Essays in Shin Buddhism,
edited by Alfred Bloom, 2004

*Of the Land and the Spirit: The Essential Lord Northbourne
on Ecology and Religion,*
edited by Christopher James and Joseph A. Fitzgerald, 2008

*Men of a Single Book: Fundamentalism in
Islam, Christianity, and Modern Thought,*
by Mateus Soares de Azevedo, 2010

Paths to the Heart: Sufism and the Christian East,
edited by James S. Cutsinger, 2002

*Remembering in a World of Forgetting:
Thoughts on Tradition and Postmodernism,*
by William Stoddart, 2008

Returning to the Essential: Selected Writings of Jean Biès,
translated by Deborah Weiss-Dutilh, 2004

Science and the Myth of Progress, edited by Mehrdad M. Zarandi, 2003

Seeing God Everywhere: Essays on Nature and the Sacred,
edited by Barry McDonald, 2003

Singing the Way: Insights in Poetry and Spiritual Transformation,
by Patrick Laude, 2005

The Spiritual Legacy of the North American Indian: Commemorative Edition,
by Joseph E. Brown, 2007

Sufism: Love & Wisdom,
edited by Jean-Louis Michon and Roger Gaetani, 2006

The Timeless Relevance of Traditional Wisdom,
by M. Ali Lakhani, 2010

The Underlying Religion: An Introduction to the Perennial Philosophy,
edited by Martin Lings and Clinton Minnaar, 2007

*Unveiling the Garden of Love:
Mystical Symbolism in Layla Majnun and Gita Govinda,*
by Lalita Sinha, 2008

Wisdom's Journey: Living the Spirit of Islam in the Modern World,
by John Herlihy, 2009

Ye Shall Know the Truth: Christianity and the Perennial Philosophy,
edited by Mateus Soares de Azevedo, 2005